THE MESS WE'RE IN

Managing the Refugee Crisis

Andrew Bennetts

Published in Australia by
Trabagem Publishing
PO Box 5068
Camberwell VIC 3124
(+61) 0412 411 829
andrew.r.bennetts@icloud.com
www.andrewbennetts.com.au

First published in Australia 2017
Copyright © Andrew Bennetts 2017

All rights reserved. No part of this publication may be reproduced, stored in a retrieval system, or transmitted, in any form or by any means without the prior written permission of the publisher, nor be otherwise circulated in any form of binding or cover other than that in which it is published and without a similar condition being imposed on the subsequent purchaser.

National Library of Australia Cataloguing-in-Publication entry

Creator: Bennetts, Andrew, author.
Title: The Mess We're In: Managing the Refugee Crisis / Andrew Bennetts.
ISBN: 9780994465207 (paperback)
ISBN: 9780994465214 (ebook)
Subjects: Refugees. Political refugees. Asylum, Right of.

Cover photography by Arthimedes
Cover layout and design by Nitsua
Book layout design and typesetting by Nelly Murariu, PixBeeDesign.com
Printed by Ingram Spark

Contents

Definitions	5
Introduction	11
PART 1. SITUATION	
Section 1.1 Global Review	21
CH 1. A Desperate Journey	23
CH 2. Disruption	37
CH 3. Vulnerable	55
CH 4. Protection	71
CH 5. Waiting	97
CH 6. Solution	131
CH 7. Home?	157
Section 1.2 Australian Review	181
CH 8. Australia's Immigration	183
CH 9. Australia's Humanitarianism	199
CH 10. Australia's Debate	227
PART 2. THE COMPLICATION, PRINCIPLES & ASSESSMENT	
Sections 2.1 & 2.2	239
CH 11. The Complication – The Main Problems	241
CH 12. Principles & Assessment Framework	251
PART 3. OPTIONS & RECOMMENDATION	
Section 3.1 Options Assessment	271
CH 13. Approach Options - Component Policies	273
CH 14. Holistic Approaches and Assessment – Current State	293
CH 15. Holistic Approaches and Assessment – Proposed	331
Section 3.2 Recommendation and Implementation	367
CH 16. Discussion and Recommendation	369
CH 17. Implementation and Australia's Lead	383
Conclusion	393
Index	395
About the Author	399
Acknowledgments	400

DEFINITIONS

Refugees and International Bodies

Approach Options: Component Policies ❯ Policies raised as possible supporting strategies to resolve the refugee situation. These may assist Holistic Approaches without being all-encompassing solutions themselves.

Approach Options: Holistic Approaches ❯ Comprehensive strategies to manage the refugee situation.

Asylum Seeker ❯ An individual who has sought protection as a refugee, but whose claim for refugee status has not yet been assessed. Every refugee has at some point been an asylum seeker.

Convention Relating to the Status of Refugees (Refugee Convention and Protocol) ❯ A United Nations multilateral treaty that defines who is a refugee. It sets out the rights of individuals who are granted asylum and the responsibilities of nations that grant asylum. The original Convention, approved in 1951, was limited to European refugees prior to 1951. The 1967 Protocol removed the timing and geographic limitations.

Countries of First Asylum ❯ Neighbouring countries close to the asylum seeker's Country of Origin. Due to their proximity, they generally hold the majority of asylum seekers.

Countries of Second Asylum ❯ The 62 countries that are not Countries of First Asylum, have over one million in population, a high or upper-middle income, and are considered free or partially free (according to Freedom House's Freedoms of the World Index). They have a combined population of over 1.7 billion, roughly 25% of the global population. These countries have the best combination of resources and willingness to create a positive impact on the plight of the world's forcibly displaced people.

Country of Asylum ❯ The country or territory that is hosting an asylum seeker or refugee.

Country of Origin ❯ The country or territory from which an asylum seeker or refugee originates.

Disruptive Causes ❯ Events resulting in people becoming forcibly displaced.

Durable Solutions ❯ A UNHCR term describing an ongoing permanent protection that is provided to a refugee. The UNHCR defines three durable solutions:
1. Voluntary Repatriation to the person's Country of Origin;
2. Local Integration within the host country of asylum;
3. Resettlement to a third country, which is a signatory nation to the Refugee Convention.

Forcibly Displaced People > Group term for refugees, asylum seekers, and internally displaced people (IDPs). Each group has a detailed specification as defined by the UNHCR.

International Covenant on Civil and Political Rights (ICCPR) > Multilateral treaty adopted by the United Nations General Assembly in 1966 committing parties to respect the civil and political rights of individuals, including the right to life, freedom of religion, freedom of speech, freedom of assembly, electoral rights, and rights to due process and a fair trial.

International Covenant on Economic, Social and Cultural Rights (ICESCR) > Multilateral treaty adopted by the United Nations General Assembly in 1966 and in force in 1976 committing parties to work toward the granting of economic, social, and cultural rights to the Non-Self-Governing and Trust Territories and individuals, including labour rights and the right to health, the right to education, and the right to an adequate standard of living.

Internally Displaced People (IDP) > People who have been forced or obliged to flee or to leave their homes or places of habitual residence as a result of generalised violence, violations of human rights, or natural or man-made disasters. They have not crossed an internationally recognised state border[1].

Local Integration > Permanent settlement of a refugee within their host community, being the Country of First Asylum.

Mandate Refugees > Refugees under the mandate of the UNHCR as defined by the Refugee Convention. The key exclusion are Palestinian refugees under the mandate of the UNRWA.

Non-refoulement > The right for refugees not to be returned to a country where they risk persecution.

Refugee > An individual who is outside their home country of citizenship because they have well-founded grounds for fear of persecution (because of their race, religion, nationality, membership of a particular social group or political opinion), and is unable to obtain sanctuary from their home country or, owing to such fear, is unwilling to avail themselves of the protection of that country; or in the case of not having a nationality and being outside their country of former habitual residence as a result of such event, is unable or, owing to such fear, unwilling to return to their country of former habitual residence[2].

---

1   Alexander Betts, Gil Loescher and James Milner, *UNHCR: The Politics and Practice of Refugee Protection* (New York: Routledge 2012, 2nd Edition) 134.
2   Article 1A(2), Convention relating to the Status of Refugees, opened for signature 28 July 1951 (entered into force 22 April 1954) read together with the Protocol relating to the Status of Refugees, opened for signature 31 January 1967 (entered into force 4 October 1967).

DEFINITIONS

Such a person may be called an "asylum seeker" until considered with the status of "refugee" by the Contracting State where they formally make a claim for sanctuary or right of asylum.

Refugee Status Determination (RSD) > The legal or administrative process by which governments or the UNHCR determine whether a person seeking international protection is considered a refugee under international law[3].

Repatriated Refugees > Refugees who have returned to their place of origin.

Resettlement > Transfer of a refugee from an asylum country to another State that has agreed to admit them as refugees with permanent residence status and to ultimately grant them permanent settlement.

Resettlement Submissions > Requests by the UNHCR for refugees to be resettled on the back of processing which determines individuals who cannot go home due to continued conflict or persecution, or have specific needs that cannot be addressed in the current place where they have sought protection.

Responsibility to Protect (R2P) > The criteria issued by the International Commission on Intervention and State Sovereignty (ICISS) in 2001 for a legitimate exercise of humanitarian intervention.

Returned IDPs > IDPs who have returned to their place of origin[4].

Secondary Movement > Movement from a Country of First Asylum to another country, often a more wealthy Country of Second Asylum.

Stateless Person > An individual not considered as a national by any state under the operation of its law[5].

UNHCR - Other People of Concern > Individuals who do not necessarily fall directly into any other groups but to whom UNHCR may extend its protection and/or assistance services. These activities might be based on humanitarian or other special grounds.

UNHCR - Population of Concern > UNHCR category including persons who are forcibly displaced (refugees, asylum seekers, IDPs etc.), those who have found a durable solution (returnees), as well as stateless persons, most of whom have never been forcibly

---

[3] UNHCR. "Refugee Status Determination." Accessed July 20, 2016, <www.unhcr.org/refugee-status-determination.html>
[4] UNHCR, *Global Trends: Forced Displacement in 2014*, 53.
[5] Hovy, Bela (2011). Bhabha, Jacqueline, ed. Human Rights and Citizenship: The Need for Better Data and What to Do about It. *Children Without a State: A Global Human Rights Challenge* (Cambridge, Massachusetts, United States: MIT Press) 90.

displaced. This categorisation is different to that of forcibly displaced persons. The figure for forcibly displaced persons worldwide, includes refugees and IDPs beyond the UNHCR mandate, and excludes returnees and stateless persons[6].

United Nations High Commissioner for Refugees (UNHCR) ❯ A subsidiary organ of the United Nations acting under the authority of the UN General Assembly. Fulfils two core purposes[7]: to ensure the international protection of refugees; and to find a solution to their plight.

United Nations Relief and Works Agency (UNRWA) ❯ A relief and human development agency that provides education, health care and social services to the five million registered Palestinian refugees from the 1948 and 1967 wars, a number that includes their descendants.

Voluntary Repatriation ❯ Voluntary return of a refugee to their Country of Origin.

Migration, Culture and Sovereignty

Cultural Assimilation ❯ The process where immigrant cultures come to resemble those of the host group. It is a one-sided process of adaptation that may be gradual or fast. Ultimately the new members of the society give up their distinctive language, culture and social characteristics to become indistinguishable from the host group.

Gross National Income (GNI) Per Capita ❯ The dollar value of a country's final income in a year, divided by its population. It reflects the average income of a country's citizens.

Human Rights ❯ A set of moral and legal guidelines that promote and protect our values, our identity and our ability to ensure an adequate standard of living. Nine core human rights treaties defining a series of human rights have been signed by the vast majority of countries.

Liberal Democracy ❯ A democratic system of government in which individual rights and freedoms are officially recognised and protected.

Multiculturalism ❯ The existence, acceptance, or promotion of multiple cultural traditions within a single jurisdiction.

---

6 UNHCR, *Global Trends: Forced Displacement in 2014*, 8.
7 Article 1, *Statute of the Office of the United Nations High Commissioner for Refugees,* UN General Assembly Resolution 428(V), 14 December 1950.

DEFINITIONS

Net Emigrant Countries > Countries with an excess of persons leaving the country each year after calculating the difference between the number of persons entering and leaving a country during that year.

Net Immigrant Countries > Countries with an excess of persons entering the country each year after calculating the difference between the number of persons entering and leaving a country during that year.

Net Overseas Migration (NOM) > The net gain or loss of population through immigration to and emigration from a country.

Secularism > The belief that religion should not be part of the affairs of the state or part of public education.

Sharia > The legal framework within which the public, and some private, aspects of life are regulated based on Islam.

Sovereignty > The full right and power of a body to govern itself without any interference from outside sources.

Theocracy > A commonwealth or state under a system of government in which God or a deity is recognised as the supreme civil ruler, the God's or deity's laws being interpreted by religious authorities.

Total Fertility Rate > A measure of an imaginary woman's fertility as she passes through her entire reproductive life (assumed to be 15-49) during one year, experiencing all the age-specific fertility rates for that year.

Australia's Programs

Australia's Offshore Program > Australia's process for resettlement of refugees directly from an asylum country to Australia. That is, they apply to Australia for settlement from outside Australia's territory (i.e. off-shore). It consists of the Refugee Program and the Special Humanitarian Program.

Australia's Onshore Program > Australia's process for Asylum Seekers who apply for protection after arrival to Australia. That is, they apply to Australia for asylum within Australia's territory (i.e. on-shore). This program processes for 'authorised' and 'unauthorised' arrivals.

Irregular Maritime Arrivals (IMAs) > Asylum seekers who arrived to Australia by a boat without the appropriate visa entry documents for Australia, should they not be seeking asylum.

Mandatory Detention ❯ Australian law requiring people within its territory found to be 'unlawful citizens' to be detained until they are granted a visa or removed from the country. The law also allows for asylum seekers who qualify as 'unlawful non-citizens', by arriving at an 'excised offshore place' such as Christmas Island, to be detained.

Operation Sovereign Borders ❯ Australian policy, since September 2013, with the aim of deterring asylum seekers from coming to Australia by denying them access to Australia. Australian naval officers are issued with orders to turn back boats carrying asylum seekers "when it is safe to do so[8]".

Pacific Solution ❯ Australian policy for offshore processing of asylum seekers who are unauthorised arrivals. This off-shore processing has been done in detention centres in other countries (Nauru and Papua New Guinea's Manus Island) and under the laws of those countries[9].

Permanent Migration Program ❯ Australia's program providing permanent entry into the country. It is divided into a Migration Part consisting of Family, Skilled and Special Eligibility components, and a Humanitarian Part consisting of Onshore, Offshore and Special Humanitarian Programs. Refugee entry is provided through the Humanitarian Part.

Temporary Migration Program ❯ Australia's process allowing international visitors to stay for 12 months or more but not permanently. It includes Temporary Business, Overseas Students, and Working Holiday Makers.

The Report of the Expert Panel on Asylum Seekers (Houston Report) ❯ Australian Report commissioned by the Gillard Government in 2012 to assess the policy options available to prevent asylum seekers risking their lives on dangerous boat voyages to Australia. It specifically related to reducing the unauthorised asylum seeker boat arrivals through the Onshore Program.

White Australia Policy ❯ A combination of various historical policies that intentionally favoured immigrants to Australia from other English-speaking countries and certain North-western European countries.

---

8 "Recent changes in Australia Refugee Policy", Refugee Council of Australia, accessed July 20, 2016. <www.refugeecouncil.org.au/wp-content/uploads/2016/07/Australia-refugee-policy-changes-July-016.pdf>
9 Ibid.

INTRODUCTION

How do we best help refugees? As a 21st century Australian resident, it is difficult not to be drawn into the plight of refugees and our country's response. For almost two decades it has been one of our country's dominant political topics and over that time the country has repeatedly changed its refugee-related policies. Each change is seemingly critiqued by local and international observers. Some focus on Australia's international obligations and adherence to human rights. Others contextualise the changes in terms of border security and controlling the numbers of asylum seekers arriving at our shores. For the casual observer, these changes appear to greatly impact the inflows of asylum seekers, the human rights they experience, and Australia's global standing.

Overlaying the debate about Australia's response to a large, long-standing and growing issue, are two global developments that are hard to ignore. The first is the rapidly growing global population, most significant in the poor and developing nations; many of these nations having consistently produced large numbers of refugees over the past 35 years. This growth suggests the scale of refugees is likely to increase significantly in the coming decades. The second is the mass migration toward Europe in the northern summer of 2015 and the ensuing friction. This event may be interpreted either as an isolated occurrence requiring a special effort to resolve, or as a harbinger of future movements should policies remain unchanged. Regardless of the interpretation, the mass migration to Europe in 2015 has crystallised for a generation the possibility of what may eventuate without a review of the current system. Such mass migration is unprecedented in recent times, and therefore its consequences unknown.

The question of how we best help refugees is one of the key issues of our time. It is a global question and has implications for the vast numbers of forcibly displaced people and, potentially, the viability of the nations who are trying to help them.

I have been torn by the dilemma facing Australia, and all nations looking to help, in response to the refugee situation. On the one hand, many Western governments (and certainly Australia) presented as not doing enough to help the world's Forcibly Displaced People and of systematically breaching key areas of human rights. On the other hand, there appears much to risk by uncontrolled and limitless immigration and refugee flows such as those to Europe in 2015. There are economic risks, which become apparent when considering the number (at least 60 million) of those forcibly displaced[10]. There are security risks, such as the coordinated Paris shootings that killed 130 in November 2015. The gunmen, known to authorities and last traced in the Middle East, appeared to have re-entered Europe through the asylum seeker channel[11]. The cultural risks are debatable and appear to be relevant over a longer term. While cultural risks are affected by asylum seeker and refugee policy, they are also related to education, migration and demographic changes.

There is clearly a moral component to this dilemma. How robust are the societies of the countries who are trying to help and what limits, if any, should they impose on themselves when helping the world's vulnerable in order to protect their own viability? What if these limits mean denying support to those who, while not being citizens, clearly need help? What if these limits infringe on the human rights of vulnerable and innocent people and breach a country's obligations under international law?

As a casual observer, I found plenty of information regarding the number of forcibly displaced people and the human rights abuses many endure. What I had more trouble finding was data relating to key demographic questions; for example, population projections and the results of how different approaches to refugee intakes may play out. Certainly the number of refugees was widely communicated, but not the potential number of future refugees or the potential consequences for countries about to take in a large number of refugees. For me, these were crucial pieces of evidence that were less prevalent in the debate seen by the general public.

Surely this gap in information must be filled to best answer the moral questions of our modern-day refugee dilemma. It is this gap that compelled me to research and write this book. My contention was that to fully explore the refugee situation, the consequences of various approaches was required to be fully appreciated. Only then can views regarding the best approach be formed. I am not an expert on refugees, nor demography, sociology or international human rights laws, nor am I aligned to a political party. In many ways this book provides a different and unencumbered perspective and has enabled a review free from adhering to political agenda and party lines. My previous experience is in management consulting and business analysis, and it is these skills I have used to draw together the information related to this issue.

This book is intended to be a resource for Australians interested in better understanding all aspects of the global refugee situation and who want to help refugees

---

10   UNHCR, *Global Trends: Forced Displacement in 2014*, 2.
11   "Paris attacks: Who were the attackers?" *BBC News*, 27 April, 2016.

INTRODUCTION

(and all other people who have been forcibly displaced) as best as possible. It is designed to be an information repository, not only regarding the facts related to refugees, but also the moral principles that must be addressed to determine what it means to best help refugees. Paris Aristotle, one of Australia's leading refugee advocates, referred to the refugee situation as an example of a Wicked Problem[12]. Wicked Problems are virtually impossible to solve as any solution usually creates other additional problems. Given the complex nature of the refugee situation, the book also presents a way of assessing the various trade-offs that must be made in finding the best possible approach. In terms of semantics, the book discusses approaches rather than solutions as there does not appear to be a solution to the refugee situation.

The topic is broad and emotional, and there are many aspects that are required to be covered. This book sweeps an expansive terrain. It aims to provide the reader with the full landscape of considerations, but given its breadth the deep dives are left for other publications. The concepts to consider include human rights law, economics, sociology, political structures, history, demography and of course, morality. Where there is clearly more to learn I refer the reader to the books I found illuminating and the footnotes provide other sources of information used in the development of this work.

I have come to believe that best helping refugees is also best helping the world. The refugee situation can no longer be isolated and managed through the status quo with no implications for the wider world. The last major change to the world's humanitarian approach occurred in the aftermath of World War II. The set of international agreements and human rights laws that were introduced with that context set a new standard in international cooperation and respect for all humans. The laws and rights brought much benefit and help to the world. However, that was a long time ago and there are growing signs that changes are necessary. There is no reason why the next generation of changes to the world's humanitarian approach cannot set a new standard that is higher again.

One of the realities in understanding the refugee situation is getting across the mounds of terminology. Some of it is short hand used to simplify the language; other terms are quite specific and precise. The most critical terms are covered in this introduction, and in the body of the book I define each new term when it is first used. In addition, a definitions section is included at the front of the book as a resource to reference along the way.

The book is set into three parts that broadly mirror a management consulting report. This structure has proved effective for decades in introducing and conveying broad and

---

[12] Paris Aristotle, 'A "wicked problem"?', Big Ideas, *ABC Radio National,* 28 June 2013 <www.abc.net.au/radionational/programs/bigideas/2013-07-01/4778140>

complex issues in a logical and methodical format. Part 1 is a situational review divided into two sections. Section 1.1 comprises seven chapters and outlines the global refugee situation. This section discusses why people are displaced and become refugees, the types of countries that traditionally produce refugees, and the likely future projections. It covers the history of international efforts in protecting refugees including the formation of the United Nations and its subsidiary organ for supporting refugees – the United Nations High Commissioner for Refugees (UNHCR). An overview of the different ways in which countries help is also provided. Efforts of supporting nations include donations to the UNHCR, the harbouring of refugees, and granting refugees a permanent residency within their lands. Benefits and costs of migration are reviewed, as is the potential economic, social and security threats that large numbers of refugees may present.

Section 1.2 covers Australia specifically. It contains three chapters that discuss Australia's migration history and current set up. Australia is one of the world's foremost nation of migrants, however this has not prevented episodes of racism and xenophobia. Since 1970 it has embraced high levels of migration and achieved a relatively harmonious society where almost half the population is either born overseas or has a parent born overseas. In this section, Australia's humanitarian history and current approach is also reviewed. The final chapter focuses on the issues and controversies regarding Australia's current humanitarian policies. Such policies include boat turn-backs, off-shore processing and the mandatory detention of all boat arrivals, including the detention of children.

Part 2 has only two chapters. Chapter 11 describes the complication, which is the summarised list of the main issues identified in the situational analysis. These issues are the essence of the problem, if they could all somehow be resolved then the plight of the world's forcibly displaced people (and the countries trying to help them) would be rectified. Unfortunately, because it is unlikely that they will all somehow be resolved, we are led to questions of trade-offs regarding competing needs.

Chapter 12 provides a set of 'questions-of-principle' that relate to these competing needs. These, questions-of-principle, require priorities to be determined that then frame how the approach options will be assessed. Many of these, questions-of-principle, are difficult as they require a subordination of an intuitive good. Responses are likely to vary among people and will lead to different views as to what approach is the best. A weakness of the current debate about the refugee situation is that it focuses on disagreements regarding approach options rather than the underlying principles from which they are developed. Such a focus may never result in an agreement as two parties that cannot understand their differences in principle are unlikely to be able to agree on an approach option.

In order to move to the options assessment I provide answers to these questions-of-principles. It is these answers that develop the assessment framework. As such, a reader who disagrees with my answers to these, questions-of-principle, will disagree with my assessment of the approach options.

Part 3 provides the options assessment and recommendation. It has two sections each with two chapters. Section 3.1 provides factual information about various policy options and approaches to help refugees. One area regards Component Policies. These are ideas that can help refugees without being complete (or holistic) approaches. The intention is to communicate the broad range of ideas being discussed and tried, both here and abroad. The other area focuses on the Holistic Approaches. These are total approaches, which may utilise some Component Policies. The book details eight Holistic Approaches from the perspective of the likely outcome if all the nations of the world that wanted to help were asked to follow each approach. Each option is described and then assessed against the framework developed in Part 2.

Section 3.2 compares the approach options and reviews the trade-offs required to be made in selecting a 'best' option. An example of one such trade-off is choosing between an approach that provides a better standard of living for more refugees but has large implementation challenges that could ultimately lead to failure, against an approach that is not as beneficial for refugees but more likely to succeed. Selecting a 'best' option is ultimately a judgement call that can only be effectively made with a full understanding of these trade-offs. The book finishes with a global recommendation as well as a road-map for action detailing how Australia can lead the way in its implementation.

There are a number of terms that invariably come up when discussing the plight of displaced people. Without proper explanation things can easily get confusing. While these terms are explained along the way and listed in the definitions section at the start of this introduction, a handful warrant specific reference here.

- **The United Nations High Commissioner for Refugees (the UNHCR).** A United Nations subsidiary organ established in 1950 to ensure the international protection of refugees and to find a solution to their plight.
- **Durable Solutions.** A UNHCR term that describes the targeted solutions to a refugee's plight. The UNHCR defines three durable solutions. Each will be described in more detail in Chapter 6:
    - **Voluntary Repatriation** of the refugee back to their Country of Origin.
    - **Integration** of the refugee locally with their host nation.
    - **Resettlement** of the refugee to a third country.

Fig 0.1 › Book Structure - Management Consulting Approach.

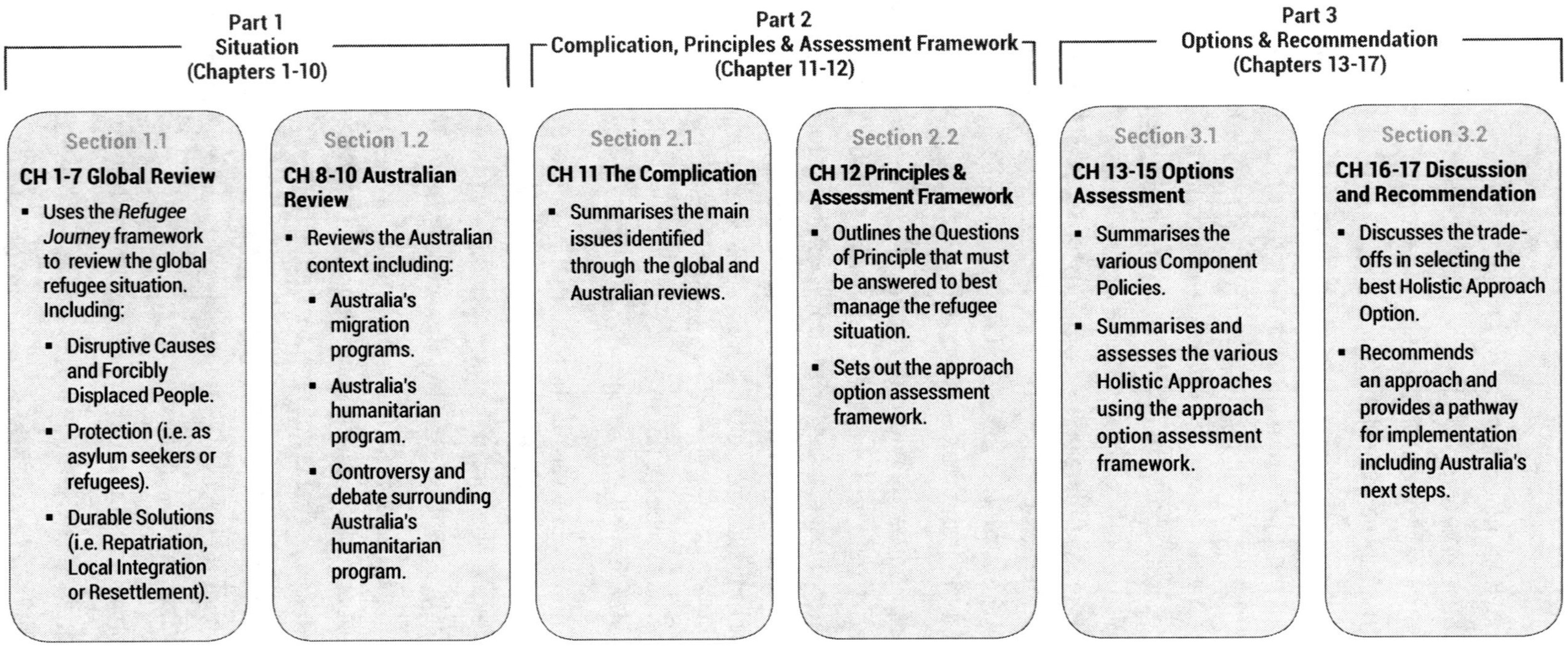

Part 1
Situation
(Chapters 1-10)

Section 1.1

CH 1-7 Global Review
- Uses the *Refugee Journey* framework to review the global refugee situation. Including:
  - Disruptive Causes and Forcibly Displaced People.
  - Protection (i.e. as asylum seekers or refugees).
  - Durable Solutions (i.e. Repatriation, Local Integration or Resettlement).

Section 1.2

CH 8-10 Australian Review
- Reviews the Australian context including:
  - Australia's migration programs.
  - Australia's humanitarian program.
  - Controversy and debate surrounding Australia's humanitarian program.

Part 2
Complication, Principles & Assessment Framework
(Chapter 11-12)

Section 2.1

CH 11 The Complication
- Summarises the main issues identified through the global and Australian reviews.

Section 2.2

CH 12 Principles & Assessment Framework
- Outlines the Questions of Principle that must be answered to best manage the refugee situation.
- Sets out the approach option assessment framework.

Part 3
Options & Recommendation
(Chapters 13-17)

Section 3.1

CH 13-15 Options Assessment
- Summarises the various Component Policies.
- Summarises and assesses the various Holistic Approaches using the approach option assessment framework.

Section 3.2

CH 16-17 Discussion and Recommendation
- Discusses the trade-offs in selecting the best Holistic Approach Option.
- Recommends an approach and provides a pathway for implementation including Australia's next steps.

INTRODUCTION

There are many categories for displaced and vulnerable people. The three key groups important to recognise up front are refugees, asylum seekers, and internally displaced people (IDPs). Each group has a detailed specification as defined by the UNHCR. For simplicity, this book describes people in these three categories collectively as Forcibly Displaced People. A simplified definition for each category is:

- **Refugee**: An individual outside their home country of citizenship because they have well-founded grounds for fear of persecution for reasons of race, religion, nationality, membership of a particular social group or political opinion, and is unable to obtain sanctuary from their home country; or who, not having a nationality and being outside the country of their former habitual residence as a result of such events, is unable or, owing to such fear, is unwilling to return to it. As at the end of 2014 there were 19.5 million refugees (14.4 million under the UNHCR mandate and 5.1 million Palestinian refugees registered by UNRWA).

- **Asylum Seeker**: An individual who has sought protection as a refugee, but whose claim for refugee status has not yet been assessed. Every refugee has at some point been an asylum seeker. As at end of 2014 there were 1.8 million asylum seekers.

- **Internally Displaced Person (IDP)**: An individual forced to flee their home but remains within their country's borders . Although often referred to as refugees they do not fall within the current legal definition of a refugee. As at end of 2014 there were 38.2 million IDPs.

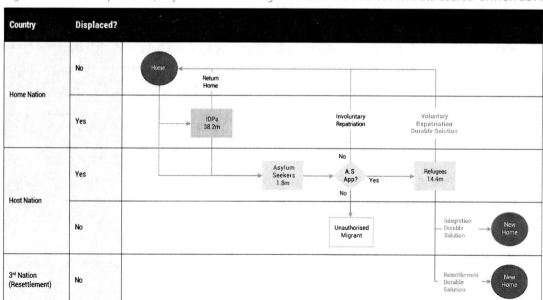

Fig 0.2 > Relationship of IDPs, Asylum Seekers Refugees and Durable Solutions. *Data Source: UNHCR 2014.*

Liberal Democracies

A cornerstone piece of this analysis is my belief that liberal democracies are a good thing for humanity. They correlate with higher GDP and have likely contributed to improved living conditions over the past 200 years. With their roots in the ancient Mediterranean empires, such democracies re-emerged in modern times within Western Europe and North America and expanded through all regions of the globe: South Korea and Japan in Asia; Chile and Argentina in South America; Latvia and Lithuania in Europe; Mauritius and Botswana in Africa; and Israel and Cyprus in the Middle East. Wherever they go they invariably lift the freedoms, rights and quality of life of the population.

According to the Museum of Australian Democracy, liberal democracies share four main principles[13].

1. A belief in the individual: since the individual is believed to be both moral and rational;
2. A belief in reason and progress: based on the belief that growth and development is the natural condition of mankind, and politics the art of compromise;
3. A belief in a society that is consensual: based on a desire for order and co-operation not disorder and conflict;
4. A belief in shared power: based on a suspicion of concentrated power (whether by individuals, groups or governments).

In his inaugural speech to the Australian Senate in March 2016, newly inducted senator James Paterson referred to classical liberals, and by extension liberal democracies, as "the custodians of a set of ideas that goes back centuries. We have inherited an incredibly proud intellectual tradition. Throughout history, liberals have fought for human progress. It was people who called themselves liberals who helped emancipate slaves, enacted religious freedom, and established the principle that all should be equal before the law[14]".

More and more countries have become liberal democracies since the start of the 20th century. However, there are still many nations that do not function in this way. Of 195 countries assessed in the Freedom in the World Report by Freedom House, 54% were rated as partly free or not free[15]. These countries house 61% of the world's population. Through the progression of such nations toward being liberal democracies, the standard

---

13 Museum of Australian Democracy, accessed 10 December, 2016 <www.moadoph.gov.au/democracy/defining-democracy/>
14 James Paterson's inaugural speech to the Australian Senate. Wednesday 16 March, 2016, 5pm.
15 "Freedom in the World Annual Report", Freedom House, accessed 10 December, 2016 <htt[s://freedomhouse.org/report/freedom-world/freedom-word-2015#.V46MZWlayK0>

of living for all humanity can be lifted and the numbers living in poverty and despair reduced.

Of course progress takes time and for the millions of refugees who are suffering today immediate help and action is required. How do we best help refugees, and best help the world? The approach must include maintaining the ongoing viability of liberal democracies as these are the cradles from which human rights will flourish throughout the world. However that does not mean more cannot be done. Our approach to help refugees can and must be improved, this book explores how.

PART 1
Situation

Section 1.1
Global Review

Part 1 — Situation (Chapters 1-10)

Part 2 — Complication, Principles & Assessment Framework (Chapter 11-12)

Part 3 — Options & Recommendation (Chapters 13-17)

Section 1.1

CH 1-7 Global Review
- Uses the *Refugee Journey* framework to review the global refugee situation. Including:
- Disruptive Causes and Forcibly Displaced People.
- Protection (i.e. as asylum seekers or refugees).
- Durable Solutions (i.e. Repatriation, Local Integration or Resettlement).

Section 1.2

CH 8-10 Australian Review
- Reviews the Australian context including:
- Australia's migration programs.
- Australia's humanitarian program.
- Controversy and debate surrounding Australia's humanitarian program.

Section 2.1

CH 11 The Complication
- Summarises the main issues identified through the global and Australian reviews.

Section 2.2

CH 12 Principles & Assessment Framework
- Outlines the Questions of Principle that must be answered to best manage the refugee situation.
- Sets out the approach option assessment framework.

Section 3.1

CH 13-15 Options Assessment
- Summarises the various Component Policies.
- Summarises and assesses the various Holistic Approaches using the approach option assessment framework.

Section 3.2

CH 16-17 Discussion and Recommendation
- Discusses the trade-offs in selecting the best Holistic Approach Option.
- Recommends an approach and provides a pathway for implementation including Australia's next steps.

Fig 1.1 > The Refugee Journey.

STEP 1: No Protection

EVENT: Disruptive Cause

STATUS: Not Protected (through country nor Refugee Convention)

- Event that triggers a person leaving their home due to a fear of persecution because of race, religion, nationality, membership of a particular social group or political opinion.
- Multiple types of events may cause disruption.
- Examples:
  - Persecution of an individual or a group. This could be caused by a government or a government may fail to protect an individual from such persecution.
  - War or conflict whereby direct threat is placed on individuals in the area.
  - Natural disasters or environmental changes.

- Displaced person no longer feels protected by their home state but has yet to be provided protection through the UNHCR or by a signatory country of the Refugee Convention.
- Examples:
  - A person who, due to civil war, is travelling on foot and heading for the border but has yet to leave their country.
  - A person who has suffered persecution due to their religion and is travelling outside their country on a boat headed for Australia.
  - A person whose home has been destroyed due to an earthquake and now is homeless.
  - An Internally Displaced Person (IDP).

2014 Population
- IDPs: 38.2 million

STEP 2: Temporary Protection

EVENT: Provision of Temporary Protection

STATUS: Temporarily Protected (through Refugee Convention)

- Event that brings a person under protection through the Refugee Convention. Initially as an Asylum Seeker.
- Examples:
  - Arriving at an emergency camp (established by the UNHCR or other organisation), be it in their own country or another country.
  - Arriving at a new country who is a signatory to the Refugee Convention and applying for asylum.

- Person is provided temporary protection outside their country of origin under the Refugee Convention by an agency, government or body whilst a durable solution is sought.
- Currently different types of protection provide different levels of quality of life and different probabilities and timelines to specific (desired) durable solutions.
- Examples:
  - Accommodation and basic provisions provided in a camp run by the UNHCR.
  - Protection provided by a country of asylum.

2014 Population
- Asylum Seekers: 1.8 million
- Refugees (UNHCR): 14.4 million
- Refugees (UNRWA): 5.1 million
- Total = 21.3 million

STEP 3: Permanent Protection

EVENT: Provision of a Durable Solution

STATUS: Permanently Protected (through Country)

- Event that provides a person with permanent protection by a state (a durable solution).
- Examples:
  - Repatriation as a citizen to the individual's home country.
  - Integration into the country of asylum (2nd country) as a citizen.
  - Resettlement into a 3rd country as a citizen.

- Person is provided ongoing protection and is not (or is no longer) considered forcibly displaced.
- Different countries provide different levels of protection and prosperity. Such differences may also increase or decrease the likelihood that disruptive events will remove the provision of this ongoing safety.
- Examples:
  - Australian citizen born in Australia.
  - Australian citizen who resettled in Australia as a refugee.
  - North Korean citizen
  - Sudanese citizen who has repatriated to Sudan after a period outside the country as a refugee.

2014 Population
- Citizens: 7.3 billion

CH 1. A DESPERATE JOURNEY

The Refugee Journey is a framework that outlines the unenviable journey a person who becomes a refugee takes from forcible displacement through to a permanent, durable solution. This book reviews information relevant to each step to ensure a complete coverage of aspects to consider with regard to the refugee situation. In Part 3 the Refugee Journey is also used in the assessment of various Holistic Approach Options for best managing the global crisis.

The Refugee Journey explained

The Refugee Journey is depicted across three steps. Each step contains an 'event' and a 'status'. The event is an occurrence that moves a person out of one status and into a new status. The status reflects the type of protection (or lack of protection) a person is receiving from a state or non-government agency like the UNHCR. The journey is thought to be an extremely long one. Although precise calculations are difficult, the current average time to move through these three stages is estimated to be eighteen years and growing. In 1993 the average was nine years[1].

Step 1: Not Protected

Step 1 Event: Disruptive Cause

A Disruptive Cause is an event that results in an individual becoming displaced and, initially at least, unprotected by a state or agency. There are multiple types of Disruptive Causes including: persecution of an individual or group by a government (or another group the government fails to keep in check); war or conflict that places a threat to an individual's life; and natural disasters such as earthquakes or environmental changes such as rising sea levels.

---

[1] Dr. James Milner, "Integrative Thinking and Solutions for Refugees" (Talk presented via TEDxRideauCanal, February 2012).

Step 1 Status: Not Protected (through country nor Refugee Convention)

Individuals who are displaced due to a Disruptive Cause do not perceive themselves to be protected by their home country nor are they protected under the Refugee Convention by an agency such as the UNHCR or another state. It is difficult to get a true measure of the number of people in this status as they do not always identify themselves, often for their own safety. Examples of people in this status include:

- 38.2 million IDPs at the end of 2014 as estimated by the Internal Displacement Monitoring Centre[2]. This includes people in emergency camps due to conflict or a natural disaster within their home country.
- People who are in their home country but are persecuted due to their race.
- People who have left their country due to religious persecution and are travelling (e.g. on foot or on a boat).
- People who have left their country and now reside in another country illegally without having registered as an asylum seeker.

Step 2: Temporary Protection

Step 2 Event: Provision of Temporary Protection

The provision of temporary protection occurs when an individual moves under the protection of a new country or an organisation such as the UNHCR. An example of this event is when a Syrian asylum seeker arrives at an UNHCR camp in Jordan. Another example is an Afghani arriving in Australia on a boat and requesting asylum.

Step 2 Status: Temporarily Protected

Individuals are protected (as asylum seekers and then as refugees) by a government or agency while a durable solution is sought. Currently the temporary protection across countries varies. Different countries provide variations in the quality of life for the refugees they harbour as well as disparate probabilities and time-lines for a durable solution if the refugees are seeking resettlement into a developed nation. This will be covered in more detail in Chapter 5.

There were 21.3 million people temporarily protected in 2014 across three categories.

- 1.8 million asylum seekers awaiting their status as a refugee to be confirmed or not.
- 14.4 million people who have been confirmed as refugees awaiting a durable solution.
- 5.1 million Palestinians registered by UNRWA.

---

2 Norwegian Refugee Council and Internal Displacement Monitoring Centre, *Global Overview 2015: People internally displaced by conflict and violence*, 7.

Step 3: Permanent Protection

Step 3 Event: Provision of a Durable Solution

The provision of a Durable Solution occurs when an individual moves back home through voluntary repatriation or is provided with permanent protection from a new country. This new country could either be the country of asylum that has provided the temporary protection to the refugee or a country of resettlement not yet inhabited by the refugee. As an example, the 12,000 Syrian refugees Australia volunteered to resettle in 2015 are being provided with durable solutions.

Step 3 Status: Permanently Protected

Individuals enjoy the protection of their state. Their state may be their Country of Origin (which has protected them continuously or since their repatriation following a period in asylum), or it may be a new state they have either migrated to (through regular migration channels) or have been resettled to (through an asylum seeking and resettlement process).

A detailed insight into the plight of refugees is beyond the scope of this book. This does not mean Forcibly Displaced People do not suffer greatly. Nor does it mean this suffering should not be taken into account. That refugees flee grave suffering, hardship and uncertainty is well established and beyond doubt. That leaving their home country is often just the beginning of a long, arduous and sometimes torturous journey has also been well established. For many people, the realisation of protection and freedom may never come again. It is a worldwide tragedy of enormous scale.

As there are many different Disruptive Causes, there are many forms of suffering and hardships. Whether it be an Afghan suffering at the hands of the Taliban, or an Iraqi being tortured under Saddam Hussein's regime or a Rohingyan enduring persecution in Myanmar, the experience can be devastating. For many, it will take their life, if not their sanity. Some are lucky enough to escape, but often with the physical and emotional scars of the terror they left behind.

The danger does not end with leaving their Country of Origin. To get to safety, an asylum seeker may have to travel across open seas or perhaps place themselves in the power and trust of people smugglers whom they have just met. Countries to which they flee, particularly non-signatories to the Refugee Convention, may show a great disinterest in helping them, or could even send them back to the country they fled.

Perhaps most alarmingly, even when asylum seekers manage to get to a country that has signed the Refugee Convention, their torment may have just begun. The most relevant example is Australia's mandatory detention centres, off-shore processing centres and range of temporary visas. Discussed further in Chapters 9 and 10, Australia's migration and humanitarian processes have been shown to cause further harm to those who have fled such terror and already endured so much.

While not detailed explicitly in this book, the pain and suffering endured by asylum seekers is a critical data point that must be front of mind when understanding the situation and determining the best Holistic Approach Option. There are many accounts that help provide insight into the plight of refugees. Four good books relating to various stages along the Refugee Journey to Australia are: *Raised In Conflict: Growing Up in Afghanistan*[3] by Essan Dileri as told by Jill Parris; *The People Smuggler*[4] by Robin De Crespigny; *From Nothing to Zero: Letters from Refugees in Australia's Detention Centres*[5] preface and chapter introductions by Julian Burnside QC; and *Lives In Limbo: Voices of Refugees Under Temporary Protection*[6] by Michael Leach and Fethi Mansouri.

Refugees and the Refugee Convention

The Refugee Convention of 1951 established the definition of a refugee. It was initially limited to a European, post World War II context. It was expanded in an update to the Convention through the 1967 Protocol. Currently the 1951 Convention or the 1967 Protocol have been ratified by over 140 countries. The convention was a thoroughly discussed and considered document that has survived for over 60 years. This longevity may be a testament to its efficacy or an example of bureaucratic inertia. Perhaps unsurprisingly given its age, there have been suggestions that potential revisions may be required given the changes to the world over the past sixty years.

Fig 1.2 › Signature Nations to the UN Refugee Convention and / or Protocol.
Source: Public Domain (via Wikipedia) https://commons.m.Wikimedia.org/wiki/File:Refugeeconvention.PNG accessed July 30, 2016.

The Convention provides the definition of a refugee that is widely used today.

---

3 Essan Dileri as told by Jill Paris. *Raised in Conflict* (Essan Dileri, 2013).
4 Robin De Crespigny, *The People Smuggler* (Melbourne: Penguin 2012).
5 *From Nothing to Zero,* compiled by Meaghan Amor and Janet Austin (Melbourne: Lonely Planet, 2003).
6 Michael Leach & Fethi Mansouri, *Lives in Limbo* (Sydney: UNSW Press, 2004).

A **Refugee** is an individual who is outside their home country of citizenship because they have well-founded grounds for fear of persecution because of their race, religion, nationality, membership of a particular social group or political opinion, and is unable to obtain sanctuary from their home country or, owing to such fear, is unwilling to avail themselves of the protection of that country; or in the case of not having a nationality and being outside their country of former habitual residence as a result of such event, is unable or, owing to such fear, is unwilling to return to their country of former habitual residence[7]. Such a person may be called an "asylum seeker" until considered with the status of "refugee" by the contracting state where they formally make a claim for sanctuary or right of asylum.

Some key terms must be expanded for a full understanding of what causes someone to be a refugee.

- **Persecution** is not defined in the Refugee Convention. It can take an infinite variety of forms but as a minimum, it encompasses threats to life and freedom. It can take on some lesser threats, such as social or economic discrimination depending on who is adjudicating. Adjudication is through a process called Refugee Status Determination (RSD), which many countries as well as the UNHCR undertake. RSD is covered in Chapter 5.

- **Fear of Persecution**. At the time the Refugee Convention was framed, the atrocities of the Nazi regime of World War II were fresh in the collective psyche, and in particular the plight of the European Jewish community. During the 1930s many requests by European Jews for immigration to countries like the United States to escape their growing persecution were declined. With the end of the war, the true horrific experience endured by the same group who had tried, often unsuccessfully, to leave prior to 1939 was evident. In this context, a rational fear of persecution became embedded as a just reason for asylum.

- **Race, religion, nationality, membership of a particular social group or political opinion.** These are the five reasons someone may claim persecution and seek asylum as a refugee. In recent times there have been calls to expand this definition to include sex (gender and/or sexual identity), but adjudicators believe such criteria is covered by the reference to a 'social group'.

---

[7] Article 1A(2), *Convention relating to the Status of Refugees,* opened for signature 28 July 1951 (entered into force 22 April 1954) read together with the Protocol relating to the *Status of Refugees,* opened for signature 31 January 1967 (entered into force 4 October 1967).

- **Outside their home country**. This specifies that obligations regarding protection of refugees only begin for signatory nations when the refugees are outside their Country of Origin. This does not mean that Internally Displaced People are any less in need of protection. However, this demarcation honours the sovereignty of the Country of Origin. By defining refugees this way, the Convention avoids sanctioning entry by foreign agencies into a country in order to support would-be refugees.

A Snapshot of the Forcibly Displaced People—end 2014

The UNHCR describes a number of differing categories under their umbrella term 'people of concern'. Three of these (refugees, asylum seekers and internally displaced people) are collectively labelled as Forcibly Displaced People[8].

Within the refugee category, there is one additional distinction:

- Palestinian Refugees registered by UNRWA relates to 5.1 million people who are displaced due to the 1948 Arab-Israeli War. This includes the still surviving 30,000 to 50,000 of the members of the original 700,000 Palestinians who were displaced, and the almost five million descendants of this original group.
- UNHCR Mandate Refugees relates to all other refugees covered by the Refugee Convention definition.

As of the end of 2014, the UNHCR estimated that 59.5 million people had a status of being forcibly displaced[9]. Unsurprisingly, the Countries of Origin across each category of forcible displacement are consistent. For example, five countries (Syria, Iraq, Democratic Republic of Congo, Sudan and Somalia) feature in the top ten Countries of Origin for each of IDPs, asylum seekers and refugees. For the asylum seeker and refugee categories, the top ten Countries of Origin account for about 75% of the total.

- 38.2 million people (almost two-thirds) were IDPs. Although arguably no less vulnerable than those outside the borders of their home countries, IDPs are not officially provided refugee status and associated protections as per the definition of the Refugee Convention. Until a person leaves their home country, they are under the jurisdiction of their home nation and no one else. This jurisdiction relates to Westphalian Sovereignty, which mandates that each nation state has the right of self-determination, that is full control over its domestic affairs to the exclusion of all other states.

---

8   UNHCR, *Global Trends: Forced Displacement in 2014*, 8.
9   Ibid 2.

- 1.8 million people were asylum seekers. These asylum seekers are provided protection while their status as a refugee is being assessed through a process known as Refugee Status Determination (RSD). In 2014 more than half of these were being conducted in four countries (South Africa, Germany, USA and Turkey).
- 19.5 million people were refugees.
    - 5.1 million Palestinian Refugees registered by UNRWA.
    - 14.4 million UNHCR Mandate Refugees, almost 8 million of these coming from three major source countries: Syria, Afghanistan, and Somalia. As we will discuss in Chapter 5, most refugees are housed in neighbouring countries, or Countries of First Asylum (COFA), which places a tremendous strain on their societies.

Calculating the Numbers of Forcibly Displaced People

The number of Forcibly Displaced People is never static. Each year a range of factors work to increase or decrease the number of people listed as IDPs, asylum seekers, or refugees.

Factors that increase the numbers include new disruptive causes such as a fresh outbreak of conflict in a country or heightened persecution of minorities within a country.

- Asylum Seeker numbers are increased by people newly presenting as asylum seekers after crossing over a border into a signatory nation.
- Refugee numbers are increased by completed Refugee Status Determinations identifying Asylum Seekers as refugees.

Perceived improvements to their possible outcomes may also increase the number of people who present as asylum seekers. A hidden number of persecuted people who are discouraged to identify as asylum seekers may occur when the probability for improvement to their conditions appears unrealistic. This hidden group shares a similarity in behaviour with hidden unemployed workforces. As conditions become more favourable they may present. The key point being that the 59.5 million forcibly displaced peoples is likely to be a large understatement of the real number of people.

Factors that decrease the numbers of forcibly displaced people include the three Durable Solutions that reduce the refugee count: repatriation home, integration into the country of asylum, or resettlement into a third country. Other factors include IDPs who voluntarily return home whether because of improved conditions or loss of hope, and people who through the Refugee Status Determination are assessed not to be refugees. Unfortunately deaths also reduce the numbers of Forcibly Displaced People.

Each year, the starting population of people who are living as forcibly displaced is altered by the net effect of the factors that increase and decrease the numbers.

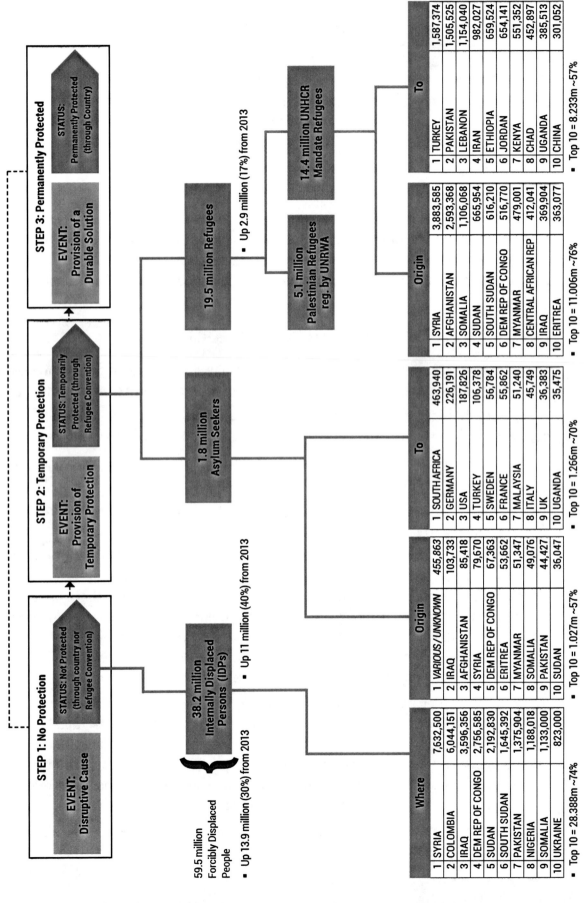

Fig 1.3 ▶ Forcibly Displaced People depicted on the Refugee Journey. *Data Source: UNHCR, Global Trends: Forced Displacement in 2014.*

The problem of Forcibly Displaced People is continuous, analogous to a puddle from a dripping tap. The 59.5 million people currently forcibly displaced are represented by the puddle that needs to be cleared by finding permanent protection for all. Newly identified Forcibly Displaced People are represented in the analogy by the drips from the tap. Helping these 59.5 million people today does not solve the problem forever – more asylum seekers are likely to present next year as nothing has been done to eliminate the disruptive causes. The key to solving the problem is stopping the events that continue to forcibly displace new people.

Growth of Forcibly Displaced People

A review of the UNHCR data can lead to a couple of contrary assessments in relation to the growth of Forcibly Displaced People. Whilst the number is growing, much of it is due to the inclusion of IDPs. Although IDPs are certainly people in need, they are not traditionally considered under the scope of the UNHCR. The UNHCR started measuring the numbers in the IDP category in 1993. Much of the growth of the population of concern is due to the large growth in IDPs, from zero in 1992 to 38.2 million in 2014. In that time, the total number of refugees has stayed relatively stable.

In general, the 1950s and 1960s had relatively low numbers of refugees. In 1971 there was a mass movement of over 10 million people from East Pakistan (now Bangladesh) into India in the first few months of the 1971 Bangladesh Liberation War. There was slow growth in the number of refugees throughout the 1970s. They came mainly from Africa (nations including Angola, Guinea, Democratic Republic of Congo and Ethiopia) and South East Asia (nations including Vietnam, Myanmar and Cambodia).

The refugee population rose dramatically in the 1980s. More than one-third of the 17.4 million refugees in 1990 were from Afghanistan (6.3 million), with over 1 million people fleeing Ethiopia and Mozambique. The 1990s saw a reduction in the refugee numbers with 12.1 million refugees listed in 2000. Afghanistan, Iraq and Bosnia & Herzegovina were the major Countries of Origin. In the first 15 years of the 21st century Afghanistan, Iraq, Somalia and now Syria are the key refugee Countries of Origin.

Removing the categories of "IDP" and "Others" shows the recent rise in numbers for UNHCR Mandate Refugees and asylum seekers is less dramatic. In fact, the total people in these two categories is less than it was in the early 1990s.

A "Wicked Problem"

The coordinated international effort in helping refugees has developed since the early 20th century, increasing significantly following World War II. In line with the growing international concern for helping those in need, so too has the world's wealth and capability through technology increased. The result is that the developed world has the means and desire to help at levels that have not previously been possible.

While these new levels of wealth, capability and desire to help represent great opportunities for alleviating the refugee situation, they do not guarantee success. It must be recognised that the presence and suffering of Forcibly Displaced People is as old as history and has yet to be solved. The efforts of the international community and the UNHCR in the past 65 years have forged into new territory, and the way forward is still being found. However, if anything, the problem seems to be growing.

The refugee situation has been referred to as an example of a "Wicked Problem"[10]. Wicked Problems are virtually impossible to solve and usually create additional problems. Difficulties in solving are due to many reasons including: incomplete or contradictory knowledge, the number of people and opinions involved, the large economic burden, and the interconnected nature with other problems. Rather than being fixed or solved, Wicked Problems should be managed to mitigate the negative consequences and position the broad trajectory of culture in a more desirable direction. This applies to the refugee situation. Given the international aspect of the issue, there are a number of contributing factors beyond the control of any one government or group of powers. There is no near-term solution, only management approaches (detailed and assessed in Part 3, Chapters 13-17).

Global Population Growth

Although the world is motivated and capable to help at levels greater than ever before, so too is the size of the problem. The global population has increased exponentially in the past 200 years, even the wars of the 20th century only had small impacts on the upward trends. Following World War II, the population doubled between 1950 and 1990. As of 2015, there are 7.3 billion people in the world.

These figures are significant as many of the present global issues are only exacerbated by more people. Examples include the depletion of natural resources like fossil fuels, the increase in pollution through industry and human activity, the reduction of natural habitats like forests, the depletion of fish populations through over-fishing, and the scarcity of food and water.

---

10   Paris Aristotle, 'A "wicked problem"?', Big Ideas, *ABC Radio National* 28 June 2013 <www.abc.net.au/radionational/programs/bigideas/2013-07-01/4778140>

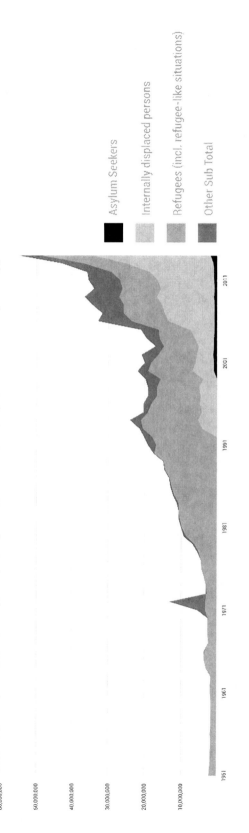

Fig 1.4 > UNHCR people of concern since 1951. *Data Source: UNHCR 2014.*

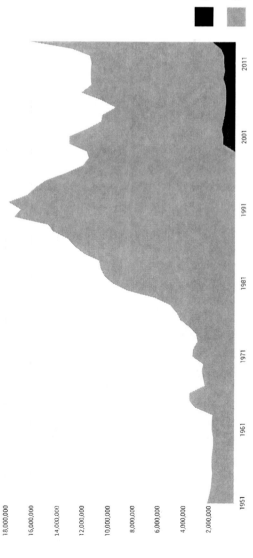

Fig 1.5 > UNHCR Mandate Refugees and Asylum Seekers since 1951. *Data Source: UNHCR 2014.*

Alternatively, there are arguments that it is the increased population that will provide the impetus and the people to solve these problems. After all, problems are opportunities and it was these same pressures which led to the population of the new world and the innovations of the last 400 years.

The growth in population is not evenly spread across all countries; poor countries are growing the fastest. At the start of the 20th century, Europe housed almost one quarter of the world's population and North America held another 5%. One hundred years later, Europe and North America housed only 17% of the world's population. Since 1960:

- Africa has increased more than threefold.
- Asia, South America, and the Caribbean have doubled.
- North America has grown by only 50%.
- Europe has grown by only 20% (and is now roughly stable).

Fig 1.6 > World Population Since 10,000 BC. *Data Source: OurWorldInData.org.*
Year of Each Additional Billion of World Population. *Source: United Nations Secretariat, 1999.*

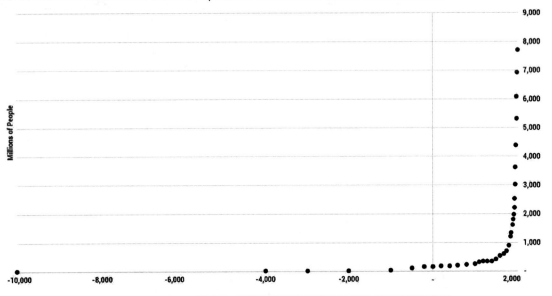

World population reached	Year	Time to add billion
1 billion	1804	
2 billion	1927	123 years
3 billion	1960	33 years
4 billion	1974	14 years
5 billion	1987	13 years
6 billion	1999	12 years
7 billion	2011	12 years

Future Population Growth

The world population grew by 1.15% in 2015 and is expected to continue to grow at a rapid rate. In fact, the projected population growth throughout the 21st century has recently been raised. During the first decade of the 21st century, it was generally thought the population would peak at about 9 billion around 2050. This estimate was based on assumptions regarding the reduction of the Total Fertility Rate (TFRs) in the remainder of the developing world where they are still high.

The TFR is a measure of an imaginary woman's fertility as she passes through her entire reproductive life (assumed to be 15-49), experiencing all the age-specific fertility rates for that year. Wealthy, developed nations tend to have lower TFRs in line with education, urbanisation and availability of contraception. The worldwide TFR has been reducing. In 1950-1955 it was 4.95 whereas in 2010-2015 it had dropped to 2.36[11].

From the 1960s the TFRs of many Asian and South American countries quickly reduced. For example, both China and Brazil experienced a drop in TFR from more than six to less than two (indicating a long-term zero population growth) in about 40 years[12]. This fast move led demographers to expect a similar experience in Africa. Statistics have been poor, but as they come in, it is apparent the decline of TFRs throughout Africa is much slower than predicted. As a result, the latest data from the UN Population Division predicts the population will continue to grow throughout the 21st century. The estimate is now for a population of around 11 billion people in 2100, with an 80% probability it will lie between 9.6 billion and 12.3 billion[13].

Inclusive in this estimate are regional predictions including:

- India's population to peak at 1.5 billion-1.6 billion in 2070.
- Most growth to occur in Sub-Saharan Africa, quadrupling from 1 billion to 4 billion – resulting in the population of Africa becoming as dense as China is today.
- Nigeria, with a population currently of 174 million, will more than quintuple to about 900 million by 2100.

These estimates are challenged by alternate views. For instance, a paper produced by Wolfgang Lutz and the International Institute for Applied Systems Analysis (IIASA) predict a population peak at 9.4 billion in 2075 and dropping to 9 billion by 2100. The approach

---

11 "Total fertility rate", UNdata, accessed 10 December, 2016 <data.un.org/Data.aspx?d=PopDiv&f=variableID%3A54>
12 Robert Kunzig, "A World With 11 Billion People? New Population Projections Shatter Earlier Estimates," *National Geographic,* September 19, 2014.
13 Ibid.

used was to gather the opinion of multiple experts on demographic related questions and input these into a model predicting the potential population growth. One of the main differences driving the reduced population estimate for Lutz's work is the inclusion of education and its role in reducing fertility rates[14].

---

[14] Ibid.

CH 2. DISRUPTION

The first step of the Refugee Journey is when a **Disruptive Cause** results in people becoming forcibly displaced with **No Protection**.

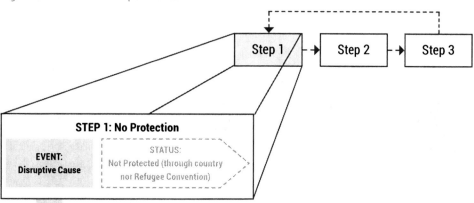

Fig 2.1 ❯ Event 1 – Disruptive Cause.

- Why are there Forcibly Displaced People?
- Disruptive Causes Relating to State Behaviour or Strength
- Colonialism, Imperialism and the West
- Intervention, Sovereignty and Responsibility to Protect
- Border Fixity and Weak Nations
- Future Projections of Forcibly Displaced People

Why are there Forcibly Displaced People?

Historically, some countries have produced many refugees consistently while other countries have not. In its global review for 2014, the UNHCR issued a matrix that displayed the top-20 refugee Countries of Origin for each year from 1980-2014. Across this 35-year period, 49 countries featured in the top-20 at least once.

Fig 2.2 ▶ The 50 major source countries for refugees in the 35 years to 2014.
Source: UNHCR Global Trends, Forced Displacement in 2014, 17.

Legend: T1 = TOP 1 | T5 = TOP 2-5 | T10 = TOP 6-10 | T20 = TOP 11-20

COUNTRY	1980	1981	1982	1983	1984	1985	1986	1987	1988	1989	1990	1991	1992	1993	1994	1995	1996	1997	1998	1999	2000	2001	2002	2003	2004	2005	2006	2007	2008	2009	2010	2011	2012	2013	2014	#TIMES IN TOP 20
AFGHANISTAN	T5	T1	T1	T1	T1	T1	T1	T1	T1	T1	T1	T1	T1	T1	T1	T1	T1	T1	T1	T1	T1	T1	T1	T1	T1	T1	T1	T1	T1	T1	T1	T1	T1	T1	T5	35
ANGOLA	T5	T5	T5	T10	T5	T10	T10	T10	T10	T10	T10	T10	T20	T20	T20	T20	T20	T20	T20	T20	T20	T10	T10	T20	T20	T20	T20	T20	T20	T20	T20	T20				32
ARMENIA													T20	T20	T20	T20	T20	T20	T20																	7
AZERBAIJAN													T20	T20	T20	T20	T20	T20	T20	T20	T10	T10	T5	T10	T10	T10	T20	T20	T20	T20	T20					15
BHUTAN																												T20	T20							2
BOSNIA AND H.												T20	T10	T10	T5	T5	T5	T5	T10	T5	T5	T5	T10	T20	T20	T20	T20									15
BURUNDI	T10	T10	T10	T20	T10	T10	T10	T10	T10	T20	T20	T10	T10	T10	T5	T5	T10	T5	T5	T10	T10	T5	T10	T5	T5	T10	T20	T10	T10	T20	T20	T20				29
CAMBODIA	T10	T20	T20	T20	T5	T20	T20	T20	T20																											8
CENTRAL AFRICAN REP																										T20	T20	T20	T20	T20	T20			T20	T10	7
CHAD	T10	T10											T20											T20	T20	T20	T20	T20								11
CHINA														T10				T10	T20	T10	T20	T10	T10	T5	T10	T10	T5	T5	T10	T10	T10	T10	T10	T10	T20	12
COLOMBIA																									T10	T10	T10	T5	T10	T10	T10	T20	T10	T10	T20	8
COTE D'IVOIRE																			T20	T10							T20				T20	T20	T20	T20	T20	3
CROATIA													T20			T20	T20	T10	T20	T20	T20															13
DEM REP OF CONGO	T20	T20	T20	T20	T20	T20	T20	T20	T20	T20	T20	T20	T10	T10	T10	T10	T10	T10	T10	T10	T10	T10	T10	T5	T5	T5	T5	T5	T5	T5	T10	T10	T10	T10	T10	30
EL SALVADOR	T20	T10	T10	T10	T10	T10	T10	T20	T20	T20						T20																				9
EQUATORIAL GUINEA	T20	T20																																		2
ERITREA															T20	T20	T20	T20	T20	T20	T20	T10	T10	T10	T10	T10	T10	T10	T10	T10	T10	T10	T10	T10	T10	24
ETHIOPIA	T1	T5	T5	T5	T5	T5	T5	T5	T5	T5	T5	T20	T10	T10	T20	T20																			T5	15
GUATEMALA			T20	T20	T20																															3
IRAQ	T20	T20	T20	T20	T20	T20	T20	T20	T20	T20	T10	T10	T20	T10	T20	T20	T20	T5	T5	T5	T5	T5	T10	T10	T10	T5	T5	T5	T5	T5	T5	T5	T5	T10	T10	35
IRAN					T20	T20	T20	T20	T20																											4
LAOS	T20	T20	T20	T20	T20	T20	T20	T20	T20	T10	T10	T20	T20																							12
LIBERIA										T20	T10	T10	T10	T10	T10	T5	T5	T5	T10	T10	T10	T10	T10	T10	T10	T10	T20									17
MALI											T20	T20																				T20	T20		T20	3
MAURITANIA											T20	T20																								2
MOZAMBIQUE	T20	T20	T20	T20	T10	T10	T5	T5	T5	T5	T5	T5	T5	T5	T20																					14
MYANMAR									T20	T20		T20	T20	T20		T20	T20	T20							T20	T20	T20	T20	T20	T10	T5	T10	T10	T10	T10	23
NAMIBIA	T20	T20	T20	T20	T20	T20	T20	T20																												8

PART 1. SITUATION > CH 2. DISRUPTION

Fig 2.2 (continued).

COUNTRY	1980	1981	1982	1983	1984	1985	1986	1987	1988	1989	1990	1991	1992	1993	1994	1995	1996	1997	1998	1999	2000	2001	2002	2003	2004	2005	2006	2007	2008	2009	2010	2011	2012	2013	2014	#TIMES IN TOP 20
NICARAGUA			T20	T20	T20			T20	T20	T20																										4
PAKISTAN																															T20			T20		1
PHILIPPINES	T20	T20	T20	T20	T20	T20	T20	T20	T20	T20																										10
RUSSIA		T20											T20	T20	T20	T20	T20		T20																T20	16
RWANDA	T10	T10	T5	T5	T5	T5	T5	T10	T10	T10	T10	T10	T10	T10	T5	T5	T10													T20	T20	T20	T20	T20	T20	22
*SERBIA													T20	T20	T20	T5	T5		T20	T10	T10	T10	T10													15
SIERRA LEONE												T20	T10	T10	T10	T10	T10	T10	T10	T10	T10	T10	T5													12
SOMALIA												T10	T10	T10	T10	T10	T10	T10	T5	T5	T5	T5	T5	T5	T5	T5	T5	T5	T5	T5	T5	T5	T5	T5	T5	27
SOUTH AFRICA	T20	T20	T20	T20																																4
SOUTH SUDAN																																		T20	T5	2
SRI LANKA												T20	T20					T20		T20	T20	T20	T5	T5	T5	T20	T20	T20	T20	T10	T10	T10	T10	T10	T10	15
***SUDAN					T20	T20	T20	T20	T10	T10	T10	T10	T10	T10	T10	T10	T5	T10	T10	T5	T5	T5	T5	T5	T5	T5	T5	T5	T5	T5	T5	T5	T5	T5	T5	32
SYRIA																																			T1	3
TIMOR-LESTE														T20						T20	T20	T20														3
TOGO																																				1
TURKEY																			T20	T20	T20	T20	T20	T20	T20	T20	T20	T20	T10	T20			T20			11
UGANDA	T10	T10	T10	T10	T10	T10	T10	T20																												8
UKRAINE																																		T20		1
****UNKNOWN	T5	T5	T10	T10	T10	T10	T5	T5	T5	T5	T5	T5	T5	T5	T5	T5	T5	T5	T5	T5	T5	T5	T10	T10	T10	T10	T10	T10	T10	T10	T10	T10	T10	T10	T20	35
VIETNAM	T5	T5	T10	T5	T10	T10	T10	T10	T10	T10	T10	T10	T10	T10	T10	T10	T10	T10	T10	T5	T5	T5	T10	T10	T10	T10	T10	T10	T10	T10	T10	T10	T10	T10	T20	35
WESTERN SAHARA	T20	T20			T20	T20	T20	T20	T20	T20	T20	T20	T20	T20	T20	T20	T20	T20	T20	T20	T20	T20	T20	T20	T20	T20	T20	T20	T20							29
YEMEN	T20																																			5

*ETHIOPIA: INCLUDES ERITREA UNTIL ITS INDEPENDENCE IN THE ABSENCE OF SEPARATE STATISTICS AVAILABLE FOR BOTH COUNTRIES.

**SERBIA AND KOSOVO. INCLUDES MONTENEGRO UNTIL ITS INDEPENDENCE IN THE ABSENCE OF SEPARATE STATISTICS AVAILABLE FOR BOTH COUNTRIES.

***SUDAN: INCLUDES SOUTH SUDAN UNTIL ITS INDEPENDENCE IN THE ABSENCE OF SEPARATE STATISTICS AVAILABLE FOR BOTH COUNTRIES.

****UNKNOWN ORIGIN: REFERS TO REFUGEES WHOSE COUNTRY OF ORIGIN IS UNKNOWN. DATA AVAILABILITY HAS IMPROVED SIGNIFICANTLY OVER THE YEARS.

Twelve countries featured as a top-20 nation in more than 20 of the 35 years:

1. Afghanistan (35)
2. Iraq (35)
3. Vietnam (35)
4. Angola (32)
5. Sudan* (32) – formerly included the land that is now South Sudan
6. Democratic Republic of Congo (30)
7. Burundi (29)
8. Western Sahara (29)
9. Somalia (27)
10. Eritrea* (24) – included within Ethiopia until independence in 1993.
11. Myanmar (23)
12. Rwanda (22)

Disruptive Causes Relating to State Behaviour or Strength

The reasons why countries produce a high number of refugees relate to the behaviour of the state, and the strength of the state.

Disruptive Causes Relating to State Behaviour

Nazi Germany is an obvious example of a strong state power that persecuted a specific population of individuals with the result that they sought asylum for their own safety. Unfortunately, Nazi Germany is not a lone perpetrator of state-based persecution. In the 1950s and 1960s people fled the Soviet Union and China based on ideological differences with the communist regimes. Given the authority and emigration controls of these regimes, the numbers were relatively low. Occasionally there were larger scale events such as the failed Hungarian revolution in 1956. Other examples include the South Vietnamese who fled at the end of the Vietnam War and, more recently, the Rohingya people of Myanmar (Burma) who have suffered systemic violence and persecution from their government. The UNHCR has estimated that 25,000 Rohingya people fled the country on boats during the first three months of 2015[1].

The civil liberties and political rights experienced by citizens vary greatly from country to country. The *Freedom of the World* annual report produced by Freedom House measures the freedom of all countries and categorises them as Free, Partly Free or Not Free. There are strong regional differences. In 2014, 86% of the population of Europe were living in free countries, 71% of the Americas, 38% of Asia-Pacific, 5% of the Middle East and North Africa and 0% of Eurasia[2].

---

1   Beh Lih Yi, "Malaysia tells thousands of Rohingya refugees to 'go back to your country,'" *The Guardian,* May 13, 2015.
2   "Freedom in the World 2015," Freedom House, accessed July 21, 2016 <https://freedomhouse.org/report/freedom-world-2015#.V5ChHPQmKnM>

PART 1. SITUATION ❯ CH 2. DISRUPTION   41

Only about 39% of the world's population live in a country classified as "Free" by the Freedom of the World Report. Countries classified as "Partly Free" contain 24% of the world's population. The remainder, about 37% of the world's population, live in countries classified as "Not Free", which are far more likely to produce refugees:

- Of the Free countries (58 of them with over one million people), only five (Serbia, Croatia, El Salvador, Namibia and South Africa) have been a top-20 refugee-producing country in any year since 1980. On average these five countries appeared in 10 of the past 35 years.

- Partially Free countries were more likely to produce refugees. They make up about 24% of the world's population, and 18 of these countries were a top-20 Country of Origin nation (with an average of 7 years in the top 20).

- Not Free countries include the top ten refugee-producing nations of 2014. Of the 50 nations that were a top-20 Country of Origin for refugees in any of the 35 years since 1980, 26 were Not Free with an average of 17 years in the top 20 (much greater than both the Free and Partially Free).

Fig 2.3 Freedoms of the World. *Source: Freedomhouse. org. https://freedomhouse.org/report/freedom-world/freedom-world-2015#.V5wmP2laySM accessed July 30, 2016.*

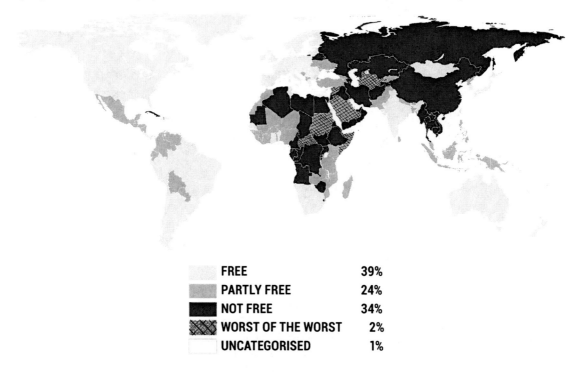

	FREE	39%
	PARTLY FREE	24%
	NOT FREE	34%
	WORST OF THE WORST	2%
	UNCATEGORISED	1%

Disruptive Causes Relating to State Strength

A weakened state power, often leading to civil war, is the Disruptive Cause that results in the most displaced people. Fighting causes a lack of security for those caught in the middle, particularly for civilians of the minority groups. Examples include the Democratic Republic of Congo, Central African Republic, Somalia, Iraq, Afghanistan and Syria.

Low wealth is a key factor increasing the risk of civil war. In his book *The Bottom Billion*, the renowned Oxford Economist Paul Collier explores the issues that affect poor countries. Collier notes, "Halve the starting income of the country and you double the risk of civil war"[3]. Additional insights from *The Bottom Billion* include:

- Slow economic growth and the dependence on a primary commodity (such as oil or diamonds) also makes a country prone to civil war.
- Areas with low population density or mountainous terrain, where rebel armies can hide, also add to the likelihood of civil war.

Interestingly, Collier reported there was little statistical evidence relating to political repression or ethnic diversity to civil war. The key point being, it is poor economics that drive the propensity for civil war. Friction toward repressive regimes or "other peoples" may be used as focus points to unite resistance movements but they are not the primary drivers for rebellion. The primary drivers are a poor economy and the resultant idleness and limited opportunities for the country's youth.

The enormous disparity of wealth across nations is an important fact given that low income and slow growth are related to civil wars that result in suffering and refugees. The World Bank uses Gross National Income (GNI) per capita to measure the relative wealth of nations. In 2015, 99.8% of the world's 7.35 billion people lived in the 158 countries with populations greater than 1 million[4]. Meaningful data relating to the income and level of freedom were available for 152 countries. Of these:

- The 46 'very high income' and 'high income' countries have a GNI per capita of US$13,020 (that of Croatia) or more.
    - Containing approximately 19% of the world's population.
    - More than half (26) were from Europe.
    - Eight were from the oil-rich Middle East, six from South America and the Caribbean, four from Asia (Chinese Hong Kong, Japan, South Korea and Singapore).

---

3 Paul Collier, *The Bottom Billion* (New York: Oxford University Press, 2007), 23 of 187. iBook edition.
4 "2015 Revision of World Population Prospects," UN Population Division, accessed 10 December, 2016 <www.un.org/en/development/desa/population/>

Fig 2.4 Country Wealth (GNI per Capita)

Source: Freedomhouse.org. <https://freedomhouse.org/report/freedom-world/freedom-world-2015#.V5wmP2laySM> accessed July 30, 2016; and World Bank, *World Development Indicators database*, 1 July, 2015. <c.ymcdn.com/sites/www.ishrworld.org/resource/resmgr/Docs/GNIPC_2014.pdf> accessed 25 October, 2016.

COUNTRY WEALTH - GNI PER CAPITA IN US DOLLARS

	VERY HIGH (17 COUNTRIES) 42,000 OR ABOVE	HIGH (29 COUNTRIES) 13,020 - 42,000	UPPER MIDDLE (39 COUNTRIES) 4,280 - 13,019	LOWER MIDDLE (37 COUNTRIES) 1,040 - 4,279	LOW (30 COUNTRIES) LESS THAN 1,020
FREE ~2.9 BILLION (39%)	NORWAY, AUSTRALIA, SWEDEN, DENMARK, USA, CANADA, NETHERLANDS, GERMANY, BELGIUM, IRELAND, FRANCE, UK, JAPAN	ISRAEL, ITALY, SOUTH KOREA, CYPRUS, GREECE, PORTUGAL, ESTONIA, URUGUAY, LATVIA, LITHUANIA, CHILE, ARGENTINA, POLAND, HUNGARY, CROATIA, CZECH REP, SLOVAKIA, FINLAND, SLOVENIA, SPAIN, AUSTRIA, SWITZERLAND, TRINIDAD AND TOBAGO, NEW ZEALAND	BRAZIL, PANAMA, COSTA RICA, MAURITIUS, ROMANIA, BULGARIA, BOTSWANA, SOUTH AFRICA, PERU, DOMINICAN REP, SERBIA, NAMIBIA, MONGOLIA, TUNISIA, JAMAICA	EL SALVADOR, GHANA, INDIA, LESOTHO, SENEGAL	BENIN
PARTLY FREE ~1.8 BILLION (24%)	SINGAPORE, KUWAIT	VENEZUELA	TURKEY, MALAYSIA, MEXICO, LEBANON, COLOMBIA, ECUADOR, BOSNIA AND HERZEGOVINA, ALBANIA, PARAGUAY, TFYR MACEDONIA	ARMENIA, GEORGIA, INDONESIA, UKRAINE, PHILIPPINES, GUATEMALA, SRI LANKA, TIMOR-LESTE, MOROCCO, NIGERIA, HONDURAS, NICARAGUA, ZAMBIA, PAKISTAN, KENYA, BANGLADESH, PAPUA NEW GUINEA, REP OF MOLDOVA, BOLIVIA	HAITI, NEPAL, BURKINA FASO, SIERRA LEONE, MALI, MOZAMBIQUE, TOGO, GUINEA-BISSAU, GUINEA, MADAGASCAR
NOT FREE ~2.7 BILLION (37%)	QATAR, UAE	RUSSIAN FEDERATION, BAHRAIN, OMAN, SAUDI ARABIA	KAZAKHSTAN, GABON, TURKMENISTAN, LIBYA, AZERBAIJAN, CHINA, BELARUS, IRAQ, ALGERIA, THAILAND, JORDAN, ANGOLA, IRAN, CUBA	EGYPT, SWAZILAND, UZBEKISTAN, SUDAN, CAMEROON, MAURITANIA, MYANMAR, TAJIKISTAN, SYRIA, YEMEN, CONGO, LAOS, VIET NAM	CAMBODIA, CHAD, SOUTH SUDAN, ZIMBABWE, RWANDA, ERITREA, UGANDA, AFGHANISTAN, ETHIOPIA, CENTRAL AFRICAN REP, BURUNDI, SOMALIA, NORTH KOREA, DEM REP OF CONGO, GAMBIA

COUNTRY FREEDOM - A PER FREEDOM HOUSE

Top ten refugee Countries of Origin in 2014.

- The remaining four countries are the United States, Canada, Australia and New Zealand.
- The 17 'very high income' countries (11% of the world's population) have an average GNI per capital of US$42,000 (that of Japan) or above.
- 39 are 'upper middle income' (ranging from Kazakhstan at US$11,670 down to Mongolia at US$4,280).
  - Containing approximately 33% of the world's population.
  - Twelve are from Asia and the Middle East.
  - Eleven are from Latin and South America.
  - Nine are from Africa, and
  - Seven are from Eastern and Southern Europe.
- A further 37 are 'lower middle income' (from El Salvador with US$3,950 to Senegal with US$1,040).
  - Containing approximately 39% of the world's population.
  - Each country in the lower middle income category has an average GNI per capita of less than one-third of Croatia (the lowest country in the high income bracket) and one-tenth of the richest 17 countries.
- Finally, 30 are 'low income' ranging from Cambodia (US$1,020) to Malawi (US$250).
  - Containing approximately 9% of the world's population.
  - Each country with an average GNI per capita less than one tenth of Croatia.

Figure 2.4 shows the relationship between freedom, wealth and stability. Free countries tend to be wealthy, and also tend to have less refugees. Of the top ten refugee-producing nations in 2014, six were low income (Afghanistan, Somalia, South Sudan, Democratic Republic of Congo, Central African Republic and Eritrea), three were lower middle income (Syria, Sudan and Myanmar) and one (Iraq) was upper middle income.

Colonialism, Imperialism and the West

Powerful outside states may contribute to the Disruptive Causes experienced within refugee-producing countries. These outside states may include both colonial powers of centuries past and modern-day powers. Three types of involvement which may have negatively impacted on today's vulnerable countries are:

1. The development of extractive political and economic systems during the colonial period which persisted after independence.

2. Military intervention, whether in defence of the human rights of the country's people or for less utilitarian, capitalistic interests.

3. The development of inappropriate State borders.

Extractive political and economic systems

In their book, *Why Nations Fail*[5], Daron Acemoglu and James A. Robinson describe how extractive political and economic systems can focus power and the accumulation of wealth to a few controlling elite. Such systems were utilised during the imperialism of the 19th and early 20th centuries. In colonial times, political and economic systems were developed to keep the political power, and therefore the economic benefits, with a narrow elite. That narrow elite was usually the monarchy of an imperialist country and its subjects employed to manage the colonial region. This occurred throughout much of Africa in the 19th century.

Following World War II, Western European imperialism was rolled back, and many African nations gained independence. Although initially democracies with free elections, many African nations quickly experienced civil wars, military coups, and often a change in political structure to dictatorships. The dictators were then able to utilise the extractive systems that were firmly established in their countries by the imperial powers. While it provided enormous wealth for the dictators and their close circle, it rendered the rest of the population to poverty and increased the propensity for civil war. An example is the Democratic Republic of Congo.

The region, known then as the Kingdom of Kongo, had been noted by 15th century European visitors as extremely poor. Historians argue this poverty was due to the extractive policies in place by the then King and his administrators. Taxes and the threat of slavery were so high that there was no incentive for the inhabitants to save for and use new technologies such as the plough. Why would they when all additional monies would be taken by the rulers? Instead people were motivated to move as far away as possible from the administrative powers.

When the region came under Belgian rule in the late 19th century, the pattern continued. This time the narrow elite extracting all the wealth was Belgian's King Leopold III and the Belgian colonists. After independence in 1960 the same systems were again adopted. The long-time economic and political institutions that funnelled wealth and power to an elite remained, it is just that the elite had changed.

---

5   Daron Acemoglu and James A. Robinson, *Why Nations Fail: The origins of power, prosperity and poverty*, (London Profile Books Ltd, 2012).

As an independent nation, the Democratic Republic of Congo experienced almost unbroken economic decline between 1965 and 1997 under the rule of Joesph Mobutu. Although the people lived in poverty, Mobutu and a narrow band of elites lived lavishly with little incentive to change the system. This decline continued through the same systems after Mobutu was overthrown by Laurent Kablia.

The Democratic Republic of Congo is just one example within sub-Saharan Africa of European imperialist powers establishing or enhancing extractive systems of economics and politics. These extractive systems funnelled wealth and power to a few at the cost of the wealth of the nation in general. Unfortunately these systems have proved to be very persistent, even following independence or the overthrowing of a dictator. Often the new controlling power – the new elite – have little incentive to change the set up and instead claim the wealth for themselves. Other examples include Angola, Cameroon, Chad, Haiti, Liberia, Sierra Leone, Sudan and South Sudan, and Zimbabwe[6].

Military intervention

The Vietnam War is an example of military intervention in defence of the interests and human rights of an inhabitant population. The governments of the USA, Australia and other allies viewed their involvement as a way to prevent the takeover of South Vietnam by the communists in North Vietnam. A consequence of this war was the forcible displacement of numerous South Vietnamese, many of whom arrived in Australia in the late 1970s as refugees. Of course, external military intervention can not be held as the sole reason for human rights abuses. It is possible that terrible suffering would also have been experienced had these nations not supported the South Vietnamese. For example, the UN decided not to intervene in the Rwandan civil war in 1994. It has since been argued that this enabled the mass slaughter of the Tutsi people by the Hutu majority.

Another example is the 2003 invasion of Iraq by coalition forces including the USA, UK, Australia and Poland. The stated intention of the Iraq invasion was to "disarm Iraq of weapons of mass destruction, to end Saddam Hussein's support for terrorism, and to free the Iraqi people"[7]. Of course, a widely held alternative belief is that the motive for many of the interventions in the Middle East is not purely in support of the populous but specifically due to the protection of capitalist interests with regard to oil. Examples include the protection of the Saudi family and Saudi Arabia, which control the world's largest known oil reserves, as well as Saddam Hussein's Iraqi regime in the 10 year war

---

6   Daron Acemoglu and James A. Robinson, *Why Nations Fail: The origins of power, prosperity and poverty*, (London Profile Books Ltd, 2012), 373.
7   George W Bush, "Operation Iraqi Freedom" (Radio address transcript accessed July 21, 2016).

against Iran. While the 2003 invasion of Iraq did succeed in ending the reign of Saddam Hussein, it is widely accepted that the subsequent power vacuum contributed to the rise of the Islamic State and much of the disruption in Syria through 2014-15.

Inappropriate State borders

One final form of outside intervention, which arguably also contributes to disruptive events is the creation of inappropriate international borders, particularly after World War II. An example of this would be the separation of Kurdish people across Iraq, Syria and Turkey. Somewhat related to this was the creation of Israel after World War II. The creation of Israel led to the 1948 Arab-Israeli War and the creation of almost 700,000 Palestinian refugees. These refugees, discussed in Chapter 5, and their descendants are treated as an exceptional case by the UN with a bespoke agency, the United Nations Relief and Works Agency for Palestine Refugees in the Near East (UNRWA), created in 1949 to support them.

Extent of these Contributions to Disruptive Causes

The extent to which these three causes have contributed to the situations that have created refugees is debatable. Certainly, it is not accurate to suggest these problems are completely manufactured by intervening powers. For example, colonial rule within Africa was for a relatively short period of time. In the case of the region now within the Democratic Republic of Congo, narrow control of political and economic power preceded the arrival of Belgian rule. Similarly, it is hard to argue that the Middle East would be peaceful if not for Western intervention. There has been a long history of fighting within the Middle East under the rule of the Ottoman Empire for hundreds of years. In comparison, Western involvement in the Middle East has been for a relatively short period of time.

If their responsibility for the creation of these Disruptive Causes is accepted, are the powerful nations of the world required to do more to help people in a situation that they helped create? If they can do more, why are they not doing so? These questions are explored further in Chapter 12.

Intervention, Sovereignty and Responsibility to Protect

If the two main drivers of disruption are the behaviour of the state, and civil war due to a weakened state. Can these situations be avoided? Can the international community help to avoid the creation of Disruptive Causes that lead to refugees in the first place? The answer, it seems, is 'sometimes but not always'. The reason help cannot always be provided lies with the concept of a sovereignty held by international law. Article 2 (4) of the United Nations Charter states that:

> *"All Members shall refrain in their international relations from the threat or use of force against the territorial integrity or political independence of any state, or in any other manner inconsistent with the Purposes of the United Nations[8]."*

This concept stems from the Treaty of Westphalia in 1648. The Treaty of Westphalia is considered a seminal agreement in regard to international diplomacy. Its concept of sovereignty, also known as Westphalian Sovereignty, remains today. Sovereignty is the monopoly on the legitimate use of force and allows sovereign states control of their own domestic affairs. Westphalian Sovereignty promotes equality amongst states and represents a common agreement among states not to interfere in one another's domestic affairs[9]. Importantly it provides states the freedom to manage their own affairs without interference from outside.

This freedom from outside interference limits the extent to which other states can intervene to prevent human rights crises within a state's border, even when such humanitarian intervention could arguably support Forcibly Displaced People. Such humanitarian intervention usually requires some form of military force to suppress the behaviour of one or more groups creating the disruption. As a sovereign nation has the monopoly of the legitimate use of force within their borders, such intervention is not allowed.

However there are occasions when a clear humanitarian crisis is occurring. For example, during the Rwandan civil war of 1994 a mass genocide of Tutsi people occurred at the hands of the Hutu majority. Should Westphalian Sovereignty be adhered to when such atrocities occur? There is clearly a balance between the rights of a state and the human rights of its inhabitants. On the one hand, loss of sovereign rights places the weaker nations at risk from the more powerful. On the other hand, international law also recognises that sovereignty cannot be used as a license to trample on human rights. The UN Secretary-General's High Level Panel on Threats, Challenges and Change concluded in its report in 2005:

> *"Whatever perceptions have prevailed when the Westphalian system first gave rise to the notion of state sovereignty, today it clearly carries with it the obligation of a state to protect the welfare of its own peoples and meet its obligations to the wider international community"*[10].

---

8   Charter of the United Nations, Chapter 1, Article (4).
9   J A Cohen, "Sovereignty in a Post-Sovereign World" (2006) 18 *Florida Journal of International Law* 907.
10   "A more secure world: Our shared responsibility, Report of the High-level Panel on Threats, Challenges and Change" (United Nations 2004), accessed 3 December 2016 <http://www.un.org/en/peacebuilding/pdf/historical/hlp_more_secure_world.pdf>

It is within this context that a set of rules exist around when an outside state or collection of states can intervene within a sovereign nation. There are four main reasons that justify intervention:

1. In response to a request from the sovereign nation.
2. In self defence.
3. Under the authority of the UN Security Council under Chapter VII of the UN Charter.
4. Due to a need for a legitimate humanitarian intervention.

The first three reasons permitting intervention are quite straight forward. Although they are open to some interpretation, in general, they allow for an easy assessment as to whether their criteria have been met or not. The fourth reason, due to a need for a legitimate humanitarian intervention, is less straight forward. A number of criteria have been issued on this front by various bodies. One of the most influential is The International Commission on Intervention and State Sovereignty (ICISS) and its 2001 *Responsibility to Protect* Report. This report established a widely referred to criteria for a legitimate exercise of humanitarian intervention[11]. It outlined six principles:

1. **Just Cause** – the justification must be an extraordinary level of human suffering (actual or imminent) from direct state action or inaction to protect its citizenry. It must entail large-scale loss of life.
2. **Right Intervention** – the primary purpose of the intervention must be to halt or avert human suffering.
3. **Last Resort** – "Every diplomatic and non-military avenue for the prevention or peaceful resolution of the humanitarian crisis must have been explored".
4. **Proportional Means** – "The scale, duration and intensity of the planned military intervention should be the minimum necessary to secure the humanitarian objective in question".
5. **Reasonable Prospects** – "Military action can only be justified if it stands a reasonable chance of success, that is, halting or averting the atrocities or suffering that triggered the intervention in the first place".
6. **Right Authority** – Intervention should be undertaken under the authority of the UN Security Council, however in exceptional cases unilateral intervention may be legitimate.

Although these principles set up a strict framework to assess the legitimacy of an intervention, the reality is there is no governing body to oversee, provide and enforce such

---

11 International Commission on Intervention and State Sovereignty, *The Responsibility to Protect,* (December 2001).

an assessment. In practice, powerful nations are still able to ignore this and intervene in sovereign nations. Two examples of contentious intervention are the military action against Iraq in 2003 by the US-led coalition (which included Australia) and the Russian annexation of the Crimea in 2014.

There have been humanitarian interventions that were more widely supported by the international community. Examples of these are:

- Indian intervention in Bangladesh (1971)
- Vietnamese intervention in Cambodia (1978)
- Tanzanian intervention in Uganda (1979)
- No-fly zones in northern Iraq (1990s)
- Kosovo (1999)

The need for an intervention implies a sovereign party in opposition to the intervention. Therefore, all interventions are disputed on some level. If all disputes toward interventions are ignored, a risk develops that powerful nations may use the guise of humanitarian intervention for their own motives. Many argue that humanitarian ideals have been provided in the past to justify colonialism, imperialism and conquest. On the other hand, moral arguments can be made that state sovereignty can be sacrificed to prevent crimes against humanity. Of course, humanitarian intervention can lead to destruction and bloodshed without the re-establishment of human rights. Given this, rather than a trade-off between human rights and sovereignty, humanitarian intervention could also be seen as a trade-off between human rights and peace. As you can see, each potential humanitarian crisis provides a dilemma for the international community regarding whether or not to intervene, and the choice is rarely clear cut.

Border Fixity and Weak Nations

Dr Boaz Atzili, a political scientist and author, has explored the prohibition on the use of force to alter international borders, what he refers to as "border fixity"[12]. This concept has only really taken hold following World War II. It seems that border fixity works very well with strong states but has unintended negative consequences in weaker states. One negative consequence is that a strong driver for social cohesion, relating to outside threats and opportunities, is lost. Another is the creation of a moral hazard by allowing weak states to perpetuate, regardless of performance.

---

12 Boaz Atzili, "When good fences make good neighbours, and when they make bad ones: The international effects of border fixity" (paper prepared for the delivery at the annual convention of the International Studies Association, San Diego, March 22-25, 2006).

The external threats to any nation help galvanise its populous together in order for mutual benefit. This may be the suppression of an external threat or indeed the capture of land from a weaker neighbour. Arguably these drivers helped create the social cohesion and shared identity that exist within Western European nations. It is clearly preferred that threats to the borders of the newly formed, ex-colonial nations of Africa and the Middle East are less than as those experienced within Europe up until 1945. However, these new nations do not experience the same drivers for social cohesion as a consequence. The result being an increased likelihood of internal conflict.

The second consequence, allowing weak states to exist in perpetuity, removes many drivers that lead to the improvement of a nation for future generations. Weak governments and people are not motivated to better organise themselves to make the state more powerful for their defence. There is less progress to improve state efficiency as there is no outside threat driving improvement. Ultimately, weak states are not absorbed and incorporated into more powerful states that can more efficiently organise people. The result is that regions under the jurisdiction of weak states remain so.

The perpetuation of weak states is not just bad for its own inhabitants but also for its neighbours and the entire international community. First, they are often susceptible to civil war or unable to control persecutions against minorities. Thus they become a source of refugees. As birth rates tend to remain high in poor nations, the supply of refugees does not abate. Second, civil conflicts can spill over to neighbouring countries. For instance, through shared ethnicity, members of a country not in civil war may align with one side of a civil conflict in their neighbouring country. Third, the weakened state encourages economic predatory activity by stronger neighbours which may ultimately spark international conflict. An example of this issue is Zimbabwe's involvement in the war over the Democratic Republic of Congo. Zimbabwe's President Mugabe encouraged the production and trade of diamonds, gold and copper from the parts of the DRC controlled by Zimbabwean troops[13].

Since the end of World War II there has been relatively little change to international borders. This has certainly reduced the devastating impact of international conflict. However, the consequences of this reducing the progressive development of stronger and more cohesive nations must also be recognised.

---

13   Ibid 24.

Future Projections of Forcibly Displaced People

The relationship between low wealth, low growth and civil war is important when considering the probability of refugee volumes in the future. As previously mentioned, projections suggest that the greatest population growth will come from the poorer nations. Alarmingly it is also the poorer nations that are more likely to fall into civil war. Ultimately this creates the potential for the displacement of very large groups of people in the future.

Not only does this increase the potential number of people that could be displaced, it also increases the number of people in the developing world relative to the developed world. This will proportionally reduce the developed world's ability to support those in need. According to data from the United Nations Population Division, since 1951 approximately 91% of the world's population growth has occurred outside the high income countries defined by the World Bank[14]. This skewed growth has decreased the proportion of the population that lives within high income countries from 32% to 19%.

Fig 2.5 > World population since 1950 (by Country Incomes). *Source Data: "2015 Revision of World Population Prospects" UN Population Division.*

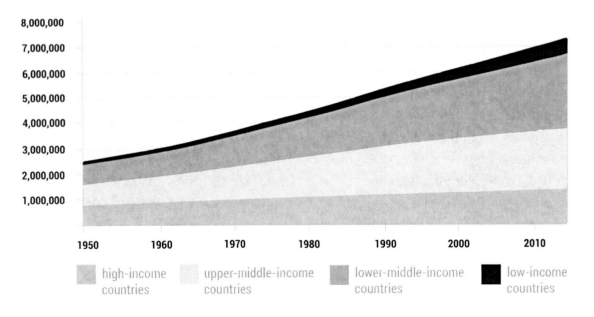

---

14   "2015 Revision of World Population Prospects," UN Population Division, accessed 10 December, 2016 <www.un.org/en/development/desa/population/>

This skewed growth reflects a general pattern where the population growth of a country reduces as the average wealth and life expectancy of its people improves. This pattern is explained by the concept of Demographic Transition, which outlines five stages in the transition from high birth rates to low birth rates. It explains that countries generally start with both high birth rates and high mortality rates. As wealth and development improves, both sanitation and medicine improves as well. The mortality rate subsequently drops but the high birth rate persists, rapidly expanding the population. Over time, the improving wealth, urbanisation and education lowers the birth rate and the population stabilises.

Demographic Transition has occurred across Europe, the United States and other parts of the industrialised west over the past 150 years. More recently it has occurred in some countries across Asia (such as Japan, South Korea), South America (such as Brazil, Argentina) and Africa (such as Kenya) as their wealth has increased. The inverse relationship between wealth and fertility rates applies across the world's major religions of Christianity, Islam, Hinduism and Buddhism[15]. However, not all religions have the same current TFR. This will be discussed in further detail in Chapter 7.

Fig 2.6 › Demographic Transition. *Source: Max Roser, "Our World In Data", accessed 25 October, 2016. <https://en.m.Wikipedia.org/wiki/Demographic_transition#/media/File%3aDemographic-TransitionOWID.png>*

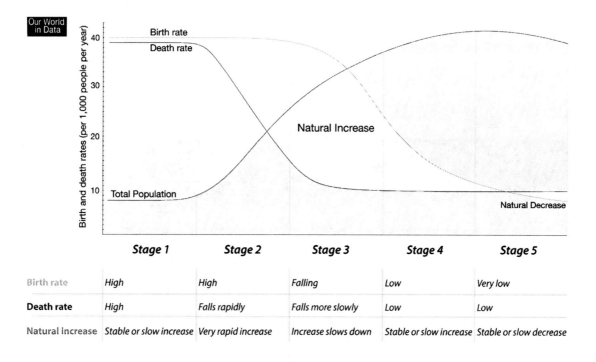

---

15 Hans Rosling, "Religion and Babies" (Talk presented via TED Tal, April 2012, Doha, Qatar).

Many poor and war-ravaged countries have yet to go through the Demographic Transition. As examples, since 2001 the population of Afghanistan has increased by 58%, the Democratic Republic of Congo by 56% and Nigeria by 45%. A key contributing factor in the Demographic Transition is the birth rate, best measured by TFR. Previous predictions about the reduction in TFR in Africa have proved to be incorrect, leading to an upward adjustment in regard to the world's 2100 population estimate by the UN Population Division. Until initiatives to reduce TFR are firmly established in the poor and developing nations the probability of rapid growth remains high. As they are also likely to be impacted by civil war, the probability of the displacement of large amounts of people in these countries also remains high.

The consecutive year count in Figure 2.7 shows that countries tend to remain as significant sources for refugees for a number of years, and that problems tend to persist. Thus, the most likely refugee Countries or Origin are the countries that are already the primary refugee-producing nations. Only a small percentage of each country's total population have become refugees or asylum seekers to date, leaving a large future potential population who may still request asylum. Those who are already IDPs would be the most likely to move. The high TFRs indicate that these countries are still growing, very rapidly. Eight of the top ten Countries of Origin for Forcibly Displaced People in 2014 have fertility rates of four or more (much higher than the worldwide average of 2.4). Thus, even if all of today's refugees are provided a durable solution, without rectifying the situations within the Countries of Origin, the future numbers of refugees from these countries could be even larger than they are today.

Fig 2.7 ❯ Top 10 Refugee Country of Origin and potential for further refugees. *Source Data: UNHCR, Global Trends: Forced Displacement in 2014.*

Country of Origin	Forcibly Displaced Population Outside Country of Origin (2014)			Country Population (2015)	% Outside Country of Origin	IDPs (2014)	Total Fertility Rate (2013)	Consecutive Years: Top 20 Refugee Country of Origin[1]
	Refugees	Asylum Seekers	Total					
Syria	3,865,720	79,670	3,945,390	18,502,413	21%	7,632,500	3.0	3
Afghanistan	2,593,368	85,418	2,678,786	32,526,562	8%	805,409	4.9	35
Somalia	1,106,068	49,076	1,155,144	10,787,104	11%	1,133,000	6.6	27
Sudan	659,395	36,047	695,442	40,234,882	2%	2,192,830	4.4	32
South Sudan	616,142	3,785	619,927	12,339,812	5%	1,645,392	4.9	2[2]
Dem Rep of Congo	516,562	67,363	583,925	77,266,814	1%	2,756,585	5.9	19
Central African Rep	410,787	14,388	425,175	4,900,274	9%	438,538	4.4	7
Iraq	369,904	103,733	473,637	36,423,395	1%	3,596,356	4.0	35
Eritrea	330,526	53,662	384,188	5,227,791	7%	-	4.7	24
Myanmar	223,891	51,347	275,238	53,897,154	1%	376,500	1.9	23

Notes: (1) Number of consecutive years in which the country has been in the top 20 countries of origin for refugees for that year.
(2) South Sudan only attained independence in 2011.

CH 3. VULNERABLE

As defined above, Disruptive Causes result in people fleeing the danger or persecution they perceive. From the commencement of this move to their attainment of temporary protection, through the UNHCR or a signature country to the Refugee Convention, these Forcibly Displaced People can be thought of as existing without protection from either their country of origin or the Refugee Convention.

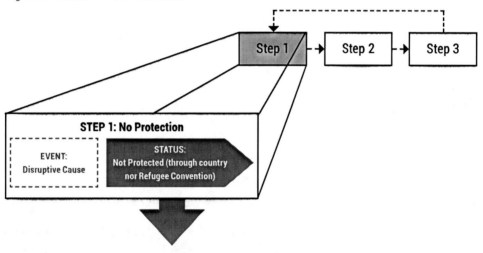

Fig 3.1 ❯ Status 1 - Not Protected.

- Three Options for the Unprotected Forcibly Displaced
- Dangerous Risks to Improve Prospects
- People Smugglers
- Internally Displaced People
- Mass Movements Since World War II
- Mass Migration to Europe in 2015
- History of Asylum Seeker Arrivals To Australia

Three Options for the Unprotected Forcibly Displaced

There are essentially three options available for Forcibly Displaced People who are not protected by their Country of Origin or a signatory country to the Refugee Convention.

One option is to make do as best they can in their home country. If they stay in their home country they may seek support through family, friends or a camp or community-based support services.

The second option is to leave their country. In this case the best outcome is often to get to a UNHCR camp or a signatory nation of the Refugee Convention and claim asylum. Both of these will provide a minimum level of comfort and protection. Failing either of these, the third alternative is to get out of harm's way by arriving at a non-signatory country of the Refugee Convention. However, these countries do not provide any guarantees in regard to minimum protection standards including support such as food and shelter.

Examples of people with no protection from either their Country of Origin or a signatory to the Refugee Convention are:

- A person whose home has been destroyed due to an earthquake and now is homeless and is living in a UNHCR emergency camp.
- A person who, due to civil war, is travelling on foot and heading for the border but has yet to leave their country.
- A person who has suffered persecution due to their religion and is travelling outside of their country on a boat headed for Australia, for instance.

The number of people forcibly displaced and with no protection is not definitively known as many in this group do not identify with an organised body. However, the IDP estimates provide a good indication as to the number and change in number of people in this status. As of 2014 there were estimated to be 38.2 million IDPs.

There are many cases where people who have been staying in a Country of First Asylum undertake a secondary movement and travel to another country in order to improve their perceived chances for a greater outcome. Sometimes the Country of First Asylum is not a signatory country, other times it is but is overwhelmed with large numbers of asylum seekers and the prospects for a durable solution are very remote. This occurrence highlights the fact that the standards of protection provided, and the probability of desired durable solutions differ according to location.

The existence of people taking such risks, especially from signatory countries that are relatively safe but with little hope of a fulfilling existence, highlights one of the limitations of the current situation. The use of people smugglers is frequent and particularly concerning as evidence shows those who use such services put themselves in danger through perilous trips often on poor boats as well as the risk of extortion and slavery.

Dangerous Risks to Improve Prospects

A large and growing number of Forcibly Displaced People are harmed due to great risks taken in attempting to reach countries that are seen to provide better safety and prospects. Two well-known dangerous routes are the Mediterranean or Aegean Sea crossings to get to Europe, and the crossing from Indonesia to Australia.

In terms of known deaths, in the first nine months of 2015 approximately 3,000 deaths were recorded in the Mediterranean Sea as over 710,000 migrants reached European shores through its crossing[1]. In the waters between Indonesia and Australia there have been 964 known deaths between late 2001 and June 2012[2].

Often these risks are taken to flee danger and persecution, such as leaving the Syrian civil war. Other times they are made once people are already safe but find themselves in hopeless situations. This appears to be the case for Alan Kurdi and his family. The tragedy surrounding Alan's family and the plight of many attempting to reach Europe entered global consciousness after his dead body was photographed washed up on a Turkish beach. Three-year-old Alan, his five-year-old brother and mother Rehan all died attempting a crossing from Turkey to the Greek island Kos in order to enter Europe on their way to Canada. Although the family was from Syria, they had been living safely in Turkey for up to three years before they attempted the crossing. This tragedy is evidence that the plight of people's prospects in countries of asylum, as well as the perceived opportunities in more wealthy resettlement countries, is often enough for people to attempt dangerous journeys.

People Smugglers

People smuggling is a term used to describe the illegal service provided by syndicates to help individuals gain illegal entry into a country. Again, in the case of people who plead asylum, any illegality is irrelevant as no documentation is required to request asylum. People smuggling differs from human trafficking in that people smuggling is voluntary whereas human trafficking is involuntary. However, there are cases where smugglers dupe clients and force them into servitude[3].

---

1 Umberto Bacchi, "EU migrant crisis: More than 3,000 deaths in Mediterranean as arrivals surpass 700,000," *International Business Times,* October 13, 2015.
2 Angus Houston, Paris Aristotle and Michael l"Estrange, "Report of the Expert Panel on Asylum Seekers", (August, 2012), 19.
3 "People Smuggling", Interpol, accessed July 23, 2016, <www.interpol.int/Crime-areas/Trafficking-in-human-beings/People-smuggling/Background>

As the service operates on the black market, it is unregulated and the levels of cost, conditions, and safety vary greatly. The operators are generally unknown to the customers, who are planning to only use the service once. This places the customers in very vulnerable situations, either because of low safety standards, or exposure to syndicates who will try to enslave and sell the customers. The methods used can be by land, air or sea and the routes can vary based on legislative changes. It has been noted that in response to Australia's crackdown on people smuggling operations during the Abbott Government, the quality of the vessels deteriorated to reduce any financial losses through confiscation. Additionally, the general age of the crew decreased to avoid legal repercussions that would only apply for adult crew members[4].

If people smugglers adhere to their agreements with their clients and move people according to their wishes (e.g. across the Mediterranean to Europe or from Indonesia to Australia) are they simply helping vulnerable people attain a greater level of safety and protection? The answer to this again has two sides.

Among those that support the mobility of asylum seekers, some suggest that governments not punish people smugglers. This results in changes that reduce safety levels and the consequences are borne by the asylum seekers. Over and above this suggestion is the need for a more formal set of regional frameworks to be created that would formalise the international movement of asylum seekers, eliminating the need for people smugglers.

Although the Australian government has portrayed people smugglers as vile and evil people, this is not consistent with the biography of Ali Al Jenabi detailed in Robin De Crespigny's book *The People Smuggler*. Jenabi was simply trying to help his family get to safety from Saddam's Regime and the Indonesia described within the book (between 1999 and 2003) was by no means a safe or prosperous place for the Iraqis trying to come to Australia[5].

Opponents to the people smuggling trade argue that many of the asylum seekers are already safe. This activity places additional strain on countries that are trying to help. For example, by requiring additional resources to detect activity and rescue services for sinking boats. Related to this point is the notion there should be no incentive for asylum seekers to leave one country of security and risk their lives to get to another perceived to have a better quality of life and more opportunities. This philosophy underpins the Houston Report (2012) recommendations that ultimately resulted in the reinstatement

---

4   Asylum Seeker Resource Centre, *Asylum seekers and refugees - myths FACTS + solutions,* 36, accessed 12 November, 2016 <https://www.asrc.org.au/pdf/myths-facts-solutions-info_.pdf>
5   Robin De Crespigny, *The People Smuggler* (Melbourne: Penguin 2012).

of the Pacific Solution and included a 'no advantage principle' for those attempting to reach Australia by boat over what outcomes they would have been provided had they stayed in their Country of First Asylum. The Houston Report and no advantage principle are covered in more detail in Chapter 9.

Turning back boats does not necessarily stop people smuggling enterprises, at least not in the short term. Instead, their activities take on a new form. Dr Antje Missbach from the Centre for Indonesian Law, Islam and Society at the University of Melbourne found that in Indonesia, people smugglers profited from a new service – that of finding the best detention centres within Indonesia that desperate asylum seekers, short on cash, can stay. The 'best' usually meaning those with vacancies and the shortest imprisonment periods. People smugglers also organise transport for the asylum seekers and collect money sent to them that can be used to buy favours within their detention centre. Her conclusion: "the only way to fight people smuggling effectively is to make the networks redundant by offering more regular and formal resettlement pathways for asylum seekers and refugees."[6]

Internally Displaced People

In recent years, the majority of IDPs have been provided some form of protection and support through the UNHCR. In 2014, it was estimated that over 32 million IDPs or people in IDP-like situations were provided protection or support from the UNHCR. This represents over 80% of the estimated global IDP population. Although IDPs are provided support, they are not protected by the Refugee Convention as the refugee definition requires a person to be outside the country of their habitual residence. Further, given the specific definition regarding a refugee (which requires fear of persecution according to race, religion, nationality, and membership of a particular social group or political opinion) not all IDPs would necessarily qualify as refugees if they seek asylum in another country.

Although there is no technical protection under the Refugee Convention, there is a growing recognition that the plight of IDPs requires international attention. The UNHCR has had some relief programs supporting people displaced in their own country since 1972. IDPs were first measured in 1989 and since then the numbers have more than doubled. The 2014 total of 38.2 million was an all-time high and 8.3 million more than 2013.

---

[6] Dr Antje Missbach, "People Smugglers in Indonesia: Definitely Not Out of Business", 25 November 2015, accessed July 23 2016, <https://www.law.ox.ac.uk/research-subject-groups/centre-criminology/centreborder-criminologies/blog/2015/11/people-smugglers>

IDPs were formally included under the UNHCR's scope in 2005 when it was appointed by the UN to lead in the protection, shelter and camp management of IDPs[7]. Where once rules regarding sovereignty precluded humanitarian aid entering countries with large numbers of IDPs, in recent years support is increasingly provided into such areas. The United Nation's support of IDPs not only manages the threat to these people's livelihoods and rights but also the threat to the stability of the region. Effective support of IDPs is hoped to mitigate and resolve their situation without them seeking asylum in other countries. Such occurrences would result in increased burdens for neighbouring countries, which could have destabilising effects.

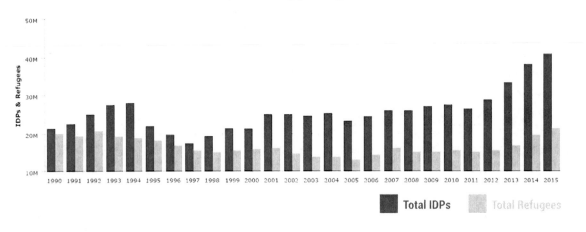

Fig 3.2 > IDP and Refugee Numbers Since 1989. *Source: International Displacement Monitoring Centre (IDMC) accessed 12 November 2016 <www.internal-displacement.org/global-figures>*

The footprint of IDPs largely correlates with the main refugee-producing countries. There were significant IDP populations in 24 countries in 2014. Over 70% are estimated to be women and children[8], presumably as men are fighting, have died, or are travelling to claim asylum before sending for their family. Although there are camps for IDPs, they are not used by the majority and about half of the IDP population are thought to be in urban areas[9]. The countries with the ten largest IDP populations account for 74% of the worldwide IDP population.

---

7   Alexander Betts, Gil Loescher and James Milner, *UNHCR: The Politics and Practice of Refugee Protection, Second Edition* (New York: Routledge, 2012), 73.
8   Norwegian Refugee Council and Internal Displacement Monitoring Centre, *Global Overview 2015: People internally displaced by conflict and violence,* <www.internal-displacement.org/assets/library/Media/201505-Global-Overview-2015/20150506-global-overview-2015-en.pdf>
9   Simone Haysom, "Sanctuary in the city? Reframing responses to protracted urban displacement," Overseas Development Institute (June 2013), accessed July 23, 2016, <https://www.odi.org/publications/7533-sanctuary-city-responses-protracted-irban-displacement>

Fig 3.3 › Not Protected.

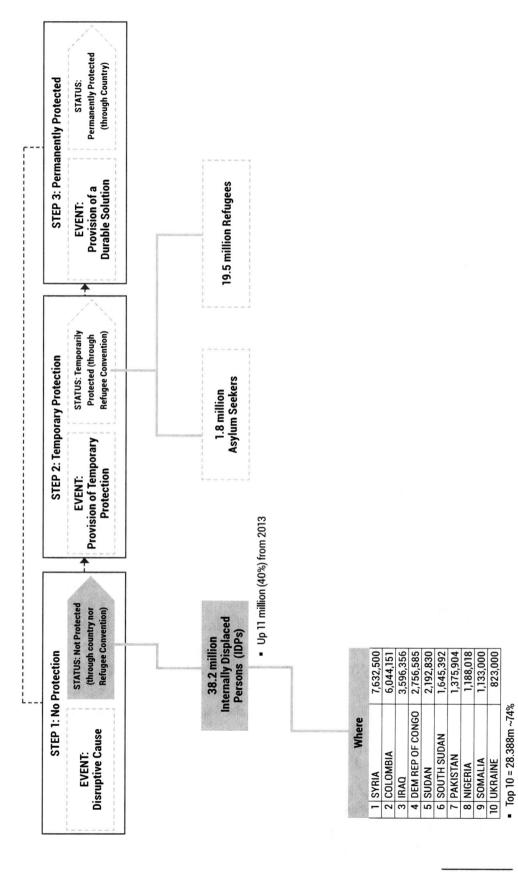

Mass Movements Since World War II

Key Examples of Mass Movements Since World War II

The Refugee Convention was established in 1951. This time corresponded with the start of the Cold War when it was envisaged many refugees would be individuals leaving regimes based on ideological differences. The displacement of masses of people is unfortunately a fairly common experience over the past 70 years since World War II. Mass movements have occurred in many regions of the world and include;

1940-60s

- **Palestine**: An exodus of about 700,000 (about 80%) of Palestinians from Arab land that became Israel. The UN set up a special agency (the UNRWA) to deal with these refugees and descendants.
- **China:** Approximately 700,000 Chinese moved into Hong Kong in the two years after the establishment of the People's Republic of China (1949[10]).
- **Hungary:** About 200,000 Hungarians fled to Austria and Yugoslavia following the 1956 invasion by the Soviet Union.
- **Algeria:** Approximately 85,000 Algerians moved into Tunisia from 1955-57.

1970-80s

- **Uganda:** Approximately 90,000 India and Pakistani community members moved from Uganda following an ultimatum from Idi Amin in 1972[11].
- **Bangladesh:** Ten million people moved from East Pakistan (now Bangladesh) into India during the 1971 Bangladesh War of Independence.
- **Afghanistan:** Constant movement from Afghanistan (over 2 million per year) since the Soviet Union invasion in 1979 to today, mainly into Pakistan.
- **Indochina:** More than three million people fled the countries of Vietnam, Cambodia and Lao in the 25 years after communist governments were established in 1975. Of these, 2.5 million were resettled (mostly in Europe and North America) and the remaining 500,000 were repatriated to their home countries. Of those resettled, Australia took in 185,700[12].

---

10   Alexander Betts, Gil Loescher and James Milner, *UNHCR: The Politics and Practice of Refugee Protection, Second Edition* (New York: Routledge, 2012), 25.
11   Mona Chhalabi, "What Happened to history's refugees?," *The Guardian*, July 25, 2013.
12   Robinson, W. Courtland *Terms of Refuge* (UNHCR, London: Zed Books, 1998 p. 270, 276, Appendix 2) Far Eastern Economic Review, June 23, 1978, p. 20.

1990s

- **Bosnia:** Approximately 200,000 people died and another 2.7 million moved due to the Bosnian war of 1992-95.
- **Rwanda:** Over two million Rwandans left in 1994 to neighbouring countries following the slaughter of 500,000 Tutsis by the Hutus.

21st Century

- **Sudan:** More than 2.5 million people in Sudan were displaced following war in the Darfur region in 2003.
- **Iraq:** Over 4.7 million Iraqis have left since the 1980 war with Iran began, peaking with the 2003 invasion.
- **Colombia:** Over four million people (about 10% of the population) were internally displaced due to conflict.
- **Syria:** Over four million refugees have fled the Syrian Civil War. It is the largest current population of refugees.

Mass Migration to Europe in 2015

Civil war has been raging in Syria since 2011. It has displaced millions of the original population of approximately 23 million. By the end of 2014, 3.9 million Syrians were refugees mainly in Turkey, Pakistan and Jordan. As detailed earlier in the chapter, mass displacement of people due to civil war or governmental pressure is unfortunately nothing new. However the response of Europe, in particular Germany, is something new, which has triggered an unprecedented movement of people across continents.

The stream of people heading for Europe from Syria and other countries of the Middle East and North Africa steadily increased through the summer of 2015. The additional asylum seekers placed pressure on border countries of Europe under the 1990 Dublin Agreement, which mandates that an asylum seeker has to apply for asylum in the first EU country that they enter and that this country is responsible for the asylum seeker's protection and Refugee Status Determination (RSD). In August of 2015 the Dublin Agreement was effectively suspended by Germany when it declared all Syrian asylum seekers were welcome to remain in Germany no matter through which country they first entered the EU[13].

Germany's announcement appeared to trigger an increase in the numbers moving into Europe. By the end of October, over 700,000 asylum claims were lodged in Europe.

---

13 Allan Hall & John Lichfield, "Germany opens its gates: Berlin says all Syrian asylum-seekers are welcome to remain, as Britain is urged to make 'similar statement'," *Independent* August 25, 2015.

Although Syria was the largest Country of Origin for the greatest number of these, it only accounted for roughly twenty percent of the total asylum seeker applicants. This is the same proportion that was measured in 2014, when Syria made up 19% of all non-EU asylum seekers presenting for asylum in the EU[14]. In short, this opportunity was taken up by many others, some arguably in just as dire circumstances as the Syrian population specifically mentioned by Germany.

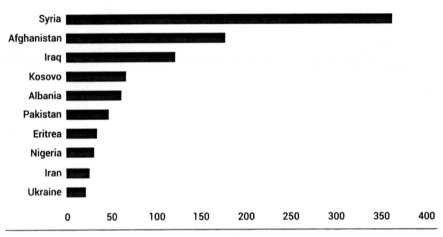

Fig. 3.4 > Top Ten Origins of People Applying for Asylum in the EU (Jan-Oct 2015, first time applications). *Data Source: BBC News - November 2015.*

The other much reported fact about the 2015 asylum seeker arrivals to Europe was that the majority were men. Reports varied the proportion between 61% and 77%[15]. UNHCR data stated that 61% were men, 15% women and 23% children (without specifying the adult age). The commonly provided rationale is the journey is dangerous for women and children, and family units may decide to send the father first then have the mother and children arrive later. The trip is certainly dangerous, in the nine months to October 2015, over 3,000 migrants were estimated to have died in the Mediterranean Sea[16]. However, the

---

14   Patrick Worrall, "Fact Check: does only one in five migrants come from Syria?," *Channel 4 News UK,* September 22, 2015.
15   Eugene Kiely, Robert Farley and D'Angelo Gore, "Facts about the Syrian Refugees, " *FactCheck.org.* November 23, 2015.
16   Umberto Bacchi, "EU migrant crisis: More than 3,000 deaths in Mediterranean as arrivals surpass 700,000," *International Business Times,* October 13, 2015.

tactic of sending the male family member out first is unlikely to explain all the discrepancy and indicates a skew towards those who are more mobile in seeking asylum in Europe.

The movement of people into Europe has triggered much debate. Supporters of policies to welcome a greater number of asylum seekers point to the Refugee Convention and other instruments of international law. These instruments provide rights to all people, regardless of their Country of Origin for protection, including the right of non-refoulement back to a country where they will be in danger. Supporters of the policy to welcome refugees note that Western-led military strikes have and are currently still occurring in some of the major Countries of Origin for refugees. These countries include Syria, Iraq and Afghanistan. They note that given the West is complicit in creating the situation so many are fleeing, they should be providing as much help as possible.

Opponents to Europe accepting a greater number of asylum seekers raise a number of concerns. One is the ability for countries to economically absorb the large numbers. A more emotive concern is that a large influx of Islamic migrants may threaten established European cultural norms of pluralism and a secular state.

Another emotive concern is that due to the large and uncontrolled numbers arriving in Europe, established and would-be jihadist terrorists are also entering. With the current mass-flow of people, it is argued authorities are unable to effectively identify terrorists and deny them entry. The large numbers (coupled with the limitations in coordinating the screening across many countries that allow movement between each other) has limited the control and identification checks of the entrants.

This lack of control increases the possibility of the entry of those with terrorist or criminal intentions. This possibility was made more real in late 2015 when a fake Syrian passport was linked to the terrorists from the November 2015 Paris attacks. This suggests the asylum inflow was utilised by some of these terrorists who were Europeans on watch lists. The lack of control enabled them to achieve re-entry into Europe from the Middle East without detection. It also suggests militant non-Europeans may have also entered this way.

History of Asylum Seeker Arrivals to Australia

Asylum seekers and refugee arrivals to Australia can be summarised in three types:

- **Offshore Program, Resettled Refugees:** Already under temporary protection and are being resettled in Australia from a UNHCR camp or another signatory nation.
- **Onshore Program, Irregular Maritime Arrivals (IMAs):** Not currently protected and arrive in Australia by boat without the necessary documents that would allow them

into Australia should they not be requesting asylum. Note. The Refugee Convention specifies that travel documents are not required by those requesting asylum.

- **Onshore Program, Non-IMAs.** Not currently protected and arrive in Australia (usually by plane or by boat) with documents that allow them into Australia on a visa such as a tourist visa, and who then request asylum.

Arrivals to Australia via the Offshore program were already protected by their Country of First Asylum. Arrivals to Australia by the methods covered by the Onshore program are not. At the time of their arrival, people covered by the Onshore program are displaced and vulnerable.

There has been much debate in Australia regarding the treatment of IMAs since the infamous MV Tampa incident of August 2001. At that time, the Howard Government of Australia refused entry to 438 would-be IMAs who were picked up by the Norwegian freighter MV Tampa. Over the preceding three years, the number of people arriving as IMAs had risen sharply from 200 in 1998 to 5,516 in 2001.

The incident proved to be a line-in-the-sand moment for the Australian Prime Minister John Howard and his government;

> *"Although the circumstances of the Tampa had not been foreseen it became, almost immediately, a powerful symbol of our determination to regain control over the flow of people into Australia"*[17].

The asylum seekers on board the Tampa were ultimately processed in New Zealand and Nauru and the incident also prompted the creation of the Pacific Solution.

---

17 John Howard, *Lazarus Rising* (Revised Edition), (Australia: HarperCollins, 2013), 325 of 765, iBooks edition.

Fig. 3.5 > Irregular Maritime Arrivals to Australia
Source. Project SafeCom, <www.safecom.org.au/pdfs/boat-arrivals-stats.pdf> accessed July 30, 2016

AUSTRALIA'S BOAT ARRIVALS 1976-2011							
YEAR	# BOATS	# PASSENGERS	% OF TOTAL ASYLUM APPS	YEAR	# BOATS	# PASSENGERS	% OF TOTAL ASYLUM APPS
1976		111		1998	17	200	2.5%
1977		868		1999	86	3,721	39.4%
1978		746		2000	51	2,939	22.5%
1979	56	304		2001	43	5,516	44.6%
1980		0		2002	1	1	0%
1981		30		2003	1	53	1.2%
1982-88		0		2004	1	15	0.5%
1989	1	27		2005	4	11	0.3%
1990	2	198		2006	6	60	1.7%
1991	6	214		2007	5	148	3.7%
1992	6	216		2008	7	161	3.4%
1993	3	81		2009	60	2,727	
1994	18	953	15.2%	2010	132	6,502	
1995	7	237	3.1%	2011	69	4,572	
1996	19	660	6.8%	2012	259	16,261	
1997	11	339	3.6%				

The Pacific Solution was an initiative to process and determine all IMA refugee claims in regions outside Australia. From 2001 these claims were processed on Nauru and Manus Island. In addition to this, a policy of turning back boats attempting to arrive in Australia was also adopted. The explicit purpose was to deter people from setting out for Australia at all by clearly showing that not even the processing of refugee claims would be done in Australia.

The number of IMAs following the 2001 introduction of the Pacific Solution suggests it worked in deterring people from attempting to come to Australia by boat. The number of arrivals dropped dramatically in 2002 and stayed low until 2008. In 2008 the Australian Government, under Prime Minister Kevin Rudd, ended the Pacific Solution and the numbers once again began to rise. This rise continued until the re-introduction of similar deterrence initiatives from 2012. These initiatives being a reintroduction of the Pacific Solution in 2012 and Operation Sovereign Borders, the process of turning back boats carrying asylum seekers to the country from which the boat departed, in 2013.

Over the past 15 years, 72,000 (or 60%) of the Onshore arrivals have been through the Non-IMA channel, with 48,000 (or 40%) arriving as IMAs. However, the year-on-year experience has fluctuated significantly. Using financial year data provided by the Parliament of Australia[18] between 2002-03 and 2007-08 the average annual number of IMAs was 73, about two per cent of Australia's total asylum seekers for that time. In 2012-13 it peaked at over 18,000 with the average across the three year period 2011-12 to 2013-14 being over 11,000, about 58 per cent of all asylum seeker requests. The variation in the number of IMA arrivals has a direct link to Australia's policies regarding the protection provided to IMA asylum seekers. This is a contentious policy area explored further in Chapters 9 and 10.

Fig 3.6 ❯ Onshore Asylum Applications to Australia.

Program Year	Non-IMA (air arrival) Protection vis (PV) applications lodged		IMA (boat arrival) refugee status determination requests received		Total
	No.	% of total applications	No.	% of total applications	
2001-02	7,026	76.0	2,222	24.0	9,248
2002-03	4,959	98.8	60	1.2	5,019
2003-04	3,485	97.6	87	2.4	3,572
2004-05	3,062	95.4	146	4.6	3,208
2005-06	3,191	96.9	101	3.1	3,292
2006-07	3,723	99.4	23	0.6	3,746
2007-08	3,987	99.5	21	0.5	4,008
2008-09	5,072	88.0	678	12.0	5,750
2009-10	5,981	56.6	4,597	43.4	10,578
2010-11	6,335	55.0	5,166	45.0	11,501
2011-12	7,063	48.8	7,373	51.2	14,436
2012-13	8,480	31.6	18,365	68.4	26,845
2013-14	9,646	51.5	9,072	48.5	18,718

Source: Asylum Seekers and refugees: what are the facts? Parliamentary Library Research Paper (2 March 2015). DIBP, Asylum Trends Australia 2010-11 Annual Publication, Canberra, 2011, p 2; Asylum Trends Australia 2012-13 Annual Publication, Canerra, 2013, p 4; and Asylum statistics Australia: quarterly tables - June quarter 2014, Canberra, 2014, p 5. Note: September and December quarter 2014 statistics not available.

Over the same time period, the number of asylum seekers arriving in Australia has been a very small fraction (between 0.5-2.3%) of the total worldwide number of asylum seekers (700,000 to 1.8 million). The fluctuation in application volume follows a similar pattern, although Australia's range varies more than the global variation. In the years since 1999, Australia's range varied 800% (between 2,000 and 16,000) whereas the OECD has varied about 200% (between 600,000 and 300,000).

---

18   Janet Phillips, "Asylum seekers and refugees: what are the facts?," *Australian Policy Online 2 March, 2015).*

Fig 3.7 ❯ Asylum Inflows. Australia vs OECD. *Data Source: Australian Parliament, Parliamentary Library.*

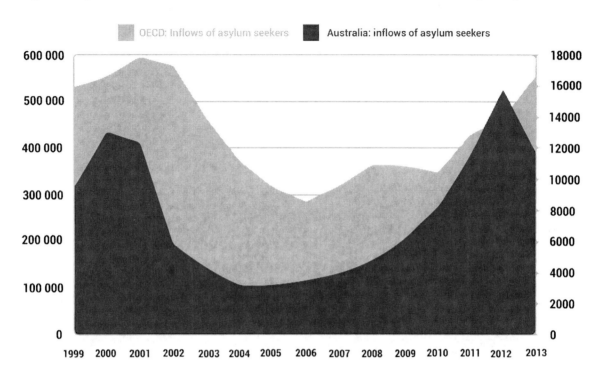

The fact the worldwide volume of asylum seekers is much larger has been used by both sides of the debate. Opponents to the current policies (those tough on IMAs in order to deter their arrival to Australia) point to Australia's small percentage share of the worldwide asylum seeker numbers as evidence of the country not doing its part to adequately share the burden. Supporters of the current policies use those same figures as evidence of the potentially overwhelming numbers that are in desperate need and could arrive on Australia's shores if Australia was perceived as a soft target.

Given Australia's island geography and remote location it is able to control its borders like few other countries. This leads to debate as to what its obligations are in relation to acceptance of asylum seekers. The debate centres around whether Australia should be obligated to accept people who could more easily have sought sanctuary elsewhere. On one hand, there is the obvious reluctance to turn people in need away, and the desire to help all those who need it.

On the other hand, accepting people who could have more easily sought asylum elsewhere creates an incentive for others to try the same approach. This promotes dangerous travel, often through people smugglers. The relative attractiveness of requesting asylum in one country, such as Australia, over another indicates a difference in protection standards and potential outcomes based on the location of application for asylum. The differences in the quality of life a refugee experiences based on where they request asylum is considered by many as a limitation of the current system (explored further in Chapter 5).

CH 4. PROTECTION

A person's period of displacement without protection ends when entering an area under the control of a body willing and able to provide protection. This area may be a camp or site under the management of a Non-Government Organisation like the UNHCR, or the area may be the territory of a signatory nation to the Refugee Convention.

Fig 4.1 ❯ Event 2 - Provision of Temporary Protection.

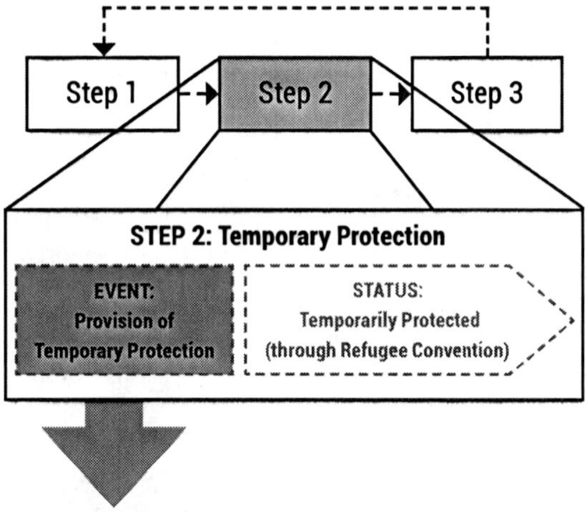

- What is Temporary Protection?
- The Refugee Convention
- European Refugees Prior to the Refugee Convention
- UNHCR Mandate
- International Law and Human Rights

What is Temporary Protection?

Temporary Protection relates to the protection provided under the 1948 Universal Declaration of Human Rights and the 1951 Refugee Convention and its 1967 Protocol. Article 14 of the Declaration of Human Rights recognises the right of every person to seek and enjoy asylum in other countries. The Declaration of Human Rights was adopted by the

United Nations General Assembly on 10 December 1948 by a vote of 48 to none. Australia was one of the original 48 nations to vote for the declaration.

Article 14 of the Declaration of Human Rights:

1. Everyone has the right to seek and to enjoy in other countries asylum from persecution.
2. This right may not be invoked in the case of prosecutions genuinely arising from non-political crimes or from acts contrary to the purposes and principles of the United Nations.

The Refugee Convention outlines the rights afforded to asylum seekers as well as those who are subsequently assessed to be refugees. This protection is guaranteed to be provided by all signatory nations to the Refugee Convention as well as by non-government agencies like the UNHCR. The process by which an asylum seeker is assessed to be a refugee is called the Refugee Status Determination (RSD). For those assessed to be refugees, the protection provided under the Refugee Convention is not necessarily permanent. It is provided while a permanent solution – one of the three 'durable solutions' the UNHCR has defined – is sought.

Fig 4.2 > Relationship of IDPs, Asylum Seekers, Refugees and Durable Solutions.

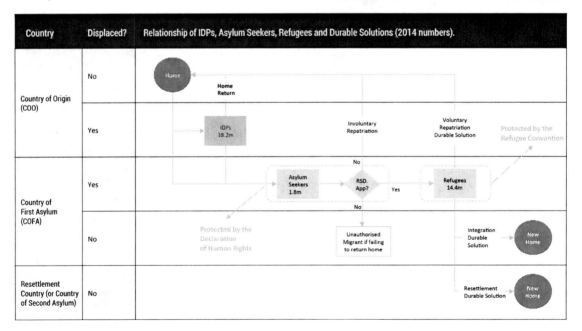

The Refugee Convention

The Refugee Convention grew out of Article 14 of the Universal Declaration of Human Rights 1948 and was originally created in 1951[1]. The Refugee Convention contained 46 Articles over seven chapters. At the time of its drafting the Convention was focused on Europe, the events of World War II, and the development of the Cold War. It only applied to people displaced prior to 1 January 1951 and countries could choose to limit their efforts to those displaced by events within Europe[2]. In 1967, the Protocol to the Refugee Convention was introduced which expanded the application of the Convention to cover refugees all over the world and from any time period.

As of 2016 there are 142 member nations to both the 1951 Convention and the 1967 Protocol. Madagascar and Saint Kitts & Nevis only signed the 1951 Convention. Although some countries only signed the 1967 Protocol, it contains a provision that specifies signature countries agree to abide by the original Refugee Convention as well. A majority of the world's countries have signed the convention. The most significant omissions from an Australian context are the Middle Eastern and Asian countries including Iraq, Saudi Arabia, Oman, Pakistan, India, Sri Lanka, Myanmar, Thailand, Malaysia and Indonesia. They are significant as they leave few viable options for a person fleeing a country in the Middle East or South Asia and looking for a signatory nation to the Refugee Convention through which to claim asylum.

As well as defining a refugee (article 1), The Refugee Convention and Protocol outline the rights provided to refugees. Some key rights are[3]:

- **Under Chapter 1 – General Provisions:** Non-discrimination based on race, religion or Country of Origin (article 3). Freedom of religion in line with freedoms of nationals of the host state (article 4).

- **Under Chapter 2 – Judicial Status:** Legal rights including free access to courts (article 16).

- **Under Chapter 3 – Gainful Employment:** The right to be employed (article 17), the right for self-employment (article 18) and the right to work in a profession should they possess suitable qualifications (article 19).

---

1   *Alternatives to Offshore Processing: Submissions to the Expert Panel on Asylum Seekers 2012,* (Australia: Labor for Refugees, 2013), 2.
2   Jane McAdam and Fiona Chong, *Refugees: Why seeking asylum is legal and Australia's policies are not,* (Sydney: NewSouth Publishing, 2014), 10.
3   *Convention relating to the Status of Refugees,* opened for signature 28 July 1951 (entered into force 22 April 1954) read together with the *Protocol relating to the Status of Refugees,* opened for signature 31 January 1967 (entered into force 4 October 1967).

- **Under Chapter 4 – Welfare:** Public support in line with that provided to nationals of the host nation including the rights to housing (article 21), public education (article 22), and social security (article 24).

- **Under Chapter 5 – Administrative Measures:** Freedom of movement within the territory (article 26), the right to travel documents to travel outside the territory (article 28), the right to not be penalised for illegal entry (article 31), the right to not be expelled unless on the grounds of national security or public order (article 32), and the right not to undergo a return to a country where their life or freedom is threatened on account of race, religion, nationality, membership of a particular social group or political opinion (article 33). This right is widely known as the right to non-refoulement.

Fig 4.3 ❯ Articles of the 1951 Refugee Convention & the 1967 Refugee Protocol
Source: UNHCR – Convention and Protocol relating to the Statute of Refugees

---

1951 Convention relating to the Status of Refugees

Chapter I – General Provisions
- Article 1 - Definition of the term "refugee"
- Article 2 - General obligations
- Article 3 - Non-discrimination
- Article 4 - Religion
- Article 5 - Rights granted apart from this Convention
- Article 6 - The term "in the same circumstances"
- Article 7 - Exemption from reciprocity
- Article 8 - Exemption from exceptional measures
- Article 9 - Provisional measures
- Article 10 - Continuity of residence
- Article 11 - Refugee seamen

Chapter II – Juridical Status
- Article 12 - Personal status
- Article 13 - Movable and immovable property
- Article 14 - Artistic rights and industrial property
- Article 15 - Right of association
- Article 16 - Access to courts

Chapter III – Gainful Employment
- Article 17 - Wage-earning employment
- Article 18 - Self-employment
- Article 19 - Liberal professions

Chapter IV – Welfare
- Article 20 - Rationing
- Article 21 - Housing
- Article 22 - Public education
- Article 23 - Public relief
- Article 24 - Labour legislation and social security

Chapter V – Administrative Measures
- Article 25 - Administrative assistance
- Article 26 - Freedom of movement
- Article 27 - Identity papers
- Article 28 - Travel documents
- Article 29 - Fiscal charges
- Article 30 - Transfer of assets
- Article 31 - Refugees unlawfully in the country of refuge
- Article 32 - Expulsion
- Article 33 - Prohibition of expulsion or return ("refoulement")
- Article 34 – Naturalization

Chapter VI – Executory and Transitory Provisions
- Article 35 - Co-operation of the national authorities with the United Nations
- Article 36 - Information on national legislation
- Article 37 - Relation to previous conventions

Chapter VII – Final Clauses
- Article 38 - Settlement of disputes
- Article 39 - Signature, ratification and accession
- Article 40 - Territorial application clause
- Article 41 - Federal clause
- Article 42 - Reservations
- Article 43 - Entry into force
- Article 44 - Denunciation
- Article 45 - Revision
- Article 46 - Notifications by the Secretary-General of the United Nations

> **1967 Protocol relating to the Status of Refugees**
> Article 1 – General Provision
> Article 2 – Co-operation of the national authorities with the United Nations
> Article 3 – Information on national legislation
> Article 4 – Settlement of disputes
> Article 5 – Accession
> Article 6 – Federal Clause
> Article 7 – Reservations and declarations
> Article 8 – Entry into force
> Article 9 – Denunciation
> Article 10 – Notifications by the Secretary-General of the United Nations
> Article 11 – Deposit in the archives of the secretariat of the United Nations

The non-refoulement right is a very important right as it protects refugees from the forcible return to places where they fear persecution. The importance of this right became apparent at the end of World War II through the violent resistance and suicides of many Eastern European and Soviet refugees who were being forced to return home against their will. As a consequence, Western powers ceased repatriating people to areas under Communist control in 1946[4]. Not all of the rights provided to refugees apply to asylum seekers. However, the right of non-refoulement does apply. This is crucial in ensuring the ongoing safety to those legitimately fleeing persecution.

There are no limits in terms of the number of asylum seekers specified by The Convention. At the time of the original draft, this uncapped obligation was discussed. Some countries, including the United States and France, argued that if governments were to adhere to the Refugee Convention then specific numbers should be[5]. However, the timing and location constraints (restricting the definition of refugees as Europeans impacting by World War II) of the 1951 Convention allayed these concerns. These concerns did not appear to be as strong at the time the Protocol expanded the Convention's scope in 1967. At this time the Cold War was at its height and the strong regimes of the Soviet Union and China tightly controlled departures from their countries.

This context may have resulted in the belief that large volumes requiring asylum was not a likely scenario. It is this uncapped obligation that now appears to be a driver for many industrialised nations to limit or deter asylum seekers through increasingly restrictive thresholds and harsh penalties. Australia has implemented such strategies. A recent insight into the potential consequences for industrialised nations through the uncapped obligation has been provided through the arrival of approximately one million people into Germany from North Africa and the Middle East in the last half of 2015.

---

[4] Alexander Betts, Gil Loescher and James Milner, *UNHCR: The Politics and Practice of Refugee Protection, Second Edition* (New York: Routledge, 2012), 11.
[5] Ibid 16.

In regard to such large numbers, an underlying understanding of the Refugee Convention is signatory countries would have the primary responsibility for protecting refugees and there would be cooperation between the states. This cooperation would play out in burden-sharing arrangements to help alleviate large volumes. The UNHCR could provide further assistance if needed, however it would be limited. Instead, the UNHCR's role is to assist and oversee the states in meeting their obligations, not taking on roles on their behalf[6]. Although there is an underlying understanding, there are no documented rules or guidelines regarding burden-sharing. Nor are there rules regarding when and in what capacity the UNHCR will provide support. Times of high volumes are assessed and responded to on an as-needs basis. For instance, with the Syrian Civil War:

- At the time of writing the UNHCR is very active in supporting the protection of the high number of asylum seekers in camps across Jordan, Lebanon and Turkey.
- After Germany accepted the approximately 1 million refugees, it sought support from other members in the EU to share the burden.

The rights provided to refugees are essentially on par with citizens of the host nation. Naturally, there is a subsequent economic cost in providing rights such as courts, housing, education, and social security. As discussed in Chapter 2, the disparities between rich and poor nations are great. It is clear to many of the world's poor that immigration to a wealthy country will improve their chances of prosperity. As many of the world's wealthy countries are difficult to immigrate to, the avenue of claiming asylum and seeking refugee status is a rational option. Significantly, Australian law recognises extreme economic deprivation may amount to persecution in and of itself[7].

European Refugees Prior to the Refugee Convention

Early Refugees

The concept of providing refuge for refugees is not a new phenomenon. All major religions highlight the importance of providing sanctuary for the persecuted. The modern day concept of refugee protection has grown primarily through a European context, along with the birth of the modern state system through The Peace of Westphalia (1648). Local monarchs sought to secure unity by creating the most homogenous state possible, thus

---

6 Alexander Betts, Gil Loescher and James Milner, *UNHCR: The Politics and Practice of Refugee Protection, Second Edition* (New York: Routledge, 2012), 82.
7 Jane McAdam and Fiona Chong, *Refugees: Why seeking asylum is legal and Australia's policies are not*, (Sydney: NewSouth Publishing, 2014), 39.

expelling minority groups[8]. The Peace of Westphalia identified refugees as people who had lost the protection of their own state. This was the first time people were able to emigrate if they held different religions to their monarch. Back then, grants were ad hoc rather than formalised and systematic.

From the late 18th century and throughout the 19th century there were large numbers of forced migrations within and from Europe. This migration flowed mainly to Britain and the USA. Key drivers were the French Revolution (1789) and the Revolutions of 1848 across Europe (including France, the German States, the Austrian Empire, the Kingdom of Hungary, and the Italian States). During the 19th century, the USA had open borders, particularly for European migrants. This provided an effective solution for many people seeking to leave their Country of Origin and was a release valve alleviating any pressures in Europe regarding the movement of people. The USA was able to utilise this new population to support its expansion into the vast spaces to the west of its original 13 states, at this time inhabited by Native Americans and Mexicans. This region included land acquired through the Louisiana Purchase (1803), the Texas Annexation (1845), the Oregon Territory Treaty with Great Britain (1846) and the Treaty of Hidalgo (1848). Such territorial expansion, and the associated population need is not a requirement for today's refugee receiving nations.

Post WW1: League of Nations and the Office of the High Commissioner for Refugees

In the aftermath of World War I, millions of people were uprooted, without legal documents and travelled from country to country in search of refuge. Fearing huge flows of displaced people, most European governments expelled thousands, closed their borders, and put up protective barriers to stop entry into their country. Immigration laws based on race, national passports and administrative barriers were introduced[9]. Eventually the USA also closed its borders in 1921 through the Emergency Quota Act, originally intended to be temporary[10].

Subsequently, in the early 1920s there was a huge refugee population in Europe. People who had fled their homes were unable to obtain the legal documentation to exist and be protected within a state. This prompted the creation of the first global refugee

---

8 Alexander Betts, Gil Loescher and James Milner, *UNHCR: The Politics and Practice of Refugee Protection, Second Edition* (New York: Routledge, 2012), 7.
9 Ibid 9.
10 Ed Krayewski, "Open Border in America: A Look Back and Forward," Reason.com, April 30, 2015, accessed 23 July, 2016, <reason.com/archives/2015/04/30/open-borders-in-america>

regime. The Office of High Commissioner for Refugees was established by the League of Nations in 1921. Its mandate was to protect specific groups of refugees, but not all. Its initial responsibilities were to refugees from the revolution and civil war in Russia, then refugees from Greece, Turkey, Bulgaria and Armenia. In later years it also included those fleeing Germany and Austria.

This regime provided refugees internationally recognised documentation to enable travel. These documents were named the Nansen Passport after the first High Commissioner for Refugees, Fridtjof Nansen from Norway.

Unfortunately, as tensions grew in the lead up to World War II, the system started to falter alongside the falling credibility of the League of Nations. The ineffectiveness of the regime was highlighted in the inadequate response to the persecution of European Jews. Impediments to its success included[11]:

- Inconsistent commitment to resolving refugee problems.
- An anti-immigration bias.
- Failure to adopt a universal term for a "refugee", which is thought to have been due to fear of being forced to accept anyone. Only some specific national groups were afforded refugee status, and they were only provided limited legal rights.
- No spending on refugees abroad (given the Great Depression).
- Low budget of the High Commissioner ensuring that the mandate was kept narrow.
- No political pressure on refugee generating countries.

Although not a lasting solution, the League of Nation's High Commissioner for Refugees served as a foundation for the next regime to deal globally with refugees.

Post-WWII: SHAEF, UNRRA and IRO

Three organisations carried the responsibility for protecting refugees from World War II until the formation of the UNHCR in 1950. During the war, the Supreme Headquarters Allied Expeditionary Force (SHAEF) was established as a temporary international effort to deal with the tens of millions of displaced people across Europe. These displaced people were seen by Allied leaders as a risk to social and political order. The SHAEF's primary focus was resettling displaced eastern Europeans back to the Soviet Union.

In 1943 the SHAEF handed over its responsibility to the United Nations Relief and Rehabilitation Agency (UNRRA). This agency, which became part of the United Nations in

---

11   Alexander Betts, Gil Loescher and James Milner, *UNHCR: The Politics and Practice of Refugee Protection, Second Edition* (New York: Routledge, 2012), 10.

1945, wasn't empowered to resettle displaced persons to third countries. Subsequently, and also due to Soviet pressure, it forcibly repatriated a large number of people back to their home countries. This sparked fierce resistance from refugees who refused to return home, resulting in violence and even the suicide of some of those resisting repatriation. Eventually this resulted in the stopping of repatriation of displaced people to areas under communist control. Today, the UNHCR policy is that all repatriation must be voluntary[12].

The United Nations was formed in 1945 at the end of the war to replace the increasingly ineffective League of Nations. Repatriation quickly became a key area of debate and drew out a fundamental difference between the ideologies of the East and West. Communist countries were concerned about un-repatriated people criticising and embarrassing their regimes. They rejected any notion their citizens would have valid reasons for not wanting to return, labelling those who resisted repatriation as war criminals and traitors. Conversely, the Western countries argued people should be able to decide for themselves whether or not they would be repatriated. Repatriation as a possible end game for refugees was completely ruled out as an option in the minds of Western leaders[13].

The UNRRA was replaced by the International Refugee Organisation (IRO) in 1947. The IRO focused on resettling rather than repatriating displaced persons, much to the disapproval of the Soviet Union. It recognised the rights of refugees not to be repatriated against their will and also agreed upon an international definition of a refugee. This definition was influenced by the horrid persecution experienced by many, including the European Jews whose pleas were ignored in the 1930s. The definition referred to "persecution or fear of persecution" rather than decreeing refugee status to specific groups by name. This was a universal catch-all definition for a refugee and it was a fundamental change. Rather than whether an individual belonged to a specific group the focus was now on the individual's experience.

There were two primary goals for the IRO:

1. Resolve the longstanding and potentially destabilising refugee issue in Europe.
2. Share the costs across many nations (including those in Western Europe, the Americas, Australia, and African nations).

The USA funded the majority of the IRO's cost and its citizens occupied most of its leadership roles. Initially the IRO was able to resettle the majority of the un-repatriated members handed over to it by the UNRRA. This was possible as nations were happy to

---

12 UNHCR, *Global Trends: Forced Displacement in 2014*, 20 <www.unhcr.org/statistics/country/556725e69/unhcr-global-trends-2014.html>.
13 Alexander Betts, Gil Loescher and James Milner, *UNHCR: The Politics and Practice of Refugee Protection, Second Edition* (New York: Routledge, 2012), 11.

receive these refugees as additional citizens and labourers for rebuilding after the war. However, by the end of the 1940s there were still hundreds of thousands of refugees unable to be resettled due to the selectiveness of the receiving nations. Additionally, there were more refugees emerging from events of the late 1940s and early 1950s across India, China, Korea and Palestine.

UNHCR Mandate

A new UN refugee agency was considered an urgent need due to the rise in the numbers of refugees across the world, the limits as to how many people could be resettled in receiving countries, and the belief that the IRO was a very expensive organisation[14]. This need was met by the United Nations High Commissioner for Refugees (UNHCR).

The United Nations High Commissioner for Refugees (UNHCR) is the main international body that deals with refugees. It is one of many subsidiary organs acting under the authority of the UN General Assembly, which itself is one of the six principle organs of the United Nations. The UNHCR was established in 1950 by the UNHCR Statute. As mentioned previously its statute outlines two key purposes:

1. To ensure the international protection of refugees; and
2. To find a solution to their plight[15].

The UNHCR operates under a number of documents and related pieces of international law which set out its scope, power, objectives and principals. These include:

- The UNHCR's three core instruments – the 1950 Statute, the 1951 Refugee Convention and its 1967 Protocol.
- Other legal instruments such as regional refugee treaties. These include: the 1969 OAU Convention for Africa, the 1984 Cartagena Declaration for Latin America, and the 2004 EU Asylum Qualification Directive.
- Other bodies of International Law including: International Human Rights Law, and International Humanitarian Law.

---

14 Alexander Betts, Gil Loescher and James Milner, *UNHCR: The Politics and Practice of Refugee Protection, Second Edition* (New York: Routledge, 2012), 13.
15 Ibid 82.

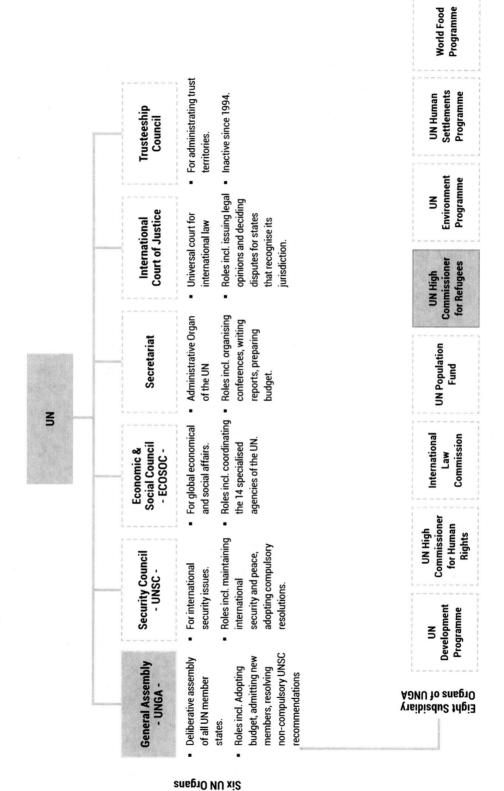

Fig 4.4 > UN Structure & UNHCR. Source: UN Charter, Chapter III – United Nations. 24 March 2008.

The 22 articles of the UNHCR Statute outline the original mandate of the UNHCR. The organisation was originally only intended to operate for 3 years (from January 1, 1951) to help the estimated one million people still uprooted by World War II. This temporary mandate has persisted and was extended in 2003 until the refugee problem is solved[16]. The UNHCR Statute outlined:

1. **General Provisions** detailing five articles such as its authority under the UN General Assembly, non-political nature, adherence to policy directives provided by the UN General Assembly of the Economic and Social Council.

2. **Functions of the High Commissioner** detailing seven articles such as the persons who fall under the UNHCR's scope, scope of protection services, and additional activities such as repatriation and resettlement.

3. **Organisation and Finances** detailing ten articles on how the office will be administered such as how the High Commissioner and Deputy are appointed, financing, and the location of the office (in Geneva).

The UNHCR mandate is to lead and coordinate international action for the worldwide protection of refugees and the resolution of refugee problems. Its primary purpose is to safeguard the rights and well-being of refugees. This includes exercising all people's rights to seek asylum and find safe refuge in another state and to return home voluntarily. The UNHCR is also authorised to support other groups of people including former refugees who have returned to their homeland, IDPs and people who are stateless or whose nationality is disputed[17].

The UNHCR's core responsibility in relation to protection of refugees has been summarised as optimising the quantity and quality of protection[18].

- **Quantity** referring to people's ability to physically access the territory of a state and claim asylum. This is represented by Event 2. Provision of Temporary Protection.

- **Quality** referring to the extent to which refugees enjoy the range of rights granted to them by the 1951 Convention, for example freedom of movement and the right to seek employment. In the Refugee Journey, this is represented by the standard of living and freedoms experienced by asylum seekers and refugees in Status 2. Temporarily Protected.

---

16   "UNHCR - Governance," UNHCR Website, accessed 23 July, 2016 <www.unhcr.org/governance.html>
17   "UNHCR - Protection," UNHCR Website, accessed 23 July, 2016 <www.unhcr.org/protection.html>
18   Alexander Betts, Gil Loescher and James Milner, *UNHCR: The Politics and Practice of Refugee Protection, Second Edition* (New York: Routledge, 2012), 85.

The UNHCR is not designed or intended to manage the needs of the world's refugees by itself. In fact, it requires the individual states to shoulder the majority of the responsibility, leaving the UNHCR to lead and coordinate activity. Thus, the ability of the UNHCR to fulfil its protection role depends on the states meeting their obligations as per the Refugee Convention. The UNHCR influences this through advocacy, capacity building (supporting nations in meeting their Refugee Convention obligations) and diplomacy. In some cases where states do not meet their obligations, the UNHCR has filled the gap by accepting new responsibilities. While the fulfilment of such needs is seemingly obvious, these additional roles have led to some criticism of the UNHCR in extending beyond its mandate. Two examples of new responsibilities are:

- **Camp Management:** Since 1980 the UNHCR has been running refugee camps and providing material assistance to refugees (outside of original mandate). These camps are argued to be detrimental to the rights of refugees in that they hold refugees against their will and do not allow them to work in the local economy[19].

- **Asylum Seeker Assessment**: The UNHCR now conducts some Refugee Status Determinations (RSDs). This adds additional strain to its resources and potential problems with host nations and Countries of First Asylum.

The UNHCR Statute details the three targeted 'durable solutions' for a refugee, which have been referred to previously:

1. Voluntary Repatriation to their Country of Origin
2. Integration locally with their host society
3. Resettlement to a third country

UNHCR Operations

As at October 2015, the UNHCR had over 9,300 staff in 123 countries. Most of the operations are in the field, which is at refugee camps. In addition, there are a number of departments that oversee and support operations, as well as non-operational activities. These departments are mainly based in Geneva, Switzerland and include: Operations, Protections, External Relations, Human Resources and Finances[20].

---

19 Tina Rosenberg, "Beyond Refugee Camps, a Better Way," *New York Times, Opinionator* September 6, 2011.
20 "UNHCR - The High Commmissioner," UNHCR Website, accessed October 2015 <www.unhcr.org/en-au/the-high-commissioner-html>

Fig 4.5 > 50 Largest Refugee Camps in the World. SOURCE: Smithsonian.com

RANK	NAME	COUNTRY	POPULATION	PRIMARY COUNTRY OF ORIGIN	REGION
1	HAGADERA	KENYA	138,102	SOMALIA	AFRICA
2	DAGAHALEY	KENYA	120,017	SOMALIA	AFRICA
3	IFO 2 WEST	KENYA	116,440	SOMALIA	AFRICA
4	IFO	KENYA	96,372	SOMALIA	AFRICA
5	NYARUGUSU	UTD REP OF TANZANIA	67,817	DEM REP OF CONGO	AFRICA
6	TAMIL NADU	INDIA	67,165	SRI LANKA	SOUTH ASIA
7	URFA	TURKEY	66,388	SYRIA	MIDDLE EAST
8	NAKIVALE	UGANDA	61,385	DEM REP OF CONGO	AFRICA
9	PANIAN	PAKISTAN	56,820	AFGHANISTAN	SOUTH ASIA
10	OLD SHAMSHATOO	PAKISTAN	53,573	AFGHANISTAN	SOUTH ASIA
11	ZAATRI	JORDAN	46,103	SYRIA	MIDDLE EAST
12	MELKADIDA	ETHIOPIA	42,365	SOMALIA	AFRICA
13	BOKOLMANYO	ETHIOPIA	40,423	SOMALIA	AFRICA
14	BREDJING	CHAD	37,494	SUDAN	AFRICA
15	BATIL	SOUTH SUDAN	36,754	SUDAN	AFRICA
16	OLD AKORA	PAKISTAN	36,693	AFGHANISTAN	SOUTH ASIA
17	BURAMINO	ETHIOPIA	35,207	SOMALIA	AFRICA
18	FUGNIDA	ETHIOPIA	34,247	SOUTH SUDAN	AFRICA
19	OURE CASSONI	CHAD	33,267	SUDAN	AFRICA
20	BELDANGI	NEPAL	31,741	BHUTAN	SOUTH ASIA
21	GAMKAL	PAKISTAN	31,701	AFGHANISTAN	SOUTH ASIA
22	KOBE CAMP	ETHIOPIA	31,656	SOMALIA	AFRICA
23	HILAWEYN	ETHIOPIA	30,960	SOMALIA	AFRICA
24	RWAMANJA	UGANDA	29,681	DEM REP OF CONGO	AFRICA
25	IFO 2 EAST	KENYA	29,421	SOMALIA	AFRICA
25	IFO 2 EAST	KENYA	29,421	SOMALIA	AFRICA
26	TOULOUM	CHAD	27,940	SUDAN	AFRICA
27	GOZ AMER	CHAD	27,091	SUDAN	AFRICA
28	BARAKAI	PAKISTAN	26,739	AFGHANISTAN	SOUTH ASIA
29	MAE LA	THAILAND	26,333	MYANMAR	SE ASIA
30	BADABER	PAKISTAN	26,227	AFGHANISTAN	SOUTH ASIA
31	GAZIANTEP	TURKEY	26,153	SYRIA	MIDDLE EAST
32	FARCHANA	CHAD	24,419	SUDAN	AFRICA
33	AM NABAK	CHAD	23,611	SUDAN	AFRICA
34	ADIHARUSH	ETHIOPIA	23,562	ERITREA	AFRICA
35	GIRDI JUNGLE	PAKISTAN	22,340	AFGHANISTAN	SOUTH ASIA
36	GAGA	CHAD	22,266	SUDAN	AFRICA
37	AZAKHEL	PAKISTAN	21,231	AFGHANISTAN	SOUTH ASIA
38	SARANAN	PAKISTAN	21,218	AFGHANISTAN	SOUTH ASIA
39	IRIDIMI	CHAD	21,083	SUDAN	AFRICA
40	KYANGWALI	UGANDA	20,678	DEM REP OF CONGO	AFRICA
41	TREGUINE	CHAD	19,957	SUDAN	AFRICA
42	MIILE	CHAD	19,823	SUDAN	AFRICA
43	KOUNOUNGOU	CHAD	19,143	SUDAN	AFRICA
44	AL KHARAZ	YEMEN	19,047	SOMALIA	MIDDLE EAST
45	DJABAL	CHAD	18,890	SUDAN	AFRICA
46	NAYAPARA	BANGLADESH	18,066	MYANMAR	SOUTH ASIA
47	KAMBIOS	KENYA	18,041	SOMALIA	AFRICA
48	ALI-ADDEH	DJIBOUTI	17,275	SOMALIA	AFRICA
49	KAYAKA II	UGANDA	17,273	DEM REP OF CONGO	AFRICA
50	WAD SHERIFE	SUDAN	16,231	ERITREA	AFRICA

In 2015, the UNHCR defined its operations across ten key activities:

1. **Advocacy**. Information dissemination, monitoring and negotiation with a view to influencing policy change and maintenance to maximise the protection of the people under UNHCR's mandate.

2. **Alternative to Camps**. Advocacy regarding the alternatives to camps (ideally used only for exceptional cases and temporarily).

3. **Assistance**. Provision of multiple life-saving items to people under its mandate including clean water, sanitation, health care, shelter material and food.

4. **Asylum and Migration**. Support to governments in handling asylum seekers, refugees and migrants coherently and practically.

5. **Capacity Building**. Support to nations in meeting their obligations under the Refugee Convention through supporting the strengthening of national laws and policies, reception and care of refugees and realisation of durable solutions.

6. **Durable Solutions**. Promotion and facilitation of the UNHCR's three durable solutions.

7. **Emergency Response**. Response to emergency zones such as those caused by conflicts or environmental disasters such as earthquakes. Response includes teams of specialists who can be deployed to the area with stockpiles of non-food items to be used in the response.

8. **Environment Climate Change**. Advocacy against and preparation for natural disasters due to climate change and the environment.

9. **Fund raising**. Fund raising to support UNHCR efforts. The UNHCR is almost entirely funded via donations.

10. **Protection.** Protection of the people under the UNHCR mandate via maintenance of basic human rights in times of displacement, ensuring non-refoulement, and finding appropriate durable solutions.

UNHCR Funding

The UNHCR does not have a permanent source of money. The 1950 Statute specifies that only the administration of UNHCR office can be paid for by the UN, all other funding must be from voluntary contributions. As the role of the UNHCR has expanded, so too has its budget through voluntary donations.

UNHCR Budgets (USD) were:

- 1950: $0.0003 billion ($300,000)
- 1970: $0.0083 billion ($8,300,000)

- 1975: $0.076 billion ($76,000,000)
- 1980: $0.5 billion ($500,000,000)
- 1990: $1.0 billion
- 2010: $3.3 billion
- 2011: $3.8 billion
- 2012: $4.3 billion
- 2013: $5.3 billion ($4.0b budget & $1.3b in supplementary appeals). US$3.2b raised
- 2014: $6.6 billion ($5.3b budget & $1.3b in supplementary budgets). US$3.6b raised

To put this in perspective, this budget has to support and provide protection for 59.5 million people. Italy, with about 61 million people as of 2014 had a GDP of 2.174 trillion, over 300 times the amount per person as budgeted by the UNHCR.

In 2014, only 55% of the US$6.6 billion final budget was funded (US$3.6 billion) leaving many of the needs of the people of concern unmet[21]. Ninety-five percent (US$6.2 billion) of the budget was split across 4 pillars.

- Pillar 1: Refugee Programs. US$4.6 billion (73%)
- Pillar 2: Stateless Programs. US$68 million (1%)
- Pillar 3: Reintegration Projects. US$258 million (4%)
- Pillar 4: IDP Projects. US$1.3 billion (22%)

The top ten donor states account for 78% of the total funding. The USA is the single largest provider, donating 37% of the 2009 amount and consistently providing >30%[22]. The practice of 'earmarking' has also grown recently. Earmarking is the placing of requirements by the donor state on how its donations can be spent. In 2009, 57% of donations were tightly earmarked, with a further 25% lightly earmarked. The concentration of donors potentially threatens the autonomy of the UNHCR. Although it must be independent to influence from the signatory nations, the UNHCR also needs these donations to fulfil its mandate. It appears a difficult balance and the scope of the UNHCR is arguably controlled by the donor states through the voluntary donation mechanism[23].

---

21 "Funding UNHCR's Programmes," UNHCR Global Report 2014, 1 accessed December 2015 <www.unhcr.org>
22 Alexander Betts, Gil Loescher and James Milner, *UNHCR: The Politics and Practice of Refugee Protection, Second Edition* (New York: Routledge, 2012), 97.
23 Alexander Betts, Gil Loescher and James Milner, *UNHCR: The Politics and Practice of Refugee Protection, Second Edition* (New York: Routledge, 2012), 99.

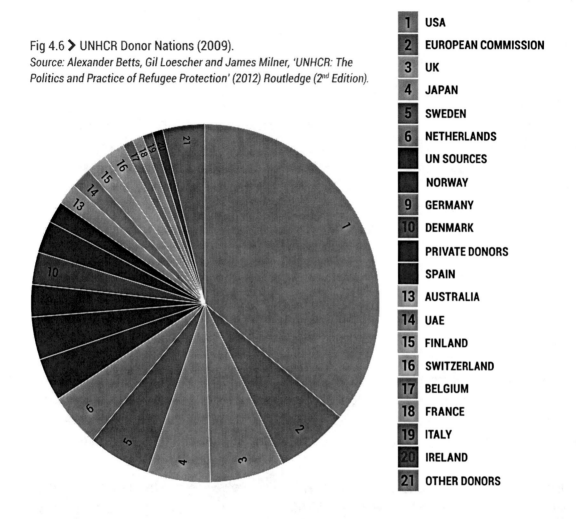

Fig 4.6 › UNHCR Donor Nations (2009).
Source: Alexander Betts, Gil Loescher and James Milner, 'UNHCR: The Politics and Practice of Refugee Protection' (2012) Routledge (2nd Edition).

1	USA
2	EUROPEAN COMMISSION
3	UK
4	JAPAN
5	SWEDEN
6	NETHERLANDS
	UN SOURCES
	NORWAY
9	GERMANY
10	DENMARK
	PRIVATE DONORS
	SPAIN
13	AUSTRALIA
14	UAE
15	FINLAND
16	SWITZERLAND
17	BELGIUM
18	FRANCE
19	ITALY
20	IRELAND
21	OTHER DONORS

UNHCR Growth during Cold War (1950-1989)

The development of the UNHCR since its establishment in 1950 can be best understood with consideration of two concepts. The first is East vs West (or Communism vs Democratic Capitalism). The inception and growth of the UNHCR occurred under the cloud of the Cold War. Many of the early policies toward refugees were made in the context of people fleeing communistic regimes. Their flight to the West was seen as beneficial in curbing the growth of communism and as an ideological stamp of approval to the democratic capitalistic countries of the West. Over time, the Cold War caused much displacement worldwide because warring factions within nations were supported by the superpowers of the East and West.

The second is North vs South (or Developed vs Developing World). The original 1951 Refugee Convention was Eurocentric with a focus entirely on the Developed World, the global north. Over time, the needs of the Developing World (referred to as the global south) became increasingly significant to the UNHCR and its donor nations. This growing need was amplified by the decolonisation of much of Africa after World War II. This had a two-fold effect. First, as the newly formed African nations joined the United Nations, their needs gained voice. Second, the process of decolonisation often led to civil wars and military coups resulting in a large number of refugees.

The UNHCR commenced in December 1950 with a much smaller scope than today. The annual budget was US$300,000 and it had a temporary three-year mandate. Its scope had geographical and temporal constraints that related to Western states dealing with arrivals from the Eastern European communist bloc. The UNHCR wasn't the only organisation working with refugees. In the early 1950s, the United States was also funding rival humanitarian organisations that were more closely aligned to its foreign policy objectives.

Through the 1950s the UNHCR was found to be effective in dealing with international humanitarian crises which led to it being provided with a greater scope. A key event was the Soviet Union's invasion of Hungary in November 1956 which led to 200,000 Hungarians fleeing to Yugoslavia and Austria. The UNHCR acted as the lead agency in raising the required funds and in coordinating governmental organisations and NGOs. Two other precedents also occurred. First, an approach that effectively ignored the temporal restrictions requiring the displacement to be due to events before 1951. Second, the suspension of RSD being done on a case-by-case basis given the volume of people to be managed. Following the perceived success of the Hungarian crisis the United Sates became the major donor to the UNHCR.

In the late 1950s and early 1960s the UNHCR became involved in humanitarian crises outside of Europe. The first time was for 700,000 people entering Hong Kong from China following the establishment of the People's Republic of China. The second was the refugees fleeing the Algerian War of Independence into Tunisia commencing in May 1957. The Algerian refugees were another first. Not only were they outside Europe but they were fleeing French-controlled Algeria rather than communist rule. The Algerian refugee situation triggered debate as to the UNHCR's role in the Developing World. Some argued the agency should adhere to its original mandate and focus on the refugees remaining in Europe. However, High Commissioner Auguste Lindt felt the precedent for action had been set in Hungary and his office had a responsibility "not only for refugees from communism". Ultimately approximately 180,000 people were repatriated back to Algeria[24].

---

24 Alexander Betts, Gil Loescher and James Milner, *UNHCR: The Politics and Practice of Refugee Protection, Second Edition* (New York: Routledge, 2012), 26.

The 1960s saw a continual increase in UNHCR activities in Africa and the Developing World. By 1964 half of the annual budget was dedicated to these areas. In 1967 the Protocol to the 1951 Refugee Convention removed the temporal and geographic limitations. However, developing countries were concerned the description in the Refugee Convention and Protocol didn't fully reflect the situation for displaced people in the Developing World. For instance, in 1969 the Organization for African Unity (OAU) drafted its own Refugee Convention and extended the definition of refugee to include "every person who, owing to external aggression, occupation, foreign domination or events seriously disturbing public order ... is compelled to leave his place of habitual residence"[25]. A similar clause was later put in the Cartagena Declaration relating to Latin American countries in 1984[26].

The UNHCR became the world's largest humanitarian organisation by the middle of the 1970s. Starting with the East Pakistan (Bangladesh) crisis in 1971, the UNHCR was used as the UN lead agency in coordinating the multiple UN agencies required to deal with large scale humanitarian crises. Significant crises also occurred in Uganda, Vietnam, Chile and Argentina. During this period, efforts were extended beyond just sending people home. First, given large-scale human rights abuses were still occurring, resettlement was re-established as an important durable solution. Second, where people were to be repatriated, their rehabilitation and support upon return were also established as standard practice. Large scale repatriations occurred in East Pakistan (Bangladesh), Sudan, Guinea-Bissau, Mozambique and Angola.

Although the UNHCR had expanded its services and found durable solutions for many people during the 1970s, by the 1980s it was becoming increasingly difficult to find durable solutions for the increasing numbers of refugees. This is considered to be due to many factors:

- More refugees through an increase in conflicts in the Developing World. Many, but not all of these, were supported by the superpowers of the East and West. Conflicts included those in Vietnam, Afghanistan, Iran and Iraq. The refugee population increased from three to seventeen million between 1977 and 1990. As funding did not expand at the same rate, the UNHCR budget per refugee halved between 1980 and 1990.

- Developing nations who were Countries of First Asylum started to turn back refugees as they felt they were unable to bear the economic and social costs of harbouring them. A consequence of this increasing number of refugees having nowhere to go was the creation and growth of refugee camps that housed people for long periods.

---

25   Ibid 30.
26   Ibid 30.

- Western nations grew resistant to the continual increase in asylum requests and created larger barriers to asylum seekers through deterrence programs, less availability of asylum programs, and removal of social benefits.

The Developed World's compassion fatigue is not without rationale. In 1980 the United States, which had already accepted 200,000 Indochinese from the Vietnam conflict that year, received close to 150,000 boat people largely from Cuba, Haiti, Iran, Nicaragua and Ethiopia. Combined with non-asylum channels, this meant 800,000 people migrated legally to the United States. It was estimated that hundreds of thousands more crossed over illegally from Mexico. Meanwhile Europe had experienced a rapid jump in asylum seeker numbers from 20,000 in 1976 to 158,000 in 1980. The majority of the migrants that were rejected still remained, many for a number of years, appealing their decisions.

Case Studies – Regional Approaches (1989)

Although the global refugee situation appeared to deteriorate during the 1980s, two regional approaches did produce positive outcomes. The first was the Indochinese Comprehensive Plan of Action (CPA) in 1989 that helped to resolve the plight of Vietnamese refugees following the communist victory in 1975.

- By 1979, 550,000 people went to regional centres in South East Asian Countries of First Asylum with 200,000 people then being resettled in the West. However, this was nowhere near enough. The regional centres in the Countries of First Asylum were overwhelmed by more people and the countries reacted by starting to turn people away. At a conference in 1979 it was agreed to re-open the regional centres with the commitment by the resettlement countries to double their intake. Although over one million people were resettled, the number of refugees in the regional centres was the same in 1988 as it was in 1979. It was suspected that pull factors were inducing economic migrants to utilise these channels.
- In 1989 a three way agreement (the Indochinese CPA) was formed which cleared the flow by 1996.
    - The Countries of First Asylum agreed to continue to keep their processing centres open.
    - The Country of Origin (Vietnam) agreed to allow orderly departure and facilitate a safe return if the refugee claim was not upheld.
    - The Countries of Second Asylum committed to resettling all successful claims up to a certain date.

The second regional approach with a positive outcome was in Central America following the 1989 International Conference on Central American Refugees (CIREFCA) designed to resolve the prolonged forced displacement in the region.

- The conference followed the 1984 Cartagena Declaration as well as the 1987 Esquipulas II peace deal for Central America. Its underlying ethos was to find durable solutions through an integrated development approach to simultaneously meet the needs of refugees, returnees, IDPs as well as the local communities.
- Participants included the Countries of Origin, First and Second Asylum, donor governments and international organisations. It created a range of projects across the many countries depending on specifics for that country. For example, Honduras had restrictions on freedom of movement which led to a UNHCR focus on camps for refugees prior to returning to Guatemala and Nicaragua.
- The success of CIREFCA is thought to be through:
  - Its collaborative approach with a number of UN agencies ensuring its programs aligned with the peace initiatives and post-conflict redevelopment in the region.
  - The UNHCR provided political leadership to help focus the various state's wider interests into a commitment to CIREFCA regarding refugee protection. This emulated the approaches used in Indochina.

The common link between these two successful approaches has been the collaboration across all countries, including countries of Origin, First Asylum and Second Asylum.

UNHCR Growth following Cold War (1990-2015)

The collapse of the Soviet Union in 1991 had major impacts on geopolitics, conflicts and the UNHCR's role in supporting displaced people. With the removal of the obstacles held in place by the Cold War, the UNHCR made repatriation a priority for the 1990s. Whereas only 1.2 million people were repatriated from 1985-90, over nine million refugees returned to their Country of Origin from 1991-96. This included the repatriation of large numbers of Afghans, Mozambicans, Ethiopians and Eritreans.

The push for repatriation was also likely influenced by the increased barriers to asylum erected by Western nations and the high refugee numbers which continued to grow in the early 1990s. By 1992 there were 18.3 million refugees and without extensive repatriation, this number would have continued to grow. This placed great destabilising risks on the host nations, which were usually poor neighbouring countries. On some occasions the repatriations were forced and arguably violated human rights. Examples of forced repatriations include the Rohingyans from Bangladesh back to Myanmar in 1994 and

Rwandans back from Tanzania in 1996[27]. This repatriation push prioritised state security and conflict resolutions above the protection of refugees. This concept is explored further in the questions-of-principle in Chapter 12.

The collapse of the Soviet Union, Yugoslavia and Czechoslovakia also resulted in millions of people becoming stateless. For example, newly-free countries like Latvia and Estonia excluded ethnic Russians from their citizenship, even though these countries had been their homes for many years. In response to the needs of these newly stateless people, the UNHCR took on responsibility for stateless people in 1995.

Another change to the global landscape was the rise in internal conflicts and the associated rise in IDPs in the early 1990s. The 1.2 million IDPs in 1982 grew to 24 million in 1992. The constraints around sovereignty made IDPs a complex issue that was not in the specific jurisdiction of any UN agency. The UN undertook a range of efforts to focus on IDPs, eventually establishing a representative for IDPs in 1992.

There was a large growth in the number of NGOs in the 1990s. Not only did these NGOs compete for funding and roles but the coordination effort required by the UNHCR with a growing number of players became more complex. For example, by the mid-1990s there were over 200 NGOs working in Rwandan refugee camps in the Democratic Republic of Congo[28]. By 1994 NGOs accounted for 10-14% of all international aid funding.

The threat of large numbers of refugees on regional stability was an increasing consideration for international bodies like the UN Security Council during the 1990s[29]. As a result, significant changes occurred in the ideas around when intervention into Countries of Origin of refugees cold be undertaken. Where once there would be little intervention into a sovereign state, on numerous occasions the UN or forces acting under its authorisation, directly intervened in intra-state conflicts in an effort to avoid mass displacements. Examples include Northern Iraq, Somalia, Yugoslavia and Haiti. There were also occasions where the international community did not intervene in humanitarian crises with disastrous consequences. The most notorious of these was the mass genocide in Rwanda in 1994. These considerations brought about the Responsibility to Protect guidelines discussed in Chapter 2. Released in 2001, the report established criteria for the legitimate exercise of humanitarian intervention.

Prior to military intervention there was also recognition of the need to provide aid and support to contain potential refugee-producing scenarios. Throughout the 1990s the governments requested the UNHCR and NGOs provide relief aid to prevent or support

---

27 Ibid 52.
28 Ibid 55.
29 Ibid 55.

a refugee crisis within their borders or their region. Critics of these actions argued the UNHCR being involved in a Country of Origin breached its non-political mandate as well as its mandate to protect refugees.

By 2005 there had been a 40% reduction in armed conflicts globally from the early 1990s. This, coupled with the push for repatriation in the 1990s, resulted in reduced refugee numbers by 2005 (9 million from a high of 18.2 million in 1992). However, in the aftermath of September 11, 2001 and further terrorist attacks including those in Spain and Bali, Western nations continued to increase their barriers toward asylum seekers. For instance, Australia's enacted offshore processing through its 'Pacific Solution'. This approach was tried by many European nations as Europe experienced 36% less asylum claims in 2004 than 2001. The result of a reduction in refugee presentation combined with less resettlements led to an increase in the average time refugees were waiting for a durable solution – an increase from nine years in 1993 to a reported eighteen years in 2010[30].

In the early 21st century, the UNHCR tried a couple of initiatives in short succession to help clear these prolonged refugee situations. One was the Agenda for Protection and the other the Convention Plus initiatives. Both achieved little success. The Convention Plus initiative was based on the structure of the successful Indochina CPA and CIREFCA initiatives. Unfortunately, it was not successful due to an inability for the poor host nations and donor Countries of Second Asylum to negotiate an agreement. The poor host nations sought more monetary assistance. The donor resettlement nations wanted more scope for refugee self-reliance in the host nations and an easier return of asylum seekers back to their Country of Origin.

In 2005 the UNHCR was assigned as the lead agency for clusters relating to IDPs. This put the responsibility for protection of IDPs firmly within UNHCR scope. Since that time the number of IDPs known to the UNHCR has grown considerably. It supported 80% of known IDPs in 2014 (from around 25% in 2005)[31].

Finally, the UNHCR also took on protection responsibilities for natural disasters. This included events like the Indian Ocean Tsunami in 2004 and the Pakistan earthquake in 2005. From 2005 to 2010 the UNHCR responded to 18 natural disasters.

---

30   Dr. James Milner, "Integrative Thinking and Solutions for Refugees" (Talk presented via TEDxRideauCanal, February 2012). <http://youtu.be/GCfr8LMx608>
31   UNHCR, *Global Trends: Forced Displacement in 2014*, 23.

International Law and Human Rights

In addition to the Refugee Convention, there are a host of treaties around international human rights law through which signatories have committed to honouring certain minimum standards in their treatment of all people. These have been developed following the Universal Declaration of Human Rights (UDHR) adopted by the UN General Assembly in 1948. The intention of the declaration was to create a new and brighter era for international relations. The UDHR listed a number of rights via its 30 articles. Most of these were political rights that were in the US constitution or had been constructed by American courts[32]. Other rights from legal traditions outside the United States were also included, such as the right to work.

Fig 4.7 › Universal Declaration of Human Rights.
Source: International Solidarity for Human Rights Inc. (www.ishrights.tumblr.com)

1. We are all born free and equal	16. I have the right to marry and found a family
2. I have the right to freedom and discrimination	17. I have the right to own private property
3. I have the right to life	18. I have the right to freedom of thought and religion
4. I have the right to freedom from slavery	19. I have the right to freedom of expression
5. I have the right to freedom from torture	20. I have the right to freedom of assembly
6. I have the right to recognition everywhere as a person before the law	21. I have the right to participate in free and fair elections
7. I am entitled to equal protection before the law	22. I have the right to social security
8. I have the right to legal assistance if my rights are being violated	23. I have the right to work
9. I shall not be subjected to arbitrary arrest, detention or exile	24. I have the right to rest
10. I am entitled to a fair and public hearing	25. I have the right to food and shelter
11. I am presumed innocent until proven guilty	26. I have the right to education
12. I have the right to privacy	27. I have the right to participate in cultural life and to the protection of author's rights
13. I have the right to freedom of movement	28. I have the right to social and international order
14. I have the right to seek and enjoy in other countries, asylum from persecution	29. I have duties in the community
15. I have the right to a nationality	30. No one can take away my rights

---

32 Eric Posner, "The Case Against Human Rights," *The Guardian,* December 4, 2014.

The UDHR was split into two treaties that were adopted by the United Nations in 1966: The ICCPR: International Covenant on Civil and Political Rights; and the ICESCR: International Covenant on Economic, Social and Cultural Rights. Two covenants were created instead of a single treaty due to an East versus West debate as to whether the economic and social rights (such as the right to work, to health-care, and to education) were aspirational rather than basic human rights. These two original treaties (plus another seven) make up the nine core international human rights treaties ratified by the vast majority of countries. The other seven treaties are:

- **ICERD:** International Convention on the Elimination of All Forms of Racial Discrimination.
- **CEDAW:** Convention on the Elimination of All Forms of Discrimination against Women.
- **CAT:** Convention against Torture and Other Cruel, Inhuman or Degrading Treatment or Punishment.
- **CRC:** Convention on the Rights of the Child.
- **ICMW:** International Convention on the Protection of the Rights of All Migrant Workers and Members of Their Families.
- **CPED:** International Convention for the Protection of All Persons from Enforced Disappearance.
- **CRPD:** Convention on the Rights of Persons with Disabilities.

As with the Refugee Convention, there is no global authority that enforces Human Rights law. As such, the treaties act as guidelines for appropriate behaviour for sovereign nations to adhere to or in monitoring other nations. In theory it can trigger humanitarian interventions, for example through the Responsibility to Protect.

Absolute and Non-derogable Human Rights

Under international law some rights are absolute. This means they cannot be limited in any way, at any time or for any reason. For example, absolute rights in the ICCPR include[33]:

- The right to be free from torture (article 7)
- The right to be free from slavery and servitude (articles 8 and 2)

---

33 "Absolute and non-derogable rigts in international law" 21 July 2011, Human Rights Law Centre, accessed 23 July, 2016 <www.parliament.vic.gov.au/images/stories/committees/sarc/charter_review/supplementary_info/263_-_Addendum.pdf>

- The prohibition on genocide (article 6)
- The prohibition on prolonged arbitrary detention (article 9)
- The prohibition on imprisonment for failure to fulfil a contractual obligation (article 11)
- The right of everyone to recognition everywhere as a person before the law (article 16)
- The right to freedom from systematic racial discrimination (articles 2 and 26)

All other rights are non-absolute. This means they are subject to limitations or restrictions that are reasonable, necessary, proportionate and demonstrably justifiable. Derogable rights are rights that can be limited by states in serious public emergencies which may threaten the viability of a nation. Any derogation of rights must be temporary, proportionate and non-discriminatory.

All absolute rights are non-derogable. Some non-absolute rights are also non-derogable. Some of the non-derogable rights in the ICCPR are[34]:

- The right to life
- Freedom from medical or scientific experimentation without consent
- Freedom of thought, conscience and religion
- The right of all persons deprived of their liberty to be treated with humanity and respect for the inherent dignity of the human person.

The significance of the classification of absolute and non-derogable human rights to the refugee situation is two-fold. First, it provides some flexibility for states to suspend the derogable human rights in a state of emergency if real threats to their viability were faced. Second, there are still many non-derogable and absolute human rights which cannot be limited. One of which, the prohibition on prolonged arbitrary detention (article 9), is arguably already being breached by Australia's Offshore mandatory detention regime.

---

34 Ibid.

CH 5. WAITING

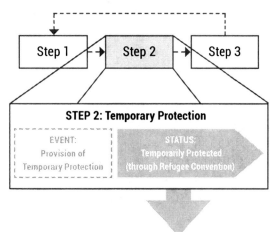

Fig 5.1 > Status 2 - Temporarily Protected.

- Countries of First and Second Asylum
- Refugee Status Determination
- Problems with the Refugee Convention

In relation to the Refugee Journey, asylum seekers and refugees are temporarily protected through either the UNHCR or a signature country to the Refugee Convention.

- For asylum seekers, this protection ends if their claims are assessed to not qualify for protection under the Refugee Convention.
- For those assessed to be refugees, protection will be provided until a permanent solution (Durable Solution), is found. This applies to both UNRWA and Mandate refugees. However, it is unlikely a durable solution for UNRWA refugees will be found prior to a peace agreement between Israel and Palestine.

Fig 5.2 ▸ Forcibly Displaced People depicted on the Refugee Journey.

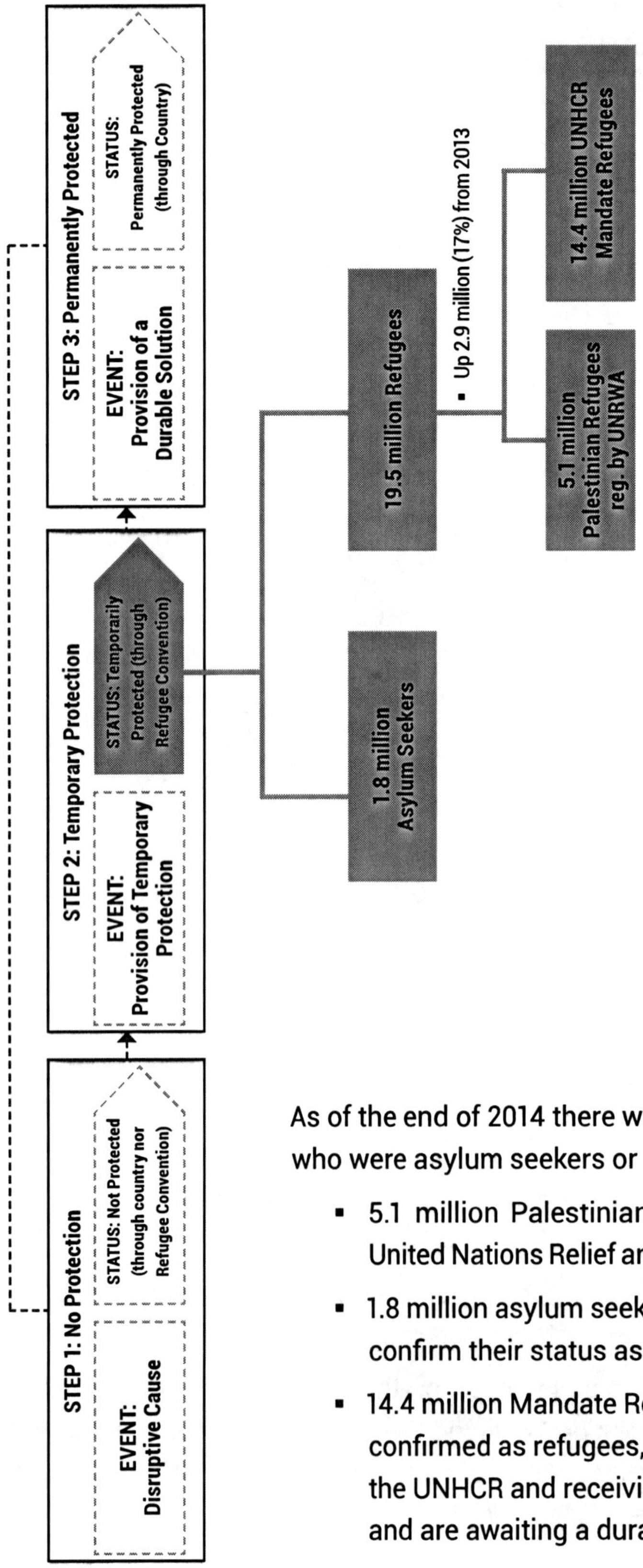

STEP 1: No Protection
EVENT: Disruptive Cause
STATUS: Not Protected (through country nor Refugee Convention)

STEP 2: Temporary Protection
EVENT: Provision of Temporary Protection
STATUS: Temporarily Protected (through Refugee Convention)

STEP 3: Permanently Protected
EVENT: Provision of a Durable Solution
STATUS: Permanently Protected (through Country)

- 1.8 million Asylum Seekers
- 19.5 million Refugees
  - Up 2.9 million (17%) from 2013
  - 5.1 million Palestinian Refugees reg. by UNRWA
  - 14.4 million UNHCR Mandate Refugees

As of the end of 2014 there were 21.3 million people who were asylum seekers or refugees.

- 5.1 million Palestinian Refugees registered by United Nations Relief and Works Agency (UNRWA).
- 1.8 million asylum seekers awaiting RSD to confirm their status as a refugee or not.
- 14.4 million Mandate Refugees who have been confirmed as refugees, are under the mandate of the UNHCR and receiving temporary protection, and are awaiting a durable solution.

Current Asylum Seeker and Refugee Statistics

Unsurprisingly, the Countries of Origin for asylum seekers, Mandate Refugees, and IDPs largely overlap. Each of these statuses is a result of the same disruptive causes discussed in Chapter 2. As of the end of 2014, there were roughly 16.2 million Mandate Refugees and Asylum Seekers who were waiting for their refugee status to be determined; 14.4 million Mandate Refugees and 1.8 million asylum seekers.

The 14.4 million Mandate Refugees were hosted across all areas of the globe. Whereas the Country of Origin of refugees is highly concentrated, (the top ten countries providing 76% of refugees in 2014) the spread of refugees across the countries of asylum is far greater. Only 57% were hosted in the top ten countries of asylum. Of the 14.4 million Mandate Refugees in 2014:

- 3.8 million people were hosted in Asia and the Pacific
- 3.7 million people were hosted in sub-Saharan Africa
- 3.1 million people were hosted in Europe
- 3.0 million people were hosted in the Middle East and North Africa
- 0.8 million people were hosted in the Americas

Although not included in the data above, the distribution of the 1.8 million asylum seekers is generally in line with the distribution of refugees.

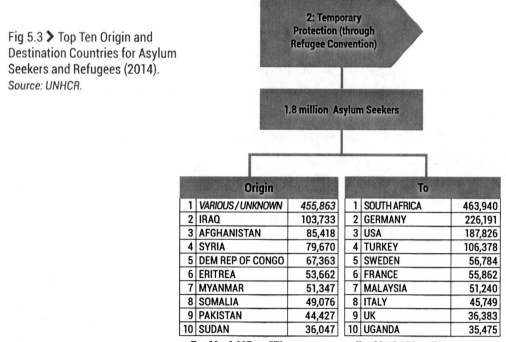

Fig 5.3 ❯ Top Ten Origin and Destination Countries for Asylum Seekers and Refugees (2014). *Source: UNHCR.*

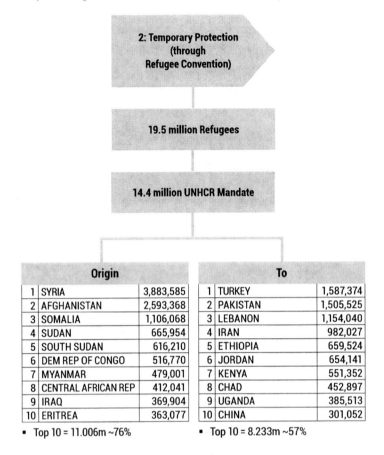

Fig 5.4 ❯ Top Ten Origin and Destination Countries for Refugees (2014). *Source: UNHCR.*

Palestinian Refugees (under UNRWA)

Due to their unique protection status the Palestinian Refugees under the protection of the UNRWA are a distinct group. The UNRWA assists Palestinian-Arab refugees and their descendants created during the 1948 Palestine War. The UNRWA, the refugees that it assists, and the prospects for their durable solutions comprise a very different situation to that of the refugees under the support of the UNHCR.

To distinguish between the two groups, in this book the 5.1 million Palestinian Refugees are always described as UNRWA Refugees whereas the 14.4 million non-UNRWA refugees are described as Mandate Refugees or sometimes just as refugees. The UNRWA has resettled or repatriated very few of the UNRWA refugees and the resolution of this protracted situation appears tied to an overall solution involving Israel and Palestine[1].

---

1 "What is the UNRWA," The MiddleEast Piece, accessed July 23, 2016 <www.middleeastpiece.com/arabrefugees_unrwa.html>

Countries of First and Second Asylum

UNHCR data for 2014 showed that there were 40 countries that hosted a combined total of more than 50,000 Mandate Refugees and asylum seekers. These 40 countries between them hosted over 14.4 million people 89% of the global total of 16.2 million. Australia is included in this group, ranking number 38 with a combined total of 57,100 asylum seekers and Mandate Refugees.

The countries are located all over the world and have different GNI per capita levels and political structures.

Geographically:

- Eight countries are in Asia and the Pacific.
- Twelve are in sub-Saharan Africa.
- Ten are in Europe.
- Eight in the Middle East and North Africa.
- Two are in the Americas.

In terms of income levels:

- Thirteen countries – including Australia – are high income, housing 2.2 million people.
- Ten countries are upper-middle income hosting 6.1 million people.
- Eight countries are lower-middle income hosting 3.5 million people.
- Nine countries are low income, hosting 2.4 million people.

Poor nations with low levels of public order and high levels of corruption generally provide fewer protections for asylum seekers and refugees. The other key indicator in regard to the quality of support an asylum seeker may find is whether the country has signed the Refugee Convention. Seven of the 40 major countries of asylum (Pakistan, Lebanon, Jordan, Bangladesh, Iraq, Thailand and Malaysia) have not signed the Refugee Convention and therefore are not giving any of the guarantees with regard to support and shelter which signatory countries do.

Most obviously, neighbouring countries are the easiest to get to. In the Middle East; Turkey, Pakistan, Lebanon, Iran and Jordan have taken the majority of refugees from Syria, Afghanistan and Iraq. In Africa; Ethiopia, Kenya, Chad and Uganda have received the majority of refugees from the nations of Somalia, Sudan, South Sudan, and the Democratic Republic of Congo.

Fig 5.5 ▶ The 38 Host countries with more than a total of 50,000 Asylum Seekers and/or Refugees (2014). Source: UNHCR.

COUNT	COUNTRY	REFUGEE CONVENTION SIGNATORY STATUS	CONTINENT	SUB CONTINENT	POPULATION 2015	INCOME GROUP	GNI PER CAPITA ATLAS METHOD (USD) 2014	FREEDOM IN THE WORLD	ASYLUM SEEKERS	SUM (REFS & REF-LIKE)	SUM (REFS REF-LIKE & AS)	COUNTRY OF 1ST ASYLUM (COFA) OR COUNTRY OF 2ND ASYLUM (COSA)
1	TURKEY	BOTH 51 & 67	ASIA	WESTERN ASIA	78,665,830	UPPER MIDDLE INCOME	10,840	PARTLY FREE	106,378	1,587,374	1,693,752	COFA
2	PAKISTAN	NO SIGNATORY	ASIA	SOUTHERN ASIA	188,924,874	LOWER MIDDLE INCOME	1,410	PARTLY FREE	5,527	1,505,525	1,511,052	COFA
3	LEBANON	NO SIGNATORY	ASIA	WESTERN ASIA	5,850,743	UPPER MIDDLE INCOME	9,800	PARTLY FREE	7,434	1,154,040	1,161,474	COFA
4	IRAN	BOTH 51 & 67	ASIA	SOUTHERN ASIA	79,109,272	UPPER MIDDLE INCOME	0	NOT FREE	42	982,027	982,069	COFA
5	JORDAN	NO SIGNATORY	ASIA	WESTERN ASIA	7,594,547	UPPER MIDDLE INCOME	5,160	NOT FREE	18,789	654,141	672,930	COFA
6	ETHIOPIA	BOTH 51 & 67	AFRICA	EASTERN AFRICA	99,390,750	LOW INCOME	550	NOT FREE	4,124	659,524	663,648	COFA
7	KENYA	BOTH 51 & 67	AFRICA	EASTERN AFRICA	46,050,302	LOWER MIDDLE INCOME	1,290	PARTLY FREE	34,011	551,352	585,363	COFA
8	SOUTH AFRICA	BOTH 51 & 67	AFRICA	SOUTHERN AFRICA	54,490,406	UPPER MIDDLE INCOME	6,800	FREE	463,940	112,192	576,132	COFA
9	USA	ONLY 67	N AMERICA	N AMERICA	321,773,631	HIGH INCOME: OECD	55,200	FREE	187,826	267,222	455,048	COSA
10	CHAD	BOTH 51 & 67	AFRICA	MIDDLE AFRICA	14,037,472	LOW INCOME	980	NOT FREE	1,800	452,897	454,697	COFA
11	GERMANY	BOTH 51 & 67	EUROPE	WESTERN EUROPE	80,688,545	HIGH INCOME: OECD	47,640	FREE	226,191	216,973	443,164	COSA
12	UGANDA	BOTH 51 & 67	AFRICA	EASTERN AFRICA	39,032,383	LOW INCOME	680	NOT FREE	35,475	385,513	420,988	COFA
13	FRANCE	BOTH 51 & 67	EUROPE	WESTERN EUROPE	64,395,345	HIGH INCOME: OECD	43,070	FREE	55,862	252,264	308,126	COSA
14	CHINA	BOTH 51 & 67	ASIA	EASTERN ASIA	1,376,048,943	UPPER MIDDLE INCOME	7,380	NOT FREE	467	301,052	301,519	COFA
15	AFGHANISTAN	BOTH 51 & 67	ASIA	SOUTHERN ASIA	32,526,562	LOW INCOME	670	NOT FREE	60	300,423	300,483	COFA
16	SUDAN	BOTH 51 & 67	AFRICA	NORTHERN AFRICA	40,234,882	LOWER MIDDLE INCOME	1,710	NOT FREE	10,209	277,833	288,042	COFA
17	CAMEROON	BOTH 51 & 67	AFRICA	MIDDLE AFRICA	23,344,179	LOWER MIDDLE INCOME	1,360	NOT FREE	11,754	264,126	275,880	COFA
18	YEMEN	BOTH 51 & 67	ASIA	WESTERN ASIA	26,832,215	LOWER MIDDLE INCOME	0	NOT FREE	8,674	257,645	266,319	COFA
19	EGYPT	BOTH 51 & 67	AFRICA	NORTHERN AFRICA	91,508,084	LOWER MIDDLE INCOME	3,050	NOT FREE	25,631	236,090	261,721	COFA
20	SOUTH SUDAN	BOTH 51 & 67	AFRICA	EASTERN AFRICA	12,339,812	LOW INCOME	940	NOT FREE	130	248,152	248,282	COFA
21	RUSSIA	BOTH 51 & 67	EUROPE	EASTERN EUROPE	143,456,918	HIGH INCOME: NONOECD	13,210	NOT FREE	3,086	235,750	238,836	COFA
22	BANGLADESH	NO SIGNATORY	ASIA	SOUTHERN ASIA	160,995,642	LOWER MIDDLE INCOME	1,080	PARTLY FREE	13	232,472	232,485	COFA
23	SWEDEN	BOTH 51 & 67	EUROPE	NORTHERN EUROPE	9,779,426	HIGH INCOME: OECD	61,600	FREE	56,784	142,207	198,991	COSA

Fig 5.5 (continued)

COUNT	COUNTRY	REFUGEE CONVENTION SIGNATORY STATUS	CONTINENT	SUB CONTINENT	POPULATION 2015	INCOME GROUP	GNI PER CAPITA ATLAS METHOD (USD) 2014	FREEDOM IN THE WORLD	ASYLUM SEEKERS	SUM (REFS & REF-LIKE)	SUM (REFS REF-LIKE & AS)	COUNTRY OF 1ST ASYLUM (COFA) OR COUNTRY OF 2ND ASYLUM (COSA)
24	CANADA	BOTH 51 & 67	N AMERICA	N AMERICA	35,939,927	HIGH INCOME: OECD	51,690	FREE	16,711	149,163	165,874	COSA
25	UK	BOTH 51 & 67	EUROPE	NORTHERN EUROPE	64,715,810	HIGH INCOME: OECD	42,690	FREE	36,383	117,161	153,544	COSA
26	MALAYSIA	NO SIGNATORY	ASIA	SE ASIA	30,331,007	UPPER MIDDLE INCOME	10,760	PARTLY FREE	51,240	99,381	150,621	COFA
27	ITALY	BOTH 51 & 67	EUROPE	SOUTHERN EUROPE	59,797,685	HIGH INCOME: OECD	34,280	FREE	45,749	93,715	139,464	COSA
28	THAILAND	NO SIGNATORY	ASIA	SE ASIA	67,959,359	UPPER MIDDLE INCOME	5,370	NOT FREE	7,931	130,238	138,169	COFA
29	DEM REP OF CONGO	BOTH 51 & 67	AFRICA	MIDDLE AFRICA	77,266,814	LOW INCOME	0	NOT FREE	1,184	119,754	120,938	COFA
30	ALGERIA	BOTH 51 & 67	AFRICA	NORTHERN AFRICA	39,666,519	UPPER MIDDLE INCOME	5,480	NOT FREE	4,874	94,128	99,002	COFA
31	NETHERLANDS	BOTH 51 & 67	EUROPE	WESTERN EUROPE	16,924,929	HIGH INCOME: OECD	51,210	FREE	6,940	82,494	89,434	COSA
32	SWITZERLAND	BOTH 51 & 67	EUROPE	WESTERN EUROPE	8,298,663	HIGH INCOME: OECD	0	FREE	20,832	62,620	83,452	COSA
33	AUSTRIA	BOTH 51 & 67	EUROPE	WESTERN EUROPE	8,544,586	HIGH INCOME: OECD	0	FREE	22,745	55,598	78,343	COSA
34	RWANDA	BOTH 51 & 67	AFRICA	EASTERN AFRICA	11,609,666	LOW INCOME	700	NOT FREE	225	73,820	74,045	COFA
35	ZIMBABWE	BOTH 51 & 67	AFRICA	EASTERN AFRICA	15,602,751	LOW INCOME	830	NOT FREE	42,426	22,494	64,920	COFA
36	CONGO	BOTH 51 & 67	AFRICA	MIDDLE AFRICA	4,620,330	LOWER MIDDLE INCOME	0	NOT FREE	3,199	54,842	58,041	COFA
37	AUSTRALIA	BOTH 51 & 67	OCEANIA	AUSTRALIA / NZ	23,968,973	HIGH INCOME: OECD	64,680	FREE	21,518	35,582	57,100	COSA
38	BURUNDI	BOTH 51 & 67	AFRICA	EASTERN AFRICA	11,178,921	LOW INCOME	270	NOT FREE	3,051	52,936	55,987	COFA
39	NORWAY	BOTH 51 & 67	EUROPE	NORTHERN EUROPE	5,210,967	HIGH INCOME: OECD	103,050	FREE	7,180	47,043	54,223	COSA
	TOTAL (TOP 38)								1,556,395	12,567,763	14,124,158	
	TOTAL (GLOBAL)								1,796,310	14,380,094	16,176,404	
	PERCENTAGE								86.6%	87.4%	87.3%	

Fig 5.6 > Top 38 countries of asylum for A.S. and Refugees (2014). Source: UNHCR Global Trends 2014.

COUNT	COUNTRY	UNHCR REGION	POPULATION	COUNTRY OF 1ST ASYLUM (COFA) OR COUNTRY OF 2ND ASYLUM (COSA)	REFUGEE CONVENTION SIGNATORY STATUS	HIGH INCOME	UPPER MIDDLE INCOME	LOWER MIDDLE INCOME	LOW INCOME	GRAND TOTAL	PROPORTION OF POPULATION
1	TURKEY	MIDDLE EAST AND NORTH AFRICA	78,665,830	COFA	BOTH 51 & 67		1,693,752			1,693,752	2.15%
2	PAKISTAN	ASIA AND PACIFIC	188,924,874	COFA	NOT A SIGNATORY			1,511,052		1,511,052	0.80%
3	LEBANON	MIDDLE EAST AND NORTH AFRICA	5,850,743	COFA	NOT A SIGNATORY		1,161,474			1,161,474	19.85%
4	IRAN	ASIA AND PACIFIC	79,109,272	COFA	BOTH 51 & 67		982,069			982,069	1.24%
5	JORDAN	MIDDLE EAST AND NORTH AFRICA	7,594,547	COFA	NOT A SIGNATORY		672,930			672,930	8.86%
6	ETHIOPIA	SUB-SAHARAN AFRICA	99,390,750	COFA	BOTH 51 & 67				663,648	663,648	0.67%
7	KENYA	SUB-SAHARAN AFRICA	46,050,302	COFA	BOTH 51 & 67			585,363		585,363	1.27%
8	SOUTH AFRICA	SUB-SAHARAN AFRICA	54,490,406	COFA	BOTH 51 & 67		576,132			576,132	1.06%
9	USA	AMERICAS	321,773,631	COSA	ONLY 67	455,048				455,048	0.14%
10	CHAD	SUB-SAHARAN AFRICA	14,037,472	COFA	BOTH 51 & 67				454,697	454,697	3.24%
11	GERMANY	EUROPE	80,688,545	COSA	BOTH 51 & 67	443,164				443,164	0.55%
12	UGANDA	SUB-SAHARAN AFRICA	39,032,383	COFA	BOTH 51 & 67				420,988	420,988	1.08%
13	FRANCE	EUROPE	64,395,345	COSA	BOTH 51 & 67	308,126				308,126	0.48%
14	CHINA	ASIA AND PACIFIC	1,376,048,943	COFA	BOTH 51 & 67		301,519			301,519	0.02%
15	AFGHANISTAN	ASIA AND PACIFIC	32,526,562	COFA	BOTH 51 & 67				300,483	300,483	0.92%
16	SUDAN	MIDDLE EAST AND NORTH AFRICA	40,234,882	COFA	BOTH 51 & 67			288,042		288,042	0.72%
17	CAMEROON	SUB-SAHARAN AFRICA	23,344,179	COFA	BOTH 51 & 67			275,880		275,880	1.18%
18	YEMEN	MIDDLE EAST AND NORTH AFRICA	26,832,215	COFA	BOTH 51 & 67			266,319		266,319	0.99%
19	EGYPT	MIDDLE EAST AND NORTH AFRICA	91,508,084	COFA	BOTH 51 & 67			261,721		261,721	0.29%
20	SOUTH SUDAN	SUB-SAHARAN AFRICA	12,339,812	COFA	BOTH 51 & 67				248,282	248,282	2.01%
21	RUSSIA	EUROPE	143,456,918	COFA	BOTH 51 & 67	238,836				238,836	0.17%
22	BANGLADESH	ASIA AND PACIFIC	160,995,642	COFA	NOT A SIGNATORY			232,485		232,485	0.14%
23	SWEDEN	EUROPE	9,779,426	COSA	BOTH 51 & 67	198,991				198,991	2.03%

Fig 5.6 (continued)

COUNT	COUNTRY	UNHCR REGION	POPULATION	COUNTRY OF 1ST ASYLUM (COFA) OR COUNTRY OF 2ND ASYLUM (COSA)	REFUGEE CONVENTION SIGNATORY STATUS	HIGH INCOME	UPPER MIDDLE INCOME	LOWER MIDDLE INCOME	LOW INCOME	GRAND TOTAL	PROPORTION OF POPULATION
24	CANADA	AMERICAS	35,939,927	COSA	BOTH 51 & 67	165,874				165,874	0.46%
25	UK	EUROPE	64,715,810	COSA	BOTH 51 & 67	153,544				153,544	0.24%
26	MALAYSIA	ASIA AND PACIFIC	30,331,007	COFA	NOT A SIGNATORY		150,621			150,621	0.50%
27	ITALY	EUROPE	59,797,685	COSA	BOTH 51 & 67	139,464				139,464	0.23%
28	THAILAND	ASIA AND PACIFIC	67,959,359	COFA	NOT A SIGNATORY		138,169			138,169	0.20%
29	DEM REP OF CONGO	SUB-SAHARAN AFRICA	77,266,814	COFA	BOTH 51 & 67				120,938	120,938	0.16%
30	ALGERIA	MIDDLE EAST AND NORTH AFRICA	39,666,519	COFA	BOTH 51 & 67		99,002			99,002	0.25%
31	NETHERLANDS	EUROPE	16,924,929	COSA	BOTH 51 & 67	89,434				89,434	0.53%
32	SWITZERLAND	EUROPE	8,298,663	COSA	BOTH 51 & 67	83,452				83,452	1.01%
33	AUSTRIA	EUROPE	8,544,586	COSA	BOTH 51 & 67	78,343				78,343	0.92%
34	RWANDA	SUB-SAHARAN AFRICA	11,609,666	COFA	BOTH 51 & 67				74,045	74,045	0.64%
35	ZIMBABWE	SUB-SAHARAN AFRICA	15,602,751	COFA	BOTH 51 & 67				64,920	64,920	0.42%
36	CONGO	SUB-SAHARAN AFRICA	4,620,330	COFA	BOTH 51 & 67			58,041		58,041	1.26%
37	AUSTRALIA	ASIA AND PACIFIC	23,968,973	COSA	BOTH 51 & 67	57,100				57,100	0.24%
38	BURUNDI	SUB-SAHARAN AFRICA	11,178,921	COFA	BOTH 51 & 67				55,987	55,987	0.50%
39	NORWAY	EUROPE	5,210,967	COSA	BOTH 51 & 67	54,223				54,223	1.04%
	GRAND TOTAL		3,478,707,670			2,226,763	5,637,499	3,478,903	2,403,988	14,124,158	0.41%

At the end of 2014 the number of refugees hosted by neighbouring Countries of First Asylum dwarfed those of the more distant, industrialised Countries of Second Asylum. The industrialised nation that took in the most refugees, the United States, hosted less than 2% of the 2014 refugee count. Even the massive influx of refugees toward Europe in 2015 – estimated at around 1 million – still only represents less than 10% of the 2014 refugee total.

In the context of the increasing restrictions adopted by industrialised nations, Germany's approach during the last half of 2015 represented a major shift in policy toward large groups of asylum seekers from more distant nations.

There are also some countries that take in very few. Saudi Arabia, the United Arab Emirates and Kuwait are close to many of the larger Countries of Origin, share many cultural characteristics and are extremely wealthy. They have a combined population of 44 million, yet housed less than 3,000 refugees or asylum seekers according to 2014 UNHCR data[2]. Although more distant geographically and culturally, Japan and South Korea with a combined population more than 175 million have a similar reluctance to take in refugees and asylum seekers, fewer than 20,000 in 2014[3].

Nations that can help

There are 65 countries of over one million in population that have both a high or upper-middle income and are categorised as Free or Partially Free by Freedom House's *Freedoms of the World Index*. They have a combined population of almost 1.9 billion roughly 25% of the global population. Three of these – Lebanon, South Africa and Turkey – are Countries of First Asylum and already overwhelmed with an influx of refugees.

The other 62 are countries that possible approach options are intended to be adopted by. For brevity they will be referred to as the 62 Countries of Second Asylum. Many of these countries already receive a large amount of refugees but others do not. These countries arguably have the resources and societies to positively impact the plight of the world's Forcibly Displaced People.

---

2 UNHCR, *Global Trends: Forced Displacement in 2014*, 44.
3 Ibid.

Fig 5.7 ▶ The 152 countries with over 1 million in population.*

Freedom of the Country

Wealth of the Country	Worst of Worse	Not Free	Partly Free	Free	
High	**1 country** • Saudi Arabia (32m)	**5 countries including:** • Russia (143m) • United Arab Emirates (9m) • Oman (4m)	**3 countries:** • Venezuela (31m) • Singapore (6m) • Kuwait (4m)	**37 countries including:** • United States of America (322m) • Japan (127m) • Germany (81m)	*46 countries* ***1,361m***
Upper Middle	**1 country** • Turkmenistan (6m)	**13 countries including:** • China (1,376m) • Iran (79m) • Thailand (68m)	**10 countries including:** • Mexico (127m) • Turkey (79m) • Colombia (48m)	**15 countries including:** • Brazil (208m) • South Africa (55m) • Peru (31m)	*39 countries* ***2,387m***
Lower Middle	**3 countries:** • Sudan (40m) • Uzbekistan (30m) • Syria (19m)	**10 countries including:** • Vietnam (93m) • Egypt (92m) • Myanmar (54m)	**19 countries including:** • Indonesia (258m) • Pakistan (189m) • Nigeria (182m)	**5 countries including:** • India (1,311m) • Ghana (27m) • Senegal (15m)	*37 countries* ***2,878m***
Low	**3 countries:** • North Korea (25m) • Somalia (11m) • Central African Republic (5m)	**12 countries including:** • Ethiopia (99m) • Democratic Republic of Congo (77m) • Uganda (39m)	**14 countries including:** • United Republic of Tanzania (53m) • Nepal (29m) • Mozambique (28m)	**1 country:** • Benin (11)	*30 countries* ***638m***
	8 countries ***166m***	*40 countries* ***2,499m***	*46 countries* ***1,726m***	*58 countries* ***2,873m***	**152 countries** **7,264m**

Overlays:
- **Rich but Oppressed** — 20 Countries, Pop'n: 1,886 million (High/Upper Middle × Worst of Worse/Not Free)
- **Rich and Free** — 65 Countries, Pop'n: 1,862 million (High/Upper Middle × Partly Free/Free)
- **Poor and Oppressed** — 28 Countries, Pop'n: 780 million (Lower Middle/Low × Worst of Worse/Not Free)
- **Poor but Free** — 39 Countries, Pop'n: 2,737 million (Lower Middle/Low × Partly Free/Free)

* Note: Excludes Côte d'Ivoire, Kyrgyzstan, State of Palestine, China Hong Kong SAR, Puerto Rico and 23 million living in other non-specified areas due to incomplete data.

Fig 5.8 > The 65 wealthy, free countries with populations greater than 1 million people.

Country	Continent	Land Size (sq km)	2015	Income Group	GNI per capita Atlas method (USD) 2014	Freedom in the World	Sum (all UNHCR POC)	Sum UN-HCR POC per Pop	Australian Policy (0.06%) Permanent Protection
Mauritius	Africa	2,040	1,273,212	Upper middle	$9,710	Free	-	0.00%	730
Tunisia	Africa	163,610	11,253,554	Upper middle	$-	Free	1,135	0.01%	6,456
Botswana	Africa	600,370	2,262,485	Upper middle	$7,240	Free	2,847	0.13%	1,298
Namibia	Africa	825,418	2,458,830	Upper middle	$5,680	Free	4,264	0.17%	1,411
South Africa*	Africa	1,219,912	54,490,406	Upper middle	$6,800	Free	576,133	1.06%	31,259
Japan	Asia	377,835	126,573,481	High income	$42,000	Free	12,491	0.01%	72,610
Mongolia	Asia	1,565,000	2,959,134	Upper middle	$4,280	Free	15	0.00%	1,698
South Korea	Asia	-	50,293,439	High income	$27,090	Free	4,866	0.01%	28,851
Malaysia	Asia	329,750	30,331,007	Upper middle	$10,760	Partly Free	270,621	0.89%	17,400
Singapore	Asia	693	5,603,740	High income	$55,150	Partly Free	3	0.00%	3,215
Cyprus	Asia	9,250	1,165,300	High income	$26,370	Free	7,593	0.65%	668
Israel	Asia	20,770	8,064,036	High income	$34,990	Free	45,284	0.56%	4,626
Kuwait	Asia	17,820	3,892,115	High income	$-	Partly Free	94,652	2.43%	2,233
Lebanon*	Asia	10,400	5,850,743	Upper middle	$9,800	Partly Free	1,167,179	19.95%	3,356
Turkey*	Asia	780,580	78,665,830	Upper middle	$10,840	Partly Free	1,694,838	2.15%	45,127
Bulgaria	Europe	110,910	7,149,787	Upper middle	$7,420	Free	17,864	0.25%	4,102
Czech Rep	Europe	78,866	10,543,186	High income	$-	Free	5,137	0.05%	6,048
Hungary	Europe	93,030	9,855,023	High income	$13,470	Free	18,675	0.19%	5,653
Poland	Europe	312,685	38,611,794	High income	$13,730	Free	29,251	0.08%	22,150
Romania	Europe	237,500	19,511,324	Upper middle	$9,370	Free	2,542	0.01%	11,193
Slovakia	Europe	48,845	5,426,258	High income	$-	Free	2,673	0.05%	3,113
Denmark	Europe	43,094	5,669,081	High income	$61,310	Free	26,807	0.47%	3,252
Estonia	Europe	45,226	1,312,558	High income	$18,530	Free	88,261	6.72%	753
Finland	Europe	337,030	5,503,457	High income	$-	Free	15,845	0.29%	3,157
Ireland	Europe	70,280	4,688,465	High income	$44,660	Free	10,578	0.23%	2,690
Latvia	Europe	64,589	1,970,503	High income	$15,660	Free	263,224	13.36%	1,130
Lithuania	Europe	65,200	2,878,405	High income	$15,380	Free	4,794	0.17%	1,651
Norway	Europe	324,220	5,210,967	High income	$103,050	Free	56,220	1.08%	2,989
Sweden	Europe	449,964	9,779,426	High income	$61,600	Free	226,158	2.31%	5,610
UK	Europe	-	64,715,810	High income	$42,690	Free	153,560	0.24%	37,125
Albania	Europe	28,748	2,896,679	Upper middle	$4,460	Partly Free	8,032	0.28%	1,662
Bosnia and H	Europe	-	3,810,416	Upper middle	$4,780	Partly Free	144,124	3.78%	2,186
Croatia	Europe	56,542	4,240,317	High income	$13,020	Free	19,809	0.47%	2,432
Greece	Europe	131,940	10,954,617	High income	$22,090	Free	42,732	0.39%	6,284
Italy	Europe	301,230	59,797,685	High income	$34,280	Free	140,277	0.23%	34,303
Portugal	Europe	92,391	10,349,803	High income	$21,320	Free	1,057	0.01%	5,937
Serbia	Europe	102,350	8,850,975	Upper middle	$5,820	Free	271,573	3.07%	5,077
Slovenia	Europe	20,273	2,067,526	High income	$-	Free	330	0.02%	1,186
Spain	Europe	504,782	46,121,699	High income	$-	Free	6,593	0.01%	26,458
TFYR Macedonia	Europe	-	2,078,453	Upper middle	$-	Partly Free	3,175	0.15%	1,192

Fig 5.8 (continued)

Country	Continent	Land Size (sq km)	2015	Income Group	GNI per capita Atlas method (USD) 2014	Freedom in the World	Sum (all UNHCR POC)	Sum UNHCR POC per Pop	Australian Policy (0.06%) Permanent Protection
Austria	Europe	83,858	8,544,586	High income	$-	Free	78,913	0.92%	4,902
Belgium	Europe	30,510	11,299,192	High income	$47,030	Free	41,684	0.37%	6,482
France	Europe	547,030	64,395,345	High income	$43,070	Free	309,414	0.48%	36,941
Germany	Europe	357,021	80,688,545	High income	$47,640	Free	455,081	0.56%	46,288
Netherlands	Europe	41,526	16,924,929	High income	$51,210	Free	91,385	0.54%	9,709
Switzerland	Europe	41,290	8,298,663	High income	$-	Free	83,528	1.01%	4,761
Dominican Rep	Latin Am & C'bean	48,730	10,528,391	Upper middle	$6,030	Free	211,354	2.01%	6,040
Jamaica	Latin Am & C'bean	10,831	2,793,335	Upper middle	$-	Free	22	0.00%	1,602
Trinidad and Tobago	Latin Am & C'bean	-	1,360,088	High income	$-	Free	170	0.01%	780
Costa Rica	Latin Am & C'bean	51,100	4,807,850	Upper middle	$10,120	Free	23,718	0.49%	2,758
Mexico	Latin Am & C'bean	1,972,550	127,017,224	Upper middle	$9,860	Partly Free	4,722	0.00%	72,864
Panama	Latin Am & C'bean	78,200	3,929,141	Upper middle	$11,130	Free	18,675	0.48%	2,254
Argentina	Latin Am & C'bean	2,766,890	43,416,755	High income	$14,160	Free	4,359	0.01%	24,906
Brazil	Latin Am & C'bean	8,511,965	207,847,528	Upper middle	$11,530	Free	47,946	0.02%	119,233
Chile	Latin Am & C'bean	756,950	17,948,141	High income	$14,910	Free	2,346	0.01%	10,296
Colombia	Latin Am & C'bean	1,138,910	48,228,704	Upper middle	$7,970	Partly Free	6,044,552	12.53%	27,667
Ecuador	Latin Am & C'bean	283,560	16,144,363	Upper middle	$6,070	Partly Free	133,744	0.83%	9,261
Paraguay	Latin Am & C'bean	406,750	6,639,123	Upper middle	$4,380	Partly Free	166	0.00%	3,809
Peru	Latin Am & C'bean	1,285,220	31,376,670	Upper middle	$6,370	Free	1,690	0.01%	17,999
Uruguay	Latin Am & C'bean	176,220	3,431,555	High income	$16,350	Free	328	0.01%	1,969
Venezuela	Latin Am & C'bean	-	31,108,083	High income	$-	Partly Free	174,027	0.56%	17,845
Canada	Northern America	9,976,140	35,939,927	High income	$51,690	Free	165,874	0.46%	20,617
USA	Northern America	9,629,091	321,773,631	High income	$55,200	Free	455,048	0.14%	184,588
Australia	Oceania	7,686,850	23,968,973	High income	$64,680	Free	57,100	0.24%	13,750
New Zealand	Oceania	268,680	4,528,526	High income	$-	Free	1,619	0.04%	2,598
								TOTAL	988,450

*Note: South Africa, Lebanon and Turkey are Countries of First Asylum.
This book refers to the other 62 as Countries of Second Asylum.

Factors Driving Countries of Asylum

Four factors appear to influence the destination for refugees.

1. **Proximity to home.** This enables an easier return home should the situation improve. It's also likely to be more culturally similar and have a larger diaspora from the homeland.

2. **Ease of access,** both in terms of travel and barriers to entry. Generally it is easier to arrive at a Country of First Asylum. Until 2015, the policies of the more distant Countries of Second Asylum were increasingly restrictive in accepting refugees from Countries of First Asylum. An example of this was the 'no advantage principle' adopted by Australia as it reintroduced the Pacific Solution following the Houston Report.

3. The **standard of living** likely to be experienced as a refugee, an example being the ability to work.

4. The **probability for successful resettlement** and the quality of life if accepted in the destination country, demonstrated by the mass movement to Germany when it opened its borders to Syrian refugees.

These factors generally lead to a distribution of refugees that places excessive strains on attractive nations which, at their extreme, may lead to social or economic breakdown causing further disruption and displacement. As of the end of 2015, the most obvious strain is that borne by Lebanon, a Country of First Asylum for Syrian refugees with over 23 refugees per 100 citizens. Germany incurred a high strain as a resettlement nation in late 2015. In the midst of over 1 million refugees arriving in a matter of months, it strongly urged its neighbours to share its burdens.

Just how many refugees a nation can successfully support is also dependent on many factors. Two critical factors are its size and wealth. Larger and wealthier countries can absorb greater numbers of people. Another factor is the level of support it provides. Poorer countries like Lebanon, Turkey, Pakistan and Kenya do not provide the same financial and material support for refugees that rich countries like Germany, Sweden, the USA and Australia (for some refugees) are able to provide. An example of this is welfare payments. Australia provides Asylum Seeker Assistance to those who are qualified to live in the community. Such payments are not provided in the Countries of First Asylum that are poorer and have many more refugees to support.

Accepting this differential of support there exist three factors that appear to influence how many refugees a willing country could absorb without undue risk to its stability.

1. **Host nation population:** an intake proportional to the overall population appears a sensible consideration in terms of maintaining culture and being able to absorb the additional people in existing infrastructure.

2. **Host nation wealth:** an intake proportional to a nation's wealth. The higher the wealth of a nation (measured GNI per capita) the more resources it has to support any intake.
3. **Host nation land and population density:** nations with smaller land size, and those already crowded, may arguably be less able to absorb an intake.

Standard of Protection

The experience of a refugee in a poor Country of First Asylum such as Lebanon or Turkey in comparison to wealthy Country of Second Asylum such as Germany, Australia or the US is vastly different. This difference in experience is based on two key factors: the quality of life as a refugee; and the probability of resettlement into a Country of Second Asylum. It is arguably this difference that provides the motivation for some people to undertake secondary movement from a Country of First Asylum to a Country of Second Asylum.

Quality of Life as a Refugee

The majority of refugee-producing countries are poor or are in the midst of conflict. These include countries such as the Central African Republic in Africa or Syria in the Middle East. As a general rule the neighbouring countries – at least those willing to accept refugees – are also relatively poor. The Central African Republic's neighbours including South Sudan and the Democratic Republic of Congo have a very low per capita GNI as do the main destinations for Syrian refugees in Turkey, Jordan and Lebanon. Given the large number of refugees and the limited infrastructure and financial resources, these countries are not well placed to sufficiently provide for the influx of refugees. Often the UNHCR and other voluntary organisations are called in to provide support and protection. Such support is essentially basic shelter and food with limited work opportunities for adults and educational opportunities for children. Refugees in these countries have the choice between remaining in a UNHCR camp with limited opportunities for education or work, or trying their chances in the main cities without any formal support.

Many refugees prefer to remain in the Countries of First Asylum for reasons including cultural similarity, increased diaspora and proximity to their home to ease the return process. However, some refugees prefer to head toward a more developed country such as Germany, Australia or the United States. For those who are able to make the journey, the Refugee Convention dictates that as refugees they must be supported to a level similar to citizens of the host nation. Countries of Second Asylum with a comparatively high social net like Australia and Germany thus become much more attractive than less wealthy Countries of First Asylum.

An example is an asylum seeker to Australia who arrives with a visa authorising their entry. A refugee in Australia on a permanent protection visa is provided unemployment benefits (if not working) and rental assistance. Although modest (approximately A$570 per fortnight in 2012) these benefits offer much more autonomy compared to what is provided to refugees in Lebanon. Additional, non-financial support is also provided in the form of orientation, assistance with sourcing accommodation and introduction to community and settlement groups and services. The full level of services is detailed in Chapter 9. Of course, this assistance is only provided to a very small subset of refugees. With the re-introduction of the Pacific Solution in 2013, asylum seekers arriving without a visa to Australia are now placed into Offshore detention with little likelihood of ever settling in Australia.

Probability of Resettlement into the Country of Second Asylum

The number of refugees who are resettled to a Country of Second Asylum is very low in comparison to the total number of refugees. In 2014, less than 1% (103,390) of the total number of refugees were resettled. For asylum seekers hoping for resettlement into a Country of Second Asylum, the odds are very slim for those who remain in a Country of First Asylum. Relatively few refugees are submitted for resettlement on the back of UNHCR processing. Of these, less than 10% are taken each year.

In contrast, arriving at the desired Country of Second Asylum often means the asylum seeker will be processed by that country. If their refugee status is confirmed during the RSD then the individual can expect eventual permanent residency. Although Australia has removed this outcome for unauthorised arrivals, it is still an avenue in many countries – most notably Germany and Sweden during 2015. As failing the RSD does not necessarily result in compulsory expulsion, there are still advantages to arriving at resettlement countries without strict border control policies.

UNHCR Camps vs Life in Cities

While the UNHCR and other agencies strive to make refugee camps available to all refugees wanting safe harbour, in many situations the majority of refugees do not opt to stay within the camps. The UNHCR estimates that more than half of all refugees live in urban areas rather than in camps. Refugees live with friends and relatives or take their chances on the street. An example of this is Jordan where nearly 90% of refugees are living in cities[4].

Reports regarding the material comforts within refugee camps supported by the UNHCR and other agencies are that they are simple, but comfortable. For example, Jordan's largest refugee camp (Za'artari) provides a standard of living described by economist Paul Collier

---

4   Paul Collier, "If you really want to help refugees, look beyond the Mediterrean," *Spectator,* August 8, 2015.

as "far superior to the African cities with which I am more familiar"[5]. Sufficient food and water is also generally available.

The biggest issue in refugee camps appears to be that refugees are not allowed to work. It is claimed that in Jordan's Za'artari camp this results in a number of undesirable consequences. "In a jobless Arab household in the camps, it is hard for parents to retain authority. Teenage girls are lured into prostitution, teenage boys drift back to Syria and to the armed gangs"[6].

While more than half of the world's Mandate Refugees live in cities, there are still many millions living in the hundreds of refugee camps worldwide. The largest fifty house almost 2 million people. The larger camps have now existed for decades as the resolution of the conflicts and issues causing displacement have not occurred. For example, the long-running Hagadera camp in Kenya was established in 1992[7].

---

5   Ibid.
6   Ibid.
7   "Hagadera Camp Profile, Dadaab Refugee Camps, Kenya," Reliefweb.int, accessed July 23, 2016 <reliefweb.int/report/kenya/hagadera-camp-profile-dadaab-refugee-camps-kenya>

Fig 5.9 ❯ **The Fifty Largest Refugee Camps (2015).** *Source: Smithsonian.com*

Rank	Name	Country	Population	Primary County of Origin	Region
1	Hagadera	Kenya	138.102	Somalia	Africa
2	Dagahaley	Kenya	120.017	Somalia	Africa
3	Ifo 2 West	Kenya	116.440	Somalia	Africa
4	Ifo	Kenya	96.372	Somalia	Africa
5	Nyarugusu	Utd Rep of Tanzania	67.817	Dem Rep of Congo	Africa
6	Tamil Nadu	India	67.165	Sri Lanka	South Asia
7	Urfa	Turkey	66.388	Syria	Middle East
8	Nakivale	Uganda	61.385	Dem Rep of Congo	Africa
9	Panian	Pakistan	56.820	Afghanistan	South Asia
10	Old Shamshatoo	Pakistan	53.573	Afghanistan	South Asia
11	Zaatri	Jordan	46.103	Syria	Middle East
12	Melkadida	Ethiopia	42.365	Somalia	Africa
13	Bokolmanyo	Ethiopia	40.423	Somalia	Africa
14	Bredjing	Chad	37.494	Sudan	Africa
15	Batil	South Sudan	36.754	Sudan	Africa
16	Old Akora	Pakistan	36.693	Afghanistan	South Asia
17	Buramino	Ethiopia	35.207	Somalia	Africa
18	Fugnida	Ethiopia	34.247	South Sudan	Africa
19	Oure Cassoni	Chad	33.267	Sudan	Africa
20	Beldangi	Nepal	31.741	Bhutan	South Asia
21	Gamkal	Pakistan	31.701	Afghanistan	South Asia
22	Kobe Camp	Ethiopia	31.656	Somalia	Africa
23	Hilaweyn	Ethiopia	30.960	Somalia	Africa
24	Rwamanja	Uganda	29.681	Dem Rep of Congo	Africa
25	Ifo 2 East	Kenya	29.421	Somalia	Africa
26	Touloum	Chad	27.940	Sudan	Africa
27	Goz Amer	Chad	27.091	Sudan	Africa
28	Barakai	Pakistan	26.739	Afghanistan	South Asia
29	Mae La	Thailand	26.333	Myanmar	South East Asia
30	Badaber	Pakistan	26.227	Afghanistan	South Asia
31	Gaziantep	Turkey	26.153	Syria	Middle East
32	Farchana	Chad	24.419	Sudan	Africa
33	Am Nabak	Chad	23.611	Sudan	Africa
34	Adiharush	Ethiopia	23.562	Eritrea	Africa
35	Girdi Jungle	Pakistan	22.340	Afghanistan	South Asia
36	Gaga	Chad	22.266	Sudan	Africa
37	Azakhel	Pakistan	21.231	Afghanistan	South Asia
38	Saranan	Pakistan	21.218	Afghanistan	South Asia
39	Iridimi	Chad	21.083	Sudan	Africa
40	Kyangwali	Uganda	20.678	Dem Rep of Congo	Africa
41	Treguine	Chad	19.957	Sudan	Africa
42	Miile	Chad	19.823	Sudan	Africa
43	Kounoungou	Chad	19.143	Sudan	Africa
44	Al Kharaz	Yemen	19.047	Somalia	Middle East
45	Djabal	Chad	18.890	Sudan	Africa
46	Nayapara	Bangladesh	18.066	Myanmar	South Asia
47	Kambios	Kenya	18.041	Somalia	Africa
48	Ali-Addeh	Djibouti	17.275	Somalia	Africa
49	Kayaka II	Uganda	17.273	Dem Rep of Congo	Africa
50	Wad Sherife	Sudan	16.231	Eritrea	Africa

Before the crisis in Syria, the majority of the major camps existed in Africa, with over one million people living across 25 camps in Kenya, Chad and Ethiopia.

Fig 5.10 › The Fifty Largest Refugee Camps by Region (2015). *Source: Smithsonian.com*

Region / Country	Camps	Sum of Population
Africa	33	1,318,891
Kenya	6	518,393
Chad	12	294,984
Ethiopia	7	238,420
Uganda	4	129,017
Utd Rep of Tanzania	1	67,817
South Sudan	1	36,754
Djibouti	1	17,275
Sudan	1	16,231
South Asia	12	413,514
Pakistan	9	296,542
India	1	67,165
Nepal	1	31,741
Bangladesh	1	18,066
Middle East	4	157,691
Turkey	2	92,541
Jordan	1	46,103
Yemen	1	19,047
South East Asia	1	26,333
Thailand	1	26,333
Grand Total	50	1,916,429

Refugee camps are still dangerous places, especially for women and children. A UNHCR report stated that "In many situations, particularly those involving the confinement of refugees in closed camps, traditional behavioural norms and restraints break down. In such circumstances refugee women and girls may be raped by other refugees, acting either individually or in gangs, and self-appointed leaders may thwart attempts to punish the offenders. In certain situations, unaccompanied women and girls have been known to enter what are called 'protection marriages' in order to avoid sexual assault. The frustration of camp life can also lead to violence, including sexual abuse, within the family"[8]. Abuse has also been reported to come from migration administration or humanitarian staff[9].

---

[8] Marja Obradovic, "Protecting Female Refugees against Sexual and Gender-based Vioence in Camps," United Nations University (November 9, 2015), accessed July 23, 2016 <unu.edu/publications/articles/protecting-female-refugees-against-sexual-and-gender-based-violence-in-camps.html>

[9] Ibid.

Burden-Sharing

Although the preamble of the Refugee Convention makes mention of international cooperation in managing "unduly heavy burdens"[10], in truth the amount of burden sharing amongst the countries of asylum is minimal. The management of the global refugee pool presents as a prisoners dilemma – it is easiest if all countries agree to share the load, but easier still for a country to opt out and let the other countries manage. The result being that few countries commit to any intake that can realistically meet the refugee numbers.

The following example highlights what is possible with burden-sharing.

- The 62 Countries of Second Asylum (which have more than 1 million people in population, are Free or Partially according to Freedom House and are high income or upper-middle income according to the World Bank) would be required to resettle refugees.

- Countries of First Asylum are required to resettle no additional refugees, (such as Lebanon, South Africa and Turkey) would be omitted from resettlement requests.

- No country is required to resettle more than 50,000 refugees each year. Thirteen countries would be capped at 50,000 resettled refugees each year: Japan, South Korea, Poland, United Kingdom, Italy, Spain, France, Germany, Mexico, Argentina, Brazil and the United States of America.

- High income Countries of Second Asylum resettle refugees equivalent to 0.20% of their population each year. This would mean Australia would resettle close to 48,000 each year.

- Upper-middle income Countries of Second Asylum resettle refugees equivalent to 0.1% of their population each year. This would mean that Malaysia with a population of 30 million would resettle close to 30,000 each year.

Through these rules over 1.2 million resettled each year, easily covering the approximate 1 million resettlement requests and well above the 100,000 each year.

Refugee Status Determination

Asylum Seekers relate to Mandate Refugees. These are people seeking protection as prescribed by the Refugee Convention and under the mandate of the UNHCR. An Asylum

---

10 *Convention relating to the Status of Refugees*, opened for signature 28 July 1951 (entered into force 22 April 1954) read together with the *Protocol relating to the Status of Refugees*, opened for signature 31 January 1967 (entered into force 4 October 1967).

Seeker is an individual who has sought protection as a refugee, but whose claim for refugee status has not yet been assessed. Every refugee has at some point been an asylum seeker. For instance, people who arrive to Australia with legal documents and request asylum are asylum seekers. Only following confirmation through the RSD are people deemed to be refugees. Those who are found to be refugees are entitled to protection and assistance from Australia given it is a signatory to the Refugee Convention. Those who are not found to be refugees nor to be in need of any other form of international protection, have no rights to protection under the Refugee Convention and can be sent back to their Country of Origin. An important detail is that people who are deemed to not be refugees through RSD may still require protection of the host country through other instruments of International Human Rights Law. For example, the right to non-refoulement exists in Article 3 of the Convention against Torture and Other Cruel, Inhuman or Degrading Treatment or Punishment[11].

There is no requirement on asylum seekers to bring documents. First, it is often not easily possible to attain these documents from the country the individual is fleeing, either due to the breakdown of the country or due to the very persecution the individual is enduring. Second, it may not be safe for the individual to explicitly identify themselves as attempting to leave to claim asylum. This may bring harm to their family and friends as a form of revenge or as a deterrent for any others considering leaving. While the absence of such a requirement is both humane and practical, it also allows for exploitation by people trying to gain entry into signatory countries who do not have claims supported by the Refugee Convention; for instance, by assuming the nationality of a country known to be more likely to lead to a confirmation of refugee status. Together with the purchase of passage to a country through people smugglers, credible stories that can help lead to a confirmation of refugee status can also be purchased[12].

The status of asylum seeker is a temporary one. The 1.8 million asylum seekers listed at the end of 2014 will no longer be classified as asylum seekers following their Refugee Status Determination (RSD). Each will then either be categorised as a refugee or not. Claims that are turned down may be appealed. In 2014 there were 1.66 million new applications for asylum or refugee status[13], of these 1.47 million were first-instance[14] requests. This means slightly more than ten percent were appeals. In line with the recent rise in refugees, the number of asylum seeker applications has almost doubled since 2011 when 0.86 million applications were received. The bureaucracy of undertaking RSD along with the appeals

---

11 *Convention against Torture and Other Cruel, Inhuman or Degrading Treatment or Punishment,* UN General Assembly, 10 December 1984, United Nations, Treaty Series, vol. 1465, 85.
12 Adrienne Millbank, "The Problem with the 1951 Refugee Convention,"Parliament of Australia (September 5, 2001).
13 UNHCR, *Global Trends: Forced Displacement in 2014,* 27.
14 Ibid.

is a vital but expensive step in the screening process. These costs are borne by the host nation or, when nations cannot provide these services, the UNHCR. The more asylum seekers, the greater the cost.

About 15% of all 2014 asylum claims were registered at UNHCR offices[15], the others are managed through a signatory nation to the Refugee Convention. There have been reported issues with RSD within the UNHCR. First, there are large backlogs due to under-staffing through funding limitations[16]. Second, asylum seekers have revealed instances where they have been required to bribe guards and officials to obtain a successful refugee status determination[17].

As of 2011, Refugee Status Determination (RSD) was performed in 171 countries[18]. Of these:

- 94 countries conduct the assessment themselves.
- 23 countries share the responsibility with the UNHCR.
- 54 countries have the UNHCR assess all claims within their borders.

The Refugee Convention does not prescribe the procedure of a Refugee Status Determination. Although the UNHCR provides guidelines, the state hosting the refugee determines and owns the process it will use. In practice, each country has developed and maintains assessment and protection programs in isolation. This fragmentation of RSD across nations is perhaps due to the humble origins of the UNHCR. Originally a small agency, and now still receiving the vast majority of its funding from donations, the UNHCR requires the support of signatory nations to shoulder the load regarding protection and assessment of asylum seekers and refugees.

Unsurprisingly this has resulted in large differences in the acceptance rates across countries. Australia's acceptance rate was relatively high – 62.2% in 2010-11 and 67.7% in 2011-12. Its acceptance rates differ greatly between plane arrivals (~44%) where the applicant will have documentation and boat (or IMA) arrivals (~90%) where the applicant often does not have documentation[19].

Australia's acceptance rate is much higher than the UNHCR global Refugee Recognition Rate of 30% in 2011. Even when using the Total Recognition Rate, which includes other forms of complementary protection (protection under other components of international

---

15 Ibid 3.
16 Michael Leach & Fethi Mansouri, *Lives in Limbo* (Sydney: UNSW Press, 2004), 35.
17 Ibid.
18 UNHCR, *Statistical Yearbook 2011*, 37.
19 Sara Davies, " "FactCheck: are Australia's refugee acceptance rates high compared with other nations?," *The Conversation*, August 20, 2013.

law), the figure of 38% is much less than Australia's acceptance rate. This global rate includes[20]:

- Europe's average across 2011 was no greater than 46% (25% initially with an additional 21% accepted through appeals).
- Canada's low acceptance rate, 38% in 2010.
- The highest acceptance rates in industrialised nations from Switzerland (72%) and Finland (67%).

The differences in the RSD acceptance rates are at least partially due to variations in legal precedents (jurisprudence) across countries. However, other factors are likely to contribute to the differences in acceptance rates:

- Differences in the Country of Origin. For example, Australia's caseload from 2008-2011 had a high proportion of asylum seekers from Afghanistan, Iran, China and Sri Lanka. Canada's caseload during the same period differed greatly, made up predominantly of people from Mexico, Hungary, China and Colombia[21].
- Difference in the ethnicity of the people who request asylum in each country. This is relevant in relation to claims of persecution based on ethnicity. For example, Australia's caseload varies from the UK in regard to asylum seekers from Sri Lanka, Afghanistan and Pakistan. The UK receives a larger proportion of Sinhalese from Sri Lanka (Australia receives predominantly Tamils). The UK also receives a larger proportion of Pashtun from Afghanistan and Pakistan (Australia receives predominantly Hazaras)[22].
- Differences in the prevalence of alternative protections provided to asylum seekers that do not appear in the refugee recognition data (such as humanitarian or compassionate visas).

Arguments exist both in support of and against the current system of having each country handle its own RSD. Arguments in support include minimising the size and funding requirements for the UNHCR. It also enables sovereign nations to maintain control over who stays as a refugee in their country or not. This includes health and security check assessments to ensure the asylum seeker does not pose an unacceptable threat.

However, there are potential negatives in the current system. First, there is a level of inefficiency worldwide as each country must develop and maintain a raft of associated procedures for such a system. Second, the differences in acceptance rates may motivate

---

20 Ibid.
21 Angus Houston, Paris Aristotle and Michael l"Estrange, "Report of the Expert Panel on Asylum Seekers", (August, 2012), 105.
22 Ibid 106.

the movement of asylum seekers beyond where it is easiest to go. This has been given the shorthand term 'asylum shopping'. As a means to reduce the attractiveness of their country to any asylum shoppers, host nations have been accused of deliberately lengthening the time taken in the RSD. The result of such policies is an increase in the period of transition and uncertainty for all asylum seekers to the country. Accounts from refugees who have gone through this process show that such periods are highly distressing[23].

RSD Claim Fails

As the figures show, there are a significant proportion of people (about 60%) whose claims for refugee status are turned down. Broadly, this is because the situation the person is in does not qualify for refugee status in the judgement of the assessor. This relates to a number of factors relating to both the individual and their Country of Origin. A subsection of this group, at least in theory, would be those who have attempted to use the refugee status as a means to immigrate into the host nation for economic reasons. This group have sometimes been called economic migrants.

When claims for refugee status fail, if there is no legal reason for the claimant to remain in the host nation, the expectation is that they would return home. However, this does not always occur. In March 2015, the UK had received 25,000 asylum seekers applications over the past 12 months. More than 60% (15,000) of these applications were refused yet less than half that number were removed or departed voluntarily over the same period[24]. Australia has previously reported similar experiences. In the 1990s, 27% of lawful non-citizens who had applied for asylum once they had arrived vanished from visibility if their claims for asylum were refused[25].

A lack of integration in systems between countries allows for people who have had their claims rejected in one country to apply in another country. This not only results in double-handling but also increases the incentive for fabricating a background in order to maximise the chance of acceptance. For example, cross-checks between Ireland and the UK in 2012 found that 1,300 of 2,000 failed asylum seekers into Ireland were known to Britain's Border Agency under a different name[26].

Just 40% of failed asylum seekers across the EU are returned to their Country of Origin. Some disappear while others exploit generous legal systems. For example, in Germany

---

23 Michael Leach & Fethi Mansouri, *Lives in Limbo* (Sydney: UNSW Press, 2004).
24 Camila Ruz, "What happens to failed asylum seekers?," *BBC News Magazine*, August 13, 2015.
25 Frank Brennan, *Tampering with Asylum* (Digitial Edition) (Australia: University of Queensland Press, 2014), 81 of 253, iBooks edition.
26 Tom Brady, "Two-thirds of failed asylum seekers had used false identities," *Irish Independent*, May 21, 2012.

three-quarters of those whose asylum bids failed are able to obtain temporary permission to stay[27].

The low return rate provides further motivation for people who are attempting to utilise the refugee process to migrate into a developed nation. Even if they are assessed to not be refugees, the likelihood of deportation being carried out remains low. For many, it appears that life as an illegal migrant in a developed nation is preferred over life in their homeland. In January of 2016, Frans Timmermans, First Vice President of the European Commission announced that over 60% of people who had arrived in Europe in 2015 as asylum seekers came from countries "where you can assume they have no reason whatsoever to ask for refugee status".

Problems with the Refugee Convention

The Refugee Convention has provided much support and help to Forcibly Displaced People over the past 65 years. It is routinely referenced when proposed changes to immigration laws are presented and any that may breach the Convention are strongly resisted by Human Rights advocates. However, it is not without critics who cite its limitations and adverse consequences.

Critics of the Refugee Convention argue the world has changed significantly since 1950 when the Refugee Convention was framed. Their argument notes that at that time the Cold War was emerging, the perceived benefit of accepting refugees was greater, refugee populations were lower and the world population was far less. The Refugee Convention reflected this international environment but now requires revision as the environment has changed. Specifically, there are mass refugee outflows and large migratory movements not previously experienced. Without such revision, the outdated aspects of the Refugee Convention prevent signatory states from responding effectively to the refugee situation.

Key criticisms include:

- An outdated Refugee Definition.
- Establishes two classes of refugees.
- Exile is embedded as a solution.
- Uncapped obligations may create overwhelming host country burdens.
- Co-opted by non-refugees as a migration channel.

---

27 "Forming an Orderly Queue," *The Economist,* February 6, 2016, 19-22.

Outdated Refugee Definition

It is widely noted the definition of a refugee in the Refugee Convention is outdated. It was drafted in the context of displacements from World War II and the emergence of the Cold War. The Convention's reference to the fear of persecution is potentially not broad enough. Since the 1980s refugees have been less likely to be individuals targeted for persecution from oppressive regimes. Instead, they are generally within large numbers of people fleeing civil war, ethnic conflicts, natural disasters or famine. Many in these groups do not fit into the categorisation of 'well-founded fear of persecution'.

Although potentially not broad enough, the criteria of 'fear of persecution' is sufficiently vague as to allow for multiple interpretations. This has led to a battle between an expansionary categorisation by Western judiciaries and a subsequent restriction through legislation by governments alarmed at the potential explosion of refugee numbers[28].

Another consequence of the definition is that a large number of people who are not able to return home do not fall under the categories outlined by the Refugee Convention. The specification for the individual to be outside the country of their habitual residence results in no right of assistance for 'internally displaced people' until they reach a signatory country[29].

A third consequence is that the Refugee Convention has led to an understanding of asylum seekers as either 'political' and deserving, or 'economic' and undeserving. It is arguably immoral to distinguish between people impelled to flee from persecution and those impelled to flee from poverty and lack of opportunity. A further complication is that asylum seekers are not generally the poorest and neediest inhabitants of their Country of Origin; they tend rather to be the younger and more enterprising.

Establishes Two Classes of Refugees

A significant criticism of the Refugee Convention argues that by legitimising irregular arrivals it effectively establishes two classes of refugees. One class being those with the mobility and resources to reach a signatory country, and the other being those without. These classes are further distinguished by the very real difference in quality of life experienced as a refugee, and by the probability of preferred durable solutions for each class. In general the probability of desired outcomes is greatly enhanced if certain signatory countries are reached.

---

28 Adrienne Millbank, "The Problem with the 1951 Refugee Convention,"Parliament of Australia (September 5, 2001).
29 Ibid.

One reason is that a considerable difference exists between the money that is spent by Western countries on their onshore asylum seekers and that which is spent by UNHCR on camp refugees. For example, in 1990 the spend of the European OECD countries and Canada on processing their refugee claims was equal to ten times the UNHCR budget for the year. Another example is Australia's annual spend on asylum seekers who were held in detention centres – A$137,317 per person in 2010/11. Chapter 9 explores the idea that mandatory detention serves deterrence and security purposes as well as the stated protection of refugees. Although it is not an enviable situation for a refugee or asylum seeker to be in, A$137,317 per year is an amount far in excess of what camps in Africa and Asia are able to spend on protecting refugees, even with UNHCR support.

One of the key drivers is the relative prosperity of the host nations. It is easy to see that the resources available to help support refugees in camps – or to assist with those who are living in the community – are likely to be far greater in the more affluent nations. This can be highlighted by a comparison of the relative prospects for refugees arriving in Australia and Kenya.

Australia has a population of about 24 million and hosts a combined number of 57,000 refugees or asylum seekers. Australia's total GDP was US$1,453.77 billion with a GNI per capita of US$64,680. Even though Kenya is not nearly the poorest of the 40 countries hosting more than 50,000, the difference in resources compared to Australia is significant. Kenya has a population (46 million) roughly twice that of Australia's and it hosted over ten times as many refugees (585,000) in 2014. In 2014 total GDP was US$60.94 billion with a GNI per capita of US$1,290, about 2% of Australia's. Additional support is provided to the refugees hosted within Kenya through the UNHCR camps. Over 70% (US$4.6 billion) of the UNHCR's 2014 budget was allocated to refugee programs. However, even with additional support it is clear that the amount of resources allocated to supporting refugees in Australia dwarfs the equivalent allocation in Kenya. Each person granted permanent protection qualifies for the same entitlements (such as social security) as citizens. The most recent budget estimates suggest that Australia expects to spend A$58,000 per refugee[30]. Not only is the quality of the material support better for those living as refugees, but the likelihood of a prosperous future through provision of a permanent visa is generally larger within a country with a higher average income.

In principle refugees should receive equal protection wherever they are; however the level of support is not the same. There is also a difference in the likely outcome. The focus of UNHCR refugee camps is repatriation, less than 30% are resettled to a third country. However, prior to the Pacific Solution, 90% of Iraqi and Afghani refugees arriving

---

30   Patrick Durkin, "Big Business wants to double Syrian refugees to 25,000," *The Australian*, Feb 3, 2016.

in Australia were resettled there. Thus the Refugee Convention, as it currently operates, gives priority to those more mobile and with a greater capacity to pay, rather than those most in need. This results in women and children making up the majority of people in the camps, and young men making up the majority of asylum seekers (detailed as 75-80% in 2001)[31].

The benefit – perceived or actual – in reaching certain countries creates a market for people smugglers who can provide a service. Critics see this legal structure as deeply immoral. In effect, refugees are taking risks due to the inequality of opportunity between staying in a camp and getting to a Country of Second Asylum. An extension of this criticism is that the West has a responsibility to not tempt asylum seekers to take dangerous trips, such as those by sea. "Paying thousands of dollars to a people smuggler for a place on a boat should not entitle a refugee to a more privileged entry to a Western nation than those who do not have money. It is profoundly unfair to the other suffering refugees"[32].

The resources spent on discouraging people smuggling can be thought of as 'diverted resources' as they provide no support to asylum seekers and constitute an opportunity cost that could be used to better the lives of those most vulnerable. The program to combat people smugglers seeks to deter asylum seekers from attempting to attain the perceived advantages of arriving at an advanced economic country. Without this deterrent it is feared uncapped obligations will grow exponentially through uncapped asylum-seeker arrivals.

A natural question that arises is whether refugees within Australia's region should be more important to Australia than those who are in other regions. An inferred outcome of the Refugee Convention is that each country should respond to the needs within its region according to its own situation as it sees fit. This allows countries to maintain sovereign control over how best to respond while still allowing for UNHCR assistance should the burden be too great for a country. However such an approach has led to inconsistent protection levels due to unbalanced spending, as in the case of Australia's detention spending. Could the money spent on programs in developed countries be better spent in Countries of First Asylum where they will potentially help more people?

---

31 Adrienne Millbank, "The Problem with the 1951 Refugee Convention,"Parliament of Australia (September 5, 2001).
32 Paul Collier, "If you really want to help refugees, look beyond the Mediterrean," *Spectator*, August 8, 2015.

Exile Embedded as a Solution to Refugee Problems

The practical implementation of the Refugee Convention by UNHCR has been reactive, exile-oriented, and refugee centric. The principal obligation of non-refoulement (article 33) reinforces and promotes this concept. Conversely, no obligation is imposed on countries to not persecute or expel their citizens, and no requirement to guarantee their safe return. There is no mechanism to stop mass outflows and the result of this is that the primary responsibility for the solution to refugee problems has been placed on host states rather than the Countries of Origin[33].

The exile-oriented focus is partly due to the legacy of the Cold War and the oppressive Eastern bloc regimes in the 1950s and 60s. The restrictions placed by these regimes on departure meant the probability of overwhelming refugee numbers was low. In addition, there were ideological advantages to accepting refugees from the East who, by fleeing, provided a vote of confidence for the western capitalist democracies. The result is that the Refugee Convention has institutionalised the idea of exile as a solution to refugee problems rather than asserting the right of individuals to stay home or to return home and enjoy basic human rights[34].

As we have seen, since the 1980s the UNHCR has advocated repatriation as the preferred durable solution. Integration into the Country of First Asylum or resettlement into a Country of Second Asylum are subordinate durable solutions[35].

Uncapped Obligations may Create Overwhelming Host-Country Burdens

The Refugee Convention provides no consideration for the capacity of the receiving states, for burden-sharing between states, for prompt assistance to those most in need, or for maximising the effectiveness of international resources. As previously noted, exits from the communist countries in the 1950s and 60s were so low that the uncapped obligations of the Refugee Convention did not imply the potential numbers they do today. The few defectors were welcomed to the Free World, where they provided much needed cheap labour as well as some ideological kudos in the height of the Cold War. Now, movements are much larger in number and the appetite for cheap labour has reduced.

Any signatory state an asylum seeker reaches is obligated to take on the associated legal responsibility. There is no cap or limit to this number, and every asylum seeker

---

33 Alexander Betts, Gil Loescher and James Milner, *UNHCR: The Politics and Practice of Refugee Protection, Second Edition* (New York: Routledge, 2012), 19.
34 Adrienne Millbank, "The Problem with the 1951 Refugee Convention,"Parliament of Australia (September 5, 2001).
35 Alexander Betts, Gil Loescher and James Milner, *UNHCR: The Politics and Practice of Refugee Protection, Second Edition* (New York: Routledge, 2012), 50.

creates a financial, social and political impact. Financially, it is expensive to host and eventually resettle a refugee. Socially, there are pressures associated with population increases, the integration of people from diverse cultures as well as people who have suffered considerable trauma.

Advocates of the Refugee Convention oppose any cap to an asylum seeker intake, and view its empowerment of individual asylum seekers over the states as its chief strength. In practice most Western governments, at least until Germany's response in 2015 to the Syrian crisis, have been spending larger sums of money to deter asylum seekers. It has been argued that if countries believed in the Refugee Convention they would assist rather than impede the people most likely to need protection in reaching their systems[36].

Although the Refugee Convention has an underlying understanding for burden-sharing arrangements to help alleviate large volumes, there are no documented rules or guidelines. Nor are there mechanisms for maximising international resources such as rules regarding when and in what capacity the UNHCR will provide support.

People can request asylum in any signatory country as the Refugee Convention obligates contracting countries to harbour and process all claims of asylum. However, as we have seen, all countries do not present the same potential benefit to an individual asylum seeker.

These discrepancies result in asylum seekers targeting specific countries rather than the load being more evenly distributed. In 2014, 57% of the world's refugees were protected in the top ten countries, and 30 in the top three. This is due mainly to proximity to Countries of Origin. Given that most of the refugee-producing countries are poor countries in developing regions, the Countries of First Asylum that harbour the majority of refugees are also developing nations. Thus, developing nations consistently receive and house the majority of refugees. This places a great deal of pressure on countries with the least financial ability to cope.

Two UNHCR measures that provide some insight into the relative burdens borne by host countries are the number of refugees per inhabitant and the number of refugees per USD GDP (PPP) per capita.

As of the end of 2014, Lebanon had by far the most refugees per inhabitants, or almost one in four. Its measure is 232 refugees per 1,000 inhabitants; Jordan was next at 87. The highest European measure was Sweden with 15, or 1.5% of all inhabitants. Australia's measure was only 1 or 0.1%[37]. Interestingly, Nauru, which has contracted to host refugees

---

36 Adrienne Millbank, "The Problem with the 1951 Refugee Convention,"Parliament of Australia (September 5, 2001).
37 UNHCR, *Global Trends: Forced Displacement in 2014* <www.unhcr.org/statistics/country/556725e69/unhcr-global-trends-2014.html>.

with Australia as part of the Pacific Solution ranks third with 39 refugees per inhabitant, or 3.9%. However, the financial burden borne by Nauru is covered through its arrangement with Australia. The UNHCR provides no formal guidelines as to the proportion of refugees per inhabitants a country can manage. The implication is that countries are to deal with situations on a case-by-case basis. Germany's experience with refugees in 2015 is an example of this. After receiving close to 1 million refugees in 2015 (roughly 125 refugees per 1,000 inhabitants or 1.25%) it announced more strict border controls and requested support from other countries in sharing the burden.

The refugees per 1 USD GDP (PPP) per capita measures the relative contribution and effort made by countries in relation to their national economy. The higher the number, the higher the relative effort as they have fewer dollars to allocate to refugee support[38]. As of end 2014, 42% of the world's refugees were hosted by countries that had per capita GDPs of less than US$5,000. The poor African nations that act as Countries of First Asylum for their neighbours dominate this measure. Ethiopia was measured to have 440 refugees per 1 USD GDP (PPP) per capita. Pakistan was measured at 316, and Chad at 203[39]. In contrast, Russia was the developed nation with the highest measurement. It ranked 34th highest with 9 refugees per 1 USD GDP (PPP) per capita. Almost fifty times less than Ethiopia by this measure. The proportion of refugees hosted by developing nations is growing. It is now at 86% when it was around 70% in the 1990s[40].

When displaced people choose to travel further their decisions tend to be even more concentrated. For example, in the early 21st century, 70% of refugees to Europe sought protection in just four countries (Germany, Britain, Switzerland and the Netherlands).

---

38   Ibid 16.
39   UNHCR, *Global Trends: Forced Displacement in 2014*, 15.
40   Ibid.

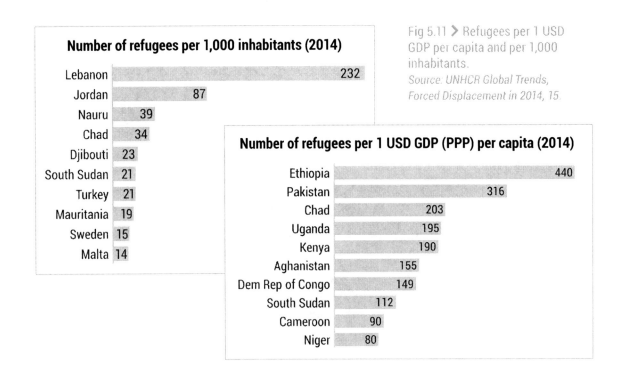

Fig 5.11 > Refugees per 1 USD GDP per capita and per 1,000 inhabitants.
Source: UNHCR Global Trends, Forced Displacement in 2014, 15.

Used as a Migration Channel and Entices People Smuggling

Providing all people the right to arrive at a country, even without documentation and request refugee status, the Refugee Convention enables the co-opting of the refugee channel as a potential mechanism to enter a country for a person who is rationally desperate to leave behind a life of poverty. Global trends are likely to increase the demand for migration from poor to rich countries. For this reason the attempted abuse of the asylum seeking channel is likely to grow in the future. Not only is the disparity between rich and poor countries likely to persist but the population of poor countries will continue to grow more rapidly than that of the rich countries. Thirdly, the diaspora of immigrants within rich nations will continue to increase, which will act to lower the perceived barriers to migrate[41].

Even when claims are clearly false, determining the difference between real refugees and migrants is difficult and costly. In 2000, Australia's budget for one tribunal in its onshore refugee determination system (the Refugee Review Tribunal) was the same as its donation to the UNHCR[42].

---

41 Paul Collier, *Exodus* (London: Oxford University Press, 2013), 23 of 159. IBook edition.
42 Adrienne Millbank, "The Problem with the 1951 Refugee Convention," Parliament of Australia (September 5, 2001).

In many countries only a minority of failed asylum seekers leave, the UK Home Office has previously reported that up to two thirds of failed asylum seekers vanish[43]. "Large scale removals may simply not be possible under liberal democracies. Without the possibility of such deportations, however, the entire process of asylum determination is, while costly, somewhat pointless"[44].

Counterpoints to the Criticisms

Whilst there are imperfections in the Refugee Convention owing to its age and the changing international landscape, the case for updating the Convention or leaving it unchanged is not clear cut. While it is not perfect, it has provided a system for protecting people at risk of persecution in their own countries. Disengagement from the Convention would likely undermine the international framework for protecting and assisting refugees.

The UNHCR is resistant to any change to the Refugee Convention as it is likely to be interpreted as a threat to the framework it has built up over the last 65 years.

> *"Governments should work, together with the UNHCR, to supplement – and not supplant – the Convention so that the protection of refugees and asylum seekers can be strengthened on the basis of already existing and widely recognised Convention principles"*[45].

---

43 Ibid.
44 Ibid.
45 Adrienne Millbank, "The Problem with the 1951 Refugee Convention,"Parliament of Australia (September 5, 2001).

CH 6. SOLUTION

A person's period of temporary protection, as either a refugee or asylum seeker, ends when they are provided ongoing (permanent) protection. These outcomes are labelled Durable Solutions. The UNHCR has defined three Durable Solutions:

1. Voluntary Repatriation back to the person's Country of Origin
2. Local Integration within the host Country of First Asylum
3. Resettlement to a third country, which is a signatory nation to the Refugee Convention.

Fig 6.1 ❯ Event 3 - Provision of a Durable Solution.

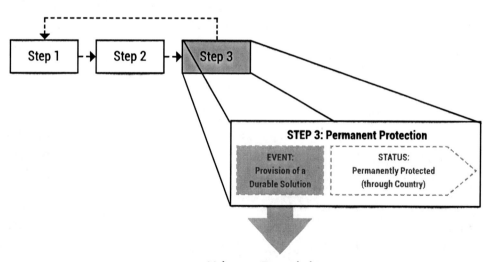

- Voluntary Repatriation
- Local Integration
- Resettlement to a Third Country
- Migration Overview
- Benefits of Migration
- Costs of Migration
- Migration Issues

1. Voluntary Repatriation

The UNHCR identifies Voluntary Repatriation as the durable solution of choice. Somewhat related, it is recognised as the approach that can resolve the largest number of refugees. Recent figures show that fourteen times as many refugees are repatriated than are resettled[1]. This is due in part to the unwillingness of signatory countries to take on ever-increasing refugee numbers as well as the growth in refugees since World War II.

Voluntary Repatriation was not considered a viable option for many decades following World War II. In the absence of Voluntary Repatriation during the Cold War, large scale resettlements occurred for hundreds of thousands of refugees fleeing conflict-torn, communist countries. It was not until the early 1990s that Voluntary Repatriation was considered a viable option and recognised as the best approach to resolve large numbers of displaced people. The fall of the Soviet Union in 1991 removed the symbolic motivations for the West in retaining defectors from the East (and vice versa), and the collapse of the Soviet Union was a catalyst for many civil wars which led to an increase in refugees that were unable to be effectively absorbed by signatory nations. Thus the study of the consequences of large scale repatriations is limited up to 1991. The one main exception being the return of ten million people from India to Bangladesh in the early 1970s.

It is important to note that thousands of refugees return home each year without any help from governments, the UNHCR or other NGOs. However, many rely on assistance to be able to return home. This may be in many forms including transportation, attaining documentation, attaining assurances that persecution will not occur, reclaiming land and homes, and finding employment or enrolling in schools. Such assistance may make a return possible; it also may sweeten the deal for a reluctant refugee to return. The UNHCR states that Voluntary Repatriation "should be exclusively based upon free and informed decisions and only when the national protection of one's rights is guaranteed"[2].

Since 1995, 18.2 million people have been repatriated through such assistance but unfortunately not without issues causing returnees to be forcibly displaced again. Methods at various levels are employed to increase the uptake of repatriation offers as well as the probability of long-term success of repatriation by ensuring there is not a repeat of forcible displacement.

- At an individual level, repatriation agreements and packages provide financial assistance and materials to returning refugees. For instance, an agreement signed

---

1   Megan Bradley, "Rethinking Return: Defining Success in Refugee Repatriation," *World Political Review* (December 3, 2013).
2   UNHCR, *Global Trends: Forced Displacement in 2014,* 20.

PART 1. SITUATION > CH 6. SOLUTION   133

in 2002 to support returning Afghan refugees from Iran included a package to each returnee of $US10 as well as food and basic tools[3].

- At a governmental level, broad agreements may be required to ensure returnees are not persecuted. In the Iran/Afghanistan example of 2002, the Afghan authorities agreed to not discriminate against returnees and to facilitate the recovery of their lost land and property. They also agreed to recognise spouses and children of returning refugees, who were not themselves citizens, to legally enter the country with their family.

- At a regional level, additional support for rehabilitation and development of any affected areas (for example due to conflict) is required to maximise the opportunity that the areas and their inhabitants thrive. Such support must be provided with long-term, as well as immediate short-term goals.

Advantages:

The advantages of Voluntary Repatriation as a durable solution include:

- It is the desire of most (but not all) refugees to return home.
- Returnees have access to family and friends to support the transition, especially in the early stages.
- Less stress is placed on host nations in absorbing large numbers of people.
- International attention is focused on the rehabilitation and redevelopment of the regions to where refugees are returning. This maximises the opportunity for a successful outcome for that region.

Disadvantages:

Voluntary Repatriation also includes a number of complex difficulties that limit the probability of long-term success.

- After long periods of exile, many returnees do not have an affiliation with their home country. Further, even if they are from rural areas, most returnees tend to stay in the larger cities due to the limited job opportunities in rural areas[4].

---

3 "Key repatriation agreement signed between Iran, Afghanistan and UNHCR," UNHCR (April 3, 2002), accessed July 23, 2016 <www.unhcr.org/news/latest/20002/4/3cab30fd4/key-repatriation-agreement-signed-iran-afghanistan-unhcr.html>

4 "Repatriation is not for everyone': the life ad livelihoods of former refugees in Liberia," Naohiko Omata, UNHCR (June, 2011) accessed July 23, 2016 <http://www.refworld.org/docid/4e55ed6e2.html>

- Many returnees struggle to reclaim their old homes. Some return to find other families have been living in their homes and on their land for many years and are unwilling to leave, often seeing the home as their own. Such disputes are not easily resolved if the state body is weak.
- Large numbers of returnees may put pressure on limited resources such as water, agricultural space, access to schools and access to medical care.
- Community grievances can arise if returning refugees receive aid that is not provided to returning IDPs or non-displaced community members.
- People who remained in the country may hold bitter perceptions toward the returning refugees as having gotten off lightly by leaving for another country.
- Grievances may also arise if returning refugees find that perpetrators of abuse prior to their departure are still roaming free. Conversely, the refugees themselves may be perceived by others to have been perpetrators of abuse.

As an example, the return of around 6 million Afghans from Iran and Pakistan since 2002 highlights the complexities of large-scale voluntary repatriations. Almost 20% of Afghanistan's 30 million population has returned in the past 13 years. Initially hopes were high that the return would help consolidate peace and stimulate development. Unfortunately, a number of issues were encountered resulting in large-scale hardship. The head of the UNHCR in Afghanistan described the return strategy as the biggest mistake the UNHCR ever made[5]. The issues included:

- Returnees struggled to reclaim or rebuild their homes.
- Returnees struggled to establish decent livelihoods.
- Conflicts arose over access to land and key resources such as water.
- Large numbers of returnees subsequently moved into slums or joined Afghanistan's IDP population.

An example from Africa: the return of Liberian refugees who had been away for over ten years in Ghana, highlights the dependency of successful repatriation on access to support networks. In this process returnees had to find their own accommodation three nights after their return to Liberia. Many with relatives were able to stay with them, some even received some financial support to smooth their transition. Those without contacts were on their own, making the period following their arrival much more precarious[6].

---

5 Megan Bradley, "Rethinking Return: Defining Success in Refugee Repatriation," *World Political Review* (December 3, 2013).
6 "Repatriation is not for everyone': the life ad livelihoods of former refugees in Liberia," Naohiko Omata, UNHCR (June, 2011) accessed July 23, 2016 <http://www.refworld.org/docid/4e55ed6e2.html>

An issue often raised is the lack of strategic coordination between the two main agency groups looking to help recovering, post-conflict countries. These agencies are the humanitarian agencies that provide short term support, like the UNHCR, and the development agencies, like the World Bank, that provide systemic support for the longer term.

The UNHCR certainly has capability in coordinating host nations, the Country of Origin to which refugees return, and other NGOs to provide a short-term environment that enables the safe return home of refugees and IDPs. However, what is often missing is strategic, longer-term developmental support such as removing socio-economic inequities that lead to conflict, and allowing returnees to benefit equally from the development gains. Examples of development agencies that must be involved are: the World Bank, United Nations Development Program and development donors. While there have been efforts in the past to coordinate humanitarian and development efforts to support return and reintegration, the results have been ineffective. Issues cited include different strategies and time lines and tendencies to compete for scope within the states they are looking to support[7].

2. Local Integration

In broad terms, Local Integration means permanently settling refugees within the communities of the Countries of First Asylum. This is realised when refugees are fully integrated as members of the community through legal, economic, social and cultural processes.

- Legally, the host government extends entitlements and rights to refugees as enjoyed by the citizens of the country. Generally this process involves naturalisation initially and the eventual provision of citizenship.
- Economically, the locally integrated refugees are included in the economy to ultimately become self-reliant through work.
- Socially and culturally, the locally integrated refugees live within communities without discrimination or exploitation.

The UNHCR reports that complete measures of local integration are not possible as only a limited number of countries report on naturalised refugees. Naturalisation often occurs before citizenship and although the numbers are not necessarily tracked, the naturalised refugee has been provided a durable solution. Only a small number of countries provide

---

7   Megan Bradley, "Rethinking Return: Defining Success in Refugee Repatriation," *World Political Review* (December 3, 2013).

data regarding the naturalisation of refugees. In 2014, 32,100 refugees were provided citizenship across 27 countries[8].

Advantages:

After long, protracted refugee situations, Local Integration may be the most practical durable solution. While it provides a realistic alternative to refugee camps, the success of Local Integration depends on the cooperation of local governments, the local community, and refugees.

A recent example of Local Integration was the 2014 resumption of granting citizenships to the United Republic of Tanzania for more than 162,000 former Burundian refugees who had fled their homeland in 1972. In the subsequent 40-odd years, this group on the whole became self-reliant taxpaying members of society[9].

Disadvantages:

Local Integration is not a viable option if it threatens the security or stability for either the local community or the refugees. In general, the interest shown by refugees in locally integrating depends on whether an individual has hopes for repatriation or resettlement into a third country. If they do have such hopes, they are less inclined to want to locally integrate. Time plays a factor in this, often refugees will view their stay initially as temporary but over time, especially if other options do not appear, this view changes and some seek to be integrated.

Local Integration as a durable solution has met increasing resistance from Countries of First Asylum over the past 30 years. Analysts have summarised the receptiveness of host governments in locally integrating refugees to depend on three key factors[10]:

1. **Real and perceived security threats:** Local Integration results in refugees bringing with them the security issues from the country they are fleeing. For that reason, some host governments seek to limit refugee movements to within camps and therefore not offer Local Integration. There is evidence that suggests refugees do bring with them security issues and crime from the regions they leave. However, this does not mean there were no problems in the host regions prior to refugee arrivals. It also appears that refugee camps often exacerbate security issues. Camps attract raids and direct attacks as well as encouraging organised crime and intimidation. Camp conditions also often lead to high rates of crime and violence towards women and children.

---

8   UNHCR, *Global Trends: Forced Displacement in 2014*, 22.
9   Ibid.
10 Karen Jacobsen, "Local Integration: The Forgotten Solution" *Migration Policy Institute,* October 1, 2003.

2. **Real or perceived economic and environmental burdens:** Local integration may result in excessive burdens on the local communities through competition for scarce resources and infrastructure. For example, communities may lose land and access to affordable homes, schools, and health facilities as a result of the population influx. Fears of environmental strains such as deforestation, water pollution and overuse of the land are also feared.

3. **Attitudes and beliefs of the refugee's length of stay (by both refugees and locals):** Naturally, when refugees are welcomed by the host communities they are generally better able to thrive. However, sometimes the host communities understand refugees are staying for a finite period until they can return home. Resentment may arise once it is understood the stay will be permanent or when more refugees arrive.

3. Resettlement to a Third Country

The UNHCR defines resettlement as the transfer of refugees from an asylum country (usually the Country of First Asylum) to another state (usually a Country of Second Asylum) that has agreed to admit them as refugees with permanent residence status and to ultimately grant them permanent settlement[11]. It is the only durable solution that moves a refugee from a country where they are already provided asylum to a third country. The number of countries that offer to resettle refugees in this way fluctuates – in 2014 it was 30. The UNHCR provides guidelines to resettlement states to promote a standardisation in the quality of refugee integration into the host community[12].

Not every refugee qualifies for resettlement. Resettlement submissions are provided on the back of UNHCR processing that determines individuals who cannot go home due to continued conflict or persecution or have specific needs that cannot be addressed in the place they have currently sought protection. Resettlement submissions are prioritised according to relative urgency. There are seven categories the UNHCR use to select refugees for resettlement. Of the 14.4 million Mandate Refugees in 2014, less than 1% (103,890) were submitted for resettlement. The reasons underpinning their resettlement outcomes were:

- 33% due to legal and/or physical protection needs.
- 26% due to lack of foreseeable alternative solutions.
- 22% survivors of violence and/or torture.
- 12% women and girls at risk.

---

11   UNHCR, *Global Trends: Forced Displacement in 2014*, 21.
12   UNHCR, "Projected Global Resettlement Needs 2016," (paper presented at 21st Annual Tripartite Consultations on Resettlement, Geneva, Switzerland, June 29 - July 1, 16.

- The remaining 7% were across the three categories of: Medical needs, Family Reunification, and Children and Adolescents at Risk.

Resettlement states are not obligated to accept a refugee who has been submitted for resettlement. Resettlement states assess each case submitted by the UNHCR and decide whether or not to resettle the individual according to their policies and regulations. The global acceptance rate in 2014 was 91%[13]. This means that almost one in ten refugees submitted for resettlement by the UNHCR are rejected by the settlement nations based on their screening criteria. Acceptance rates vary according to the Country of Origin and the submission category.

Fig 6.2 ❯ Resettlement Submission Acceptance Rates.
Source: UNHCR Projected Global Resettlement Needs 2016 (Page 55).

Country of Origin	Cases Submitted	% Cases Accepted
Myanmar	5,207	97.9%
Syria	5,040	92.1%
Dem Rep of the Congo	4,676	95.2%
Iraq	4,355	87.2%
Somalia	3,358	82.5%
Afghanistan	1,753	81.3%
Bhutan	1,649	99.4%
Eritrea	1,543	94.4%
Iran	1,517	92.4%
Sudan	938	88.2%
All Others	3,065	79.3%
Grand Total	33,101	91.3%

Submission Category	Acceptance Rate
Children and Adolescents at Risk (CHL)	87.6%
Family Reunification (FAM)	97.3%
Lack of Foreseeable Alternative Durable Solutions (LAS)	91.3%
Legal and/or Physical Protection Needs (LPN)	92.5%
Medical Needs (MED)	87.3%
Others/Unspecified	79.5%
Survivors of Violence and/or Torture (SVT)	89.3%
Women and Girls at Risk (AWR)	90.3%

---

13 UNHCR, *"Projected Global Resettlement Needs 2016,"* (paper presented at 21st Annual Tripartite Consultations on Resettlement, Geneva, Switzerland, June 29 - July 1, 55.

Advantages:

Resettlement states provide refugees with legal and physical protection. This includes rights similar to those enjoyed by citizens across civil, political, economic, social and cultural spheres[14].

Resettlement acts as a form of burden-sharing. To that end, the countries taking in the largest amounts are usually not Countries of First Asylum, which are often stretched and looking to lower the numbers of refugees they are hosting. Not all of the 103,890 refugees submitted for resettlement in 2014 were provided places in resettlement countries. Some were not accepted by the resettlement states, and others were not taken due to capacity constraints. In all, the UNHCR assisted the resettlement departures of 73,331 refugees, about 71% of the submissions.

Fig 6.3 ❯ Resettlement Submission Vs Departures.
Source: UNHCR Projected Global Resettlement Needs 2016 (Page 48).

	2014	2013	2012	2011	2010
Submissions	103,890	93,226	74,835	91,843	108,042
Departures	73,331	71,411	69,252	61,649	72,914
Countries of Asylum	90	80	80	79	86
Countries of Origin	70	69	79	77	71
Countries of Resettlement	30	25	26	22	28

The key countries involved in 2014 resettlements are shown in figure 6.4 below.

- The Country of Asylum refers to the host nation, usually the Country of First Asylum, where the refugee was being protected prior to their departure to the country of resettlement. In 2014, Malaysia, Turkey and Nepal had hosted over 29,000 (almost 39%) of these resettled refugees.

- The Country of Origin refers to the home country of the refugee prior to their forcible displacement.

- The Country of Resettlement refers to the country receiving the refugees and ultimately granting them permanent residence. In 2014, the US provided the clear majority of these places. The United States along with Canada, Australia and Germany was the destination for 90% of the total UNHCR assisted resettlement departures.

---

[14] "UNHCR - Resettlement," UNHCR, accessed July 23, 2016 <wwwunhcr.org/resettlement.html>

Fig 6.4 > UNHCR Assisted Resettlement Departures in 2014. *Source: UNHCR Projected Global Resettlement Needs 2016 (Page 51).*

COUNTRY OF ASYLUM	PERSONS
MALAYSIA	10,976
TURKEY	8,944
NEPAL	8,582
THAILAND	7,170
LEBANON	6,285
KENYA	4,913
ETHIOPIA	4,514
JORDAN	3,319
RWANDA	2,569
SYRIAN ARAB REPUBLIC	1,889
ALL OTHERS	14,170
TOTAL	73,331

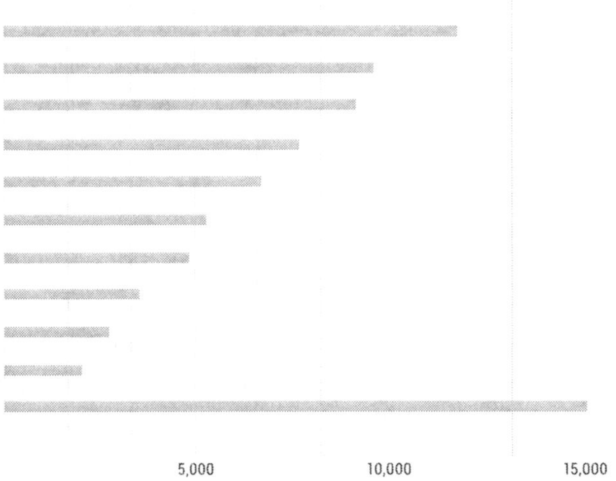

COUNTRY OF ORIGIN	PERSONS
MYANMAR	17,596
IRAQ	10,985
SOMALIA	9,929
BHUTAN	8,395
SYRIAN ARAB REPUBLIC	7,021
DEM. REP. OF THE CONGO	6,245
AFGHANISTAN	3,331
ISLAMIC REPUBLIC OF IRAN	2,536
ERITREA	2,386
COLOMBIA	982
ALL OTHERS	3,925
TOTAL	73,331

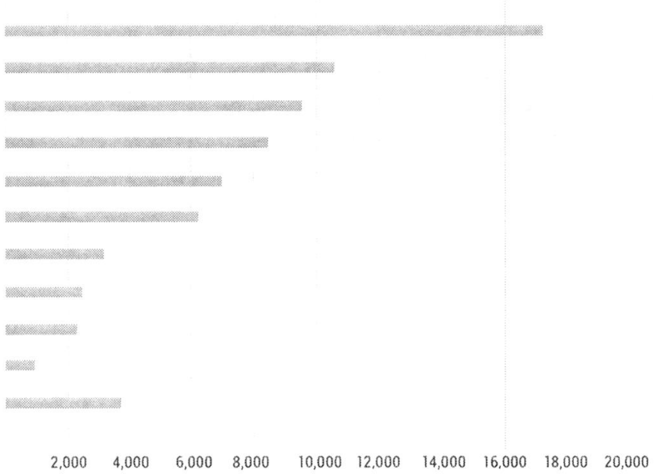

COUNTRY OF RESETTLEMENT	PERSONS
UNITED STATES	48,911
CANADA	7,234
AUSTRALIA	6,162
GERMANY	3,467
SWEDEN	1,812
NORWAY	1,188
FINLAND	1,011
NETHERLANDS	743
NEW ZEALAND	639
UNITED KINGDOM	628
ALL OTHERS	1,536
TOTAL	73,331

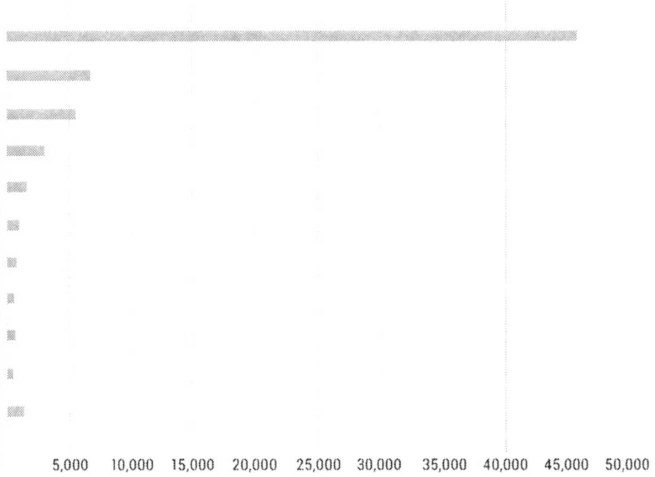

There are also refugees who resettled to Countries of Second Asylum without any assistance from the UNHCR. In 2014 the combined total number of refugees who resettled with or without UNHCR assistance was 105,200. The relative numbers across the resettlement states remains very similar, with the US resettling a total of 73,000 refugees, Canada 12,300 and Australia 11,600.

In response to the Syrian crisis in 2015, many nations undertook commitments to resettle a special additional volume of refugees to provide as much help as possible. Canada committed for an additional 25,000, Australia an additional 12,000 and the USA an additional 10,000. A total of 28 countries confirmed in 2015 they would receive Syrian refugees[15].

Resettlement as a durable solution provides advantages for the host nation over the process of providing protection to refugees as they arrive to their land. Those to be resettled can be screened and accepted from a pool of candidates. It also means refugees can be flown to the new country, avoiding the danger and expense of using people smugglers. The countries accepting the most resettled refugees are some of the wealthiest in the world. In this regard the resettled refugees are likely to receive some of the best support available. Many resettlement nations offer integration services that include cultural orientation, language and vocational training, as well as programs to support access to education and employment[16].

Fig 6.5 > Annual Resettlement Departures. *Source: UNHCR Projected Global Resettlement Needs 2016.*

	2010	2011	2012	2013	2014
COUNTRIES WITH REGULAR RESETTLEMENT PROGRAMMES					
ARGENTINA	23	24	5	7	21
AUSTRALIA	5,636	5,597	5,079	11,117	6,162
BELGIUM	2	19	1	100	32
BRAZIL	28	23	8	56	44
CANADA	6,706	6,827	4,755	5,140	7,234
CHILE	6	22	3	3	0
CZECH REP	48	0	25	1	4
DENMARK	386	606	324	475	332
FINLAND	543	573	763	665	1,011
FRANCE	217	42	84	100	378
GERMANY	457	22	323	1,092	3,467

---

15 UNHCR, "Projected Global Resettlement Needs 2016," (paper presented at 21st Annual Tripartite Consultations on Resettlement, Geneva, Switzerland, June 29 - July 1, 10.
16 "UNHCR - Resettlement," UNHCR, accessed July 23, 2016 <wwwunhcr.org/resettlement.html>

	2010	2011	2012	2013	2014
COUNTRIES WITH REGULAR RESETTLEMENT PROGRAMMES					
HUNGARY	0	0	1	0	4
ICELAND	6	0	9	0	4
IRELAND	20	36	40	62	98
ITALY	58	0	9	0	0
JAPAN	27	18	0	18	23
LUXEMBORG	0	0	0	0	28
NETHERLANDS	430	479	262	362	743
NEW ZEALAND	535	477	719	682	639
NORWAY	1,088	1,258	1,137	941	1,188
PORTUGAL	24	28	21	6	14
SOUTH KOREA	23	11	20	31	14
ROMANIA	38	0	0	0	44
SPAIN	0	0	80	0	30
SWEDEN	1,789	1,896	1,483	1,832	1,812
SWITZERLAND	19	39	54	78	139
UK	695	424	989	750	628
USA	54,077	43,215	53,053	47,875	48,911
URUGUAY	17	0	5	14	52
COUNTRIES WITH SPECIAL RESETTLEMENT PROGRAMMES					
AUSTRIA	0	0	0	4	269
LIECHTENSTEIN	0	0	0	0	5
MEXICO	0	0	0	0	1
PALAU	3	0	0	0	0
PARAGUAY	13	13	0	0	0

Disadvantages:

The main negative of resettlement as a durable solution is the very low annual number of refugees provided with this outcome. Over the past 20 years about 1.8 million refugees have been resettled. For context, ten times as many refugees (18.2 million) were repatriated in that period and the current number of Mandate Refugees is eight times as many (14.4 million).

Many countries are reluctant to accept more resettlement refugees given they are dealing with large numbers of refugees and illegal immigrants.

Migration Overview

Durable Solutions and Migration

For refugees unable to return home due to ongoing conflict or persecution, the durable solutions of Local Integration and Resettlement offer immediate outcomes that enable them to begin to rebuild a life. Such a rebuild is not possible for asylum seekers or refugees given the temporary nature of their protection. These people might be in a UNHCR camp or residing in a country such as Australia for the time being, but with no assurances they will be able to stay. The volume of Forcibly Displaced People was 59.5 million as of the end of 2014. If they are unable to go home, why couldn't these people be provided with such a durable solution?

The answer is that refugees provided the durable solutions of either Local Integration or Resettlement are effectively a type of migrant to their new country and that most countries control their level of immigration. Countries control their immigration because of a perceived set of related costs and benefits.

It is due to these controls that the proportion of people living as immigrants in the world has remained relatively stable at around 3% in recent decades[17]. As of 2015, there were about 244 million migrants living across the world – about 3.3% of the population[18]. Net Overseas Migration (NOM) is a common measure used in monitoring and controlling migration amounts. It is the net amount of the number of immigrants arriving to a country minus the number of emigrants leaving. Australia, as an example, has one of the highest proportion of immigrants in the Western world. As of 2015 about 28% of Australian's were immigrants with a further 20% of inhabitants having at least one parent born overseas[19]. Even with this high proportion, Australia has controlled its NOM, since World War II this number has generally ranged between 0.5% and 1.5% of Australia's total population.

---

[17] Stephen Castles, Hein De Haas and Mark J. Miller, *The Age of Migration,* Fifth Edition, (London: The Guilford Press, 2014), 1 & 9.
[18] "International Migration 2015," United Nations, accessed July 23, 2016 <www.un.org/en/development/desa/population/migration/publications/wallchart/docs/MigrationWallChart2015.pdf>
[19] Ibid.

Fig 6.6 ❯ Australian Net Overseas Migration as a percentage of population (1860 – 2010).
Source: *Migration to Australia since Federation, a guide to the statistics.*

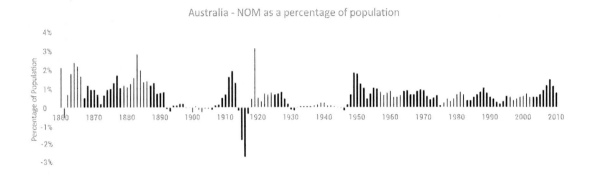

Migration History

Historically, the main drivers of migration have generally been war and the deportation of conquered people, the search for economic opportunities, and forced movement due to the creation of states and empires.

Migration across continents increased with the expansion of European power following the discovery of the New World in 1492. The subsequent colonisation meant millions of Europeans were able to build new lives in different regions – originally Africa and Asia, then to the Americas and finally to Australia and Oceania[20].

Much of the colonial migration prior to 1800 was supported by commerce and global companies like the Dutch East India Company. Work in the remote, often tropical areas occupied by these commercial outposts was dangerous and there were high mortality rates. However, for many migrants it was the only way to escape poverty. Slaves and indentured labour were also large components of migration at this time.

Slaves were widely used to support commodity production – mainly sugar, cotton, tobacco, coffee, cotton and gold – from the late-17th to the mid-19th centuries. Slavery increased British and French power in the 18th century as well as imprisoning and moving millions of Africans to the new world. Approximately 12 million slaves were taken to the Americas by 1850[21]. Slave trading was progressively abolished during the 19th century,

---

20 Stephen Castles, Hein De Haas and Mark J. Miller, *The Age of Migration,* Fifth Edition, (London: The Guilford Press, 2014), 86.
21 Stephen Castles, Hein De Haas and Mark J. Miller, *The Age of Migration,* Fifth Edition, (London: The Guilford Press, 2014), 86-93.

starting with the British Empire in 1807, the rest of Europe by 1815, British colonies by 1834, Dutch colonies by 1863 and US Southern States by 1865.

Following the abolishment of slavery, indentured workers were used as the main source of plantation labour. Generally young and with limited capital, indentured workers paid for their migration to the New World by working for an employer for a defined number of years. Colonial powers used indentured workers in dozens of countries. About half of the white immigrants to the American colonies during the 17th and 18th centuries were indentured workers, and estimates suggest that between 12-37 million workers migrated this way between 1834 and 1941[22]. Whilst the conditions were tough, people made the choice in the search for a better life. Other examples of indentured workers include Indians moving to the sugar plantations in the Caribbean and to the mines and railways in South East Asia and East Africa, Chinese 'coolies' moving to South East Asia, and Japanese moving to Hawaii, USA, Brazil and Peru.

The Industrial Revolution prompted a new burst of migration. Great Britain and Germany, who underwent the Revolution first, were the largest providers of early emigrants. The peak period of their migration to America being between 1800 and 1860 (about 66% of migrants to the USA during that time were from Britain, 22% from Germany). From 1850-1914 most migrants came from areas that went through Industrialisation later (including Ireland, Italy, Spain, and Eastern Europe). The growth in migration was extraordinary. It is estimated that less than 1 million immigrants came to the USA from Europe between 1600 and 1799. Following industrialisation it steadily increased to where more than 30 million Europeans migrated across to the USA from 1836 to 1914. One of the cornerstones of the new national identities of the new world was the battle against the indigenous people. The associated mythology of the pioneers triumphing over the native peoples has been posed by scholars as a possible foundation stone for the perceived xenophobic and racist cultures of the Western colonialists[23].

As Western Europeans went to the New World to escape the poverty and squalor of the industrialised towns, workers from peripheral areas such as Ireland, Italy and Poland were drawn to Western Europe as replacement labour. For example, over 15 million Italians emigrated between 1876 and 1920, almost 7 million of these went to other European countries[24].

The period between World Wars I and II, had little labour migration. There were two main contributing factors – economic stagnation and increased hostility towards migrants.

---

22 Ibid.
23 Ibid.
24 Ibid.

Groups in the US claimed that Southern and Eastern Europeans were 'unassimilable' and Congress passed laws in the 1920s limiting entries outside those from Western Europe – National Origins Quota System[25]. France was the notable exception in Western Europe. It was in a demographic deficit exacerbated by heavy war losses. In response to this, foreign labour systems were refined by the government and employers. Between 1920 and 1930 almost 2 million foreign workers entered, mainly from Italy, Poland, Spain and Belgium. A law removed the barriers for Algerian Muslims to enter, although they remained non-citizens. Between 1921 and 1931, 75% of population growth was through immigration[26] by 1931, 6.6% of population were foreigners (2.7 million).

In the two decades following World War II, the demand (Pull) for immigrants by the US and European economies was large enough to stimulate large-scale migrations from the poorer economies of the periphery (including Mexico, Turkey, North-Africa). These labour migrations were initiated and legitimised by the receiving states through programs like Western Europe's Guest Worker's Program and United States' Bracero Program.

The economic slowdown following the first oil shock of 1973-74 resulted in labour migrations being seen as a negative. However the flow of migration, even during times of economic contraction did not stop. The reasons for this included:

- Employers in the western intake countries wanted to retain their "guest workers" indefinitely.
- The dependence of the sending countries of multi-billion dollar migrant remittances.
- The supply-push from the sending nations reached new heights as the populations of the peripheral countries (like Turkey, Mexico, and Algeria) grew very rapidly even as their economies slowed.
- Migration networks developed, helping spread information about job opportunities, modes of entry, and residence in receiving countries[27].

Thus, immigration has continued at historically high levels, forcing governments to scramble to redesign immigration control and refugee admission policies to cope with the rising tides.

---

25   Stephen Castles, Hein De Haas and Mark J. Miller, *The Age of Migration,* Fifth Edition, (London: The Guilford Press, 2014), 96-98.
26   Ibid.
27   James F. Hollifield, Philip L. Martin and Pia M. Orrenius, *Controlling Immigration: A Global Perspective,* Third Edition (United States, Standford Univerity Press, 2014).

Migration Drivers

There are multiple models that outline what drives people to migrate. The most intuitive models look at Push Factors and Pull Factors. Push Factors push people away from their homeland. Pull Factors pull people to a new country. It is the combination of Push and Pull Factors that compel an individual to migrate. As different people are motivated by different things, not all factors apply to all people. Some factors that push one person away from a state may attract another.

Push Factors that generally motivate people to emigrate out of a country include:

- Population Density: high population density suppresses the utility of citizens through increased congestion, crowds and waiting times, lack of access to amenities, and lack of exposure to nature. Interestingly, some places of very high density (e.g. Singapore) also attract migrants.
- Lack of Economic Opportunity: lack of opportunity to work and support oneself and family is an obvious driver for emigration.
- Political Repression: limitation of opportunities, or worse still a threat regarding to one's well-being.

Pull Factors that generally motivate people to immigrate into a country include:

- Demand for Labour: greater opportunity to work and better pay abroad.
- Availability of Land: to improve standard of living.
- Economic Opportunities: enabling a better standard of living.
- Political Freedoms: enabling one to express their true self and to access a full suite of opportunities and protections available to a citizen.

Each of these drivers can be debated as to their influence on decisions to migrate. For example, the effect of population density has been questioned as in recent times people have tended to move from areas of lower population to higher population. For instance, Germany has a much greater population density than Afghanistan or Eritrea[28].

Migrants often tend to come from particular sub-sections of populations. For example, the young and higher-skilled people tend to migrate more often. This is somewhat explained by the concept of individuals deciding to invest in migration much like investing in education. As people vary in terms of age, knowledge, skills, networks and capability, each makes a decision on whether and where to migrate based on their own unique cost/benefit calculation.

---

28 "Demography does not Explain the Migration Crisis," Matt Ridley, Rational Optimist, published September 6, 2015, accessed July 23, 2016 <www.rationaloptimist.com/blog/demography-does-not-explain-the-migration-crisis/>

It is when the combination of the Push and Pull Factors outweigh the costs or barriers to moving that an individual will decide to migrate. Barriers to moving include cost, fear of the unknown and isolation from their culture and support network. This cost barrier contributes to the relationship that exists between the development of a country and the level of migration it experiences. Developed countries tend to have higher levels of internal and international migration.

As a country develops, individuals within the country gain capabilities to migrate (income, education, access to information) as well as increased aspirations (increased awareness of lifestyles and opportunities elsewhere due to education and access to information). This can lead to a paradox for a developing country where a jump in its wealth and productivity coincides with a jump in emigration of its citizens away from it.

Migration Rate

In his book on 21st century immigration *Exodus*[29], economist Paul Collier states that the rate of migration also changes according to three factors. The first is the gap in wealth between two nations, the bigger the gap the bigger the drive to migrate. The second is the wealth of the emigrant country, as with more wealth people are better able to overcome the obstacles to emigrate. The third is the diaspora of the emigrant peoples in the destination country. A further insight was that all these factors were required to generate big flows of migrants. That is, big movements required a wide gap, with a large diaspora and an adequate level of income[30].

Clearly a larger income gap and standard of living will greatly entice people to move to a more developed country. Advancements in smart-phones and the Internet has led to an increase in the knowledge and aspirations of many in the developing world.

The percentage of migrants in the developed world has steadily increased since the 1960s. Between 2000 and 2015 it has increased from 8.7% to 11.2%. Once a critical number of migrants have settled in an area, they tend to draw others from their social network to that area. This is due to the reduction in barriers to moving including cultural isolation, fear of the unknown and isolation from a support network.

Benefits of Migration

The benefits and costs of migration are both immediate – therefore easier to see; as well as long term, and therefore harder to identify. The general consensus among scholars is

---

29 Paul Collier, *Exodus* (London: Oxford University Press, 2013), 18 of 159. IBook edition.
30 Ibid, 24 of 159.

that migration is on the whole a good thing. It provides economic advantages for the host nation as well as providing new opportunities for the incoming migrant. However, it has also been compared to food, in that although necessary, too much of it may be harmful[31]. Arguments for and against migration consider a whole range of stakeholders including the migrant and their family, the nation of emigration, the nation of immigration, and the rest of the world.

Social Benefits

The perceived benefits of migration include the fulfilment of the wishes of the person who seeks to migrate. Freedom of choice and freedom to travel and move to wherever one wants in order to enjoy their life to the greatest possible extent is desirable provided it does not negatively impact other individuals or societies as a whole.

Migration enriches society. Though a values-based judgement, diversity is generally considered a benefit to society through cultural additions such as food, art, customs and products. It also increases the influence and power of the intake nation. All else being equal, the larger a country's population, the more influence and power they have in asserting their interests.

Economic Benefits

In terms of the economy, although debatable, most analysts arrive at a mild economic benefit of larger migration intakes. Key insights include:

- Migrants are generally found to be better educated than the average in the host populations (in part because they are on-average younger than the host population, and younger people are generally better educated).
- Migrants are able to fill labour market gaps in the host country. For example, immigrants filled 22% of entries in strongly-growing occupations in the USA (and 15% in Europe). They also filled 28% of entries in strongly-declining industries in the USA (and 24% in Europe), these jobs are considered as unattractive or lacking in career prospects by domestic workers[32].
- There is debate about whether migration enhances the GDP per capita. Recent studies of OECD countries suggest the impact of migrants over the past 50 years is on average close to zero, rarely exceeding plus or minus 0.5% of GDP per capita.

---

31   Paul Collier, *Exodus* (London: Oxford University Press, 2013), 17 of 159. IBook edition.
32   "Is migration good for the economy?," OECD Migration Policy Debates, May 2014, accessed July 23, 2016 <www.oecd.org/els/mig/OECD%20Migration%20Policy%20Debates%20Numero%202.pdf>

Immigrants are neither a burden nor a help to the public purse[33]. Two recent reports regarding the UK economy found that higher levels of net migration (for the UK 200,000–225,000) lead to higher GDP per capita (2.7-3%) and a lower net debt as a percentage of GDP[34]. Regarding this, migrants arriving to work have a much more favourable fiscal position than asylum seekers and refugees. Employment is the single biggest determinant of a migrant's net fiscal contribution, particularly in countries with generous welfare[35].

In terms of a country's age profile, migration improves (through lowering) the dependency ration. That is, it reduces the number of people 65 years of age or above for every 100 people of working age (15-64). Thus it should lower the burden each working-age adult must bear to support retirees. Migrants are generally in the younger age categories. This helps support the ageing population many Western countries are faced with.

Fig 6.7 ▶ Countries receiving the largest remittance payments. *Source: Wikipedia (2 source cited).*

Countries with the largest remittance in comparison to GDP (Percentage of 2013 GDP)	Countries receiving the largest dollar amounts (USD Billion, 2013)
1. Timor-Leste (216%)	1. India (70.0)
2. Tajikistan (42.1%)	2. China (59.5)
3. Kyrgyzstan (31.5%)	3. Philippines (26.7)
4. Nepal (28.8%)	4. France (23.3)
5. Moldova (24.9%)	5. Mexico (23.0)
6. Lesotho (24.4%)	6. Nigeria (20.9)
7. Samoa (23.8%)	7. Egypt (17.8)
8. Haiti (21.1%)	8. Germany (15.2)
9. Armenia (21.0%)	9. Pakistan (14.6)
10. The Gambia (19.8%)	10. Bangladesh (13.9)
11. Liberia (18.5%)	11. Belgium (11.1)
12. Lebanon (17.0%)	12. Venezuela (11.0)
13. Honduras (16.9%)	13. Ukraine (9.7)
14. El Salvador (16.4%)	14. Spain (9.6)
15. Kosovo (16.1%)	15. Indonesia (7.6)

One benefit that is perhaps not immediately obvious is that migration creates the opportunity for remittance payments to be made. Remittances are transfers of money migrants have earned in their host nation back to their Country of Origin. This money supply is very important to developing countries. In 2014, there was approximately US$580

---

33 Ibid.
34 Carlos Vargas-Sliva, "Hard Evidence: are migrants good for the economy?," *The Conversation,* August 19, 2014.
35 "Is migration good for the economy?," OECD Migration Policy Debates, May 2014, accessed July 23, 2016 <www.oecd.org/els/mig/OECD%20Migration%20Policy%20Debates%20Numero%202.pdf>

billion in remittance payments, approximately US$430 billion of this being transferred to developing countries, in many cases dwarfing the amount received by foreign aid[36]. The US is the largest source country of these remittance payments over the past decade. Russia, Saudi Arabia and Switzerland have been the next largest source countries.

Costs of Migration

There are also less positive views toward the use of migration. In the past, migration was used as large scale recruitment of labour by governments or organisations to support national objectives. An example being indentured workers used as the main source of colonial plantation labour. Arguments are made that migration is used to mobilise cheap labour and serves to boost profits of the employers of host nations while depriving the emigration states of valuable labour and skills. This structural control is argued to be a legacy of colonialism and the result of war and international inequalities.

An extension of this view is that states have set up a two-tiered regime that encourages migration for the economic elite while keeping the lower classes unable to move easily. While immigration regimes fail to curb migration as long as labour demands persist, they lead to an increase in illegal migration and subsequently increase the vulnerability of migrants who are then exploited in labour markets.

Economic Costs

The perceived costs of migration include impacts to society through overcrowding. The high levels of migration needed to attain any economic benefit have detrimental social impacts such as overcrowding of public facilities (e.g. roads, schools, hospitals), limited supply of housing and a strain on natural resources (e.g. water).

Alternatively, the cost of expanding durable assets to cover the expansion required by population growth is very expensive. Durable assets include items like roads, dams, train lines, houses, schools, shopping centres and the education of a skilled workforce. Development economist Jane O'Sullivan estimates that a population increase of 1% per year uses about 7% of GDP. Immigration contributes over 50% of Australia's population growth, which has recently averaged about 1.5% of the total population each year. The cost of such growth is about 10% of GDP[37].

---

36   Dilip Ratha, "The hidden force in global economics: sending money home" (Ted Talk, presented in Rio de Janeiro, Brazil, October, 2014).
37   Geoff Davies, "The huge, hidden cost of population growth,", The Sydney Morning Herald, February 22, 2016.

Migration of low-skilled labour results in lower wages for the working class. The increase worker supply lowers the average pay.

Social Costs

Migration can risk the inhabitants losing control of their land through unforeseen consequences. An example of such unforeseen consequences is the Texas Annexation from Mexico. Texas had been part of the Spanish empire for over 300 years since it was first mapped in 1519. After Mexico won its Independence from Spain in 1821 it invited Anglo-American immigrants to Mexico Texas to populate its sparsely inhabited land. Following a series of events and complexities, ultimately Texas declared independence from Mexico in 1836 and was eventually incorporated into the United States in 1845. In hindsight, the allowance of immigrants into their land proved disastrous for Mexico. Another example of unforeseen and negative consequences of immigration is the British arrivals to India in the early 18th century. This form of immigration ultimately led to the subjugation of the Indian peoples.

As migrants tend to be the young, educated and motivated people of the emigrant country, migration results in a "brain drain" from developing countries. By luring the best and brightest away from poor nations, migration slows the development of these nations which is needed to provide the greatest good for the entire population.

Large inflows of migration may impact the notion of Mutual Regard which has been described by Paul Collier in his book *Exodus*. Mutual regard is the contribution and support all members of society provide each other in order for society to work cohesively and optimally. Collier describes two key aspects of mutual regard:

- The first is the 'willingness of the successful to finance transfers to the less successful' through solidarity with other members of the community who are less fortunate.

- The second is cooperation 'to provide public goods that would otherwise not be well supplied by a purely market process'. Collier provides the example of England's National Health Service and a traditional, unwritten convention of restraint by the general public when dealt a minor error from the service. Through this cooperation, the NHS is able to maximise its resources on health services rather than legal battles and compensatory claims.

Both of these aspects may decrease with large intakes of immigration. Such changes are not likely to be a step change, but rather happen gradually over many years. How and why it does is complex and involves cultural and political aspects as well as just numbers. However, a sense of solidarity that is felt with numbers of migrants that are perceived to be manageable to a society may be evaporated with larger numbers that are perceived to be overwhelming. Similarly, a sense of mutual trust and cooperation can be decreased when immigration is so rapid that it impacts cultural norms and lessens a sense of community.

Large inflows of migrants, particularly from other cultures, also risks cultural clashes through pure xenophobia and some potentially through an inability of cultures to co-exist. The extent of such clashes is debatable, and once again based on many factors outside pure numbers alone.

- In 1968 a British Tory parliamentarian Enoch Powell made two infamous speeches in regard to Britain's immigration of 'coloured' people from its former colonies (mainly the Indian sub-continent and Caribbean). He predicted violence and cultural clashes as 'the people of England will not endure it'. Many of Powell's predictions regarding the population of immigrants and their descendants in the UK have proved to be correct. However, while there has been racial and cultural violence in the UK since 1968, it has not been at the levels Powell implied would occur.
- Other areas of Europe have also seen a rise in seemingly cultural violence in the past two decades. Most notably countries like France, the Netherlands and Sweden who all have large and growing Muslim populations. Islam and the West is further explored in Chapter 8.
- Australia, Canada and the United States all have very high immigrant numbers but with minimal instances of cultural disruptions or violence.

Migration Issues

Migration Amounts

United Nations data shows that migrants made up over 28% of Australia's population in 2015. This is quite high in the developed world. Migrant percentages in 2015 for other OECD countries include: 22% in Canada, 15% in the USA and Germany, 13% in the UK and 12% in France. In general, the developing world has much less immigrant populations: less than 1% in Mexico, Nigeria and 0.1% in Indonesia. Other relatively low migrant populations exist in Russia (8%), Iran (3%) and Japan (2%). Many of the rich oil states including the United Arab Emirates (88%), Kuwait (74%) and Saudi Arabia (32%) have large migrant worker populations.

Demographic Ignorance

As is the case in many countries, the size of Australia's migration program is not widely known by the general public. This has been supported by a number of studies over the past fifty years[38]. One cause of the ignorance may be that demography is not widely taught in Australia, another is that the figures are not easily accessible, or understood once accessed. Gary Freeman, an American scholar, suggests this is because most liberal democracies run immigration rates higher than the electorate prefers[39].

The argument continues that immigration produces concentrated benefits and diffused costs, resulting in vested interest groups lobbying for higher immigration rates. The concentrated benefits are in the forms of new customers for housing developers, more customers for retailers, and cheaper labour for employers. The diffused costs include increased housing costs, increased congestion, lower wages and less environmental amenity.

Life Boat Ethics

Life boat ethics is a metaphor for resource distribution proposed by Garrett Hardin in 1974. Hardin was the American ecologist who had famously brought William Forster Lloyd's 'Tragedy of the Commons' metaphor into popular consciousness in 1968. Life boat ethics was the next generation of Hardin's exploration into population and immigration. It can be used to provide a perspective on the case for limiting migration amounts (including asylum seekers).

If the world is roughly divided into rich and poor nations, about 80% of the population would be poor and only 20% would be rich. Metaphorically, each rich nation can be seen as a lifeboat full of comparatively rich people. In the ocean outside each lifeboat swim the poor of the world. The metaphor then asks who should get in, or at least have a share of some of the wealth. What should the lifeboat passengers do?

- Firstly, the limited capacity of the lifeboat must be recognised. For example the land, water and other resources of a nation have a theoretical carrying capacity. Hardin asked the reader to assume a life boat representing the USA with 50 people in it, and a carrying capacity of 60. The example then poses the question of what to do with 100 people of the poor nations swimming in the water outside.
- **Option 1. Take on everyone.** Helping all in need would result in taking all 100 people onto the boat. The result would be having the life boat designed for 60 carrying 150, swamping the boat and drowning everyone.
- **Option 2. Take on ten people to fill up capacity.** In this case, Hardin asks which ten would come on board? Are the 'best' ten chosen or are the first come taken? What

---

38 Katharine Betts,"Attitudes to Immigration and population growth in Australia 1954 to 2010: An Overview," *People and Place, vol. 18, no. 3, 2010: 34.*
39 Ibid.

is said to the other 90? Hardin then points out that if all ten spots are taken, putting the life boat at its theoretical maximum carrying capacity, the safety factor of a buffer amount under the carrying capacity is lost. Thus, mishaps affecting crops such as a drought or a new plant disease could have disastrous consequences.

- **Option 3. Take on less than ten.** If a small buffer is preserved to provide a carrying capacity safety factor, then survival of the life boat is possible but only when constantly guarding against boarding parties.
- Hardin argued that Option 3 was clearly the only means for survival. He also recognised that it is morally abhorrent to many people. His response was to tell them to, 'get out and yield your place to others'.

The much higher fertility rates of the poorer nations also impact the life boat model. The richest 20% of nations are doubling every 80-odd years, whereas the poorest 80% are doubling every 30-40 years, twice as fast. The growth rates imply that the difference in average wealth between the rich and the poor nations will most likely increase. In 'sharing with all according to their needs', 'their needs' are determined by population size, which in turn is determined by the fertility rate. This is a sovereign right of every nation, poor or not. The burden of sharing (be it foreign aid or immigration into rich countries) on rich nations will continue to increase until the population growth of the poorest nations is stabilised as they go through the demographic transition.

Mutual Regard

Collier posits that mutual regard is reduced when immigrants remain outside the mainstream society. Although a diversity of migrants creates a greater diversity, a loss of mutual regard will have detrimental impacts on public institutions that require cooperation to best operate[40].

The Liberal Paradox

Along with an increase in immigration, since World War II liberal democracies have expanded the rights for marginal and ethnic groups, including foreigners[41]. As we have seen, this originated with the adoption of the Universal Declaration of Human Rights in 1948. These expanded rights have constrained governments in their attempts to control borders and exclude specific individuals or groups from membership in society.

---

40 Paul Collier, *Exodus* (London: Oxford University Press, 2013), 35 of 159. IBook edition.
41 James F. Hollifield, Philip L. Martin and Pia M. Orrenius, *Controlling Immigration: A Global Perspective*, Third Edition (United States, Standford Univerity Press, 2014), 8-9..

The continued immigration drive by the Push and Pull Factors combined with the expanded rights since World War II have highlighted some difficulties liberal democracies are having with controlling immigration. In 1992, academic James Hollifield raised the 'liberal paradox': How can a society be open for economic reasons and at the same time maintain a degree of political and legal closure to protect the social contract?[42] Initiatives made by many states to regain control of their borders have included the rollback of some civil and human rights. Examples of such rollbacks include the United States' 1996 Illegal Immigration Reform and Immigrant Responsibility Act which increased restrictions on immigrants; Germany's amendment to Article 16 of the Basic Law which restricted the blanket right of asylum; and the Pasqua and Debre laws in France of the 1990s[43]. Since World War II there has also been a rise in nationalist, anti-immigration movements. A prime example is the French Front National Party, but similar parties exist in many countries with high immigration.

Scholars have suggested there is a trade-off between immigrant numbers and rights. States may have more foreign workers with fewer rights; alternatively they may have fewer foreign workers with more rights. However they cannot have both. That is, more foreign workers through open labour markets, and high rights for all[44]. However, if not all members of a society are citizens with the same rights, many argue the society is not a truly liberal society.

---

42 Ibid.
43 Ibid.
44 Ibid.

CH 7. HOME?

Attainment of permanent protection through a durable solution represents the completion of the Refugee Journey. The person now has a permanent home where they enjoy or will in time, the full rights of a citizen. The person may have returned to their Country of Origin by Voluntary Repatriation, been accepted as a permanent resident with their host state and Locally Integrated or have been accepted for Resettlement into a third country (many of which are Countries of Second Asylum).

Fig 7.1 > Status 3 – Permanently Protected

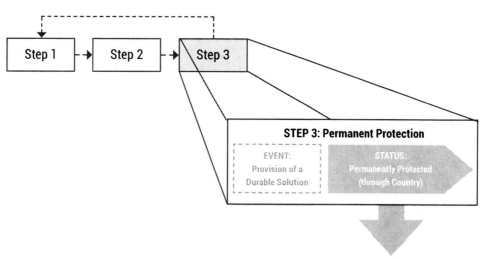

- Statistical Overview of Durable Solutions
- Sizing the Problem
- Cultural Assimilation versus Multiculturalism
- Islam and the West

Statistical Overview of Durable Solutions

Voluntary Repatriation

Since the 1970s, the available data shows that Voluntary Repatriation numbers are consistently higher than resettlements either through local integration to a host country or resettlement to a third country[1]. For every refugee who is resettled, 14 repatriate[2]. During the past 20 years, 18.2 million refugees have repatriated to their Country of Origin. Unfortunately the rate has decreased significantly. Thirteen million refugees voluntarily repatriated between 1995 and 2004, but less than half this amount (5.2 million) repatriated between 2005 and 2014. The result being more pressure on Countries of First Asylum or Second Asylum and more refugees remaining in exile for protracted periods.

Fig 7.2 > Annual Voluntary Repatriations. *Source: UNHCR Global Trends, Forced Displacement in 2014, 20.*

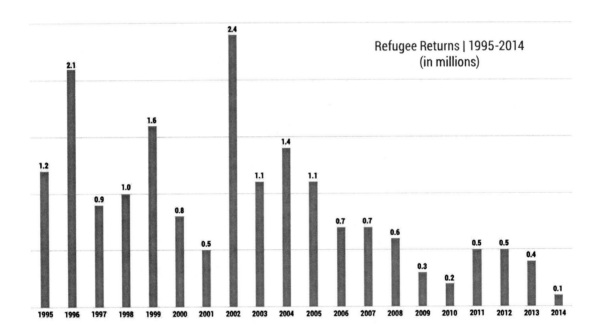

In 2014, only 126,800 people were voluntarily repatriated – the lowest number since 1983 and much lower than the previous year of 414,600. The persistence of wars and political instability are considered the drivers for these lower numbers. The refugees who Voluntarily Repatriated in 2014 returned to 37 countries. Ninety-five percent of those returnees went to eight countries.

---
1 UNHCR, *Global Trends: Forced Displacement in 2014*, 20.
2 Megan Bradley, "Rethinking Return: Defining Success in Refugee Repatriation," *World Political Review* (December 3, 2013).

- ~25,000 (20%) to Democratic Republic of Congo
- ~21,000 (17%) to Mali
- ~18,000 (14%) to Afghanistan
- ~14,000 (11%) to Angola
- ~13,000 (10%) to Sudan
- ~12,000 (9%) to Cote d'Ivoire
- ~11,000 (9%) to Iraq
- ~6,000 (5%) to Rwanda

Local Integration

The annual statistics regarding Local Integration are less accurate as only a limited number of countries publish statistics on naturalised refugees. The 27 countries that did provide statistics confirmed the granting of citizenship to 32,100 refugees during 2014. By far the largest was Canada granting 27,200 people with citizenship. France (2,400) and the United Republic of Tanzania (1,500) were the only other countries to confirm the granting of citizenship to more than 1,000 refugees.

Resettlement

Although the annual number of refugees who have been resettled over the past two decades has fluctuated, each 10-year period (1995-2004 and 2005-2014) has seen about 900,000 refugees resettled. Although the number of UNHCR assisted resettlement departures has increased recently, the total numbers of resettled refugees in 2014 (105,200) is not as great as it was in 1992 when almost 125,000 people were resettled.

Fig 7.3 > Resettlement of Refugees: 1992 - 2014. *Source: UNHCR Global Trends, Forced Displacement in 2014, 21.*

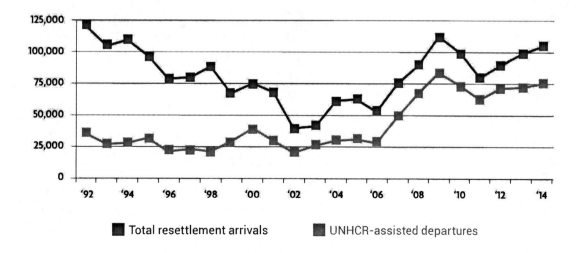

In the years from 2010-2014, the number of countries operating resettlement programs and the people they took in remained stable – 73,331 with UNHCR assistance are recorded as resettlement departures. The biggest change took place in Germany, which raised its resettlement intake more than 700% to 3,467 in 2014. This increase in the willingness to take in refugees continued in 2015 with its open intake of Syrian refugees.

Fig 7.4 › Annual Resettlement Departures. *Source: UNHCR Projected Global Resettlement Needs 2016 UNHCR Resettlement Departures by Resettlement Country 2010-2014.*

	2010	2011	2012	2013	2014
Countries with regular resettlement programs					
Argentina	23	24	5	7	21
Australia	5,636	5,597	5,079	11,117	6,162
Belgium	2	19	1	100	32
Brazil	28	23	8	56	44
Canada	6,706	6,827	4,755	5,140	7,234
Chile	6	22	3	3	-
Czech Rep	48	-	25	1	4
Denmark	386	606	324	475	332
Finland	543	573	763	665	1,011
France	217	42	84	100	378
Germany	457	22	323	1,092	3,467
Hungary	-	-	1	-	4
Iceland	6	-	9	-	4
Ireland	20	36	40	62	98
Italy	58	-	9	-	-
Japan	27	18	-	18	23
Luxembourg	-	-	-	-	28
Netherlands	430	479	262	362	743
New Zealand	535	477	719	682	639
Norway	1,088	1,258	1,137	941	1,188
Portugal	24	28	21	6	14
South Korea	23	11	20	31	14
Romania	38	-	-	-	44
Spain	-	-	80	-	30
Sweden	1,789	1,896	1,483	1,832	1,812
Switzerland	19	39	54	78	139
UK	695	424	989	750	628
USA	54,077	43,215	53,053	47,875	48,911
Uruguay	17	-	5	14	52

Countries with special resettlement programmes/ad-hoc resettlement intake					
Austria	-	-	-	4	269
Liechtenstein	-	-	-	-	5
Mexico	-	-	-	-	1
Palau	3	-	-	-	-
Paraguay	13	13	-	-	-
Grand Total	**72,914**	**61,649**	**69,252**	**71,411**	**73,331**

Once again, it is worth noting that the countries that offer the highest number of resettlement places per capita tend to be the countries that are not Countries of First Asylum. Those countries are usually stretched just to meet the demands of the refugees they are hosting. A comparison using 2014 data highlights the magnitude of the burden borne by the Countries of First Asylum. Australia had the lowest proportion of resettled refugees per population with 1 resettled refugee per 3,636 inhabitants. In comparison, Lebanon had the highest proportion of hosted refugees per population with one refugee per 4.3 inhabitants.

While this difference is truly enormous and clarifies why Countries of First Asylum do not involve themselves with the intake of resettled refugees, it should be noted the service and support provided to the two groups is very different. Refugees in Countries of First Asylum are under temporary protection, many in camps who are waiting for a Durable Solution. Resettled refugees have been provided permanent residency and are afforded all the rights and obligations of a citizen of a host country.

Fig 7.5 > Per Capita Resettlement. *Source: UNHCR Projected Global Resettlement Needs 2016, 54.*

Country of Resettlment	Persons Resettled in 2014	National Population*	Population per Refugees Resettled
Australia	6,162	22,404,000	3,636
Norway	1,188	4,891,000	4,117
Canada	7,233	34,126,000	4,718
Sweden	1,812	9,382,000	5,178
Finland	1,011	5,368,000	5,310
USA	48,911	312,247,000	6,384
New Zealand	632	4,368,000	6,911
Liechtenstein	5	36,000	7,200
Denmark	332	5,551,000	16,720
Luxembourg	28	508,000	18,143
Netherlands	743	16,615,000	22,362
Germany	3,467	83,017,000	23,945
Austria	269	8,402,000	31,234

Ireland	98	4,468,000	45,592
Switzerland	139	7,831,000	56,338
Uruguay	52	3,372,000	64,846
Iceland	4	318,000	79,500
UK	628	62,066,000	98,831
France	378	63,231,000	167,278
Belgium	32	10,941,000	341,906
Romania	44	21,861,000	496,841
Portugal	14	10,590,000	756,429
Spain	30	46,182,000	1,539,400
Argentina	21	40,374,000	1,922,571
Hungary	4	10,015,000	2,503,750
Czech Rep	4	10,554,000	2,638,500
South Korea	14	48,454,000	3,461,000
Brazil	44	195,210,000	4,436,591
Japan	23	127,353,000	5,537,087
Mexico	1	117,886,000	117,886,000

Sizing the Problem

The most striking statistic which emerges when analysing the Durable Solutions is just how inadequate the numbers are. Only a small proportion of all refugees are provided a Durable Solution each year. The total number of refugees has increased in each of the past four years. Mandate Refugees have grown from 10.4 million in 2010 to 14.4 million in 2014 and it is estimated to be 5.1 million in mid-2015. Against this demand for protection the supply of durable solutions has met only a small percentage. In 2014, available data shows that about 260,000 refugees were provided with durable solutions. That's less than 2% of the total number of refugees.

- 126,800 people were voluntarily repatriated.
- 32,100 refugees were confirmed to be locally integrated through the receipt of citizenship.
- 105,200 refugees were resettled (with or without UNHCR assistance).

The average length of displacement is a difficult calculation to make. A 2004 UNHCR document provides an estimate that the average duration of major refugee situations, protracted or not, had increased from 1993 to 2003 from 9 to 17 years. The document admits the estimate is crude. It appears this reference is the source of the widely accepted understanding that 17 years is the average time of displacement for a refugee[3]. If true, 17 years is a very long time to lead a life in limbo. Even assuming the recent years where the most durable solutions were provided can be emulated consistently each year (2.4 million voluntarily repatriating as in 2002 and resettling 125,000 people as in 1992) it would still take over five years to provide durable solutions to all current refugees.

The inadequacy of the current durable solutions is further exacerbated with the recognition that the current volume of Mandate Refugees is likely to be just the tip of the iceberg. The requirement is to find many more durable solutions for the 14.4 million Mandate Refugees of 2014. Unfortunately, but inevitably, each year a new cohort of people are forcibly displaced. This may be due to new conflicts or new experiences of persecution. It may also be due to persistent conflicts and regimes that continue to displace their citizens. The major Countries of Origin for refugees very often have high fertility rates. This means the consistent addition of new Forcibly Displaced People is unlikely to cease until the root cause of these issues are resolved. These issues are varied and complex and unlikely to be resolved soon, leaving us with the question, is there a better way to manage such large numbers of refugees?

It is also possible the number of Mandate Refugees is a large understatement of those actually needing protection. In most instances the number of refugees from a country is just a small percentage of its total population. There may be many others who have not presented as refugees as they harbour little hope of it being an effective resolution for their problems. A percentage of these would be within the 38.2 million internally displaced people in 2014. Economists speak of the hidden unemployed – those who have given up looking for work. As they have stopped looking they are no longer counted as unemployed. However, when the economy improves, they re-commence the search. This sometimes creates paradoxical statistics where many new jobs were created but the unemployment rate rose. The same mechanism may well apply with refugees. If a more effective process of providing durable solutions was implemented, it is quite possible many more people in need would present. These people currently are the hidden number of would-be refugees.

Finally, there is also the spectre of economic refugees. This group of people do not fall under the current definition of refugees but seek a better life for economic reasons. Hundreds of millions of people live in countries with such dire poverty that many rationally would be motivated to attempt to utilise the asylum framework to migrate to an industrialised country. Including hundreds of millions of would-be economic migrants into the scope of the problem to solve further highlights the inadequacy of the current durable solutions.

---

[3] "Protracted Refugee Situations: Executive Committee of the The High Commissioner's Programme," UNHCR, June 10, 2004, accessed July 23, 2016 <www.unhcr.org/40c982172.pdf>

Resettlement Costs

Social Costs

Any negative social impact of locally integrated or resettled refugees relates to how much the overall immigrant intake is increased and to what annual level it rises. This total level is debatable, as is the proportion that could be made up of refugees.

History has shown that at the levels Australia has historically taken in, no such impacts have occurred. However, the intakes in Europe over 2015 have been much larger. With the continent already experiencing increased cultural violence since September-11, there is a significant chance such a large intake may have negative social consequences.

Economic Costs

The financial cost of resettling refugees varies from country to country. A cost will be based on the level of welfare a country provides its citizens as well as the additional services a country may choose to provide refugees who have been given permanent protection. For instance, Australia offers a range of integration and post trauma-related services. A total cost also depends on how long the average resettled refugee takes to become self-sufficient within the society.

The estimates across Australia, Canada and the United States are between US$37,000 and $US65,000 (assuming exchange rates as of March 2016).

- In 2015, the Australian government budgeted for A$700 million for the 12,000 Syrian refugees it will be resettling[4]. This equates to about $58,000 or $14,500 each year for four years.
- The US organisation the Center for Immigration Studies estimated in November 2015 that each Middle Eastern resettled refugee would cost US$64,370 over five years[5].
- The Government of Canada's plan to resettle 25,000 Syrian refugees was budgeted for CAD$1.2 billion or CAD$48,000 over six years.

To put the Australian figures into context, the 2013/14 Australian Government receipts were A$360 billion[6]. The A$700 million budgeted for the Syrian refugees is about 0.2% of the government revenue for 2013/14. While this figure may seem very small, it is worth noting

---

4   Patrick Durkin, "Big Business wants to double Syrian refugees to 25,000," *The Australian,* Feb 3, 2016.
5   "The hgh cost of resettling Middle Eastern Refugees," Centre for Immigration Studies, November 2015, accessed July 23, 2016 <cis.org/High-Cost-of-Resettling-Middle-Eastern-Refugees>
6   "Budget 2014-15, Statement 5: Revenue," Australian Government, accessed July 23, 2016 <www.budget.gov.au/2014-15/content/bp1/html/bp1_bst5-01.html>

that this 12,000 intake is in addition to the 13,750 that Australia already commits to provide permanent visas for, as well as the 51,700 asylum seekers and refugees that it harbours.

Cultural Assimilation Vs Multiculturalism

Countries with high numbers of immigrants now have a growing diversity of ethnicities and cultures[7]. In many cases, settlers are from numerous source populations and cultures. The differences in culture can be broad and multi-faceted. Examples of differences include:

- Type of society (e.g. agrarian-rural vs urban-industrial)
- Traditions
- Religions
- Political institutions
- Language
- Cultural practises
- Appearance (including dress)

One increasingly important question is how immigrants and their descendants can become incorporated into host nations. This question has become more important in the 21st century with a number of 'home grown' attacks committed by immigrants or descendants of immigrants. Examples include the 2005 London bombings, the 2013 Boston Marathon bombings and the 2015 Paris shootings. The approach options for the incorporation of migrants and migrant cultures into the host nation can be summarised along a spectrum running from Cultural Assimilation, through Integration and all the way to Multiculturalism.

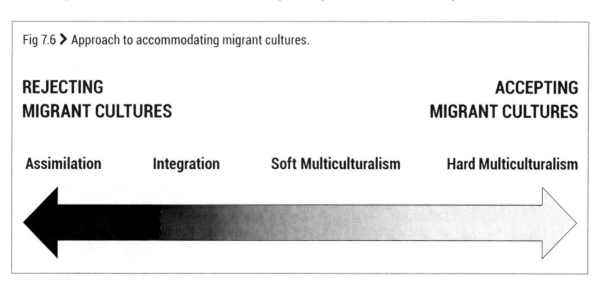

Fig 7.6 > Approach to accommodating migrant cultures.

---

7   Stephen Castles, Hein De Haas and Mark J. Miller, The Age of Migration, Fifth Edition, (London: The Guilford Press, 2014), 3.

Cultural Assimilation

Cultural Assimilation describes the process where immigrant cultures come to resemble those of the host group. It is a one-sided process of adaptation that may be gradual or fast. Ultimately the new members of the society give up their distinctive language, culture and social characteristics to become indistinguishable from the host group. The metaphor of a melting pot is often used to describe Cultural Assimilation whereby different elements melt together to create a harmonious and common culture.

Integration

Integration describes a slower and gentler process of assimilation. Some aspects of the immigrant cultures remain and some formations of immigrant communities are accepted as part of the gradual process of assimilation. There may also be some degree of adjustment from the host society.

Multiculturalism

Multiculturalism describes the existence, acceptance or promotion of multiple cultural traditions within a single jurisdiction. These cultural traditions are usually associated with the cultures of ethnic groups. It is often described with the analogy of a salad bowl. Individual groups maintain their distinctive characteristics and together these many groups form a society much like the many ingredients that make up a salad. Multiculturalism can occur when jurisdictions amalgamate two or more different cultures (e.g. French and English Canada) or when immigration from different areas arrive at one jurisdiction (e.g. USA, Brazil or Australia).

This meaning describes the demographic fact that inhabitants come from many different ethnic backgrounds. A second meaning refers to policies around ethnic and cultural diversity. Australian historian John Hirst has described potential policies across a spectrum bookended by soft and hard multiculturalism[8]. Hard multiculturalism values immigrant cultures for their own sake, and so promotes affirmative action, quotas, ethnic separatism, and even separate laws. Soft multiculturalism approaches cultural assimilation as it promotes tolerance of cultural and ethnic diversity and makes newcomers welcome while easing the path to integration.

Those in favour of hard multicultural policies argue that they avoid the inequality that inadvertently comes when applying the law universally without regard to background

---

8   Katherine Betts, "Population and Multiculturalism: Immigration, integration and crime," on *The Greens: Policies, Reality and Consequence*, ed. A. McIntyre (Ballan, Connor Court, 2011), 110.

circumstance including cultural differences. The argument proposes that equality oppresses minorities as it is based on individual rather than group rights and that only differentiated citizenship can remedy the injustice of individual equality[9].

Supporters of soft multiculturalism or cultural assimilation argue that hard multiculturalism promotes groups and diversity at the expense of individual rights and social cohesion. This relates back to the concept of mutual regard. With the creation of separate and distinct groups within a society the level of solidarity and cooperation between peoples is potentially reduced.

It is argued that you cannot have equality and multiculturalism, for multiculturalism dictates that you put a group's welfare and preservation of its culture above the rights of the individuals within the group[10]. The liberal state should be neutral on how best to live, and such matters should be left to citizens to decide for themselves. The state should be 'difference blind' and recognise individuals only in terms of their common citizenship[11].

History of Assimilation vs Multiculturalism

The United States, Canada and Australia accepted a high proportion of immigrants up to and shortly after World War II. Their approach was to accommodate new migrants into society through assimilation. Effectively these countries were a melting pot that melded all to a homogeneous culture. Differing cultural habits were accepted as a partial phase on the way to full assimilation. This approach was often reinforced by the selection process. For example Australia had the White Australia policy, while Canada and the United States also had policies to keep out non-Europeans.

During the 1970s multicultural policies gathered momentum. They originated in Canada and were taken up elsewhere including in Australia, the Netherlands and Sweden. Governments moved away from cultural assimilation and towards granting minorities cultural and political rights.

This continued in the main until the attacks on September 11, 2001. Since these and subsequent 'home grown' attacks, debates regarding whether multiculturalism actually works have increased. In 2010, German Chancellor Angela Merkel announced that multiculturalism had utterly failed and that the new arrivals to Germany had to do more to integrate. In 2013, a task force chaired by British Prime Minister David Cameron said the

---

9   Katharine Betts, "Multicultural muddles," review of *Transforming a 'White Australia': Issues of Racism and Immigration by L. Jayasuriya*, Australian Universities' Review vol.54, no. 2, 2012.
10 Bruce Bawer, *The New Quislings* (New York: HarperCollins, 2012), 73 of 81, EPUB.
11 Geoffrey Brahm Levy, "Nothing 'hard' about Australian multiculturalism," abc.net.au February 24, 2014, accessed July 23, 2016 <www.abc.net.au/religion/articles/2014/02/24/3950661.htm>

policy of treating different cultures as separate and distinct had been a mistake[12]. National security concerns held by Western governments have reduced their focus on celebrating and maintaining diversity and increased their insistence for integration based on ideas of social cohesion and national values[13].

One-way Multiculturalism

While multiculturalism thrived in the West, it was not adopted universally. One way Multiculturalism describes the existence of tolerant, multicultural societies in the high-immigrant Developed World, while the high-emigrant Developing World maintains intolerant (and ethnically less diverse) societies.

In countries new to immigration, such as the oil-rich gulf states, Japan and South Korea, immigrants are seen as temporary visitors who should not be integrated at all[14]. Parts of the Muslim world like Iran and Saudi Arabia are increasingly intolerant of other cultures. For example, the practice of non-Muslim religions is prohibited in Saudi Arabia[15]. Commentators like the late Christopher Hitchens have demanded the West insist on reciprocity at all times. As an example, he suggested banning any Saudi-sponsored propaganda within the US until Saudi Arabia also permits Jewish, Christian and secular practises[16].

Because of this one-way multiculturalism one of the common criticisms made of multiculturalism is that with the large numbers of immigrants, the liberal democracies of the West are erroneously expecting people arriving from intolerant and singular cultures to easily assimilate with a secular environment.

Key Values in Western Culture

Multicultural policies usually include expectations to conform with certain key values[17]. These include the rule of law, secularism, freedom of speech and religion, equality of sexes, and minority rights. Although these expectations may be established, the implementation and enforcement of them is not guaranteed.

---

12 James Slack, "Mistake of multiculturalism aided extremists says PM," *Daily Mail Australia,* December 5, 2013.
13 Stephen Castles, Hein De Haas and Mark J. Miller, *The Age of Migration, Fifth Edition,* (London: The Guilford Press, 2014), 270.
14 Ibid 265.
15 "International Religious Freedom Report 2008: Saudi Arabia," U.S. Department of State, accessed July 23, 2016 <m.state.gov/md108492.htm>
16 Christopher Hitchens,"Facing the Islamist Menace," review of *America Alone: The End of the World As We Know It,* by Mark Steyn. City Journal, Winter 2007.
17 Stephen Castles, Hein De Haas and Mark J. Miller, *The Age of Migration, Fifth Edition,* (London: The Guilford Press, 2014), 270.

Islam and the West

Is Islam Different?

Although any different culture could prove difficult to accommodate into Western society, in practice it is Islam which is currently creating the biggest problems. These problems most obviously manifest in the terror attacks conducted under the banner of Islamic extremism, also known as Islamism. Problems have been most apparent in Western Europe, corresponding to the largest growth of Muslim populations in the West. In 2001 there were between 15 and 17 million Muslims in Western Europe where fifty years earlier there had been virtually none[18].

The unique issues around Islam are examined by author Christopher Caldwell through comparing the Muslim community in Europe with the Latino community in the United States[19]. In total, the proportions of immigrants into the two regions are similar. However, the cultural differences each group has with the host region differ greatly. Latino culture, he argues, is comparable to the American working class culture of the 1960s and 70s. The result of mass Hispanic immigration has required no subsequent fundamental reform of American cultural practises or institutions, "Latinos have less money, higher labour-force participation, more authoritarian family structures, lower divorce rates, more frequent church attendance (...primarily Catholic...), lousier diets and higher rates of military enlistment"[20]. Caldwell suggests that Islam in Europe is different in that it has led to adjustments of many European customs and laws. These include minor adjustments like the elimination of post-work drinks or the creation of women-only swimming hours at public pools, as well as more fundamental changes like the banning of the veil in French schools[21].

However, Muslims are not the first people labelled by inhabitants of Western nations as undesirable or not being able to assimilate. Such fears, held against many groups including Irish, Southern Europeans and the Chinese, are now identified as foolish and xenophobic.

- Irish immigrants fleeing the potato famine and arriving in 19th century England were subjected to racism and misrepresentations of their culture and beliefs. Misrepresentations arguably very similar to the descriptions being used regarding Muslims today. Benjamin Disraeli, future prime minister of the UK wrote in 1836 that the Irish[22]: "...*hate our order, our civilisation, our pure religion. This wild, reckless,*

---

18 Christopher Caldwell, *Reflections on the Revolutions in Europe* (London: Penguin, 2009), 17 of 301, iBook edition.
19 Ibid 18 of 301.
20 Ibid 17 of 301.
21 Christopher Caldwell, *Reflections on the Revolutions in Europe* (London: Penguin, 2009), 18 of 301, iBook edition.
22 Robert Blake, *Disraeli* (London, Faber and Faber, 1966), 152-153.

indolent, uncertain and superstitious race have no sympathy with the English character. Their ideal of human felicity is an alternation of clannish rolls and coarse idolatry. Their history describes an unbroken circle of bigotry and blood."

- Following large scale immigration after World War I, Southern and Eastern Europeans were specifically restricted from entering the United States through legislation passed in the early 1920s. These restrictions did not apply to Northern Europeans.

- Chinese migrant workers in the United States in the late 19th and early 20th centuries were subjected to prejudice and used as scapegoats for depressed wage levels. Chinese men were also portrayed as dangerous to young white women, resulting in harassment within Chinese communities[23].

- Australia too was not immune from such xenophobia. At the end of World War II, 80% of the population opposed Jewish migration and 70% opposed Italian migration[24].

Many Branches of Islam

This section provides an overview of whether and, if so how, Islamic ideas clash with core Western values and what ramifications this might have on refugee resettlement. An important contextual point to specify upfront is that like any religion, there are many different branches of Islam. Further, Islamic laws are open to interpretation and debate, somewhat like aspects of the constitution of the US. The result is that Islam and its various branches are too varied and nuanced to clearly define in a brief overview.

Islam and Islamism

Maajid Nawaz, a British activist, author and politician, as well as a former member of radical Islamist group Hizb ut-Tahrir has been prominent in leading open discussion on the difference between Islam and Islamism. Nawaz has proposed the following definitions for Islam, Islamism and Jihadism[25]:

- Islam: a religion (with its problems like any other).
- Islamism: a desire to impose any version of Islam over society.
- Jihadism: the use of force to spread Islamism.

Nawaz continues by stating "... imposing any version of Islam over the other, whether 'moderate' form (headscarf) or rigid form (burka) is inherently theocratic and therefore

---

23 Huping Ling, *Chinese St Louis: From Enclave to Cultural Community* (Temple University Press, 2004), 68.
24 Paris Aristotle, 'A "wicked problem"?', *Big Ideas*, ABC Radio National, 28 June 2013 <www.abc.net.au/radionational/programs/bigideas/2013-07-01/4778140>
25 @maajidNawaz, *twitter feed*, July 20, 2015, 5:12PM.

repugnant. Anyone who in principle aspires to resurrecting a Caliphate – now or in the future – is inherently a theocrat and therefore part of the problem."

These assertions are useful as they separate Islamism and its use of violence from Islam. At the same time it is useful to note that although they are not the same, they are related.

Rising Population

In 2010, there were 1.6 billion Muslims in the world, making it the second largest of all religions behind Christianity. Muslims are also the fastest growing religious group in the world, with the population of Muslims expected to grow by 73% by 2050. Across all regions, Muslims currently have a higher fertility rate than non-Muslims. This, coupled with net immigration from Muslim countries, results in an expected increased proportion of Muslims within the citizenry of the liberal democracies of the West. Although increasing, the proportion of Muslims in the West will still be a small percentage. Researchers have projected that Muslims will make up 10% of the European population in 2050[26].

Eight countries house approximately 1.26 billion (roughly two thirds) of the world's Muslim population: Indonesia, Pakistan, India, Bangladesh, Egypt, Nigeria, Iran and Turkey[27]. Through immigration, the proportion of the population that is Muslim is growing in Western developed nations. Muslims represent 7.5% of the population in France, up to 5.5% in Germany, 5% in Sweden, 4.8% in the UK and 3.7% in Italy. Outside of Europe the proportions are smaller: up to 3.2% in Canada, 2.2% in Australia, and 0.8% in the United States.

The population of France from 1997-2016 grew from 57 million to 67 million, a 15% increase. In the same period the Muslim population (which has always had mixed numbers) grew from about 3-4 million to 5-6 million, an increase of between 25%-100%. This means the French Muslim population growth is increasing somewhere between 2-6 times the French average. 25% of high school pupils are now Muslim[28].

---

26 Michael Lipka, "Muslims and Islam: Key findings in the U.S. and around the world," PewResearch Centre, last updated July 22, 2016, accessed July 23, 2016 <www.pewresearch.org/fact-tank/2016/07/22/muslims-and-islam-key-findings-in-the-u-s-and-around-the-world/>
27 "Muslim Population by Country: The Future of Global Muslim Population," *Pew Research Centre* (December 22, 2011).
28 Michael Gurfinkiel, "Latest Survey Finds 25% of French teenagers are Muslims," *PJmedia*, March 14, 2016.

Fig 7.7 ❯ Fertility Rates (Muslim / Non Muslim). *Source: Pew Research Centre (December 7, 2015).*

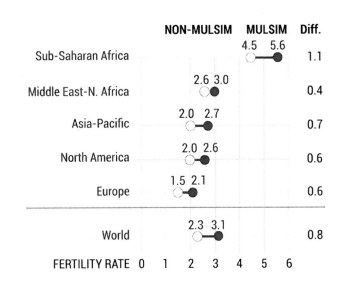

Although still a small percentage of the overall population in Europe, areas of concentrated Muslim population have formed. This should not be surprising as naturally, people enjoy living with those of their diaspora and culture. This trend highlights the possibility that some areas within Western European countries may soon have a Muslim majority, with that majority having the ability to determine local politics and law. Some potential areas would be within Birmingham (estimated to be 21% Muslim in 2026)[29], Bradford (UK), Duisburg (Germany), Molenbeek (Belgium), Marseilles (France), and Malmo (Sweden). If Muslim majorities do attain such power, arguments have been made that it may be possible some tenets of Islamic faith opposed to Western egalitarian and liberal traditions could be proposed as laws. The full manifestation of this would be Sharia Law.

Muslim Community Separation and Isolation

Commentator Christopher Caldwell points out there has been a growing recognition in the EU countries with the largest Muslim populations of the development of 'ghettos' – places where at least two thirds of residents belonged to a specific ethnic group. For instance, in the British towns of Bradford and Leicester, almost 15% of the ethnic Pakistanis surveyed were living in ghettos[30]. Whether this is segregation, self-segregation or a combination of both, the result increases the likelihood of parallel societies developing. Examples of such parallel societies Caldwell lists include:

- In 2002, an imam in Roubaix France refused to meet the mayor of Lille, Martine Aubry, in his neighbourhood as it was Muslim territory and it would be unclean to welcome her there.

- In the city of Dreux in Denmark, there were protests over the serving of non-halal meat in school cafeterias.

- In the Rosengard housing estate just outside Malmo, Sweden, ninety percent of women went veiled. This included those who were not veiled before arriving to Sweden.

Another example of the development of parallel societies within Europe is the report referenced by UK Prime Minister David Cameron in January 2016 which showed that 22% of Muslim UK women spoke little or no English[31].

---

29 Christopher Caldwell, *Reflections on the Revolutions in Europe (London: Penguin, 2009)*, 81-82 of 301, iBook edition.
30 Ibid 86 of 301.
31 Brendan Cole, "Muslim women in the UK 'must integrate and speak English' says David Cameron," *International Business Times*, January 18, 2016, accessed July 24, 2016.

Outcomes of Isolationism

Development of parallel societies sits within a hard multicultural context. It suggests a low level of mutual regard and certainly does not promote assimilation or even integration. Some negative outcomes of such isolationism have been referenced by writers and commentators. One example is a survey showing 27% of British Muslim sympathise with the motives behind the Charlie Hebdo attacks[32]. Another is the rising occurrence of genital mutilation in the UK with around 500 new cases per month[33].

Isolation of migrants within migrant communities

Muslims in Australia are a much smaller population in number and percentage and appear to be more integrated into Australian life than in Europe. However, many young immigrants or children of immigrants to Australia may also be shielded from inclusion within the broader society in which they live. Following the Paris attacks of 2015, a Muslim Masters Student in Terrorism and Security at Charles Sturt University wrote about her experience growing up in Australia following her family's migration from Pakistan in the mid-1980s when she was a young girl.

> *"While people associate Western life with certain freedoms and civil liberties not guaranteed to all in other parts of the world, my reality as a young Pakistani girl in Australia was very different[34]."*

Upon arriving in Australia, Anooshe Mushtaq noted that her family were no longer complete masters of their own lives. Instead, they became prisoners of their need to be accepted in their communities. For example, relatives and the local Muslim community became dominant voices in where Anooshe would attend school or if she could go to certain school functions. Many of the freedoms she had in Pakistan had actually been taken away in Australia. An experience not unique among migrants who engage in a community created for cultural and religious preservation. Anooshe's assessment is that acceptance within such communities is paid for by seclusion from the broader society.

The isolation can potentially be further exacerbated by the power of the imams and muftis who interpret the Qur'an for followers. Their interpretations are considered beyond reproach. Though not all imams promote a hatred of the West, some imams constantly deliver anti-West sermons. Criticising the West's actions against Muslims in

---

32   Matthew Holehouse, "Quarter of British Muslims sympathise with Charlie Hebdo terrorists," The Telegraph (February 25, 2015).
33   Mark Tran, "Female genital mutilation increase in England 'only tip of iceberg,'" *The Guradian* April 30, 2015).
34   Anooshe Mushtaq, "Radicalisation: the tone of Muslim community discussion must change," Sydney Morning Herald (November 18, 2015).

Gaza, Afghanistan and Iraq is a main theme in these anti-West, isolationist messages. These messages are then discussed throughout the local community[35].

Secularism vs Sharia (Islamic Law)

Western European democracies are based on Secularism, a value system that holds that religion should not be part of the affairs of the state or part of education (separation of church and state). A small but not insignificant number of the Western European Muslims are calling for theocracy, namely Sharia. For example 37% of British Muslims between sixteen and twenty-four want an introduction of Sharia and 57% of Irish Muslims want Ireland to become an Islamic State[36].

A theocracy is a system of government in which priests rule in the name of God or a god. Sharia is a legal code based on the Qur'an and other Islamic scripture. In Arabic, Sharia means "the clear, well-trodden path to water", and it is very broad[37]. Unlike other legal codes, Sharia covers private behaviour and beliefs as well as public behaviour. There are many Islamic states that are theocracies (including Afghanistan, Iran, Mauritania, Saudi Arabia, Somalia, Sudan and Yemen).

Fig 7.8 > Practice of Sharia. *Source: Pew Research Centre (December 7, 2015).*

- ■ Countries and members of the Organisation of Islamic Cooperation where sharia plays no role in the judicial system.
- ■ Countries where sharia applies in personal status issues (such as marriage, divorce, inheritance, and child custody).
- ■ Countries where sharia applies in full, covering personal status issues as well as criminal proceedings.
- ■ Countries with regional variations in the application of sharia.

---

35   Ibid.
36   Christopher Caldwell, *Reflections on the Revolutions in Europe (London: Penguin, 2009),* 145 of 301, iBook edition.
37   Lin Taylor, "What exactly is Sharia Law? And is it in conflict with the Australian way of life?," SBS News.com.au (last updated October 23, 2014). Accessed July 23, 2016 <www.sbs.com.au/news/article/2014/09/23/explainer-what-sharia-law>

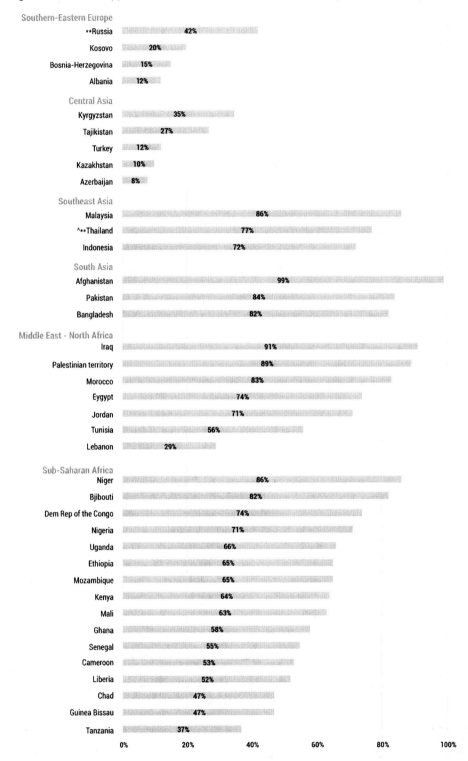

Fig 7.9 > Muslim Support for Sharia. *Source: Pew Research Centre (December 7, 2015).*

Data for all countries except Niger from "Tolerance and Tension: Islam and Christianity in Sub-Saharan Africa".

^ Interviews conducted with Muslims in five southern provinces only.

** Question was modified to ask if sharia should be the law of the land in Muslim areas. This question was not asked in Uzbekistan.

Sharia is not strictly codified. As such there is not one set of laws that can be examined and understood. Instead, it is a system of laws based on the Qur'an, Hadith (a collection of traditions containing sayings of the prophet Muhammad) and centuries of debate and Islamic jurisprudence known as 'fiqh'. Although Sharia is unchanging as it is enshrined in the Qur'an, fiqh can vary according to the situation at hand. This means Islamic law can adapt to remain applicable to modern life[38]. Within Muslim communities — both inside and external to countries that have Sharia Law — there is significant support for Sharia Law.

A concern held in Western secular countries regarding the possible introduction of Sharia is that some of the beliefs of Islam appear to clash with core Western values. These include:

- Separation of church and state.
- Equality: for example Wahhabi Islam in Saudi Arabia subjugates women and bans homosexuality (which is punishable by death).
- Freedom of speech: many interpretations of Islam forbid blasphemy. The most telling evidence is the January 2015 murders of the *Charlie Hebdo* cartoonists for drawing pictures of Muhammad deemed forbidden in some interpretations of Islam.
- Freedom of religion: some interpretations of Islam rule apostasy as a crime.

Sharia also has some less contentious components. For example halal butchers and sharia-conforming stock funds that do not invest in alcohol, tobacco, pork or gambling. Taken one by one, it is argued the elements of Islam that seem incompatible with the West (for example the veil or halal) actually are not. A counterpoint is that taken one by one the pieces of a gun are harmless as well. It is the way everything fits together in Sharia that makes assimilation difficult.

The key concern raised by detractors of Sharia in the West appears to surround whether the adherence to Sharia will no longer remain private and voluntary but rather will become something recognised and mandated by the State. The point was made by Dutch justice minister, Piet-Hein Donner in 2006 that if two-thirds of the voting public wanted Sharia Law, then there could be no objection under the law. Although not aligned with Western liberal values, it is the essence of democracy to implement this[39].

---

38   Ibid.
39   Christopher Caldwell, *Reflections on the Revolutions in Europe (London: Penguin, 2009),* 145 of 301, iBook edition.

According to University of Sydney legal academic, Dr Ghena Krayem, Australian Muslims do not want Sharia to be implemented into the Australian legal system.

> *"What might surprise most Australians is that most Muslims live according to Sharia everyday of their lives. They live harmoniously. They're not living in defiance of the Australian law. They're not seeking to set up a parallel legal system[40]."*

Instead, a suggestion is to accommodate Islamic principles in the Australian legal system so the system can be culturally appropriate for people of Islamic faith. In practice an adoption of hard multiculturalism. How broad those changes would need to be has not been specified.

Islam and Women's Rights

Author Richard Dawkins articulated the inconsistency between feminism and Islam in early 2016, *"That is one of the scandals of our age that feminists are so muted about the appalling things that are done to women in Islamic theocracies. It is shocking that Western feminists are so pusillanimous about condemning misogyny in Islam[41]."*

Terrorism

Since the September 11, 2001 there there have been numerous terrorist attacks perpetrated in the Europe in the name of Islamic Jihad. These include the Madrid train bombings in 2004, the London 7/7 attacks in 2005, the Charlie Hebdo and Paris Shootings in 2015 and the Brussels attacks of 2016.

Western countries outside Europe have also experienced attacks. Attacks in the United States include the Boston Marathon in 2013 and the San Bernardino attack of 2015. Attacks in Australia have been much smaller, these have included the Sydney hostage crisis in 2014 (two hostages died) and the 2015 Parramatta shooting where a 15-year-old Iranian-born Iraqi-Kurdish boy murdered a 58-year-old accountant. However, Islamist attacks in the West are much less than what occurs in the developing world. In March 2016 alone, the month of the Brussels attacks, eight other terrorist attacks occurred in the developing world.

---

40   Ibid.
41   Rachael Sylvester and Alicew Thompson, "Richard Dawkins: 'It's time feeble feminists started to condemn the misogyny in Islam,'" The Times (last amended February 4, 2016) accessed July 24, 2016 <www.thetimes.co.uk/tto/news/uk/article4678093.ece>

Repercussions and Response

There is a growing consensus among European leaders that multiculturalism is not working. Within Europe the key friction is with the Muslim community. As noted by author and political commentator Douglas Murray, *"at a time when all leaders have said that there is a problem with part of the Muslim community, Europe is letting in an unprecedented amount of Muslims. What's the plan?"[42]* In 2016, there does not appear to be a coherent, publicly available plan.

One response, at least in part, to immigration and associated terrorism has been the rise of Nationalist parties with strong anti-immigration policies in Western democracies. In Europe, parties with anti-immigration ideologies have attained more than 10% of the popular vote in many countries including Denmark (Danish People's Party – 21.1%), Austria (Freedom Party of Austria – 20.5%), Finland (Finns Party – 17.7%), Norway (Progress Party – 16.3%), France (National Front – 13.6%) and the UK (United Kingdom Independence Party – 12.6%). The US Presidential Primary debates, especially among the Republicans, focused heavily on illegal immigration control and possible restrictions on Muslim arrivals to the United States.

Another response to terrorist attacks and fear of rising immigration is rising public hostility to immigrant populations. This plays out in abuse on the street, direct violence, or vandalism and damage of property. All of which adds to feelings of isolation and separatism. Refugee intakes contribute to such tensions in so much as they contribute to the overall Muslim population. In western societies, since World War II refugees have traditionally been a small proportion of the total population. This has changed with the flood of Muslim refugees to Germany and western Europe in 2015.

Saudi Arabia and Wahhabism

According to former MI-6 agent and author Alastair Crooke, with the influx of oil wealth, the Saudi Arabian goal has been to spread Wahhabism, a branch of Sunni Islam, across the Muslim world. This would ultimately reduce the various branches of Islam into a single religion and transcend national divisions[43].

Saudi Arabia and the West have worked together on many Western objectives including countering socialism, Ba'athism, Soviet influence and Iranian influence. Saudi leadership has effectively managed Sunni Islam on behalf of Western objectives. During this

---
42 "On the Maintenance of Civilisation: A Conversation with Douglas Murray," samharris.org, November 22, 2015, accessed July 24, 2016 <https://www.samharris.org/podcast/item/on-the-maintenance-of-civilisation>
43 Alistair Crooke, "You can't understand ISIS if you don't know the History of Wahhabism in Saudi Arabia," *Huffington Post*, last updated June 3, 2016.

collaboration, Western leaders have chosen to view Saudi Arabia for its wealth, modernity and influence and not its Wahhabism. Part of this may be that such radicalisation is more effective in combating the enemies of the West. A result of this is that British and American policy has been bound to Saudi aims and heavily dependent on their direction in the Middle East.

The irony of the relationship between the West, Saudi Arabia and Wahhabism is that Wahhabism is particularly puritanical. According to author and associate professor at the University of California at Riverside, Laila Lalami, the influence of spreading Wahhabism has been to regress many Islamic regions as well as giving rise to Islamic extremism[44]. She writes:

> "When I was a child in Morocco, no clerics told me what to do, what to read or not read, what to believe, what to wear. And if they did, I was free not to listen. Faith was more than its conspicuous manifestations. But things began to change in the 1980s. It was the height of the Cold War and Arab tyrants saw an opportunity: they could hold on to power indefinitely by repressing the dissidents in their midst – most of them secular leftists – and by encouraging the religious right wing, with tacit or overt approval from the US and other Western allies.... Into the void created by the decimation of the Arab world's secular left, the Wahhabis stepped in, with almost unlimited financial resources."

---

44   Laila Lalami, "When terror striikes, Saudi Arabia evades reponsibility," *The Age*, November 18, 2015.

PART 1
Situation

PART 1.2
Australian Review

Part 1 — Situation (Chapters 1-10)

Section 1.1
CH 1-7 Global Review
- Uses the *Refugee Journey* framework to review the global refugee situation. Including:
- Disruptive Causes and Forcibly Displaced People.
- Protection (i.e. as asylum seekers or refugees).
- Durable Solutions (i.e. Repatriation, Local Integration or Resettlement).

Section 1.2
CH 8-10 Australian Review
- Reviews the Australian context including:
- Australia's migration programs.
- Australia's humanitarian program.
- Controversy and debate surrounding Australia's humanitarian program.

Part 2 — Complication, Principles & Assessment Framework (Chapter 11-12)

Section 2.1
CH 11 The Complication
- Summarises the main issues identified through the global and Australian reviews.

Section 2.2
CH 12 Principles & Assessment Framework
- Outlines the Questions of Principle that must be answered to best manage the refugee situation.
- Sets out the approach option assessment framework.

Part 3 — Options & Recommendation (Chapters 13-17)

Section 3.1
CH 13-15 Options Assessment
- Summarises the various Component Policies.
- Summarises and assesses the various Holistic Approaches using the approach option assessment framework.

Section 3.2
CH 16-17 Discussion and Recommendation
- Discusses the trade-offs in selecting the best Holistic Approach Option.
- Recommends an approach and provides a pathway for implementation including Australia's next steps.

CH 8. AUSTRALIA'S IMMIGRATION

Complementary to the global review and before determining the specific problems and the approaches we will now take a look at the Australian context. The next three chapters will explore Australia's migration program, humanitarian program, as well as the current issues and debate around Australia's humanitarian program.

Australia lives in the shadows of the xenophobic White Australia policy and its discriminatory treatment of the Indigenous Australians. Along with this shameful past Australia also has a record of accepting many immigrants and refugees creating a pluralistic society, to date free of much of the social tensions and violence apparent in the United States and Europe.

The following three chapters aim to provide context to Australia's migration and refugee past. They also aim to provide a broad understanding of how Australia's current 2016 programs are structured (as they constantly change) and what issues and concerns have been raised. This context is vital not only when understanding Australia's relative contribution in managing the refugee situation, but also when reviewing options for a way forward. It helps crystallise what has been attempted before, what has worked, what hasn't, and why it hasn't.

Australia's Migration History

Along with countries such as the USA and Canada, Australia is described as a land of migrants. Although the Aboriginal culture still lives with the Indigenous population, the sober fact is that the prevailing culture experienced and shared by the vast majority is one that has been brought to the land and developed since the arrival of the First Fleet in 1788. As of 2009, Australia and Switzerland were the two countries with the highest proportion of immigrants in the Western world. In 2015, 28% of Australians were born overseas[1] and approximately 20% more had a parent born overseas[2].

---

[1] "Migration, Australia 2014-15," Australian Bureau of Statistics, accessed July 24, 2016 <www.abs.gov.au/ausstats/abs@.nsf/mf/3412.0>.

[2] "2011 Census reveals one in four Australians is born overseas," Australian Bureau of Statistics, accessed July 24, 2016 <abs.gov.au/websitedbs/censushome.nsf/home/CO-59>.

Fig 8.1 ❯ Australia, Net Overseas Migration (1860 – 2010). *Source: Migration to Australia since Federation, a guide to the statistics.*

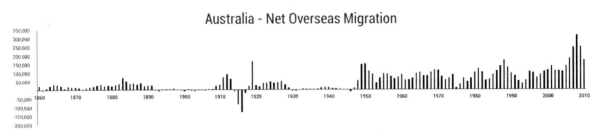

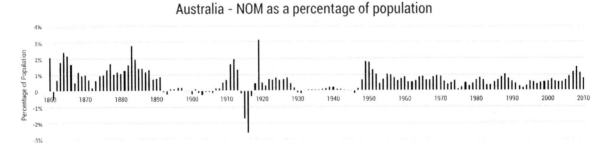

White Settlement, Colonialism, Inter War Period

White settlement (1788-1850)

Soon after Australia's settlement as a penal colony, it was integrated into the British Empire to supply raw materials such as wool and wheat. Convicts, men and women, were used to support the expansion. Due to the scarcity of women in the colonies (over three men to one woman during much of the 1820s), special schemes were introduced to bring out single women for domestic services and to be wives of settlers.

Colonial Australia (1850-1901)

Immigration was controlled and measured by each of the individual Australian colonies. With the expansion in the 1850s due to the discovery of gold, British immigrant labour could no longer meet the demand of all the available jobs. Employers called for non-British labour to keep wages from skyrocketing and to minimise the power of trade unions[3]. Subsequently, labour was supplied by immigrants from other parts of the British Empire

---

[3] James F. Hollifield, Philip L. Martin and Pia M. Orrenius, *Controlling Immigration: A Global Perspective,* Third Edition (United States, Standford Univerity Press, 2014), 129.

such as China, India and the islands of the South Pacific. Organised labour within Australia was strongly opposed to these new migrants. Propaganda arose accusing the Chinese of undercutting wages, spreading disease and coveting white women. There was violence towards Chinese and Asian workers and racist slogans for wages to be 'fit for white men'.

In response to this opposition, the colonial governments of Victoria, New South Wales and South Australia introduced measures to exclude Chinese immigrants. This is noted as a key moment in the emergence of a link between racism, Australian identity and nationhood[4]. By the 1901 census 22.6% of the 3.8 million people in Australia were born overseas. Of these, people born in Britain or Ireland accounted for almost 80% of all migrants whereas Chinese-born people represented only 3.5%.

Federation to World War II (1901-1945)

The Immigration Act (1901) was one of the first laws passed by the new Federal Parliament. It established the 'White Australia' policy which was universally included by all the major parties as the first plank in their platforms[5]. A royal commission report in 1904 advised the only way of being able to 'people the vast areas of the continent which are capable of supporting large populations' is by increasing the population through high birth rates, high immigration, or both. Expansionary population policy was built on keeping out the Asian races and enlarging the Anglo-Celtic immigrant population to defend the young nation.

Immigration control remained State-based and disparate until after World War I when it was consolidated under the Commonwealth. During the 1920s, the British plan was to use Australia to 'stock the dominions' of the empire the target population of 100 million was widely accepted. Settlers were encouraged to Australia through assisted Empire Settlement Schemes. A large number of migrants (349,000) came to Australia from Britain during this decade. However, there were dissenting voices regarding the Australian continent's carrying capacity. For example Thomas Griffith Taylor argued that Australia could only support a number considerably less than this 100 million, he suggested 65 million and later further reduced the figure down to 20 million.

In the lead up to World War II, immigration greatly reduced with the declining fertility rates in Britain. Hopes for population growth were replaced with concerns of decline. The 1947 Census showed that the percentage of the 7.6 million Australians born overseas had plummeted to 9.8%, British and Irish immigrants still dominated and European immigration was very low. In the years between 1901 and 1945 a subdued number of approximately 700,000 permanent migrants arrived in Australia.

---

4   Ibid.
5   Doug Cocks, *People Policy: Australia's Population Choices,* (Sydney, University of New South Wales Press, 1996), 1.

Fig 8.2 > Top 10 countries of birth for migrants (1901 & 1947).
Source: Migration to Australia since Federation, a guide to the statistics, 29 October 2010, 22 & 23
(a) Excludes full-blood indigenous persons. (b) prior to the 1954 Census persons born in the Republic of Ireland and Northern Ireland are recorded together under Ireland

Birthplace	1901 Census No.	%
1. UK (b)	495,074	57.7
2. Ireland (b)	184,085	21.5
3. Germany	38,352	4.5
4. China	29,907	3.5
5. New Zealand	25,788	3.0
6. Sweden & Norway	9,863	1.2
7. India	7,637	0.9
8. USA	7,448	0.9
9. Denmark	6,281	0.7
10. Italy	5,678	0.7
Top ten total	810,113	94.5
Other	47,463	5.5
Total overseas born	857,576	100
Total population (a)	3,788,123	
% of Australian born overseas		22.6

Birthplace	1947 Census No.	%
1. UK (b)	496,454	66.7
2. Ireland (b)	44,813	6.0
3. New Zealand	43,610	5.9
4. Italy	33,632	4.5
5. Germany	14,567	1.7
6. Greece	12,291	1.1
7. India & Sri Lanka	8,160	0.9
8. Poland	6,573	0.9
9. China	6,404	0.8
10 USA	6,232	0.8
Top ten total	672,736	90.4
Other	71,451	9.6
Total overseas born	744,187	100
Total population (a)	7,579,358	
% of Australian born overseas		9.8

Post World War II

Australia's first federal immigration department was established in 1945 resulting in greater planning on immigration policy. In recent decades it has specifically targeted skilled migration while continuing to allow a certain amount of family and humanitarian migration. The year on year immigration numbers have fluctuated based on Government priorities. In general, the annual Net Overseas Migration (NOM) ranges between 0.5% ad 1.5% of the population. The highest relative NOM was in 1950 (1.83% or 147,000). The highest annual NOM post World War II has been in 2008 at over 315,000. Since 1946 the lowest relative NOM was in 1975 (0.10% or 13,000). The percentage of the Australian population born overseas has steadily risen from 9.8% in 1947 to 20% in the 1980s and now approaching 30% in 2015.

1945-1975

After World War II, Australia attempted to grow the population and manufacturing industry in order to stimulate economic development and protect national sovereignty in the event of another war. This was communicated to the populous under the slogan 'populate or perish'. As labour demand once again outstripped the British supply of newcomers, a new policy – widely supported by the community – included immigrants from Europe. In comparison to the 700,000 who arrived in the 45 years up to 1945, about one million European migrants arrived in each decade after 1950. The Department of Immigration began by recruiting displaced persons from European camps, then from Italy, Greece and Malta. Any Trade Union opposition to non-British immigrants was mitigated by promises that immigrants would be tied to unskilled jobs for two years and would not displace Australian workers[6].

The post-war economic boom ran from the late 1940s through to the early 1970s. During this time, political debate focused on the size of the migrant intake that could be absorbed each year rather than any long-term target population for the continent. An annual immigration goal of 1% of the population was widely accepted during this time[7], however this was cut with the recession of the early 1970s. Permanent settler arrivals, which had averaged well over 100,000 each year since 1949, had dropped to 54,000 by 1975. Priority was now given to skilled labour and the White Australia policy was officially replaced by a non-discriminatory selection model based on the Canadian points system. Australia also followed Canada in introducing multiculturalism as a basis for its immigration policy[8].

The mid-1970s saw the arrival of the first Vietnamese boat people. The Australian government developed a resettlement program in support of these asylum seekers and its humanitarian intake peaked at about 20,000 refugees each year from 1979-1982.

A National Population Inquiry was conducted in the first half of the 1970s and reported in 1975. The Inquiry included an assessment of similar countries to Australia, a study of modern population theories, and economic, social, and environmental consequences of various levels of population growth. The inquiry questioned the feasibility and benefits in setting an optimum population or population growth rate. Rather, it advised letting the population adjust according to efforts associated with other goals relating to a humane and equal society[9].

1976-1989

The 1980s was a period of relatively high immigration, with family reunion being the largest component. There was broad political consensus for non-discriminatory immigration

---

6   James F. Hollifield, Philip L. Martin and Pia M. Orrenius, *Controlling Immigration: A Global Perspective*, Third Edition (United States, Standford Univerity Press, 2014), 130.
7   Doug Cocks, *People Policy: Australia's Population Choices*, (Sydney, University of New South Wales Press, 1996), 2.
8   James F. Hollifield, Philip L. Martin and Pia M. Orrenius, *Controlling Immigration: A Global Perspective*, Third Edition (United States, Standford Univerity Press, 2014), 130.
9   Doug Cocks, *People Policy: Australia's Population Choices*, (Sydney, University of New South Wales Press, 1996), 2.

policies and multicultural policies towards ethnic communities. As a result, the 1991 Census showed Australia's immigrant population had risen once again to over 20% of the population, however Britain and Ireland did not dominate as before. Although the UK represented the largest single-source country, the mix was much more spread than the first half of the century. Italy, Yugoslavia, Greece, Germany and the Netherlands now accounted for over 20% of the immigrant population, whilst Vietnam, China and the Philippines made up 6.4%.

With these high immigration levels came some signs of growing anti-immigration sentiments. These included a warning by historian Geoffrey Blainey against the 'Asianisation of Australia' in 1984, and a 1988 announcement from then opposition leader John Howard on limits on Asian immigration (he subsequently stepped down following accusations of racism). In the late 1980s the Federal Government under Bob Hawke divided the immigration program into the three main streams, which are still used in 2016; Family, Skilled, and Humanitarian[10].

1990-2010

From 1996, the Liberal-National Coalition government under John Howard emphasised bringing in skilled migrants and reducing the numbers associated with family reunions. During the 1980s and 1990s, the family migrant intake exceeded the skilled migrant intake, this was effectively reversed from the late 1990s. One result of this was a short-term uplift to the economy. The economic contribution of migrants was unsurprisingly closely linked with their employment status, skilled migrants in general providing a net contribution to the economy almost immediately.

During this period stricter measures were also employed with regard to Asylum Seekers and Australia shifted away from multiculturalism. Additionally, more emphasis has also been placed on temporary migrant visas, which since 2001 have exceeded permanent visas.

During this time the mix of immigrants from Asia increased; China, Vietnam, India and the Philippines now made up 14.3%. The top countries of previous citizenship show the increasing Asian footprint of new migrants to Australia.

---

[10] "Parliamentary Library: Migration to Australia since federation: a guide to the statististics," Parliament of Australia, Department of Parliamentary Services, last update October 29, 2010, accessed July 24, 2016 <www.aph.goc.au/binaries/library/pubs/bn/sp/migrationpopulation.pdf>, 10.

Fig 8.3 ❯ Permanent migrants to Australia (since 1985).
Source: Migration to Australia since Federation, a guide to the statistics

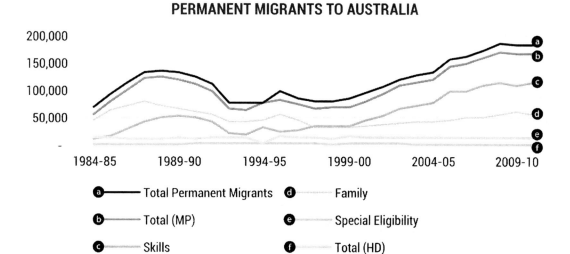

With the change in government to the Australian Labor Party in 2007, immigration again increased. The nominal Net Overseas Migration (NOM) has been at an all-time high in the past decade and the proportion of NOM to overall population has only been surpassed by the 1850s Gold Rush, the 1880s and post-World War II.

Birthplace	1991 Census No.	%
1. UK (b)	1,107,119	30.0
2. New Zealand	264,094	7.2
3. Italy	253,332	6.9
4. Yugoslavia	160,479	4.4
5. Greece	136,028	3.7
6. Vietnam	121,813	3.3
7. Germany	111,975	3.0
8. Netherlands	94,692	2.6
9. China	77,799	2.1
10. Philippines	73,144	2.0
Top ten total	2,400,475	65.1
Other	1,288,653	34.9
Total overseas born	3,689,128	100
Total population (c) (d)	16,770,635	
% of Australian born overseas		22.0

Fig 8.4 ❯ Top 10 countries of birth for migrants (1991 & 2006). *Source: Migration to Australia since Federation, a guide to the statistics, 29 October 2010, 24.* (a) Excludes full-blood indigenous persons. (b) prior to the 1954 Census persons born in the Republic of Ireland and Northern Ireland are recorded together under Ireland. (c) Excludes overseas visitors. (d) Includes birthplace not stated

Fig 8.4 (continued)

Birthplace	2006 Census No.	%
1. UK (b)	1,038,162	23.5
2. New Zealand	389,467	8.8
3. China	206,593	4.7
4. Italy	199,124	4.5
5. Vietnam	159,848	3.6
6. India	147,111	3.3
7. Philippines	120,534	2.7
8. Greece	109,989	2.5
9. Germany	106,528	2.4
10. South Africa	104,132	2.4
Top ten total	2,581,488	58.5
Other	1,834,548	41.5
Total overseas born	4,416,036	100
Total population (b) (c)	19,855,288	
% of Australian born overseas		22.2

Prime Minister Kevin Rudd announced in 2009 that he was in favour of a 'big Australia' following a report that estimated Australia's population would reach 36 million by 2050 due in part to high immigration rates. The large growth estimates for Australia were met with negative responses[11]. After taking over as Australian leader from Kevin Rudd, Prime Minister Julia Gillard moved away from the concept of a big Australia and couched her position as seeking a sustainable population strategy. However, in September 2011 the government released a paper which advocated continued rapid rates of population growth[12].

One of the key insights into Australia's migration intake is the diversity of source countries. There is a correlation with a dominant second culture and social tensions within societies. Examples include Northern Ireland, Fiji, Belgium and Canada. Thus a widely spread intake of migrants helps to limit any negative social consequences from a large and vocal second cultural group that sees itself as distinct from the main society. With such a high migration rate Australia faces all the benefits and costs described in Chapter 6. To date it appears that both economically and socially Australia has been a great beneficiary of the high recent intakes. However, the proportion of migrants within the Australian society leads all OECD countries and is the largest in Australia for over 100 years.

---

11 Nicholas Stuart, "A bigger Australian population will not gurantee more prosperity," *The Canberra Times,* March 31, 2014.
12 Franklin, Matthew, "Big Australia back on the Agenda, says Craig Emerson," *The Advertiser,* September 30, 2011.

Australia's Migration Program

Australia has one of the highest percentages of immigrants in the Western world and its NOM has hovered around 100,000 people since the 1980s, or somewhere around 0.5% of population. Between 2005 and 2010 the figure increased peaking at 315,000 in 2008 (or 1.47% of population). In addition to the natural rate (births minus deaths), Australia's population grew 2.2% during this year (the largest growth since 1971).

In 2010-11, about 170,000 migrants to Australia came from 185 different countries. The top ten countries of origin were:

- China 29,547 (17.5%)
- United Kingdom 23,931
- India 21,768
- Philippines 10,825
- South Africa 8,612
- Malaysia 5,130
- Vietnam 4,709
- Sri Lanka 4,597
- South Korea 4,326
- Ireland 3,700

Australia's population has grown significantly since 2005. Although the country's fertility rate has increased, the growth has mainly been due to the increased NOM. This increase has been through overseas students, temporary skilled migrants as well as Australian residents returning home from overseas due to the economic downturn. From 1985-2010 NOM contributed on average 39% of Australia's population growth. This increased significantly from 2005-2010, to approximately 65% of 2008-09 population growth.

Components of Australia's Migration Program

Australia's Migration Program is split into Permanent and Temporary Migration Programs.

1. **The Permanent Migration Program** is for people who have been granted visas enabling permanent residency and eventually citizenship.

2. **The Temporary Migration Program** is for people who have been granted access to Australia on a long-term basis (that is, greater than 12 months) but not permanently. Temporary visas are not required by New Zealanders, who have the right to free entry and are sometimes only temporary labour. The number of temporary visas has recently grown, and since 2001 exceeds the permanent migration visas.

Long-term temporary migrants have steadily increased and now outnumber permanent arrivals each year. Temporary migration is increasingly becoming the first step towards permanent settlement in Australia for many people. Unlike permanent migration, the level of temporary migration is not determined by the government, rather it is demand driven.

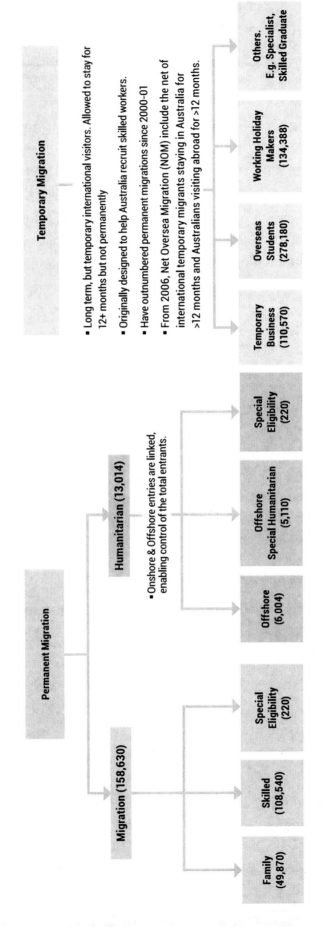

Fig 8.5 > Overview of Australia's Migration Program (2007-08).

Fig 8.6 Permanent Migration and Temporary Migration Programs.
Source: Philips, Klapdor, and Simon-Davies (2010) but expanded by Holliifiled.

Year	1996-97	1997-98	1998-99	1999-00	2000-01	2001-02	2002-03	2003-04	2004-05	2005-06	2006-07	2007-08	2008-09	2009-10	2010-11
Total Permanent Migrants	85,762	79,145	79,286	86,040	94,353	105,439	120,595	128,183	133,248	157,084	161,217	171,644	184,825	182,393	182,450
Overseas Students (TM)	113,000	108,827	110,894	119,806	146,577	151,894	162,575	171,616	174,786	190,674	228,592	278,180	320,368	NA	NA
Temporary Business (TM)	25,786	30,880	29,320	31,070	36,900	33,510	36,800	39,500	49,590	71,150	87,310	110,570	101,280	NA	NA
Combined (OS & Bus TM)	138,786	139,707	140,214	150,876	183,477	185,404	199,375	211,116	224,376	261,824	315,902	388,750	421,648	NA	NA

Permanent Migration Program

Fig 8.7 › Australia's Permanent Migration Program (2007-08)

Permanent Migration

Migration (158,630)

Family (49,870)
- Reunification of families within Australia to a member already resident within Australia..
- No test for English language or professional skills

Skilled (108,540)
- Variety of streams including Employer sponsored, General Skill, Business Skill & Distinguished Talent.
- Includes dependents of the skilled worker (55% of total)

Special Eligibility (220)
- Covers former residents who had not yet acquired Australian Citizenship, seeking to return.

Humanitarian (13,014)

- Onshore & Offshore entries are linked, enabling control of the total entrants.

Offshore (6,004)
- Refugees resettled from overseas through the UNHCR.

Offshore Special Humanitarian (5,110)
- People not qualifying as refugees but who have experienced violation of their human rights within their home country.

Special Eligibility (220)
- Asylum sought after arrival to Australia.
- Majority by air, some by boat.

Since the mid-1980s, the Permanent Migration Program has settled almost 4 million people. The program is divided into a Migration Program and a Humanitarian Program that includes refugees. Almost nine out of ten places come through the Migration Program (89% between 1984 and 2011). Both parts can be further sub-categorised. The numbers processed within each part and the contributions of the sub-categories have fluctuated across the years.

The Migration Program (89%)

The Migration Program has accounted for 89% of the intake of the Permanent Migration Program. It has three distinct sub-components which were first classified and created in the 1980s.

1. **Family Migration (~47.5%):** for relatives of people already settled in Australia.
2. **Skilled Migration (~51.5%):** for people entering Australia to meet skilled labour needs.
3. **Special Eligibility (~1.0%):** for relatively rare and specialised cases (e.g. former residents who had not gained citizenship seeking to return to Australia).

The figures for the Family and Skilled streams include the primary applicant as well as any dependents. Thus, if a worker receiving a Skilled Migrant Visa has a spouse and two children also included on the application, all four family members will receive Skilled Migrant Visas. The outcome being that not all entrants on the Skilled Migrant Visa are actually skilled migrants. For example, in 2008-09, 55% of the 115,000 Skilled Migrant Visas were granted to dependents of the primary applicant[13].

The Humanitarian Program (11%)

The Humanitarian Program has accounted for 11% of the Permanent Migration Program since 1984. It was categorised separately for the first time by the Keating Government in 1993 and the intake has been around 14,000 each year. There are essentially three core components which relate to various tenets of the Refugee Convention. They are covered in more detail in Chapter 9 but are included here for context.

1. **The Onshore Program** is used for Asylum Seekers who apply after arrival to Australia. Historically the majority of people applying for asylum in this way have arrived via plane and with a visa authorising entry (e.g. as a tourist or student). It is also the program that processes claims for asylum made by those arriving to Australia by

---

13 James F. Hollifield, Philip L. Martin and Pia M. Orrenius, *Controlling Immigration: A Global Perspective,* Third Edition (United States, Standford Univerity Press, 2014), 134.

boat. In some years claims by boat arrivals have exceeded those arriving by plane. It is the policies in processing these asylum seekers that has caused much controversy in the past 15 years.

2. **The Offshore Program** is used for people who have already been processed and granted refugee status elsewhere but are in need of resettlement as they are unable (or unwilling) to go back to their own country. The majority of these applicants are referred to the Australian Government by the UNHCR (United Nations High Commissioner for Refugees).

3. **The Special Humanitarian Program** is technically a specific section within the Offshore Program. It is used for people who, while not technically refugees according to the definition in the 1951 Refugee Convention, are subject to substantial discrimination, amounting to a gross violation of their human rights in their Country of Origin. They must be living outside their home country and have 'compelling reasons' to resettle in Australia.

Fig 8.8 > Permanent Migrant Program by components. *Source: DIAC (2012).*

| Year | Permanent Migration Program |||||| |
| | Migration Program |||| Humanitarian Program || |
	Family	Skill	Special Eligibility	Total	Humanitarian	Total	
1984-85	44,200	10,100	200	54,500	14,207	68,707	20.7%
1985-86	63,400	16,200	400	80,000	11,700	91,700	12.8%
1986-87	72,600	28,500	600	101,700	11,291	112,991	10.0%
1987-88	79,500	42,000	600	122,100	11,392	133,492	8.5%
1988-89	72,700	51,200	800	124,700	11,309	136,009	8.3%
1989-90	66,600	52,700	900	120,200	12,415	132,615	9.4%
1990-91	61,300	49,800	1,200	112,300	11,284	123,584	9.1%
1991-92	55,900	41,400	1,700	99,000	12,009	111,009	10.8%
1992-93	43,500	21,300	1,400	66,200	11,845	78,045	15.2%
1993-94	43,200	18,300	1,300	62,800	14,070	76,870	18.3%
1994-95	44,500	30,400	1,600	76,500	14,858	91,358	16.3%
1995-96	56,700	24,100	1,700	82,500	16,252	98,752	16.5%
1996-97	44,580	27,550	1,730	73,860	11,902	85,762	13.9%
1997-98	31,310	34,670	1,110	67,090	12,055	79,145	15.2%
1998-99	32,040	35,000	890	67,930	11,356	79,286	14.3%
1999-00	32,000	35,330	2,850	70,180	15,860	86,040	18.4%
2000-01	33,470	44,730	2,420	80,620	13,733	94,353	14.6%
2001-02	38,090	53,520	1,480	93,090	12,349	105,439	11.7%
2002-03	40,790	66,050	1,230	108,070	12,525	120,595	10.4%
2003-04	42,230	71,240	890	114,360	13,823	128,183	10.8%
2004-05	41,740	77,880	450	120,070	13,178	133,248	9.9%
2005-06	45,290	97,340	310	142,940	14,144	157,084	9.0%
2006-07	50,080	97,920	200	148,200	13,017	161,217	8.1%
2007-08	49,870	108,540	220	158,630	13,014	171,644	7.6%
2008-09	56,366	114,777	175	171,318	13,507	184,825	7.3%
2009-10	60,254	107,868	501	168,623	13,770	182,393	7.5%
2010-11	54,550	113,850	300	168,700	13,750	182,450	7.5%
	1,356,760	1,472,265	27,156	2,856,181	350,615	3,206,796	
	47.5%	51.5%	1.0%	89.1%	10.9%		

Temporary Migration Program

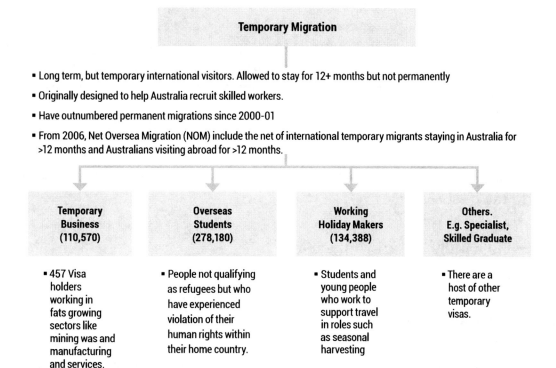

Fig 8.9 Australia's Temporary Migration Program (2007-08)

Long-term temporary migrants are international visitors allowed to stay for 12 months or more but not permanently. The program was originally designed to recruit skilled workers (managers, IT personnel, technicians) including working holiday makers, entertainers, and sports people. Australia now has around 650,000 temporary migrants, most of whom make a significant contribution to the labour force[14]. This represents a shift from the historical settler model. The perspective of people on temporary visas is likely to be different with regard to settlement and citizenship compared to those with permanent visas.

Three major categories have been utilised in recent years:

1. **Temporary business (long stay) Subclass 457** was introduced in 1996. The number of 457 visa holders is now over 100,000 and nearly equals the permanent skilled migrants. It is highly responsive to economic conditions with the quantity issued being directly related to the level of demand by the employers (and their willingness to sponsor such workers). It has no annual cap.

---

[14] James F. Hollifield, Philip L. Martin and Pia M. Orrenius, Controlling Immigration: A Global Perspective, Third Edition (United States, Standford Univerity Press, 2014), 133.

2. **Overseas student** visas are now the largest group of temporary visa holders (386,523 student visa holders in the 12 months to June 2009) and exceeds the number of people arriving for permanent settlement. These temporary migrants are highly beneficial to the Australian economy, as well as the higher education schools to which they pay their fees. In 2007, Australia accounted for 11% globally of the international student population and had experienced a three-fold increase in student numbers over the previous 10 years. The main countries of origin of the students are China, India and South Korea.

3. **Working Holiday Makers** are students and other young people (mainly from Britain, Europe and North America) who work temporarily while holidaying in Australia. They generally work in the agricultural and tourism industry. There were 130,000 of these visas in 2007-08.

Australia's Multiculturalism Policy

The Australian Government Department of Social Services describes multiculturalism as "a term which describes the cultural and ethnic diversity of contemporary Australia". Currently the government has three dimensions of multicultural policy:

1. Cultural Identity: the right of all Australians, within carefully defined limits, to express and share their individual cultural heritage, including their language and religion;

2. Social justice: the right of all Australians to equality of treatment and opportunity, and the removal of barriers of race, ethnicity, culture, religion, language, gender or place of birth; and

3. Economic efficiency: the need to maintain, develop and utilise effectively the skills and talents of all Australians, regardless of background.

There are also stated limits to Australian multiculturalism:

1. Multicultural polices are based upon the premises that all Australians should have an overriding and unifying commitment to Australia, to its interests and future first and foremost;

2. Multicultural policies require all Australians to accept the basic structures and principles of Australian society – the Constitution and the rule of law, tolerance and equality, Parliamentary democracy, freedom of speech and religion, English as the national language and equality of the sexes; and

3. Multicultural policies impose obligations as well as conferring rights: the right to express one's own culture and beliefs involves a reciprocal responsibility to accept the rights of others to express their views and values.

CH 9. AUSTRALIA'S HUMANITARIANISM

Australia voluntarily ratified the Refugee Convention in 1954, and ratified its Protocol in 1973, and in signing, assumed the obligations held under the Convention. However, these obligations are not bound by any enforceable law as Australia operates under a 'dualist' system. This means that international law and domestic law operate on two parallel planes. The significance being that obligations borne out by the Refugee Convention and other UN treaties (international law), do not automatically become part of Australian law unless Parliament passes domestic law to give them effect.

Australia's only enforceable obligation to protect refugees relates to what has been incorporated into the Migration Act 1958, which is Australia's domestic immigration legislation. This is different to some countries, particularly in Europe, which have a 'monist' system where international obligations automatically become part of their domestic laws.

By ratifying the Refugee Convention, Australia has promised all other signatory parties that it will uphold the tenets of the treaty. This includes three critical components critics of government policy cite as being breached:

- Respect the principle of non-refoulement.
- Affording refugees a certain legal status that includes access to employment, education and social security.
- Not punishing refugees for entering illegally, i.e. without passports or visas.

This section provides a brief overview of the Australian policies and processes for managing unauthorised arrivals. Many of these are controversial and with much debate (covered in Chapter 10).

The generosity and compassion of Australia's humanitarian program is hotly debated. Criticisms are raised regarding the human rights violation of Australia's offshore detention centres as well as its low intake of refugees through its Onshore Program. With regard to providing temporary protection, Australia supported just 0.43% of the world's refugees in 2014, ranking it 22nd globally, 27th on a per-capita basis and 43rd relative to GDP. Conversely in terms of a durable solution, Australia has resettled an estimated 822,924 refugees – providing them protection as permanent residents – between Federation in 1901 and June 2014. This number is among the highest worldwide. Australia is still recognised as a major contributor to the UNHCR Refugee Resettlement program, with at times the highest resettlement intake of refugees from refugee camps per capita in the world. Australia resettled 11,570 refugees in 2014, ranking it third overall and first on a per-capita basis and relative to GDP.

Prior to the policies enacted in response to refugees fleeing the Syrian War in 2015, the total size of Australia's Refugee and Humanitarian Program was capped at around 13,750 each year. With the special intake of 12,000 Syrian refugees, the intake increased to around 25,750. Australia's Humanitarian Program has three core components: The Onshore Program and the two components of the Offshore Program. Different visas are associated with the different components. As Australia has been operating to a target cap, the numbers across the three groups vary but the total intake remains relatively consistent. As the Onshore Program is not able to be controlled, the Offshore Program (with its Offshore and Special Humanitarian components) varies to maintain a consistent overall intake.

Fig 9.1 › Australia's Humanitarian Program (2007-08)

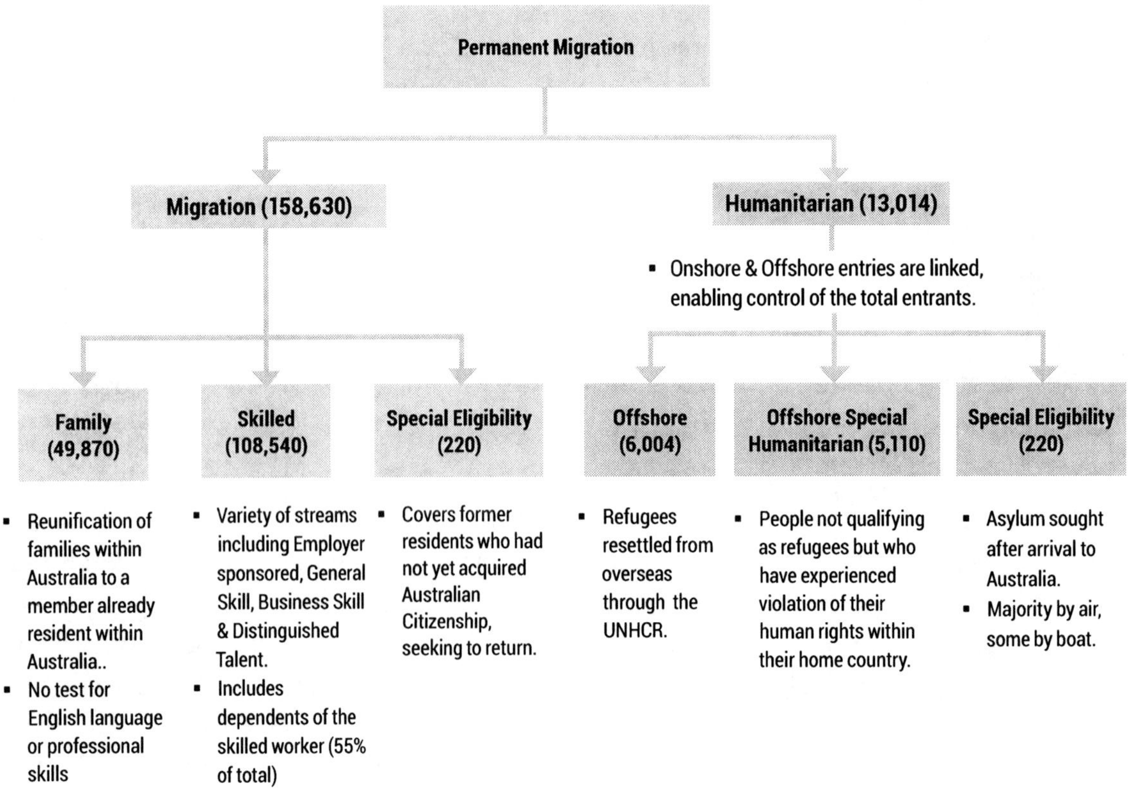

Permanent Migration

- **Migration (158,630)**
  - **Family (49,870)**
    - Reunification of families within Australia to a member already resident within Australia.
    - No test for English language or professional skills
  - **Skilled (108,540)**
    - Variety of streams including Employer sponsored, General Skill, Business Skill & Distinguished Talent.
    - Includes dependents of the skilled worker (55% of total)
  - **Special Eligibility (220)**
    - Covers former residents who had not yet acquired Australian Citizenship, seeking to return.

- **Humanitarian (13,014)**
  - Onshore & Offshore entries are linked, enabling control of the total entrants.
  - **Offshore (6,004)**
    - Refugees resettled from overseas through the UNHCR.
  - **Offshore Special Humanitarian (5,110)**
    - People not qualifying as refugees but who have experienced violation of their human rights within their home country.
  - **Special Eligibility (220)**
    - Asylum sought after arrival to Australia.
    - Majority by air, some by boat.

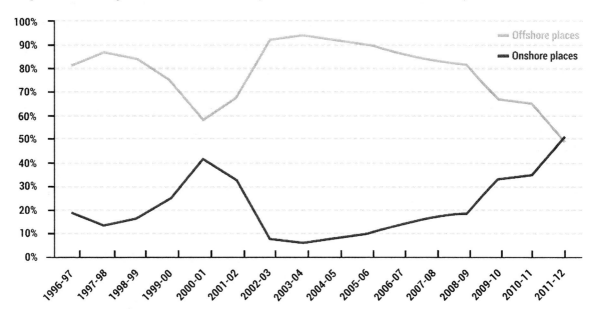

Fig 9.2 › Percentage of Offshore and Onshore places. *Source: DIAC, data received on 7 July 2012.*

Onshore Program

The Onshore Program is used for Asylum Seekers who apply for protection after arrival to Australia. That is, they apply for asylum in Australia's territory or 'on shore'. In theory the volume of Asylum Seekers processed through the Onshore Program is limitless and cannot be controlled by the Australian Government. In practice, given that Australia is an island that is distant from much of the world's trouble-spots, the numbers arriving to Australia has been less than other developed areas such as Europe.

Authorised and Unauthorised Arrivals

The process that is followed for assessing asylum seeker claims and the associated visas differ according to whether the person arrived with a visa that legally allowed them to enter if they were not seeking asylum. To demarcate this distinction the terms 'authorised' and 'unauthorised' arrivals are used.

- Authorised Arrivals are asylum seekers who arrived as visitors or students using the associated authorisation to enter the country following a regular process prior to applying for asylum.

- Unauthorised Arrivals are asylum seekers who arrived to Australia without the appropriate visa documents to enter Australia (should they not be seeking asylum.)

Unauthorised arrivals can arrive in Australia by planes, however most enter via boats. The term 'Irregular Maritime Arrivals' (IMAs) is used to categorise these asylum seekers. The colloquial term 'boat people' has also been attached to this group. Although not legally allowed to enter Australia for migration, holiday, or any other purpose, under the Refugee Convention people are allowed to enter Australia (as a signatory country) if claiming asylum.

The Onshore Program is not one simple program that is followed for all applicants covered by its mandate. Different procedures and rights apply to applicant types. Confusingly the Onshore Program has onshore processing and offshore processing. Onshore processing is for authorised arrivals, offshore processing for unauthorised arrival. Adding to the complexity is that the process seems to continually change for each applicant type. Recent changes have related to:

- Where the applicant is held or located during the waiting period. From July 2013 IMAs are detained and processed 'off shore', on Manus Island, PNG (until the PNG government ruling in April 2016 that such detention was illegal[1]) and Nauru.
- Providing more short-term bridging visas as opposed to keeping people in immigration detention. These allow asylum seekers to work and access health care whilst waiting for resolution of their claims.
- The type of visa available if approved as a refugee. The Temporary Protection Visa (TPV) was a previously controversial visa that has been slightly amended and reintroduced in 2015 for those found to be refugees by RSD.
- The ultimate resettlement location. In 2013 it was announced that all unauthorised arrivals were to be processed.

Authorised Arrivals

In recent years, the asylum seeker process for authorised arrivals has changed the least. It is more transparent and straight forward, and less punitive than the process for unauthorised arrivals. There are three steps:

Step 1. The process for asylum commences when the asylum seeker applies for a Protection Visa.

- Applications are required to be made in writing to the Department of Immigration and Citizenship (DIAC). The application is assessed by an officer of the department (who

---

[1] Eric Tlozek and Stephanie Andersen, "PNG's Supreme Court rules detention of aslyum seekers on Manus Island is illegal," ABC News, updated April 27, 2016, accessed Juy 24, 2016 <www.abc.net.au/news/2016-04-26/png-court-rules-asylum-seeker-detention-manus-island-illegal/7360078>.

technically has been delegated power by the Minister for Immigration and Citizenship) to determine if the applicant qualifies as a refugee. The assessment is Australia's RSD and it is made against the Refugee Status Determination System established by the 1958 Migration Act. Determination is targeted to be made within 90 days.

- Legal support is provided for each application. This helps maximise the time of the decision makers by clarifying the request of the applicant, as well as screening out applicants when their claim has no legal merit.
- A Bridging Visa may be provided, allowing the applicant to stay lawfully within the community (rather than detention) while the application is being processed. In some cases the applicant is allowed to work, but generally they are not.

Step 2. The asylum seeker applicant undergoes health, character and security checks.

- Health Check: a check of the applicant's medical health.
- Character Check: a review of the applicant's criminal record and activity. Protection can be denied to people who have committed (or are suspected of having committed) certain kinds of crimes, or have engaged in certain types of activity.
- Security Check: a security assessment is conducted by the Australian Security Intelligence Organisation (ASIO) to ensure the refugee does not pose a risk to national security.

Step 3. A Protection Visa is either granted or not granted.

- All applicants who have been assessed as qualifying as refugees and passing the health, character and security tests will be granted a Protection Visa and can remain in Australia as permanent residents.
- Applicants who are not granted a Protection Visa may seek for a review or appeal the decision provided they arrived in Australia on a valid visa. An independent review is conducted by the Administrative Appeals Tribunal (AAT)[2].
- Applicants who receive a negative outcome from the AAT may apply for a review of the tribunal's decision by a court. However, an appeal will only be allowed if it can be shown that the tribunal has made an error of law[3].

---

2   "2012 Face the Facts: Chapter 3," Australian Human Rights Commission, accessed July 24, 2016 <https://www.humanrights.gov.au/publications/face-facts-2012/2012-face-facts-chapter-3>.
3   Ibid.

Unauthorised Arrivals

The asylum seeker process for unauthorised arrivals is more punitive than for authorised arrivals. It has also undergone more changes in recent times. Australia's Migration Act of 1958 requires all 'unlawful non-citizens' (that is, people who are not Australian citizens and do not have permission to be in the country) such as unauthorised arrivals, be detained regardless of circumstances until they are granted a visa or leave the country.

Mandatory Detention

Australia was the first country to legislate mandatory detention and is one of the few democratic countries to have such a policy[4]. Mandatory detention was introduced as a policy in 1992 by the Keating Government and has been maintained by successive governments. It was initially an exceptional measure for the influx of Indo-Chinese arrivals (mainly Cambodian) and detention was to be for a maximum of 273 days. The policy was extended in 1994 to all unlawful non-citizens and the time cap was removed. It now applies to many groups, including asylum seekers who arrive in Australia by boat without authorisation. All groups of people covered by its scope are held in a detention facility until they are granted a visa or are removed from Australia. This means all unauthorised asylum seekers to Australia, including to its territories like Christmas Island, are placed in a form of immigration detention. This includes children.

Mandatory detention has an administrative component to mitigate risk while health, character and security checks are run. It has also been used as a mechanism to deter more people from arriving by boat to Australia to qualify for the Onshore Program. Minister Gerry Hand told parliament in 1992:

> "I believe it is crucial that all persons who come to Australia without prior authorisation not be released into the community. Their release would undermine the government's strategy for determining their refugee status or entry claims. The government is determined that a clear signal be sent that migration to Australia may not be achieved by simply arriving in this country and expecting to be allowed into the community[5]."

As previously discussed, there is no way to control the numbers of asylum seekers arriving to Australia's shores to apply via the Onshore mechanism. Deterrence, though an

---

[4] Jane McAdam and Fiona Chong, *Refugees: Why seeking asylum is legal and Australia's policies are not*, (Sydney: NewSouth Publishing, 2014), 90.
[5] Frank Brennan, *Tampering with Asylum (Digitial Edition)* (Australia: University of Queensland Press, 2014), 76 of 253, iBooks edition.

unpleasant system is seen as one way to limit IMAs. The evidence since 2001-2 (covered in Chapter 3) shows a correlation between government policy and the number of boat arrivals. However, the efficacy, legality and ethics of these policies attract considerable debate. This is discussed in Chapter 10.

Australian law requires that people within its territory found to be 'unlawful citizens' be detained until they are granted a visa or removed from the country. Thus, Immigration Detention applies to other individuals as well as to asylum seekers covered by the Onshore Program. Unlawful Citizens include:

- Asylum Seekers without a valid visa (unauthorised arrivals).
- Recognised refugees yet to have satisfied the visa-related health, character or security clearances.
- People who have overstayed their visa. In the early 2000s, there were 60,000 overstayers each year, only about 15,000 were located each year[6].
- Non-citizens whose visas have been cancelled.

The law also allows for asylum seekers who qualify as 'unlawful non-citizens' by arriving at an 'excised offshore place' such as Christmas Island, to be detained. Although not a mandatory requirement in the law, the Australian Government's current policy (since 1992) is to detain all such asylum seekers. In total, asylum seekers make up about 95% of people in immigration detention centres[7].

There are five different types of immigration detention:

- Immigration Detention Centres (held) – most widely used.
- Immigration Residential Housing (confined).
- Immigration Transit Accommodation (confined).
- Alternative Places of Detention.
- Community Detention.

Centres are generally in remote areas that impede access to health care, lawyers, meaningful activity and reliable phone and internet access. There are limited employment and educational opportunities.

---

6   Ibid 96 of 253.
7   Jane McAdam and Fiona Chong, *Refugees: Why seeking asylum is legal and Australia's policies are not,* (Sydney: NewSouth Publishing, 2014), 89.

Fig 9.3 ❯ Australian immigration detention centres. *Source: Australian Human Rights Commission.*

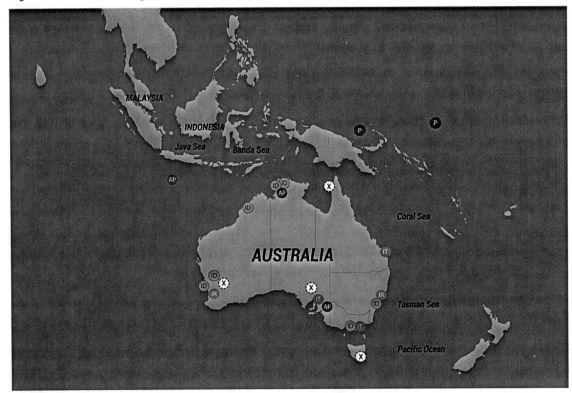

- **ID** Immigration Detention Centres (IDCs)
- **IR** Immigration Residential Housing Centres (IRHC)
- **IT** Immigration Transit Accommodation Centres (ITAC)
- **AP** Alternative Places of Detention (APOD)
- **P** Pacific Solution Facilities (PSF)
- **X** Closed Facilities

Types of Immigration Detention Centres[8]

Immigration Detention Centres are the most widely used and highest security form of immigration detention in Australia. Staff are required to sign confidentiality agreements, preventing them from speaking about what goes on within detention centres[9]. It is the conditions within these centres that caused the 2015 protests of medical professionals regarding the poor standards of medical care provided to the asylum seekers. People held in these centres are not free to come and go, having similarities to a prison. As of May 2012, immigration detention centres were located at:

---

8   "2012 Face the Facts: Chapter 3, Section 11," Australian Human Rights Commission, accessed July 24, 2016 <https://www.humanrights.gov.au/publications/face-facts-2012/2012-face-facts-chapter-3>.

9   Jane McAdam and Fiona Chong, *Refugees: Why seeking asylum is legal and Australia's policies are not,* (Sydney: NewSouth Publishing, 2014), tbc.

- Melbourne (Maribyrnong) – (M)
- Sydney (Villawood) – (V)
- Perth – (P)
- Northern (in Darwin) – (N)
- Curtin (near Derby, Western Australia) – (C)
- Wickham Point (near Darwin) – (W)
- Yongah Hill, Western Australia – (Y)
- Note: Pontville (Tasmania) and Scherger (near Weipa, northern Queensland) were both closed in 2014

Immigration Residential Housing are closed facilities but with less intrusive security measures. Often used for families or unaccompanied children, they are more flexible, less institutionalised settings. For example people can prepare their own meals. Those detained here are able to leave for short periods to shop or for recreation. However, these excursions must be under the supervision of officers from the detention services provider. As of May 2012, these facilities were located in:

- Sydney – (S)
- Perth – (P)
- Note: Port Augusta (South Australia) closed in 2014

Immigration Transit Accommodation are also closed facilities but with less intrusive security measures than immigration detention centres. They are now used to detain families and unaccompanied minors. In May 2012, immigration transit accommodation facilities were located in:

- Brisbane – (B)
- Melbourne – (M)
- Adelaide – (A)

Alternative Places of Detention include correctional centres, hospitals, hotels, psychiatric facilities and foster care arrangements. The conditions and restrictions that apply to these people vary on a case by case basis.

There are also a number of low-security immigration detention facilities classified by the Department as alternative places of detention. People detained in these facilities are supervised and not free to come and go.

- Christmas Island – (C)
- Darwin – (D)

- Inverbrackie (South Australia) – (I)
- Note: Leonora (Western Australia) closed in 2014

Community Detention allows for people to live in specified residences in the community. People in community detention are generally not under supervision and can move freely about in the community. Legally, however, they remain in immigration detention.

Certain conditions and requirements are attached, such as reporting regularly to the Department, sleeping at a specified residence every night and not engaging in paid work or formal study. Introduced in 2005, by 2013 about one-third of people were accommodated this way. The cost per asylum seeker is about $100,000 per year, or $40,000 if on a bridging visa. By contrast immigration detention centres cost about $239,000 and offshore processing centres $400,000 per refugee[10]. It also provides asylum seekers with the greatest freedom and quality of life.

Standardising Unauthorised Plane and Boat

Prior to 2012, unauthorised asylum seekers arriving via plane or boat (IMAs) were processed differently, effectively disadvantaging IMAs. In March 2012, the Gillard government streamlined arrangements that unified the process for all unauthorised arrivals (plane or boat).

The Houston Report

The Houston Report was commissioned by the Gillard Government in 2012 to assess 'the policy options available ... to prevent asylum seekers risking their lives on dangerous boat voyages to Australia'. Thus, it specifically related to reducing unauthorised asylum seekers arriving on boats (IMAs) managed through the Onshore Program.

The drivers for the report included the number of lives lost at sea by attempted IMAs (964 between late 2001 and June 2012)[11], and the recent increase in IMAs up until 2012. The report was overseen by Air Chief Marshal Angus Houston AC, AFC (retired) and was produced over a six week period after consultation with a wide range of political leaders, other members of Parliament, agencies and departments of government, non-government organisations (NGOs), academics and other experts as well as those in the wider community including refugee communities in Australia and refugees who travelled to Australia more recently through irregular means.

---

10   Jane McAdam and Fiona Chong, *Refugees: Why seeking asylum is legal and Australia's policies are not*, (Sydney: NewSouth Publishing, 2014), 182.
11   Angus Houston, Paris Aristotle and Michael l"Estrange, "Report of the Expert Panel on Asylum Seekers", (August, 2012), 19.

The Houston Report, released on 13 August 2012, provided 22 recommendations to prevent asylum seekers from risking their lives on dangerous boat voyages to Australia. The recommendations included:

- Increasing Australia's Humanitarian program to 20,000 (and potentially a further increase to 27,000) to assist in making asylum in Australia work better. These targets are approximately 0.1% of the population or 15-20% of Australia's recent NOM.
- Disincentives to IMAs through a 'no advantage principle' whereby asylum seekers gain no benefit by choosing not to seek protection through established mechanisms.
- Incentives and disincentives together being the most effective way to discourage asylum seekers from risking life on dangerous sea voyages.

The government reacted swiftly to the recommendations of the report. In particular it re-established offshore processing centres in PNG and Nauru. It endorsed the recommendation to increase the humanitarian intake by 50% to 20,000 each year but provided the caveat that costs needed to be managed.

The Pacific Solution

The Pacific Solution was initially developed by the Howard government in 2001 after the Tampa incident. It excised almost 5,000 islands from Australia's migration zone and declared that any asylum seeker who was an unauthorised arrival (without a valid visa) would be transferred to Papua New Guinea (PNG) or Nauru for detention and processing through RSD. This first incarnation of the Pacific Solution was closed down in 2008 by the Rudd government.

The second incarnation of the Pacific Solution was introduced following the Houston Report. One of the key justifications for the reincarnation was the 'No Advantage' Principle that sought to ensure those who chose irregular maritime voyages to Australia to claim asylum would not be advantaged for doing so over those who pursued regular mechanisms.

Fig 9.4 ▶ Summary of the 22 recommendations of the Report of the Expert Panel on Asylum Seekers, August 2012.
Source: Report of the Expert Panel on Asylum Seekers, August 2012.

TERMS OF REFERENCE

To provide advice on:

How best to prevent asylum seekers risking their lives by travelling to Australia by boat;

Source, transit and destination country aspects of irregular migration;

Relevant international obligations;

The development of an inter-related set of proposals in support of asylum seeker issues, given Australia's right to maintain its borders;

Short, medium and long term approaches to assist in the development of an effective and sustainable approach to asylum seekers;

The legislative requirements for implementation; and

The order of magnitude of costs of such policy options

RECOMMENDATIONS

PRINCIPLES

Recommendation 1. Policies shaped on the following principles:

Strategic, comprehensive and integrated approach establishing short, medium and long term priorities

Incentives for asylum seekers to seek protection through a managed regional system

Regional cooperation and protection framework that is consistent in processing asylum claims, assisting during assessment period and achievement of durable outcomes.

No benefit to be gained through circumventing regular migration arrangements (aka 'no advantage').

Promotion of a credible, fair and managed Australian Humanitarian Program.

Adherence by Australia to its international obligations.

HUMANITARIAN PROGRAM

Recommendation 2. Australia's Humanitarian Program to be increased to 20,000 per year (and potentially to 27,000).

REGIONAL ENGAGEMENT

Recommendation 3. Australia expands relevant capacity-building initiatives in the region.

Recommendation 4. Bilateral cooperation on asylum seeker issues with Indonesia advanced urgently, including resettlement from Indonesia and surveillance and response controls

Recommendation 5. Develop cooperation with Malaysia on asylum issues, including the management of refugees to be taken annually from Malaysia.

Recommendation 6. A more effective whole-of government strategy be developed for engaging with source countries for asylum seekers to Australia, focus on increased resettlement places for Middle East and Asian regions.

REGIONAL PROCESSING

Recommendation 7. Legislation to support transfer of people to regional processing arrangements be introduced as a matter of urgency.

Recommendation 8. Capacity be established in Nauru to process claims of IMAs transferred from Australia consistent with Australian and Nauruan responsibilities under international law.

Recommendation 9. Capacity be established in PNG to process claims of IMAs transferred from Australia consistent with Australian and Nauruan responsibilities under international law.

Recommendation 10. The 2011 Malaysia Agreement be built on further, rather than discarded or neglected.

FAMILY REUNION

Recommendation 11. Remove family reunion concessions in the SHP for proposers who arrive through irregular maritime voyages., these proposers to instead utilise the family stream of the Migration Program.

Recommendation 12. Future arrivals through irregular maritime means should not be eligible to sponsor family under the SHP.

OTHER RECOMMENDATIONS

Recommendation 13. More active coordination strategies among traditional and emerging resettlement countries.

Recommendation 14. Amend the Migration Act 1958 so that arrival anywhere on Australia by irregular maritime means will not provide individuals with a different lawful status that those who arrive iin an excised offshore place.

Recommendation 15. Conduct a thorough review of Refugee Status Determination.

Recommendation 16. Develop a whole-of-government strategy to negotiate better outcomes on removals and returns on failed asylum seekers.

Recommendation 17. Continue disruption strategies as part of any comprehensive approach to people smuggling and relevant Australian agencies be resourced with appropriate funding.

Recommendation 18. Law enforcement agencies in Australia continue their activities in countering involvement of Australian residents who are engaged in funding or facilitating people smuggling operations.

Recommendation 19. Note that the conditions necessary for effective, lawful and safe turn-back of irregular vessels carrying asylum seekers to Australia are not currently met, but that this situation could change in the future.

Recommendation 20. Develop joint operational guidelines for managing Search and Rescue (SAR) activities in the region.

Recommendation 21. The linkage between the onshore and offshore components of the Humanitarian Program be reviewed within two years.

Recommendation 22. Address the incompleteness of the evidence base on asylum issues through a well-managed and adequately funded research program engaging government and non-government expertise.

The cornerstone of the Pacific Solution is the offshore processing of asylum seekers who are unauthorised arrivals. This offshore processing is done in detention centres in other countries (Nauru and until recently, Papua New Guinea's Manus Island) and under the laws of those countries[12]. The policy also intends that such people who are found through RSD to be refugees will be settled in a country other than Australia. In July of 2013 the Rudd government announced that asylum seekers arriving by boat would be sent to PNG for processing and also resettlement. In August of 2013, Nauru entered a similar agreement by committing to resettle some (but not all) asylum seekers it processes on its shores.

As of August 2015, 1,589 people were detained in Offshore facilities due to Australian immigration and asylum seeking policies, 936 on Manus Island (PNG) and 653 on Nauru. Some of these detainees were children. The detention of child asylum seekers is an emotive and contentious issue and is covered in Chapter 10.

Cost of Offshore Detention

According to the Department of Immigration and Border Protection, the costs of offshore detention centres have three components:

1. Operational expenditure, which includes paying contractors to run the centres.
2. Department expenditure to run the government bureaucracy.
3. Capital expenditure to build the offshore facilities.

The total cost of all components was A$1.3 billion for the 2013-14 financial A$1.1 billion for the first ten months of the 2014-15 financial year. The future annual costs are expected to fall to under $A400 million as the bulk of the costs relate to operational expenditure, which is predicted to decrease with the deterrence measures, and the capital expenditure will slow down as the infrastructure is established[13].

Children in Detention

Australia's system of mandatory detention includes children. Most of the children in immigration detention arrived to Australia as IMAs, that is, on a boat and without a visa. Some of these children arrived without any family. The majority of children are now

---

12 "Recent changes in Australian refugee policy," Refugee Council of Australia, last updated July 2016, accessed July 24, 2016 <www.refugeecounil.org.au/wp-content/uploads/2016/07/Australia-refugee-policy-changes-July-2016.pdf>.
13 "Fact Check: Does Australia spend more on offshore processing than the UN spends on refugee programs in South East Asia?," *ABC News*, last updated July 21, 2015, accessed July 24, 2016 <www.abc.net.au/news/2015-07-14/cost-of-offshore-processing-united-nations-fact-check/6609764>.

held in community detention, this is a result of the recent focus to move children into alternatives to closed detention facilities[14].

According to statistics published by The Department of Immigration and Border Protection as of November 30, 2015 there were 505 children in detention:

- 70 in the Regional Processing Centre in Nauru.
- 104 in closed immigration detention facilities in Australia.
- 331 in community detention in Australia.

Australia ratified the Convention on the Rights of the Child (CRC) in 1990. The CRC sets out that the best interests of the child should be a primary consideration in all decisions that affect them. Specific requirements regarding the protection of the liberty of children in the CRC include:

- Children must be detained as a measure of last resort.
- Children must only be detained for the shortest appropriate period of time.
- Children should not be detained unlawfully or arbitrarily.
- Children in detention have the right to challenge the legality of their detention before a court or another independent body.

Enhanced Screening

In response to an increase in the number of boat arrivals from Sri Lanka, Enhanced Screening was introduced on 27 October 2012. Enhanced Screening is a controversial process regarding asylum seekers who arrive by boat to Australia. It involves an interview conducted between the potential asylum seeker and officers of the Immigration Department to determine whether or not they may engage in Australia's protection obligations. If 'screened in' (determined that they may engage in Australia's protection obligations) the potential asylum seeker can make a claim for a protection visa. If asylum seekers do not raise concerns, which suggest they may not have a valid protection claim they are 'screened out' and returned to their Country of Origin without the opportunity to formally lodge a protection claim[15]. More than 1,000 people have been screened out since the system was introduced.

---

14 "Information about children in immigration detention," Australian Human Rights Commission, last updated January 6, 2016, accessed July 24, 2016 <https://www.humanrights.gov.au/information-about-children-immigration-detention>.
15 "Recent changes in Australian refugee policy," Refugee Council of Australia, last updated July 2016, accessed July 24, 2016 <www.refugeecouncil.org.au/wp-content/uploads/2016/07/Australia-refugee-policy-changes-July-2016.pdf>.

Fig 9.5 > Convention on the Rights of the Child. *Source: Unicef.org.au*

Article 1 — Everyone under 18 years of age has all the rights in this Convention.

Article 2 — The Convention applies to everyone whatever their race, religion, abilities, whatever they think or say, whatever type of family they come from.

Article 3 — All organisations concerned with children should work towards what is best for each child.

Article 4 — Governments should make these rights available to children.

Article 5 — Governments should respect the rights and responsibilities of families to guide their children so that, as they grow up, they learn to use their rights properly.

Article 6 — Children have the right to live a full life. Governments should ensure that children survive and develop healthily.

Article 7 — Children have the right to a legally registered name and nationality. Children also have the right to know their parents and, as far as possible, to be cared for by them.

Article 8 — Governments should respect a child's right to a name, a nationality and family ties.

Article 9 — Children should not be separated from their parents unless it is for their own good. For example, if a parent is mistreating or neglecting a child. Children whose parents have separated have the right to stay in contact with both parents, unless this might harm the child.

Article 10 — Families who live in different countries should be allowed to move between those countries so that parents and children can stay in contact, or get back together as a family.

Article 11 — Governments should take steps to stop children being taken out of their own country illegally.

Article 12 — Children have the right to say what they think should happen when adults are making decisions that affect them and to have their opinions taken into account.

Article 13 — Children have the right to get and to share information, as long as the information is not damaging to them or to others.

Article 14 — Children have the right to think and believe what they want and to practise their religion, as long as they are not stopping other people from enjoying their rights. Parents should guide children on these matters.

Article 15 — Children have the right to meet with other children and young people and to join groups and organisations, as long as this does not stop other people from enjoying their rights.

Article 16 — Children have the right to privacy. The law should protect them from attacks against their way of life, their good name, their family and their home.

Article 17 — Children have the right to reliable information from the media. Mass media such as television, radio and newspapers should provide information that children can understand and should not promote materials that could harm children.

Article 18 — Both parents share responsibility for bringing up their children and should always consider what is best for each child. Governments should help parents by providing services to support them, especially if both parents work.

Article 19 — Governments should ensure that children are properly cared for and protect them from violence, abuse and neglect by their parents, or anyone else who looks after them.

Article 20 — Children who cannot be looked after by their own family must be looked after properly by people who respect their religion, culture and language.

Article 21 — When children are adopted the first concern must be what is best for them. The same rules should apply whether children are adopted in the country of their birth or if they are taken to live in another country.

Article 22 — Children who come into a country as refugees should have the same rights as children who are born in that country.

Article 23 — Children who have any kind of disability should receive special care and support so that they can live a full and independent life.

Article 24 — Children have the right to good quality health care, clean water, nutritious food and a clean environment so that they will stay healthy. Richer countries should help poorer countries achieve this.

Article 25 — Children who are looked after by their local authority rather than their parents should have their situation reviewed regularly.

Article 26 — The Government should provide extra money for the children of families in need.

Article 27 — Children have the right to a standard of living that is good enough to meet their physical and mental needs. The government should help families who cannot afford to provide this.

Article 28 — Children have the right to an education. Discipline in schools should respect children's human dignity. Primary education should be free. Wealthier countries should help poorer countries achieve this.

Article 29 — Education should develop each child's personality and talents to the full. It should encourage children to respect their parents, their cultures and other cultures.

Article 30 — Children have the right to learn and use the language and customs of their families, whether or not these are shared by the majority of the people in the country where they live, as long as this does not harm others.

Article 31 — Children have the right to relax, play and to join in a wide range of leisure activities.

Article 32 — Governments should protect children from work that is dangerous or that might harm their health or education.

Article 33 — Governments should provide ways of protecting children from dangerous drugs.

Article 34 — Governments should protect children from sexual abuse.

Article 35 — Governments should make sure that children are not abducted or sold.

Article 36 — Children should be protected from any activities that could harm their development.

Article 37 — Children who break the law should not be treated cruelly. They should not be put in a prison with adults and should be able to keep in contact with their family.

Article 38 — Governments should not allow children under 15 to join the army. Children in war zones should receive special protection.

Article 39 — Children who have been neglected or abused should receive special help to restore their self-respect.

Article 40 — Children who are accused of breaking the law should receive legal help. Prison sentences for children should only be used for the most serious offences.

Article 41 — If the laws of a particular country protects children better than the articles of the Convention, then those laws should override the Convention.

Article 42 — Governments should make the Convention known to all parents and children.

The Convention on the Rights of the Child has 54 articles in all. Articles 43-54 are about how adults and governments should work together to make sure that all children get all their rights.

Operation Sovereign Borders

Operation Sovereign Borders was undertaken after the commencement of the Abbott Government (September 2013), with the aim of deterring asylum seekers from coming to Australia by denying them access to Australia. Australian naval officers are issued with orders to turn back boats carrying asylum seekers 'when it is safe to do so'[16].

It reflects a strategy employed by the Howard government after the Tampa incident in 2001 (through Operations Relex and Relex II). Essentially boats that would otherwise carry unauthorised arrivals to Australian shores are intercepted in Australia's contiguous zone and sent back to the edge of the territorial waters from where they came (generally speaking this is Indonesia). The result is that IMAs do not even arrive at Australia and are not processed through the Onshore Program. In August 2015, the Australian government revealed that 20 boats carrying 633 people had been turned back since late June 2013.

The Offshore Program (~11,000 places)

The Offshore Program is used for resettlement of refugees directly from an asylum country to Australia. These refugees apply to Australia for asylum and resettlement from outside her borders. In recent years it has provided permanent residency in Australia to approximately 11,000 people each year. It consists of two main parts:

- The Refugee Program (~6,000)
- The Special Humanitarian Program (SHP) (~5,000)

Australia is consistently recognised as one of the most generous countries in regard to resettlement of refugees. According to UNHCR data, Australia received 11,600 refugees for resettlement into its Offshore Program in 2014, ranking 3rd overall in the number of refugees it resettled. The USA took in 73,000 and Canada 12,300. Sweden, ranked fourth, took in considerably less refugees for resettlement (2,000). The Refugee Program is the only component that resettles refugees. Although part of the Offshore Program, visas provided under the Special Humanitarian Program are given to people who are not technically refugees.

The Refugee Program (~6,000)

The Refugee Program resettles refugees from outside Australia. The visas provided by the Refugee Program are specifically for refugees. That is, people subject to persecution in their own country and in need of resettlement. At the end of 2014 there was 14.4 million

---

16 Ibid.

refugees under the UNHCR mandate. The majority of these applicants are referred to the Australian Government by the UNHCR. Four sub-classes exist[17]:

1. **Subclass 200 – Refugee Visa.** People subject to persecution in their Country of Origin and are in need of resettlement.

2. **Subclass 201 – In-Country Special Humanitarian Program Visa.** People subject to persecution in their Country of Origin who have not been able to leave that country to seek refuge elsewhere.

3. **Subclass 203 – Emergency Rescue Visa.** People who satisfy refugee criteria and whose lives or freedom depend on urgent resettlement.

4. **Subclass 204 – Woman at Risk Visa.** Female applicants and their dependents that are subject to persecution or are of concern to the UNHCR. They are living outside their home country without the protection of a male relative and are in danger of victimisation, harassment or serious abuse because of their gender.

The Special Humanitarian Program (~5,000)

The Special Humanitarian Program (SHP) is for people who are not refugees according to the definition in the 1951 Refugee Convention, but are subject to substantial discrimination amounting to a gross violation of their human rights in their Country of Origin. They must be living outside their home country and have 'compelling reasons' to resettle in Australia. When introduced in 1981, this visa was designed for 'quasi-refugees'. Recipients are provided a Subclass 202 – Special Humanitarian Program Visa. The compelling reasons can include:

- arbitrary interference with the applicant's privacy, family, home or correspondence
- deprivation of means of earning a livelihood, denial of work commensurate with training and qualifications and/or payment of unreasonably low wages
- relegation to substandard dwellings
- exclusion from the right to education
- enforced social and civil inactivity
- removal of citizenship rights
- denial of a passport, or
- constant surveillance or pressure to become an informer

---

17 "Offshore - Resettlement," Australian Government: Department of Immigragtion and Border Protection, accessed July 24, 216 <https://www.border.gov.au/Trav/Refu/Offs>.

Applicants for the Special Humanitarian Program Visas must be supported by a proposer (an Australia citizen or comparable) who is responsible for the cost of their settlement. The visas are usually provided to family members of refugees and humanitarian entrants already in Australia. Overseas refugees are included in this intake, but usually account for less than 50% of the annual allocation of visas under the Humanitarian Program.

Both the Refugee Program and SHP have 'split family' provisions. These allow visa holders to sponsor their immediate family members (i.e. their partner and dependent children or, if the proposer is an unaccompanied minor, their parents) for resettlement in Australia. Generally, visas are granted in the same category as the proposer's visa; e.g. immediate family members of a proposer who was resettled in Australia on a Refugee Visa (subclass 200) will also be granted a Refugee visa. The main exception is Protection Visa holders (via the Onshore Program), whose immediate family members are granted SHP visas.

Support Provided Within Australia

There are a variety of government and non-government agencies that offer support for some asylum seekers and those provided with a permanent visa. These include refugees or humanitarian visa holders via the Offshore Program and or protection visa holders via the Onshore Program. For those who qualify, the support provided within Australia is very generous in comparison to other countries.

Government Agencies

The Department of Human Services provides a range of support services for refugees and asylum seekers which includes:

- information in first language and interpretation services;
- Multicultural Support Officers to facilitate access to relevant support networks and services;
- financial support;
- accommodation or rental assistance.

Support for Permanent Visa Holders

Those provided permanent visas (including refugees on Protection Visas, people on Special Humanitarian Program Visas, and those on Refugee Visas) have the same entitlements to social security as all other Australian permanent residents[18]. Two key payments are unemployment benefits and rental assistance. These payments are modest and in 2012 amounted to approximately A$570 per fortnight (for a single person in shared accommodation). Additional, non-financial support is also provided in the form of orientation, assistance with sourcing accommodation and introduction to community and settlement groups and services.

Support for Asylum Seekers

Support is also provided to asylum seekers, the level of which is dependent on whether they have a Bridging Visa, or are in community detention or immigration detention.

All Bridging Visa holders and some Protection Visa applicants qualify to live in the community and as such are able to receive payments under the Asylum Seeker Assistance (ASA) Scheme. These payments are equivalent to 89% of the unemployment and rental assistance benefits (that permanent visa holders receive). The ASA provides asylum seekers with case work support for their asylum claim. It also provides health care, pharmaceuticals, and referrals to other agencies including social, counselling and education[19].

Additional services may also be provided through the Community Assistance Support (CAS) program to support people who are particularly vulnerable, often women, children, and the elderly. Examples of such people include those who have suffered trauma or domestic abuse, have a mental health problem, have serious health issues or are elderly.

All asylum seekers in community detention are provided housing, payment for living expenses (70% of the unemployment payments as accommodation is provided), education for children, health care services, and community and social support networks. This support is provided through Non-Government Organisations (NGOs) via funding that is provided by the Department of Immigration and Citizenship (DIAC), the main agency being the Australian Red Cross[20].

Asylum seekers in immigration detention do not receive financial assistance as all services, even if basic, are provided for them. These services include accommodation

---

18 Luke Buckmaster, "Australian Government assistance to refugees: fact v fiction," Parliament of Australia (September 28, 2012), accessed July 24, 2016 <www.aph.gov.au/About_Parliament/Parliamentary_Departments?Parliamentary_Library/pubs/BN/2012-2013/AustGovAssistRefugees>.
19 Ibid.
20 Ibid.

with bedding and bathing facilities, food according to religious or cultural beliefs, access to religious practitioners, access to media and educational facilities, supply of clothes, footwear and personal hygiene items. A points system provides some the ability to 'shop' at stores at the centres. Most centres are run by a private company, Serco, which is contracted by the Australian government.

Non-Government Agencies

For asylum seekers provided with a Bridging Visa that allows them to stay within the community while their claims are being assessed, life is still difficult. They are most likely feeling that they are in a foreign place with a foreign culture, with very few contacts. Most will have no right to work[21] and must live off the payments and support under the ASA Scheme discussed above. In response, a variety of non-government, not-for-profit agencies have been established across Australia to provide some support to asylum seekers.

There are numerous NGOs operating in Australia, many (for example the Australian Red Cross) are directly contracted by the government to support asylum seekers and refugees. These agencies are connected through a national umbrella body, the Refugee Council of Australia (RCA). The RCA was formed in 1981 and works on a modest budget of ~A$1 Million[22] sourced primarily through donations and memberships with some funding from the Australian Federal Government (the level and presence of this fluctuates over time). The RCA's stated five key areas of focus are:

1. Policy
2. Support for Refugees
3. Support for its Members
4. Community Education
5. Administration

There are over 200 organisational members of the RCA and over 900 individual members. It is not possible for this review to detail all agencies; however, there is significant overlap in what they do. A review of two of the larger organisations – the Asylum Seeker Resource Centre (ASRC) and the Refugee and Immigration Legal Centre (RILC) – provides a good insight into the services provided.

---

21 Jane McAdam and Fiona Chong, *Refugees: Why seeking asylum is legal and Australia's policies are not*, (Sydney: NewSouth Publishing, 2014), 109.
22 "Refugee Council of Australia, Annual Report 2014/15," Refugee Council of Australia, accessed July 24, 2016 <www.refugeecounil.org.au/wp-content/uploads/2015/11/RCOA-Annual-Report-2015-WEB.pdf>.

Fig 9.6 ▶ Australian NGOs supporting asylum seekers and refugees. *Source: Refugee Council of Australia.*

ACT (4)
- Australian Catholic Migrant and Refugee Office
- Canberra Refugee Support Inc
- Companion House
- MARSS (Migrant and Refugee Settlement Services)

NT (3)
- Alice People Services
- Anglicare NT Refugee and Migrant Settlement Services
- Melaleuca Refugee Centre

Qld (23)
- 4walls Ltd
- Access Community Services
- Barnabas Relief Education and Development
- Catholic Diocese of Toowoomb Social Justice Commission
- Centre for Multicultural Pastoral Care
- Community Queensland Ltd
- Fedeation of Liberian Communities in Australia
- Friends of Heal Foundation
- George St Neighbourhood Centre Association
- Inala Community House
- Milpera State High School
- Multicultural Development Association
- Multilink Community Services Inc
- ProEmpowerment International
- QPASTT (Queensland Program of Assistance to Survivors of Torture and Trauma)
- RAILS (Refugee and Immigration Legal Service)
- Refugee Claimants Support Service
- St Vincent de Paul Society Queensland
- TAFE Queensland English Language and Literacy Services
- Townsville Multicultural Support Group
- TRAMS (Toowoomba Refugee and Migrant Support Service)
- Uniting Church in Australia – Queenslan Synod
- World Wellness Group Ltd

SA (10)
- Anglican Dioceses of Adelaide
- Australian Refugee Association
- Bhutanese Australian Association of South Australia
- Centacare Catholic Family Services
- Circle of Friends Australia Inc
- Diompillor Kissia SA Inc
- Lutheran Community Care
- Migrant Resource Centre of South Australia
- STTARS (Survivors of Torture and Trauma Rehabilitation Service)
- Unitarian Church of South Australia

Tas (5)
- Centacare Tasmania
- Migrant Resource Centre (Northern Tasmania)
- Migrant Resource Centre (Southern Tasmania)
- Multicultural Council of Tasmania
- The Tasmania Opportunity

NSW (67)
- Ahmadiyya Muslim Association of Australia Inc
- Anglicare Migrant and Refugee Services Sydney
- Anglicare North Coast
- Armidale Sanctuary Humanitarian Settlement
- Assyrian Australian Association
- Asylum Seekers Centre
- Auburn Diversity Services
- Australian Catholic Social Justice Council
- Australian Federation of Islamic Councils
- Australian Karen Organisation Inc
- Balmain for Refugees
- Blue Mountains Refugee Support Group
- Burmese Rohingya Community in Australia
- Cabramatta Community Centre
- Catholic Education Office Wollongong
- Catholic Immigration Office, Sydney
- Centacare Wagga Wagga
- Centre for Refugee Research, University of NSW
- Circassian Association of Australia
- Coexistence Inc.
- Community Migrant Resource Centre
- Domestic Violence NSW Service Management Ltd
- Dominican Sisters of Eastern Australia & the Solomon Islands
- Edmund Rice Centre for Justice and Community Education
- Executive Council of Australia Jewry
- Franciscan Friars of the Province of the Holy Spirit – JPIC Committee
- God's Dwelling Place Bethany City Church Ic
- Granville Multicultural Community Centre
- Horn of Africa Relief and Development Agency
- House of Welcome
- Illawarra Multicultural Services
- Immigrant Women's Speakout
- Immigration Advice and Rights Centre
- Jesuit Refugee Services Australia
- Lao Community Advancement NSW Cooperative
- Liverpool Migrant Resource Centre
- Mercy Works Ltd
- Mt Druitt Ethnic Communities Agency
- Multicultural Council of Wagga Wagga
- Neighbours and Friends
- Nepean Migrant Access
- Nothern Settlement Services
- NSW Community Relations Commission
- NSW Council for Civil Liberties
- NSW Refugee Health Service
- NSW Teachers Federation
- Pax Christi Australia (NSW) Inc
- Psychiatry Research & Training Unit, Liverpool Hospital
- Queanbeyan Multilingual Centre
- RACS (Refugee Advice and Casework Service)
- Rural Australians for Refugees (Braidwood NSW)
- SCARF (Strategic Community Assistance to Refugee Families)
- Settlement Services International
- Sister of St Joseph of Orange, California
- St Anthony's Family Care
- St Bede's Social Justice Group
- St George Migrant Resource Centre
- St George Youth Services
- St James' Church, King St, Sydney
- St Vincent de Paul Society Refugee and Asylum Seeker Services
- STARTTS (NSW Service for the Treatment and Rehabilitation or Torture and Trauma Survivors)
- Sydney Multicultural Community Services
- SydWest Multicultural Services
- The Mercy Foundation
- The Multicultural Network
- Waverley Council
- West Wagga San Isidore Refugee Committee

Unspecified (40)
- ACFID (Australian Council for International Development)
- Act for Peace (National Council of Churches in Australia)
- ActionAid Australia
- Adventist Development and Relief Agency Australia Ltd
- Amnesty International Australia
- ANCORW (Australian National Committee on Refugee Women)
- Association for the Wellbeing of Children in Health
- Australian Council of Trade Unions (ACTU) – International Section
- Australian Education Union
- Australian Red Cross
- Baptist Care Australia
- B'nai B'rith Australia / New Zealand
- Caritas Australia
- Catholic Religious Australia
- Catholics in Coalition for Justice and Peace
- ChilOut
- Coptic International Union Ltd
- Foundation House (Victorian Fooundation for Survivors of Torture)
- International Commission of Jurists, Australian Section
- Islamic Relief Australia
- Josephite Community Aid
- Life Without Barriers
- Marist Sisters
- Marist Youth Care
- Missionaries of the Sacred Heart, Justice and Peace Centre
- Occupational Opportunities for Refugees and Asylum Seekers Inc
- Overseas Services to Survivors of Torture and Trauma
- Oxfam Australia
- Salvation Army
- Sanctuary Australia Foundation
- Save the Children Australia
- Sisters of Charity of Australia
- Sisters of Mercy in Australia, Institute Mission Team
- Sisters of the Good Samaritan
- South Australian Refugee Health Network
- St Vincent de Paul Society National Council of Australia
- Tasmanian Catholic Justice and Peace Commission
- Uniting Church National Assembly
- Uniting justice Australia
- World Vision Australia

Vic (40)
- Aireys Inlet Rural Australians for Refugees
- AMES (Adult Multicultural Education Services)
- Asylum Seekers Resource Centre
- Australian Karen Foundation
- Ballarat Community Health
- Ballarat Regional Multicultural Council
- Bhutanese Organisation in Australia Inc
- Brotherhood of St Laurence Ecumenical Migration Centre
- Centre for Multicultural Youth
- Cohealth
- Diversitat
- FamilyCare
- Fitzroy Learning Network
- Good Shepherd Mission and Justice
- International Society for Human Rights Australia Inc
- Jesuit Social Services
- Jewish Aid Australia
- Lentara UnitingCare Asylum Seeker Program
- Liberians for Empowerment and Development
- Liverpool Campaspe Multicultural Services
- Melbourne Catholic Migrant and Refugee Office
- Mercy Community Services SEQ Ltd
- New Hope Foundation
- Oromia Support Group in Australia
- Pratt Family Foundation
- RILC (Refugee and Imigration Legal Centre)
- SCAAB (Springvale Community Aid and Advice Bureau)
- SEAAC (Southern Ethnic Advisory and Advocacy Council)
- SORA (Sudanese Online Research Association) & SAIL (Sudanese Australian Integrated Learning Program)
- Southern Migrant and Refugee Centre
- Spectrum Migrant Resource Centre
- St Macartan's Parish Social Justice Group
- UnitingCare Cutting Edge
- Victorian Arabic Social Services
- Victorian Multicultural Commission
- Western Region Ethnic Communities Council
- Whittlesea Community Connections
- Wimmera Development Association (Wimmera Settlement Association)
- Women's Health in the South East
- Wyndham Community and Education Centre

WA (15)
- ASeTTS (Association for Services to Torture and Trauma Survivors)
- Baptcare
- CARAD (Coalition for Asylum Seekers Refugees and Detainees)
- Centacare Inc
- Communicare
- Edmund Rice Centre, Mirrabooka
- Fremantle Multicultural Centre
- ISHAR Multicultural Women's Health Centre
- Life Support Ministries Inc.
- Metro Migrant Resource Centre
- Multicultural Services Centre of WA
- Organisation for Support to underprivileged Children and Women of Afghanistan, Inc
- SCALES Community Legal Centre
- St Vincent de Paul Society Migrant and Refugee Committee
- The Humanitarian Group

NGO Example 1 – ASRC

The Asylum Seeker Resource Centre (ASRC) is Australia's largest asylum seeker advocacy, aid and health organisation with an aim to promote and protect the human rights of asylum seekers. Its stated vision is that all those seeking asylum in Australia have their human rights upheld and that those seeking asylum within the Australian community receive the support and opportunities they need to live independently[23].

ASRC Core Principles:

- Assist all asylum seekers regardless of race, religion, gender, health or sexuality.
- Advocate for asylum seekers without fear or favour, and work at both an individual and structural level in trying to create the most just refugee determination system possible.
- Empower asylum seekers and foster their independence and self-determination.
- Engage, educate and work with the community as the key to creating social change.
- Work from a holistic model of practice that sees the entire person.
- Work from a social justice model that is committed to human rights.
- Remain an independent organisation at all times and do not accept funding that will compromise independence or work quality.
- Value an organisational culture which is responsive to the needs and wants of asylum seekers and involves volunteers as the heart of the work force.

ASRC Services:

- **Client Services:** case management to educate an individual regarding services and legal rights as well as connect them with relevant support networks.
- **Legal Services:** legal support and assistance through the individual's protection visa application process.
- **Food and Aid:** provision of culturally specific food and meals as well as basic bedding and clothing (important as asylum seekers have no guarantee to income).
- **Health Services:** a broad range of health services, mostly provided pro-bono.
- **Employment, Training and Skills Development:** training and education (including language, skills, systems within Australian society) to help maximise employment opportunity.

---

23   "Asylum Seeker Resource Centre: About Us," Asylum Seeker Resource Centre, accessed July 24, 2016 <https://www.asrc.org.au/about-us/>.

- **Social Enterprise:** employment of Asylum Seekers through two enterprises (ASRC Catering, ASRC Cleaning).
- **Community Enterprises:** community engagement programs to educate and raise awareness of the situation faced by asylum seekers and to raise funds for such programs.

NGO Example 2 – RILC

The Refugee and Immigration Legal Centre (RILC) is Australia's largest provider of legal services regarding refugee and immigration law, including key legal assistance to those who could not otherwise obtain it due to financial and other forms of disadvantage (such as cultural, linguistic and exposure to trauma and torture). It has about ten full-time staff members and a team of volunteers that assist around 5,000 people each year[24].

RILC Services:
- **Telephone Advice:** dedicated immigration advice line open 8 hours per week.
- **In-person Advice:** weekly face-to-face Evening Advice Service.
- **Casework:** full application casework/legal representation service.
- **Special Projects:** include monthly Offshore Refugee 'Family Reunion' Visa clinics.
- **Community Education:** extensive professional and community-based education programs.
- **Advocacy:** active and wide-ranging advocacy and law reform program.
- **Volunteer Program:** involving around 80 legal and non-legal volunteers.

The range of casework and advice undertaken by RILC includes:
- Applications for:
  - Protection Visas (refugee status) in Australia.
  - Sponsorship under the Family Stream, including of spouse, fiancé, children and other family members from overseas.
  - Change of status for those seeking permanent residence in Australia.

---

[24] "Refugee Legal: Overview," Refugee & Immigration Legal Centre, accessed July 24, 2016 <www.rilc.org.au/About-Rilc/Overview>.

- Advice on:
  - How to propose people overseas under the Refugee and Special Humanitarian program.
  - Options for people held in immigration detention, including local and remote detention centres.
  - All other migration visa categories, including re-entry or return visas.
  - Conditions attached to visas, such as permission to work, Medicare eligibility and 'no further stay'.
  - Visa cancellation matters.
  - Options for over-stayers and other 'unlawful non-citizens'.
- Representation in cases before:
  - The Department of Immigration and Citizenship (DIAC).
  - The migration tribunals (Refugee Review Tribunal and Migration Review Tribunal).
  - The Administrative Appeals Tribunal (AAT) on visa cancellation and refusals on 'character' grounds.
- Involvement in 'test case' litigation.
- Referrals for:
  - Legal advice and representation on appeals to the Courts, including to the Federal Magistrates Court, Federal Court or High Court of Australia.
  - Counselling and assistance on related health and welfare issues such as accommodation, medical care, social security, and counselling for torture and trauma survivors.

History of Australia's Humanitarian Program

During the nineteenth century various groups arrived in Australia fleeing religious persecution in Europe. The first group is considered to be the Lutherans from Eastern Prussia, (modern day Russia, Poland and Lithuania) who arrived in South Australia in 1837. Other significant groups in the nineteenth century included Hungarians, Italians and Poles[25].

---

25 "History of Australia's refugee program," Refugee Council of Australia, accessed July 24, 2016 <www.refugeecouncil.org.au/getfacts/history-australias-refugee-program/>.

Between Federation and World War II, refugees could settle as unassisted migrants so long as they were considered acceptable within the criteria of the White Australia Policy. Such migrant arrivals during this period were small, the main groups being Russians, Greeks, Bulgarians, Armenians, Assyrians and Jews. From 1933 to 1939, 7,000 Jews fled Nazi Germany to Australia. In 1937, the Australian Jewish Welfare Society pioneered Australia's first refugee settlement support service with financial assistance from the Australian Government. However, it was short lived as it ended with the outbreak of the war.

1945-1975

The aftermath of World War II saw high numbers of displaced people seeking to emigrate from Europe. This corresponded with Australia seeking to increase its population as protection against the threat of invasion from the northern 'Yellow Peril'. In 1947 Australia made an agreement with the International Refugee Organisation (the precursor to the UNHCR discussed in Chapter 4) and 170,000 people were resettled in the following seven years. The largest groups were from Poland, Yugoslavia, Latvia, Lithuania, Estonia, Ukraine, Czechoslovakia and Hungary.

The Refugee Convention, drafted in 1951, was ratified by Australia in 1954. Although Australia assumed the obligations held under the Convention, as discussed earlier these obligations are not bound by any enforceable law. The next influx of refugees to Australia followed the failed Hungarian revolution of 1956.

When the Dutch transferred West Papua over to Indonesia in 1963, Australia's first ever land border to a potential group of refugees was created. This was in the form of West Papuans fleeing Indonesian persecution into Papua New Guinea, which up until its independence in 1975 was under Australian administration. This event aroused some fear about the numbers that might present to Australia. The Minister for Foreign Affairs, Sir Garfield Barwick told his department officers that they 'should not be too infected with the British notion of being a home for the oppressed'[26].

This governmental concern was reflected in Australia's hesitance in signing the 1967 Protocol to the Refugee Convention. Australia agreed to recognise refugees beyond Europe but did not sign the protocol based on concerns of unlimited obligations towards asylum seekers. Australia 'was unhappy about allowing to stay within her borders, as the Protocol might well have required her to do, any number of Papuans or West Irianese'[27].

---

26 Frank Brennan, *Tampering with Asylum (Digitial Edition)* (Australia: University of Queensland Press, 2014), 24 of 253, iBooks edition.
27 Ibid.

The Whitlam Government eventually signed the Protocol in 1973 but with a caveat that the provisions were not extended to Papua New Guinea. The implication being that Australia did not see itself as a Country of First Asylum.

Refugees arrived from many areas during the late 1960s and early 1970s. In 1968 there were refugees following the invasion of Czechoslovakia; in 1972, Asian refugees expelled from Idi Amin's Uganda; in 1973 Chilean refugees following its military coup; in 1974, Cypriot refugees following Turkish invasion; and in 1975 East Timorese refugees.

1975-1990

With the 1975 fall of South Vietnam and the widespread flight from that country, Australia was prompted to change its refugee program. The Australian Senate's Standing Committee on Foreign Affairs and Defence identified an urgent need for a new approach to refugee settlement. The Senate's committee made recommendations regarding refugee settlement which ultimately resulted in a dedicated and planned humanitarian program. During the next twenty years, over 100,000 refugees came from various Asian countries. During that time, Australia took more Indo-Chinese refugees per capita than any other nation[28]. Only a very small portion, approximately 2,000, came to Australia directly by boat.

Australia's first planned humanitarian program commenced in 1977. The National Refugee Policy was established including procedures for responding to refugee situations. Approaches were made to voluntary agencies for their involvement. In addition to this policy, the Galbally Report in 1978 reviewed the post-arrival programs and services, and made a series of recommendations. Implementation of these recommendations included language teaching, settlement services and other migrant services. In 1978 the Government set up the Determination of Refugee Status (DORS) committee to act as Australia's RSD and determine onshore refugee claims[29].

The early 1980s were the high point with regard to refugee intake numbers. The annual intake rose to 22,000, the largest number since the introduction of the National Refugee Policy. The bulk of these refugees were Vietnamese who were resettled from camps in Asia.

The mix of refugee Country of Origin grew greatly in the mid to late 1980s. One hundred and six Ethiopians were included in the 1984 refugee program, being the first significant group of Africans to enter Australia by this mechanism. There were increased intakes from Eastern Europe, the Middle East, Afghanistan, Sri Lanka, East Timor and Latin America

---

28 John Howard, *Lazarus Rising (Revised Edition)*, (Australia: HarperCollins, 2013), 321 of 765, iBooks edition.
29 Frank Brennan, *Tampering with Asylum (Digitial Edition)* (Australia: University of Queensland Press, 2014), 35 of 253, iBooks edition.

off-setting the declining intake from Indochina. There was also significant change in the Refugee Status Determination process. In 1985, the High Court determined that ministerial decisions were reviewable by Courts, this meant the refugee status was now to be a matter of the law and paved the way for the Administrative Appeals Tribunal (AAT) and the Refugee Review Tribunal (RRT)[30].

The first Torture and Trauma Services Centres opened in 1989. This was in response to the recognition of the need to treat the psychosocial impacts of persecution and conflict. The Women at Risk Visa was introduced in 1989. Since then, 8,800 refugee women and their children have been resettled.

1991-2000

The Mandatory Detention Policy was introduced in 1992. This detained all 'unlawful non-citizens' (those without visas) who arrived at an 'excised offshore place'. Perhaps surprisingly, the initial focus of the Mandatory Detention was not deterrence but rather to isolate them from lawyers so that their public description as economic migrants would hold[31].

The Humanitarian Program was separated from the Migration Program in 1993. The new process, existing today, is for the places available under both programs to be reviewed and adjusted by the Government on an annual basis. In 1996 the Howard government separately identified and linked the 'Onshore' and 'Offshore' programs. The linkage of these two programs meant the total number of places allowed across both programs can be controlled to a target. This enables budgetary and resettlement services to be planned. So effectively, for every additional onshore visa granted, one less offshore visa is available.

2001-2016

Just one month before the September 11 attacks in 2001, Australia refused to take in 434 potential 'unauthorised arrivals'. They were rescued from a boat that had left Indonesia by the Norwegian ship MV Tampa. International attention was drawn to the incident and Australia's obligations to people in distress as a signatory to the Refugee Convention. Ultimately these people were processed in New Zealand and Nauru. The Tampa incident was not an isolated event, the number of asylum seekers presenting as IMAs had grown from under 500 in 1995 to 5,500 in 2001. In response to the growing number of IMAs,

---

30 Ibid.
31 Ibid, 37 of 253.

and very shortly after the Tampa incident, the Pacific Solution was commenced by the Howard Government. This involved the excising of 5,000 islands from Australia's migration zone, and the formal policy of processing of IMAs in Papua New Guinea and Nauru. In conjunction with these actions, Operation Relex commenced, which effectively turned back IMAs. Suspected Illegal Entry Vessels (SIEVs) were intercepted and denied entry to Australian waters. In the context of post September 11 security concerns, these initiatives were broadly accepted by the Australian public.

From 2002, the number of IMAs had returned to low levels. By this time, the refugee Countries of Origin had become predominantly African, around 70%. In 2008 the Pacific Solution was closed down by the Rudd Government. From this point the number of asylum seekers arriving as IMAs increased immediately and rapidly from 2,700 in 2009 up to 16,000 in 2012. The number of arrivals again became a political issue and several policy options were explored. In 2011, the Malaysia Agreement, announced by the Australian Government that July was blocked by the Australian High Court in August. The Report of the Expert Panel on Asylum Seekers (Houston Report), commissioned by the Gillard Government to stop asylum seeker deaths at sea, was released in August 2012. Among a number of policy changes it recommended the reintroduction of the Pacific Solution. Offshore processing was re-introduced in 2013 by the Rudd Government.

Following the 2013 election, Operation Sovereign Borders was introduced by the newly-elected Abbott Government. Like Operation Relex under the Howard Government, Operation Sovereign Borders aimed to deter asylum seekers to Australia by denying them access. This was done through intercepting the boats and turning them back. The limited information regarding these operations, as well as whether there have been any boat arrivals, has been criticised. Between December 2013, and August 2015, the Government reported that 20 vessels were turned back containing 633 people[32]. By 2014, the refugee intake split in even thirds across Africa, Asia and the Middle East[33].

---

32 Hasham, Nicole, "In a rare disclosuure, Abbott goverment admits turning back 633 asylum seekers," *The Sydney Morning Herald,* August 6, 2015.
33 "History of Australia's refugee program", Refugee Council of Australia, accessed 3 December 2016 <http://www.refugeecouncil.org.au/getfacts/seekingsafety/refugee-humanitarian-program/history-australias-refugee-program/>..

CH 10. AUSTRALIA'S DEBATE

Australia's Offshore Program that contributes to the UNHCR's resettlement program is of little controversy. It should not be confused with the offshore processing component of Australia's Onshore Program. Australia continues to be one of the world's largest voluntary recipients of refugees and people qualifying for Special Humanitarian visas. As detailed above, once within Australia, these people are provided with a very high-quality level of support through Australia's welfare system, which is generous by world standards. Various NGOs also assist refugees and humanitarian visa holders to access a range of community support networks. The contention with the Offshore Program is regarding how many refugees Australia should take in each year.

Conversely, there is much controversy surrounding the Onshore Program and its system of deterrence toward people who would be Irregular Maritime Arrivals (IMAs). Opponents of the system raise concerns regarding the high cost, the efficacy in deterring would-be asylum seekers, and most critically the arguable violations of the human rights of the asylum seekers.

Offshore Program

Australia is a significant contributor to the UNHCR resettlement program, one of the countries providing the highest number of placements each year. However, Australia's full contribution towards refugees, including both resettlement as well as onshore arrivals, is far less generous in comparison to other nations. Indeed, Australia's remoteness and strict policies towards IMAs limits the number of asylum seekers in the Onshore Program when compared to other countries. It is these low numbers within the Onshore Program that enable Australia to have one of the most generous resettlement programs in the world. Even though resettlement through Australia's Offshore Program is one of the most generous in the world, is it large enough?

Australia's Humanitarian Program provided 13,750 visas each year, of which 11,000 per year were resettlement places. In 2012-13 they were lifted to 20,000 overall as per the recommendation of the Houston Report before being wound back to 13,750 with the change of government in 2013. Outside of the special 12,000 places provided to Syrian refugees, the intake via the Offshore Program is budgeted to be 11,000 people per year until 2016-17 with an indication of increases to 16,250 and 18,750 in 2017-18 and 2018-19 respectively. These numbers are still lower than those recommended by the Houston Report, which was to increase the Humanitarian Program to 27,000 by 2018[1].

The number of refugees that a wealthy country can bring in annually is open to debate. Germany's acceptance of over one million refugees (roughly 1.25% of their population) in 2015 has sparked concern from many residents and commentators that it risks damaging its culture and security. Indeed, this proportion of refugees is larger than what most countries accept as immigrants annually. Canada and Australia, two countries in the developed world with the largest number of migrants, generally accept around 1% of their population in migrants each year. Only a small proportion of this has traditionally been refugees.

Onshore Program

Australia's annual cost of detention and processing of asylum seekers totalled A$2.9 billion in 2014-15[2]. This is under 1% of the nation's total budget revenue[3]. Much of this expense was due to maintaining the high cost of offshore processing and Mandatory Detention Centres. Detention centres, be they offshore or within Australia, cost much more than processing refugees in community detention or allowing them to live in the community on Bridging Visas.

The per asylum seeker costs are:

- A$400,000 each year in offshore detention.
- A$239,000 each year in detention centres within Australia.
- A$100,000 each year in community detention.
- A$40,000 each year to live on a Bridging Visa[4].

Supporters of the high cost of detention centres point to their deterrence functions. Although the average cost per asylum seeker is more, the logic is that these centres will ultimately cost the government less by reducing the number of asylum seekers that arrive each year.

---

1   Angus Houston, Paris Aristotle and Michael l"Estrange, "Report of the Expert Panel on Asylum Seekers",(August, 2012), 14.
2   "2015-16 Federal Budget in Brief: What it means for refugees and people seeking humanitarian protection," Refugee Council of Australia, accessed Juy 24, 2016 <www.refugeecouncil.org.au/wp-content/uploads/2014/08/2015-16-Budhet.pdf>.
3   "Budget 2014-15, Statement 5: Revenue," Australian Government, accessed July 23, 2016 <www.budget.gov.au/2014-15/content/bp1/html/bp1_bst5-01.html>
4   Jane McAdam and Fiona Chong, *Refugees: Why seeking asylum is legal and Australia's policies are not,* (Sydney: NewSouth Publishing, 2014), 182.

Efficacy of Deterrence

The questions of whether Mandatory Detention is successful in deterring asylum seekers from coming to Australia, and the ethics of such a system if indeed successful, garner conflicting views. Defenders of the efficacy of recent deterrence policies cite data including:

- The introduction of the first Pacific Solution under the Howard government in 2001 quickly reduced the number of IMAs to less than 100 per year after a number of years of increasing arrivals (up to 5,516 in 2001)[5]. IMA arrivals stayed low until 2008-09 when the program was withdrawn by the Rudd Government. This was followed by a rise in arrivals growing each year to 18,000 in 2012-13. After the second incarnation of the Pacific Solution was reintroduced in 2012 the IMA numbers once again reduced. With the implementation of Operation Sovereign Borders, arrivals are seemingly approaching zero. At the time of writing (October 2015), the last IMA transferred to immigration officials had occurred in December 2013.

- The large number of asylum seekers from the Middle East and North Africa who arrived in Europe in 2015 is an indication of the vast number of people who have an incentive — be it security or economically-driven — to seek a better life in a developed country. That few have tried to enter Australia may be taken as evidence of the efficacy of the program's deterrence effect.

- Another aspect from the European refugee crisis since 2015 is that technology is increasingly used to share information among people who are seeking asylum. Information regarding what channels work and how to best achieve entry and claim for asylum is now flowing almost instantaneously. This supports an argument that information regarding the relative attractiveness of a country's humanitarian channels is now quickly communicated.

Critics of the effect of deterrence policies argue:

- The diabolical state of affairs many asylum seekers face in their homeland, or indeed the countries on the way to Australia, are so poor that their current situation outweighs any disincentives that may be faced upon arrival. Even though Australia has one of the toughest detention regimes in the Western world, people still attempt entry because of a lack of alternatives.

- Studies reveal asylum seekers seem to know very little about the policies of the countries of refuge before they arrive[6].

---

5 John Howard, *Lazarus Rising (Revised Edition)*, (Australia: HarperCollins, 2013), 322 of 765, iBooks edition.
6 Jane McAdam and Fiona Chong, *Refugees: Why seeking asylum is legal and Australia's policies are not*, (Sydney: NewSouth Publishing, 2014), 104.

- Detention is a public demonstration that the Department has Australia's borders "under control" - even if it does not in terms of the number of onshore illegal immigrants[7].

Ethics of Deterrence

Regardless of how much the deterrence framework of Australia's Onshore Program costs, or how effective it is, there is also much debate regarding the ethics of a deterrence framework. In essence the debate is about whether access to Australia should be constrained, the conditions made less hospitable, and the chance of resettlement into the country be limited in order to deter more potential asylum seekers from arriving, even if not all of them are truly refugees.

Critics of Australia's deterrence policies argue they are unethical and breach a host of international conventions, most notably individual human rights as set out in the 1948 Declaration of Human Rights. Conversely, defenders of the deterrence policies point out there is a potential overwhelming number of would-be asylum seekers that would arrive in Australia without such policies in place. Such numbers could greatly threaten Australia's economic and social stability, and ultimately the human rights of the inhabitants of that nation. It also risks the many lives that would attempt the journey to arrive as an IMA.

Issues with Australia's Onshore Program

As discussed previously, due to Australia's dualist system, none of its international commitments are enforceable by domestic law unless they are also included in Australia's 1958 Migration Act. Regardless of whether or not any breaches are enforceable, there are a number of human rights concerns that have been raised regarding Australia's asylum seeker process. In particular, unauthorised arrivals in the Onshore Program. Jane McAdam's and Fiona Chong's book *Refugees: Why seeking asylum is legal and Australia's policies are not*[8] does an excellent job at identifying the key concerns.

Enhanced Screening

The Enhanced Screening approach has attracted criticism from the UNHCR as being unfair and unreliable. For instance, asylum seekers are not provided with the information that they have the right for legal representation unless they specifically ask. Arguments have also

---

[7] Frank Brennan, *Tampering with Asylum (Digitial Edition)* (Australia: University of Queensland Press, 2014), 41-42 of 253, iBooks edition.
[8] Jane McAdam and Fiona Chong, *Refugees: Why seeking asylum is legal and Australia's policies are not,* (Sydney: NewSouth Publishing, 2014).

been raised about the high risk of this step in wrongly 'screening out' legitimate refugees[9]. These arguments are supported by a case involving 41 Sri Lankan asylum seekers in July 2014. Their boat was intercepted attempting to enter Australia and the asylum seekers were processed through advanced screening. They were screened out at sea, denied access to Australia and were returned to Sri Lanka. Some subsequently fled to Nepal where the UNHCR found them to be legitimate refugees, indicating the enhanced screening may have incorrectly 'screened out' the asylum seekers in the view of the UNHCR[10].

Mandatory Detention

Mandatory Detention applies to a large range of people who are deemed to be 'unlawful citizens' by events such as overstaying their visa or having their visa cancelled. However, in practice, it is used mainly for asylum seekers who arrive without a valid visa. For example, the majority of people who are unlawful citizens through overstaying their visa are provided Bridging Visas. Thus, 95% of people in Immigration Detention are asylum seekers[11].

Although the Migration Act 1958 allows for a system of Mandatory Detention, critics of the process argue it violates international human rights as without liberty a person is unable to enjoy other human rights.

Mandatory Detention breaches Article 9 of ICCPR which prohibits arbitrary detention[12]. Critics of mandatory detention argue that in Australia criminals are treated to a fairer detention process than asylum seekers. Criminals receive a transparent judicial process that takes into account their individual circumstances in sentencing, are provided a finite sentence, and are provided the opportunity to appeal. By contrast, even though asylum seekers have not committed any crime, they are detained automatically and possibly indefinitely. Moreover, their detention cannot be reviewed to assess whether it is necessary or reasonable.

Mandatory detention also breaches a number of articles of the Convention of the Rights of the Child (CRC) including Article 37(b) which states that no child shall be deprived of his or her liberty arbitrarily[13], and Article 31 of the Refugee Convention which prohibits imposing penalties through entering without authorisation[14].

---

9   Ibid 47.
10 "Recent changes in Australian refugee policy," Refugee Council of Australia, last updated July 2016, accessed July 24, 2016 <www.refugeecounil.org.au/wp-content/uploads/2016/07/Australia-refugee-policy-changes-July-2016.pdf>.
11 Jane McAdam and Fiona Chong, *Refugees: Why seeking asylum is legal and Australia's policies are not*, (Sydney: NewSouth Publishing, 2014), 89.
12 UN General Assembly, *International Covenant on Civil and Political Rights*, December 16, 1966, United Nations, Treaty Series, vol. 999, 171.
13 UN General Assembly, *Convention on the Rights of the Child*, November 20, 1989, United Nations, Treaty Series, vol. 1577, 3.
14 *Convention relating to the Status of Refugees*, opened for signature 28 July 1951 (entered into force 22 April 1954) read together with the *Protocol relating to the Status of Refugees*, opened for signature 31 January 1967 (entered into force 4 October 1967).

Under international law, detention is only lawful if it is reasonable, necessary and proportionate in all circumstances, and can be periodically reviewed. Asylum seekers can raise alleged breaches with the Commonwealth Ombudsman or the Australian Human Rights Commission. If the Commission determines a breach has occurred it can issue recommendations but it cannot enforce them. This lack of judicial oversight of Mandatory Detention breaches Article 2(b) of ICCPR[15]. In August 2013, the UN Human Rights Committee said that in certain circumstances, Australia's indefinite Mandatory Detention breached article 7 of ICCPR, torture or cruel, inhuman or degrading treatment or punishment as well as Article 10 of ICCPR treating people with humanity and with respect to their inherent dignity[16].

Asylum seekers have no clear idea how long they will stay in the centres. Not surprisingly, the prison-like environment and uncertainty for the future create huge mental strains. As early as in 1993 cases of depression and anxiety were reported among some of the detainees. There is now significant and mounting evidence of psychological harm associated with detention of asylum seekers through the Onshore Program. This applies regardless of whether the processing is onshore or offshore. Already vulnerable because of the events in their home countries that caused them to leave, these people continue to meet with danger, fear and sustained uncertainty throughout their bid for asylum. The available evidence indicates that the effects are often cumulative and can lead to psychiatric impairment, creating new disorders or exacerbating existing problems[17].

> "It's hard to wake up in the morning knowing I am in jail separated from the world and from life by razor wire as if I have committed the worst offence imaginable." (Jamil, Iraqi refugee)[18]

The Pacific Solution

> "The idea underpinning the policy of the Pacific Solution is that inferior conditions on Nauru and Manus Island, the lack of legal advice, the absence of well-developed processing and review mechanisms, and delayed resettlement times (around five years) would deter asylum seekers from getting on boats to Australia[19]."

---

15 Jane McAdam and Fiona Chong, *Refugees: Why seeking asylum is legal and Australia's policies are not*, (Sydney: NewSouth Publishing, 2014), 95.
16 Ibid 96.
17 *Alternatives to Offshore Processing: Submissions to the Expert Panel on Asylum Seekers 2012*, (Australia: Labor for Refugees, 2013), 24.
18 Jane McAdam and Fiona Chong, *Refugees: Why seeking asylum is legal and Australia's policies are not*, (Sydney: NewSouth Publishing, 2014), 95.
19 Ibid 120.

The Pacific Solution raises concerns regarding the adequacy and efficacy of both the Nauru and Manus Island sites. These concerns include the countries not signing (or providing conditional signing to) many international conventions. Given this, there is a chance of many human rights infringements to asylum seekers including chain refoulement due to an absence of robust refugee status determination procedures in Nauru and PNG[20]. While the Refugee Convention doesn't prohibit offshore processing, it is probable the drafters didn't envisage it occurring. Asylum seekers whose protection claims are processed offshore do not have the same speed of access to the lawyers and non-government agencies as those processed onshore. Nor do they have the same rights of review (for example the RRT) as those who are processed onshore.

> "If other countries were to emulate the Pacific Solution, asylum seekers would be routinely traded across the world by first-world countries anxious to maintain the integrity of their borders. Asylum seekers would be exported to third-world countries desirous of improving their terms of trade[21]."

In October of 2015, the High Court heard a case regarding a Bangladeshi woman detained on Nauru who came to Australia for medical complications late in her pregnancy. It was the lead case linked to a series of challenges on behalf of 260 asylum seekers who were detained in Nauru but brought to the Australian mainland for medical emergencies. It is an example of the moving goalposts concerning the practice and legality of the Pacific Solution.

The case originally challenged the lawfulness of the Australian government spending money on offshore detention centres in a foreign jurisdiction. The Abbott Government passed legislation that retrospectively provided it that authority. The case then challenged whether Australia had the constitutional power to detain people on foreign soil. Two days before that hearing it was announced that the Nauru centre was open and asylum seekers who were sent there were now free to move around the island[22]. In February of 2016 the High Court found the arrangements valid under the Constitution[23].

---

20   Ibid 128.
21   Frank Brennan, *Tampering with Asylum (Digitial Edition)* (Australia: University of Queensland Press, 2014), 95 of 253, iBooks edition.
22   Paige Taylor, "Christmas Island braces for High Court detention judgement," *The Australian,* February 1, 2016.
23   Elizabeth Byrne and Stephanie Anderson,"High Court throws out challenge to Nauru offshore immigration detention," *ABC News,* updated February 8, 2016.

Children in Detention

Australia has obligations to ensure alternative care for children who arrive as unaccompanied asylum seekers. A key element is providing effective guardianship in the absence of the child's parents. Under Australian law, the legal guardian for 'non-citizen' unaccompanied children is the Federal Minister for Immigration and Border Protection. As the legal guardian, the Minister has the primary responsibility for the upbringing and development of the child and is under a CRC obligation to act in the best interests of the child.

The Australian Human Rights Commission raised concerns the Minister's role as guardian of unaccompanied children creates a conflict of interest. The Minister is also responsible for administering immigration detention, granting visas and transferring children to Nauru. Given these other responsibilities, the Commission argues it is difficult for the Minister to make the best interests of the child the primary consideration[24].

The National Inquiry into Children in Immigration Detention was conducted by the Australian Human Rights Commission in 2014. It found that prolonged, mandatory detention of asylum seeker children causes them significant mental and physical illness and developmental delays. This is in breach of Australia's international obligations[25].

By holding children in detention for longer than is strictly required to conduct health, identity and security checks, three articles of the CRC were found to be violated[26]:

- Article 3(1) requires that all actions concerning children, the best interests of the child should be the primary consideration.
- Article 24(1) provides all children have the right to the highest attainable standard of health.
- Article 37(b) requires children should only be detained as a measure of last resort, and for the shortest appropriate period of time.

The inquiry also found that at various times children in immigration detention were not in a position to fully enjoy their rights under[27]:

- Article 6 provides that children have a right to live a full life and governments should ensure that children survive and develop healthily.
- Article 19 requires governments to ensure children are properly cared for and protected from violence, abuse and neglect by their parents, or anyone else that looks after them.

---

24 "Information about children in immigration detention," Australian Human Rights Commission, last updated January 6, 2016, accessed July 24, 2016 <https://www.humanrights.gov.au/information-about-children-immigration-detention>.
25 Ibid.
26 Ibid.
27 Ibid.

- Article 24 provides children have the right to good quality health care, clean water, nutritious food and a clean environment so they will stay healthy.
- Article 27 provides children have the right to a standard of living that is good enough to meet their physical and mental needs.
- Article 37 provides children who break the law should not be treated cruelly. They should not be imprisoned and should be able to keep in contact with their family.

The numbers of children in closed immigration detention centres were at unprecedented levels in the months leading up to this inquiry, reaching 1,992 in July 2013. Since the inquiry the numbers have reduced significantly. Only 174 children were in closed immigration centres in November 2015.

Operation Sovereign Borders

Operation Sovereign Borders risks breaching international refugee law and human rights law if it turns back boats without assessing refugee claims made by those on board. An additional issue arose with an allegation that in May 2015 Australian Security Intelligence Service officials made payments to people smugglers to return 65 asylum seekers, who were intercepted on a boat heading towards Australia, back to Indonesia[28]. Amnesty International argues that not only did this put lives at risk but is also a transnational crime[29]. The Australian Government refused to comment on these claims 'for security reasons'[30].

Character Check

The Character Check conducted as part of the Onshore Program is controversial as protection may be denied for certain kinds of crimes or conduct (or suspicion of), which are not specified in the Refugee Convention. If Australia denies a refugee a protection visa on character grounds, and the refugee cannot be sent home due to non-refoulement obligations, unless another country is willing to resettle the refugee, the refugee will end up in indefinite detention.

This is arguably a violation of human rights and at times potentially a wholly disproportionate response to the original crime committed or perceived risk. Examples of such conduct include actions as innocuous as property damage and spitting[31].

---

28 "Recent changes in Australian refugee policy," Refugee Council of Australia, last updated July 2016, accessed July 24, 2016 <www.refugeecounil.org.au/wp-content/uploads/2016/07/Australia-refugee-policy-changes-July-2016.pdf>.
29 "Report: Evidence of public officials' involvement in criminal activity," *Amnesty International*, October 29, 2015.
30 "Recent changes in Australian refugee policy," Refugee Council of Australia, last updated July 2016, accessed July 24, 2016 <www.refugeecounil.org.au/wp-content/uploads/2016/07/Australia-refugee-policy-changes-July-2016.pdf>.
31 Jane McAdam and Fiona Chong, *Refugees: Why seeking asylum is legal and Australia's policies are not*, (Sydney: NewSouth Publishing, 2014), 75.

Security Assessment

The Refugee Security Assessment is conducted by the Australian Security Intelligence Organisation (ASIO) to ensure the refugee does not pose a risk to national security. ASIO does not have to satisfy a high burden of proof and can issue an adverse assessment even if the risk of danger is relatively low. Decisions can only be reversed if errors of the law have been made, not if errors of fact have been made.

An example case was more than 50 Tamils from Sri Lanka who were denied protection visas due to an adverse security assessment by ASIO. They could not be removed from Australia because they faced the risk of persecution or significant harm in Sri Lanka. As a result they faced an indefinite detention in Australia, most have been detained for nearly five years. Several attempted suicide. Many comparable countries (including the United Kingdom, Canada and New Zealand) do not permit indefinite detention and have developed more humane alternatives[32].

Bridging Visas

Bridging Visas usually do not provide an asylum seeker the right to work. Various forms of assistance are available to people on Bridging Visas but often only to those most vulnerable. Regardless, without the ability to work life becomes mundane and demoralising. Arthur Brooks, president of the American Enterprise Institute, argues that 'earned success' is the key to human happiness[33]:

> *"The happiness rewards from work are not from the money, but from the value created in our lives and in the lives of others - value that is acknowledged and rewarded".*

Temporary Protection Visas (TPVs)

Temporary Protection Visas (TPVs) existed between 1998 and 2008. They were granted to people who had arrived by boat and allowed the recipient to remain in Australia for three years. After that time the recipient would have to apply for protection. However, there were a number of restrictions on the visa and it subjected the recipient to a high degree of uncertainty. Subsequently, there were a number of negative impacts on the recipients in terms of health, wellbeing and settlement outcomes[34]. The TPVs proved impractical,

---

32   Ibid.
33   Arthur C. Brooks, *The Conservative Heart: a new vision for the pursuit of happiness, earned success, and social justice*, (New York: HarperCollins, 2015), 19 of 134. IBook edition.
34   "Recent changes in Australian refugee policy," Refugee Council of Australia, last updated July 2016, accessed July 24, 2016 <www.refugeecounil.org.au/wp-content/uploads/2016/07/Australia-refugee-policy-changes-July-2016.pdf>.

because few people were ever able to return home in such a short period. By late 2007, 9,500 of the 11,300 TPVs granted had been granted permanent visas.

TPVs were reintroduced with some changes in 2015 for all people found to be owed protection, but who arrived in Australia without a prior visa. The new TPVs allow people to reapply for another TPV after three years but do not allow application for permanent protection. TPV holders are allowed to work and have access to Medicare and other assistance services like trauma counselling. However, they are not eligible for the full range of settlement services provided to other humanitarian entrants, like resettled refugees. For example, TPV visa holders cannot sponsor family members to come to Australia nor can they return to Australia if they leave.

Are Boat People Queue Jumpers?

For many years, people who have arrived in Australia without a valid visa and requested asylum have been labelled as queue jumpers. The terminology goes back at least to 1990 in a Bob Hawke interview on Channel 9's A Current Affair with Jana Wendt in regard to Cambodian boat people:

> "...we have an orderly migration program. We're not going to allow people just to jump that queue by saying we'll jump into a boat, here we are, bugger the people who've been around the world. We have a ratio of more than 10 to 1 of people who want to come to this country compared to the numbers we take in[35]."

Just as frequently as this label is used, counterpoints in defence of these arrivals, allowed for under the Refugee Convention, are made. The most direct being, that there is no queue. The two arguments can be summarised as follows:

The case why boat arrivals are not queue jumpers.

- The Refugee Convention mandates that people who arrive at a country and seek asylum are entitled to that protection and all other asylum rights as described under the Refugee Convention.
- The linking of Australia's Offshore Program's resettlement numbers with the Onshore Program's numbers within an overall humanitarian quota creates an artificial relationship between the two so that providing a visa to an Onshore arrival

---

[35] Frank Brennan, *Tampering with Asylum (Digitial Edition)* (Australia: University of Queensland Press, 2014), 38-39 of 253, iBook edition.

reduces the resettlement places by one. Thus, the notion of a resettlement spot being taken away by the actions of an IMA is due to policy alone.

- In many cases, the asylum seekers have no choice but to make the journey as an IMA as they are in grave peril.
- For those not in grave peril, there is no orderly queue where refugees simply wait their turn. Firstly, there are far more refugees than places. Secondly, there is no first-in first-out queue, instead resettlement submissions are given to priority cases similar to a hospital emergency department triage system. Given this process, as well as reports and opportunities for bribing and corruption, and people may simply be overlooked year after year.
- The inefficiencies of an under-resourced UNHCR mean there is no guarantee of being resettled in any reasonable time-frame, thus any rational person would consider risking their life to attempt to move into the Onshore Program by arriving as an IMA.

The case why boat arrivals are queue jumpers.

- There is a process by which refugees can apply for resettlement into a country of their choice through the UNHCR. Each year about 10% of those put forward for such resettlement are actually resettled in a new country.
- For the 90% who are not resettled, there is no guarantee they will ever be provided a place. The resettlement selection is not done via a first-in first-out queue mechanism. Thus, some people can wait for an indefinite length of time. Current obligations under the Refugee Convention mean that if a refugee arrives (e.g. as an IMA) at a country, they can apply for refugee status immediately and effectively utilise the protection of that country without having to wait to be selected for resettlement.
- By arriving as an IMA, the asylum seeker can bring forward the timing of their protection from a desired country. For countries that have a capped quota for their total refugee intake (as Australia has had since the mid-90s) then the place taken up by IMAs would be at the expense of those waiting for resettlement.

PART 2
The Complication, Principles & Assessment

Sections 2.1 & 2.2

Part 1 — Situation (Chapters 1-10)

Section 1.1
CH 1-7 Global Review
- Uses the *Refugee Journey* framework to review the global refugee situation. Including:
  - Disruptive Causes and Forcibly Displaced People.
  - Protection (i.e. as asylum seekers or refugees).
  - Durable Solutions (i.e. Repatriation, Local Integration or Resettlement).

Section 1.2
CH 8-10 Australian Review
- Reviews the Australian context including:
  - Australia's migration programs.
  - Australia's humanitarian program.
  - Controversy and debate surrounding Australia's humanitarian program.

Part 2 — Complication, Principles & Assessment Framework (Chapter 11-12)

Section 2.1
CH 11 The Complication
- Summarises the main issues identified through the global and Australian reviews.

Section 2.2
CH 12 Principles & Assessment Framework
- Outlines the Questions of Principle that must be answered to best manage the refugee situation.
- Sets out the approach option assessment framework.

Part 3 — Options & Recommendation (Chapters 13-17)

Section 3.1
CH 13-15 Options Assessment
- Summarises the various Component Policies.
- Summarises and assesses the various Holistic Approaches using the approach option assessment framework.

Section 3.2
CH 16-17 Discussion and Recommendation
- Discusses the trade-offs in selecting the best Holistic Approach Option.
- Recommends an approach and provides a pathway for implementation including Australia's next steps.

CH 11. THE COMPLICATION – THE MAIN PROBLEMS

With Part 1 Situation complete, what does this all mean? This next section will develop the background research to create a clear set of questions that must be answered to improve the refugee situation. It will also provide a framework for assessing the approach options that will be reviewed in Part 3.

Part 1 reviewed the steps of the Refugee Journey as well as Australia's Migration and Humanitarian Programs. From this review the main issues are now able to be identified. Collectively these issues make up the Complication. Identifying no issues would imply there is no Complication and the refugee situation was operating perfectly. This is not the case.

The framework of The Refugee Journey is again used, this time to catalogue the issues. One additional category is added – that of the affected party. The affected party is the individual or group that most suffers as a result of an issue. Although there are many potential affected parties, only two were relevant to the issues identified: those who have been forcibly displaced; or the countries attempting to help. Sometimes multiple parties were affected; in these cases only the most affected party is identified.

The output is the Complication – a list of ten issues that relate to the refugee situation. Each issue catalogued is within one of the three steps of The Refugee Journey and according to the party it most affects. From this list, the questions needed to be answered can then be created and the objectives of approach options detailed. These next steps are covered in Chapter 12.

STEP 1 ISSUES: No Protection

1. Large and growing number of Forcibly Displaced People.

With the inclusion of IDPs, the number of Forcibly Displaced People (59.5 million as at the end of 2014) is the largest of any time since World War II. These are people in desperate situations. Unfortunately, even this number is likely to be an understatement as many vulnerable people are likely to be hidden through discouragement of their situation and will only present themselves if and when more viable options are provided.

In addition to the current numbers of Forcibly Displaced People, the future need is quite likely to be greater still. Alarmingly, the countries that are most likely to produce refugees are growing the fastest. Of the top ten Countries of Origin of Forcibly Displaced People, eight of them have TFR of four or more against a global average of 2.4.

2. People harmed due to grave risks taken to improve prospects.

A large and growing number of Forcibly Displaced People are harmed due to great risks taken in attempting to reach the developed world to improve their prospects. Some of these risks are taken in the immediate need to get to an area of safety and protection. Others are taken in the hope of improving one's prospects given the discrepancies between locations regarding the protection provided and the probability of a desirable durable solution.

The risks taken by an increasing number of people include dangerous sea voyages such as the crossing the Mediterranean Sea (about 3,000 deaths in the first nine months of 2015) or the Indian Ocean to Christmas Island and Australia (964 deaths between 2001 and 2012). Many more are saved through expensive rescue efforts. Desperate people are also often compelled to place great trust in people smugglers, which could possibly lead to theft, extortion and even enforced servitude.

3. Government policies and resultant asylum seeker behaviour divert finite resources from improving the plight of refugees.

Deterrence measures such as Australia's boat turn-back policy and the newly constructed fences in Europe increase the danger for people attempting to make asylum claims. While they help to maintain control of inflows of asylum seekers to specific countries, these policies lengthen the period of vulnerability and the risk of disaster for the impacted asylum seekers. These policies are an inefficient use of resources as they divert monies and efforts from supporting asylum seekers.

Some asylum seekers now apply for asylum in multiple countries hoping to maximise their chances of being accepted in one and, if fortunate enough to be accepted by more than one country, choose the best country for their needs. Cases have also been found where the same person, after being denied asylum in one country changed their identity (including their nationality) and presented in a different country. While this is rational and understandable behaviour for a person desperate to improve their prospects of a better life, it diverts resources from a more efficient use as the same people are being processed by multiple bureaucracies.

STEP 2 ISSUES: Temporary Protection

4. Temporary protection standards are inconsistent across regions and sometimes breach individual human rights.

The quality of life as well as the prospects and wait for a favourable durable solution vary enormously according to the location of a refugee. For example, a refugee in Australia on a Bridging Visa has relatively large benefits and support in comparison to a refugee in a Kenyan camp. Such differences occur due to the relative wealth of the host country as well as the number of refugees they are attempting to protect. In addition to the quality of life experienced as a refugee, the prospects for a durable solution also differ. For example, the chance for resettlement to a developed country is much higher for the refugee in Australia on a Bridging Visa than that for the refugee in Kenya.

Other differences arise due to government policy rather than wealth or refugee numbers. For example, in order to deter asylum seekers from making dangerous sea voyages and risking death at sea, Australia's Humanitarian Program breaches international covenants including the Refugee Convention. This breach is at least in spirit if not technically. Australia's program seems to be at least partially based on a deterrence motive. These breaches include incorrectly turning away legitimate asylum seekers through high-level enhanced screening, and arbitrarily detaining asylum seekers, including children.

Finally many nations, including India, Malaysia and Indonesia, are simply not signatories of the Refugee Convention so do not provide any guarantees to a minimum standard of protection. In addition, whether they are signatories or not, some countries through factors including poverty, disorder or corruption, just don't provide adequate support or justice for asylum seekers and refugees. One would expect the experience of asylum seekers and refugees in such countries to be far worse than those within ordered countries that adhere to the Refugee Convention.

5. Refugee numbers are much larger than previously accepted.

Since World War II there have been numerous occasions of mass movements of refugees. The largest of these was the movement of ten million East Pakistanis (now Bangladeshis) into India during the 1971 Bangladesh War of Independence. Outside of this, no other movement above five million refugees has occurred. These numbers are far less than the mid-2015 count of 15.1 million refugees within the 59.5 million Forcibly Displaced People.

The ability of developed nations to house, process and absorb such large numbers is untested. Beyond the issue of the current volume of refugees or IDPs is the possibility these numbers will increase. If the demographic trajectory of both the developed intake nations and the Countries of Origin remain unchanged, the population of intake countries will be increasingly dwarfed by the population of the outflow countries. International agreements such as the Refugee Convention do not address the possible consequences of overwhelming populations of vulnerable people.

6. Inconsistent and overwhelming country burdens.

Asylum seeker and refugee numbers are borne unevenly across countries of asylum. This inconsistency of burden is driven by factors including a country's proximity to refugee Countries of Origin, the country's prospects for a favourable refugee outcome, and their policies around deterrence. The most burdened Country of First Asylum is Lebanon where almost one fifth of the current inhabitants are refugees. The most burdened Country of Second Asylum is Germany, which in 2015 accepted about one million asylum seekers (over 1% of its total population) from regions as far off as the Middle East and North Africa.

Such large intakes, especially in the Countries of First Asylum, have negative consequences. The presence of asylum seekers threaten the immediate peace as often fighting follows refugees, especially if the country neighbours a state in conflict. The economic stability of an intake country is threatened through the financial cost of housing and feeding so many people as well as the potential impacts on the labour market if refugees enter the black market as cheap labour in order to earn money. The social stability is also threatened through large pressures resulting from great influxes of people. These pressures are potentially heightened with cultural differences that may invoke fear, some likely unwarranted and xenophobic and others likely to be rational. The uncapped obligation of the Refugee Convention provides little protection or guidance regarding overwhelming asylum seeker inflows.

Although Australia's voluntary Resettlement of Refugees is one of the largest in the world, its intake of Onshore refugees is comparatively low. By this measure, Australia could do more if it was to contribute in line with its relative wealth. In 2014, Australia housed approximately 36,000 refugees (approximately 0.15% of its population). Although a greater proportion than the US and close to the proportion of the UK, this proportion is far less than many other wealthy nations. For instance, Canada houses 0.42% of its population in refugees, France 0.39%, and Sweden 1.45%.

7. Many people with no refugee claim attempt to utilise the asylum seeker avenue to enter a developed nation.

Many economic migrants attempt to utilise the asylum seeker pathway. The factors driving migration from the developing to the developed world are at an all-time high. The population of the developing world includes over 3.5 billion with an average GNI of less than US$4,000. These countries, particularly within Africa, the Middle East and South Asia, continue to grow much faster than developed nations. The increasing availability and usefulness of the internet to potential migrants, and the diaspora of emigrants within the developed world, lower the fears associated with movement more than ever before. Although most developed nations have increased the barriers for migration into their countries, the asylum seeker path provides an alternate pathway into the developed world.

Economic migrants, although not technically refugees, are rationally motivated to improve their quality of life by moving to a country with more wealth and prospects. In early 2016, EU officials revealed that at least 60 percent of people who arrived in the EU as asylum seekers in 2015 were economic migrants[1]. A high prevalence of migrants adds cost and complexity to the Refugee Status Determination process. Additionally, a substantial proportion of those determined to not be refugees do not consequently leave the country. Indeed, in many cases the countries they left are less than willing to accept their return, an example occurring in December 2015 where the Pakistan government refused 31 of 50 deportees from Greece as they were "unverified"[2]. There may be multiple reasons why the Countries of Origin refuse to re-admit a failed asylum seeker. One reason is financial. Remittance payments from expatriates living in the developed world provide more to the GDP of many poor countries than foreign aid.

Not all illegal entrants are economic migrants and some unfortunately have militant intentions. The European experience of 2015 highlights that providing open pathways for asylum seekers into a developed nation results in large influxes of refugees and migrants. The large numbers arriving in Europe, coupled with the limitations in coordinating the screening of many people across the various countries of Europe (where internal movement is allowed), resulted in limited control and identification of the entrants. This lack of control risks the entry of those with criminal or terrorist intentions. Providing such open pathways appears to have allowed the re-entry into Europe of some of the terrorists involved in the Paris attacks of November 2015.

8. Exponential increase in the UNHCR budget.

The annual budget of the UNHCR has grown exponentially since the 1950s. Chapter 4 detailed the budget grew from US$300,000 at its inception in 1951, to half a billion in 1980, one billion in the 1990s, over 3 billion in 2010 and over 6 billion in 2014. In addition to the growing number of Forcibly Displaced People, this increase is also due to its expanded scope. This expanded scope, including camp management and asylum seeker assessment (RSD), has been taken on to fill the gaps not fulfilled by the supporting countries. Even with an expansion in budget, the UNHCR services are stretched across the globe, limiting the

---

[1] Peter Cluskey, "Most fleeing to Europe are 'not refugees', EU official says," *Irish Times*, January 26, 2016, accessed July 23, 2016 <www.irishtimes.com/news/world/europe/most-fleeing-to-europe-are-not-refugees-eu-official-says-1.2511133>

[2] Oliver JJ Lane, "Pakistan refuses to take back Europe's rejected migrants," *Breitbart*, December 4, 2015.

availability of such services like RSD. This expanding budget requires donor nations to continually contribute more, in addition to providing their own support to asylum seekers and refugees. The provision of such donations is not limitless.

STEP 3 ISSUES: Permanent Protection

9. Average waiting time is very long.

The average waiting times for refugees is very long due to limitations with each of the three durable solutions. Although difficult to calculate, the average wait appears to be well over ten years and potentially growing when considering the data detailed in Chapter 7. The number of refugees in 2014 (14.4 million) was over fifty times the number of durable solutions provided that year (264,100). The long wait time is driven from the limited number of places provided by each of the three durable solutions. During their wait refugees are generally living in temporary accommodation, have little access to work, and have no certainty of their future.

A. Voluntary Repatriation has had limited success.

Voluntary Repatriation is viewed as the durable solution with the largest volume potential. However, it has had limited long-term success, often resulting in a repeat of the forcible displacement. The issues limiting the success of previous repatriation attempts relate to the disputes over vacated property, pressures regarding limited resources and jobs, and community grievances. Community grievances can arise when returning refugees are provided with benefits that those who remained at home (often enduring hardship) are not provided. They may also arise when it seems that perpetrators of crimes prior to the forcible displacement are seemingly unpunished and free within the rehabilitating country.

B. Local integration increasingly resisted by host countries.

Host nations are less willing to locally integrate refugees due to three key drivers:

1. Real and perceived security threats from refugees bringing the security issues of the country they are fleeing with them;
2. Real and perceived economic and environmental burdens through competition for scarce resources and infrastructure; and
3. Poorly managed expectations as to the number and length of stay of the refugees. Resentments often arise once it is understood the stay will be permanent or when many more refugees than expected arrive.

C. Resettlement places cater for <1% of the refugee population.

Voluntary Resettlement is now undertaken by almost thirty countries but the annual number accepted is vastly inadequate. Although very successful in offering a permanent solution to those it helps, Resettlement caters for only 10% of the identified candidates. This is less than one percent of the total number of refugees. Even including the additional Resettlement placements offered by countries such as Australia, Canada and the US in 2015 following the Syrian crisis, it is still well short of the total number of refugees. Mandating quotas on nations to resettle refugees would increase the number resettled but would impinge on national sovereignty, as well as exposing nations to potential disruptions in harmony as well as social and economic stability. Any quota system is unlikely to truly accommodate all relevant variables regarding the prosperity of a nation.

10. Western nations with large cultural diversity are experiencing increasing incidents of intolerance.

Western nations have never been more culturally diverse. With this increase in diversity is a correlation (not necessarily causation) of intolerance. Examples of intolerance include the perpetuation or increase of voluntary segregation, the rise of anti-immigration nationalist parties, the rise of home-grown terrorist attacks in the name of Islam, and increasing distrust between cultural groups. Chief among the concerns of the secular Western nations is the compatibility of Islamic cultures and the growing Muslim population. European leaders have declared multiculturalism as dead, yet the number of immigrants (including refugees) from Islamic countries is continuing at high levels.

Summary of Issues

Figure 11.1 plots the ten main issues relating to the refugee situation across the Refugee Journey. It also associates the problem with the affected party who most experiences the negative consequence of the problem. The affected party is either the individual asylum seeker or the country (and their residents) who are attempting to help.

The Ten Complications of the Refugee Situation

Disruptive causes and unprotected Forcibly Displaced People

1. The number of Forcibly Displaced People is large and is growing.
2. People are harmed due to grave risks taken in an attempt to improve their prospects.
3. Government policies and resultant asylum seeker behaviour divert finite resources from improving the plight of refugees.

Temporary Protection of Asylum Seekers and Refugees

4. Temporary protection standards are inconsistent across regions and sometimes breach individual human rights.

5. Refugee numbers are much larger than what developed countries have previously been willing to accept and resettle.

6. The burdens borne by countries of asylum are inconsistent and sometimes overwhelming.

7. Many people with no refugee claim attempt to utilise the asylum seeker avenue to enter a developed nation.

8. The UNHCR budget has increased exponentially over the past 30 years and continues to grow.

Durable Solutions and permanently protected people

9. The average time spent waiting in limbo as a refugee for a durable solution is very long.

10. Western nations with large cultural diversity are experiencing increasing incidents of intolerance.

Fig 11.1 › Ten Complications of the Refugee Situation.

Affected Party	STEP 1: No Protection		STEP 2: Temporary Protection		STEP 3: Permanent Protection	
	EVENT: Disruptive Cause	**STATUS:** Not Protected (through country nor Refugee Convention)	**EVENT:** Provision of Temporary Protection	**STATUS:** Temporarily Protected (through Refugee Convention)	**EVENT:** Provision of a Durable Solution	**STATUS:** Permanently Protected (through Country)
Forcibly Displaced People	1. Large and Growing number of Forcibly Displaced People. 2. People harmed due to grave risks taken to improve prospects. 3. Government policies and asylum seeker behaviour divert finite resources from improving the plight of refugees.		4. Temporary protection standards are inconsistent across regions and sometimes breach individual human rights.		9. Average waiting time is very long. 　A. *Voluntary Repatriation has had limited success.* 　B. *Local integration increasingly resisted by host countries.* 　C. *Resettlement places cater for <1% of the refugee population.*	
Countries attempting to help	▪ Nil		5. Refugee numbers much larger than previously accepted. 6. Inconsistent and overwhelming country burdens. 7. Many people with no refugee claim attempt to utilise the asylum seeker avenue to enter a developed nation. 8. Exponential increase in the UNHCR budget.		10. Western nations with large cultural diversity are experiencing increasing incidents of intolerance.	

CH 12. PRINCIPLES & ASSESSMENT FRAMEWORK

The issues that make up the complication, outlined in Chapter 11, provide the basis on which the questions to answer regarding the refugee situation will be created. The task is to then identify the approach option that best answers the questions. Identifying this best approach option is achieved by assessing each option against a suite of criteria within an assessment framework. The eventual goal being a recommended approach option supporting nations, including Australia, can adopt to best manage the needs of Forcibly Displaced People. Thus the establishment of the questions and the assessment framework by which they will be measured are critical in the determination of how to best handle the refugee situation.

Although the issues provide the basis for both the questions and assessment framework, they are not the whole story. The determination of the questions and assessment framework is also dependent on a number of principles. These principles are values-based judgements that can differ from person to person. Accordingly, the set of questions and objectives that are developed from the list of issues are likely to differ between two individuals based on their principles.

The questions-of-principle require a priority between two desired objectives that may, but not necessarily, require a different approach. The hope is that both objectives can be simultaneously met, but where they cannot pragmatism requires a selection of a priority. The following question provides an example of how principles may impact the questions and assessment framework:

Is the optimal outcome to ensure the protection of the human rights for as many people as possible today OR to ensure the protection of humans rights for as many people as possible considering today's population and posterity?

If the answer to this question is 'to ensure the protection of as many people as possible today', then an emphasis would be on rescuing as many people from situations of vulnerability. Strategies would ignore any issues regarding signals that impact future asylum seeker behaviour or any long-term consequence on the nations enlisted to help who are taking in refugees. Approaches where supporting countries took in ever larger volumes of people would be preferred as the most vulnerable people are provided protection.

Alternatively, if the answer is 'to ensure the protection of humans rights for as many people as possible considering today's population and posterity', the objectives are broadened to consider the long-term viability and perpetuation of nations that currently provide human rights to their population. All approach options are then assessed in accordance with how they may impact the world over a number of generations. An approach to take in very large numbers of people over the next 10-20 years but that bears the risk of such nations falling apart due to the subsequent burdens, would be considered suboptimal through this principle. The loss of human rights for future generations would be a detrimental outcome.

So the questions and the assessment framework are reliant on a set of principles. And those principles may vary across different people. Therefore, before any approach option can be assessed, the principles must be defined. A feature of the current debate about the refugee situation is that it focuses on disagreements regarding approach options rather than the underlying principles from which they are developed. Such a focus may never reach an agreement as two parties that cannot understand their differences in principles are unlikely to be able to agree on a preferred approach option.

Thus, there is great value in identifying the complete set of principles relating to the refugee situation. If areas of contention and differing opinions are identified, the debate can then focus on how to progress, be it through compromise or authoritative direction. In order to develop the principles, a series of six sets of questions-of-principle have been outlined. Each set relates to a concept of protection: what, who, why, how, where and when to protect.

The following section outlines the six sets of questions-of-principle. Some are straightforward but many are contentious and difficult to answer. In order to frame the questions and assessment framework relating to the refugee situation, this book provides a position for each question-of-principle. The principles are the critical components of what policies should be aiming to achieve and how various approach options will be assessed. Where you agree with the answer provided you will also agree with the associated assessment criteria. Where you disagree with the answer provided, you will most likely disagree with the associated criteria.

SUMMARY OF PRINCIPLES

Q1. What (or whom) to protect?

Since World War II, protection has meant the granting of access into a country, as well as the provision of accommodation, safety and potentially a durable solution as a permanent resident. Ideally all populations should be protected, as every life is important. However, if this is not possible and a trade-off was required, which population should be given the priority? Key questions-of-principle to define priorities regarding what to protect include:

- Should the populations of refugees and asylum seekers be prioritised over those of the intake nations?
- Should refugees and asylum seekers be prioritised over economic migrants and/or IDPs?
- Should specific groups of refugees and asylum seekers be treated differently? For example, should refugees from areas of geopolitical instability be given priority or should refugees who arrive at a signatory nation's borders be given priority?
- Should protection plans focus on the current numbers of refugees OR should they be scalable to deal with all potential volumes?

The Position of this Book:

Refugees and asylum seekers are to be protected, but the populations and core cultural aspects of the supporting intake nations should be protected as a priority.

- The stability and viability of the supporting nations must be paramount as you cannot help others if you're hurt yourself. This relates to the concept of Lifeboat Ethics discussed in Chapter 6. In a scenario where there may be ever-increasing refugees, countries attempting to help must limit their support at the extent of their perceived capacity to help. Much like a lifeboat allowing in only the number of people it is able to safely carry. To do more risks the stability and ongoing viability of the nations providing help. The viability of these nations must be maintained as the paramount priority as if they fall, then there is even less help available in the future. Such priority does not exclude more being done to help Forcibly Displaced People. In fact, as much help as possible should be provided to the forcibly displaced, this includes focusing efforts and resources on helping rather than deterring asylum seekers. However, the consequences of all policies on the supporting nation must be understood and determined to not be critically adverse.
- Only where compatible should cultures of immigrant populations be allowed to perpetuate within the intake nation. Where cultures are potentially non-compatible

then the cultural practises of the refugee (and immigrant) populations must be subordinated and assimilation to the culture of the host nation is required. This requirement exists for immediate and longer-term horizons. The term 'compatible' is vague and must be strictly defined with the criteria of requirements to be as narrow as possible. Two key examples cited as a potential source of incompatibility between some branches of Islamic culture and secular liberal democracies are the equality of women and freedom of religion. If the desire of the intake nation is to maintain these cultural norms then great attention must be given regarding the intake numbers and cultural assimilation. The size of the annual volumes arriving should not be so great as to threaten change to the cultural norm, and potentially the democratically elected law, of the nation.

Refugees and asylum seekers who are outside their Countries of Origin should be prioritised over economic migrants and IDPs.

- Economic migrants should not be given support through the refugee framework. Although their plight may be severe, it is beyond the ability of the developed nations to help all the people of a rapidly-growing developing world by allowing them to emigrate. It is up to the populations within these countries to bring about the changes necessary to develop their economy. Developed nations have tried and will continue to try to help. It is not the responsibility of developed nations to provide a better life to all that want it, nor is it possible given the large and growing populations in poor nations. This position is no different to that outlined in the Refugee Convention.

- Refugees and asylum seekers, who are outside of their countries, should be provided priority treatment over IDPs. Westphalian Sovereignty dictates that intervention within another state's jurisdiction can only occur in exceptional circumstances. Only in these circumstances would IDPs be prioritised equally with asylum seekers and refugees. Lines need to be drawn in terms of humanitarian help, and the lines of international borders presently provide the greatest utility. This position is no different to that outlined in the Refugee Convention.

All refugees and asylum seekers should be treated equally:

- Ideally refugees from all areas should be treated with equal priority. In situations where there are important geopolitical pressures, prioritising refugees from certain areas may occur, but only if it alleviates a threat to global stability, especially through threats to the viability of intake nations. This follows the principle of protecting the population of the intake nations as a priority.

- Refugees who arrive to a country should not be prioritised over refugees who remain in refugee camps. A refugee's ability to travel the distance required does not make them more in need or more deserving of the potentially limited spots in a country offering to help. The existence of such location-based prioritising has attracted large volumes of people movement (such as towards Germany in 2015), which diverts resources from an efficient allocation.

Protection approaches should be scalable:

- Protection plans should be scalable to account for larger numbers of refugees than are currently presenting. The framework in dealing with ever-increasing numbers is best created in advance of such events rather than having to deal with them on the spot. It is recognised that plans are subject to change and it is possible that approaches for larger numbers of refugees may still require adjustment should that reality ever eventuate. However, it would be short-sighted to ignore planning for larger numbers and may lead to errors that could affect the lives of millions of refugees and the viability of nations enlisting to support.

Q2. Who is protecting?

Nation States do the protecting with the support of non-government agencies, the most prominent of which is the UNHCR. Although desirable, not all nations are able or willing to help. Some are in a state of disintegration and conflict like many of the refugee Countries of Origin. Others have limited money and resources or are not willing to help for reasons beyond their resource capacity. Key questions-of-principle to define priorities regarding who should be protecting include:

- Should all nations help OR just the rich and liberal nations?
- Should contribution be relative to resources (for example money, population, proximity and land)?
- Should contribution be dependent on responsibility or obligation?

The Position of this Book:

As many Nation States as possible should be contributing to the protection of Forcibly Displaced People.

- Although mandatory requirements that impinge on state sovereignty should not exist, pressures should be put on countries to contribute to workable approaches to this international problem. Some vulnerable countries may not be able to help in the short term. Countries of Origin must feel strong international pressure to provide as much help and cooperation as possible. Large non-governmental agencies, such as the UNHCR, can also help.

Contribution should be relative to resources.

- To maintain sovereign controls for supporting countries, relative contributions will remain voluntary, existing in the form of guidelines and international pressure. Proximal Countries of First Asylum should be expected to house the majority of refugees as they provide a number of advantages including enabling the best chance for repatriation. Outside of proximity, guidelines regarding the contribution by both Countries of First Asylum and Second Asylum should be based on the country's population, land size and GDP per capita. This applies to both the physical housing of refugees and the financial support to other countries (such as Countries of First Asylum) and the non-governmental agencies (such as the UNHCR).

The contribution of countries should not be dependent on any perceived responsibility they had in creating the plight of the refugees.

- Regardless of causal responsibilities, countries should do all they can without excessively threatening their ongoing viability. While this clearly includes economic, social and environmental factors, the determination of excessive threat is vague, complex, and must always remain a sovereign decision.

Q3. Why to protect?

The concept of protecting refugees has existed for centuries. Since World War II, the UNHCR has been increasingly visible in coordinating the effort of the world's nations to support Forcibly Displaced People. Key questions-of-principle to define priorities regarding the rationale for protecting include:

- Should it be to maintain and expand the basic human rights of all people as a cornerstone for civilisation – that helping others is helping ourselves OR should it be as a component in maintaining or enhancing global stability? If motives exist for both, is one more important?
- Should protection be provided as a symbol of support for what is right and fair OR to affect a practical outcome?

The Position of this Book:

Protection should be provided to maintain and expand human rights.

- On occasion this will require the subordination of the human rights of refugees to the maintenance and enhancement of global stability, specifically the enhancement and stability of liberal democracies. The human rights of refugees should be pursued with full commitment by all contributing nations of the world. However, if such pursuit threatens a nation's viability, especially liberal democracies, then it must

- be brought back to a point where it no longer does. Ultimately, liberal democracies are a good thing for humankind and it is through the protection and expansion of these societies that human rights will be provided to the greatest number of people.
- The weakness with such a priority is that an important component of liberal democracies is the protection of human rights for all. Allowing a government to override the human rights of some people for a stated goal of 'protecting a liberal democracy' allows great potential for abuse. This weakness is countered by two responses. First, in a world where a nation cannot control the population of those external to its borders, it cannot be expected to always protect an infinite number of non-citizens should they arrive to its territories. Second, the alternative is worse if protection policies threaten the viability of the countries that are helping. Maintaining an objective to protect the human rights of refugees could result in a liberal democracy critically damaging itself, which could lead to hardship in its own population or even its breakdown. This is the same dilemma as presented in the Life Boat Ethics question. In some scenarios, to help everyone would result in a destruction of the society trying to help. Ideally, the two needs would never require a choice, but this is simply not always the case. The number of refugees descending on places like Lebanon, Germany and Sweden has prompted discussion regarding the principle of protecting the populations of the intake nations (if necessary) over protecting those who request asylum.
- The obligations required under the various international treaties should be adhered to as much as possible. However, there are examples where they are too onerous and need to be re-framed in order to enable supporting countries to honour the treaties as well as prioritise their own protection. Specifically, the uncapped obligation the Refugee Convention places on signatory countries to process all refugees that arrive to their land. The right of Non-refoulement, considered a non-derogable right, is covered in both the Refugee Convention and the Convention against Torture and Other Cruel, Inhuman or Degrading Treatment or Punishment. While the principle is noble, it creates situations of incredible stress on countries (such as in Lebanon in 2015), large numbers of long-distance movement towards countries (such as towards Germany in 2015), or new policies specifically designed to thwart movements towards countries perceived to be an easy or favourable option (such as Australia's policies since 2013).
- Part of the issue is the age of the various treaties. For instance, the Refugee Convention is over 60 years old and its Protocol is approaching its 50th anniversary. In functioning societies, laws change all the time. They change because they have unforeseen consequences that are negative for society or at least contradict the

intention of some aspects of law. International laws are no different and they too can be improved with change. The complication is that they are hard to change quickly given the complexities of international agreements and relations. Ideally, the international laws such as the uncapped obligation of the Refugee Convention would be changed to enable the necessary room for countries to protect themselves first.

Protection should be provided to affect a practical outcome.

- Good intentions and symbols do not help the world's vulnerable people, nor the citizens of the nations tying to help, if they do not achieve the desired outcome. To this end, all approach options must be reviewed through a lens regarding how likely they are to be effective. This includes the ability of an individual nation, such as Australia, to implement a change in isolation.

Q4. How to protect?

The obligations of signatory nations with regard to the protection of refugees are set out in the Refugee Convention. In addition, many nations have additional obligations due to the instruments of international human rights law (covered in Chapter 4). In the current situation where protection standards are inconsistent and often in breach of human rights, what trade-offs, if any, are possible? Key questions-of-principle to define priorities regarding how nations should be protecting refugees include:

- Should protection be based on emotion, logic or both?
- Should protection be under the tenets of various treaties such as the Refugee Convention and the various human rights instruments OR should protection be more flexible to enable the protection of more refugees but encompassing less rights?
- Should protection standards and prospects for durable solutions be dependent on location OR standardised regardless of location?
- Should the numbers accepted for protection and a durable solution be standardised regardless of the asylum seekers OR should the numbers be dependent on characteristics deemed to affect assimilation. For example: culture, race or location?
- Should protection seek voluntary repatriation as the primary option or resettlement and local integration?
- Should protection efforts include interventions to improve the stability and viability of refugee Countries of Origin? Or, should a policy of non-intervention be followed?

The Position of this Book:

The impetus for protection efforts can be derived from emotions, but the efforts themselves should be logic-based .

- Emotions are powerful in that they invoke our humanity and can compel us to act for the betterment of an individual's plight, as well as humanity in general. How we act has consequences, and the best actions are those that produce the best outcomes.

- The refugee situation appears to have no approach that helps all. Those that help the most refugees appear to create unacceptable threats to core foundations of society that are imperative for the long-term perpetuation of human rights. Those that best protect the societies of the helping nations fail to support all people in need.

- Logic must be used in order to rationally arrive at the approach that provides the greatest good. Emotion is certainly an aspect of this logic and must play a part in the construction of the best approach, but its relative weight must be appropriately in line with all other data points. This logic must then be followed in responding to acute situations that evoke emotions. To acquiesce to emotion may provide a short-term visible good and perhaps an alleviation of emotional strain. However, if it differs from the best logical response, it is, to the extent of our knowledge, a lesser outcome that incurs harm and damage that could otherwise have been avoided.

It should be possible for additional aspects of the various international treaties to be subordinated to meet a need to protect more asylum seekers.

- International law does make a distinction between absolute, non-derogable and derogable laws (derogable laws being those that can be limited in times of emergency). However, the extent of derogable laws, if not broad enough, can result in situations that potentially threaten the ongoing viability of supporting nations. A key example is the obligation for signatory nations to protect an uncapped number of refugees. As a consequence, housing a very large number of refugees can be potentially detrimental to a country's economy. Again, in emergency situations where a large number of people arrive very quickly, this movement could result in social friction, as well as being open to exploitation by those with ulterior motives, for example, terrorists. Conversely, subordinating human rights increases the potential for exploiting asylum seekers. The ideal outcome is an update to the international conventions to increase their flexibility with regard to derogable rights and when they can be enacted.

Protection standards and prospects for durable solutions should be standardised regardless of location.

- For example, an asylum seeker arriving solo to Australia on a plane and one arriving with a large group to Kenya on foot should be provided with a similar quality of life and similar opportunities for a durable solution. All asylum seekers should be treated equally, and the ability to travel to certain countries should not result in better outcomes for a refugee. The outcome of such a principle would be that Australia does not just 'do as good as it can' for the refugees that arrive at her shores but helps all regions to achieve a bare minimum. To achieve this a large amount of money and resources must continue to be invested in the Countries of First Asylum, usually coming from the richer and more distant Countries of Second Asylum. Naturally large transfers of money are not always going to be used effectively and such a system will be vulnerable to abuse. Robust mitigation steps would need to be in place.

The volumes accepted should not be changed according to characteristics perceived by a governmental body to affect assimilation.

- As discussed in **Q1. What (or whom) to protect?** Assimilation of migrants and refugees to a narrow set of cornerstone principles should be a non-negotiable for any arrivals to a country. For Australia, these would include: equality of sexes, races and sexuality; freedom of religion; and the rule of law. Assimilation considerations should limit the annual intake of refugees and migrants each year into a society. Too large an intake may potentially threaten societal norms that are considered by the population to be desirable. It may be perceived that people of cultures more closely aligned to the intake nation will generally assimilate more easily. However, there should be no changes to accepted volumes based on perceptions regarding ease of assimilation.

Protection efforts should seek repatriation as the primary option rather than local integration or resettlement.

- Sovereign nations, through the collective will of their inhabitants, have the right to control their population numbers and limit the amount of immigrants each year. Large numbers of integrating or resettling refugees potentially place a great burden on such intake societies. Sovereign nations should not be obligated to provide permanent residence to never-ending numbers of refugees in perpetuity. In order to minimise the local integration and resettlement requirements, repatriation must be pursued as the desired option.

Protection efforts should, where possible, include interventions to improve the stability and viability of refugee Countries of Origin.

- The presence of large amounts of refugees places a burden on the international community. Such a burden at some point must result in a loss of sovereign rights. Although sanctioned, any intervention strategy must be carefully assessed to be effective in improving the stability and viability of the country. The goal of such interventions must be to reduce the outflow of refugees, and commence the process of rehabilitation to allow the return of repatriating refugees.

Q5. Where to protect?

In addition to asylum seekers and refugees, there are Forcibly Displaced People who are still within their Country of Origin. In 2014 the number of IDPs (38.2 million) was much larger than the number of refugees (14.4 million) – 70% were estimated to be women and children. Once outside their Country of Origin, 80% of asylum seekers and refugees are housed in neighbouring countries. Neighbouring countries provide a range of benefits such as proximity and cultural similarities. However, the large volumes located in Countries of First Asylum, which are usually poor, also result in rudimentary conditions as the already limited resources are stretched. Key questions-of-principle to define priorities regarding where nations should be protecting refugees include:

- Should protection be provided within the countries in which people are being persecuted? Or, only once they are outside?
- Should protection be provided as close to their Country of Origin? Or, spread equally across all supporting nations?

The Position of this Book:

Protection should most often be provided outside the Countries of Origin.

- As covered in **Q2. Who to protect?** Westphalian Sovereignty dictates that intervention within another state's jurisdiction can occur only in exceptional circumstances: 1. When requested by the sovereign nation; 2. In self-defence; 3. Under the authority of the UN Security Council; and 4. In a legitimate humanitarian intervention (guidelines for which are provided under the R2P report). **Q4. How to protect?** Proposes that at some point the presence of large populations of IDPs and large flows of refugees must result in a loss of a nation's sovereign rights. However, the thresholds for such interventions will need to be very high in order to mitigate the risk of abuse. As such, protection of forcibly displaced people by the international community must remain largely outside the Country of Origin.

Protection for refugees should be provided as close as possible to their Country of Origin without over-burdening the Countries of First Asylum.

- Neighbouring countries (such as Lebanon in 2015) must be monitored and alleviated before they reach a critical level that places too great a risk on the economic and social viability of the host nation. This alleviation requires support from Countries of Second Asylum as well as the Country of Origin.

Q6. When to protect?

Chapter 3 discussed forcible displacement throughout history and the high fertility rates of the countries that have repeatedly produced the most refugees. It is highly likely the problems regarding Forcibly Displaced People are going to perpetuate and arguably grow. Key questions-of-principle to define priorities regarding when nations should be protecting refugees include:

- Should protection approaches consider only for today's refugees? Or, should they consider the refugees of future years and generations?

The Position of this Book:

Protection approaches should consider future generations of displaced people and not just today's refugees.

- History has shown that forcible displacement, although unfortunate, is a continually repeated event. It is almost certain to happen in the future. Thus, protection approaches should be designed where possible to exist in perpetuity. The resolution of the problems of today's refugees should not be at the expense of future generations, both of refugees and host nations. This question was discussed at the beginning of this chapter. As suggested in that example, approaches must enable the long-term viability and perpetuation of nations that currently provide human rights to their population and are able to support others in need.

Summary of Principles

The following principles have been derived from the priority questions. It is these principles that will be used as the framework for assessing the approach options across each of the three key questions.

Set 1. What (or whom) to protect?

- Refugees and asylum seekers are to be protected, but the populations and core cultural aspects of the supporting intake nations should be protected as a priority.
- Refugees and asylum seekers outside their Countries of Origin should be prioritised over economic migrants and IDPs.
- All refugees and asylum seekers should be treated equally. Refugees who arrive to a country should not be prioritised over refugees who remain in refugee camps. In situations with important geopolitical pressures, prioritising refugees from certain areas may occur, but only if it alleviates a threat to global stability, especially through threats to the viability of intake nations.

- Protection approaches should be scalable to account for larger numbers of refugees than are currently presenting.

Set 2. Who is protecting?

- As many nation states as possible should be contributing to the protection of Forcibly Displaced People.
- Contribution should be relative to resources.
- The contribution of countries should not be dependent on any perceived responsibility had in creating the plight of the refugees.

Set 3. Why to protect?

- Protection should be provided to maintain and expand human rights. On occasion this will require the subordination of the human rights of refugees to the maintenance and enhancement of global stability, specifically the enhancement and stability of liberal democracies.
- Protection should be provided to affect a practical outcome. All approach options must be reviewed through a lens of effectiveness.

Set 4. How to protect?

- The impetus for protection efforts can be derived from emotions, but the efforts themselves should be logic-based.
- It should be possible for additional aspects of the various international treaties to be subordinated to meet a need to protect more asylum seekers.
- Protection standards and prospects for durable solutions should be standardised regardless of location.
- The volumes accepted should not be changed according to characteristics perceived by a governmental body to affect assimilation.
- Protection efforts should seek repatriation as the primary option rather than local integration or resettlement.
- Protection efforts should, where possible, include interventions to improve the stability and viability of refugee Countries of Origin.

Set 5. Where to protect?

- Protection should most often be provided outside of the Countries of Origin.

- Protection for refugees should be provided as close as possible to their Country of Origin without over-burdening the Countries of First Asylum.

Set 6. When to protect?
- Protection approaches should consider future generations of displaced people and not just today's refugees.

Assessment Framework

The main issues making up The Complication and the principles determined in this chapter drive the creation of an assessment framework for eight approach options to the refugee situation we will review. Each approach option is assessed according to the same approach questions and is provided with four scores:

- The first is an **Effectiveness Score,** which is based on questions linking to one of the three steps of the Refugee Journey reflecting the issues outlined in Chapter 11. A fourth approach question relates to the persistence and scalability of the approach.
- Second is the **Human Rights Score** which outlines the adherence of the approach to the tenets of the Refugee Convention and other human rights instruments.
- The **Cost Score** outlines the financial and resource costs for countries to implement each approach.
- Finally the **Implementation Success Score** outlines the likelihood of successful implementation that would enable an approach to achieve its Effectiveness Score.

Together, these four scores help compare and contrast the different approach options, highlighting the advantages and disadvantages of each.

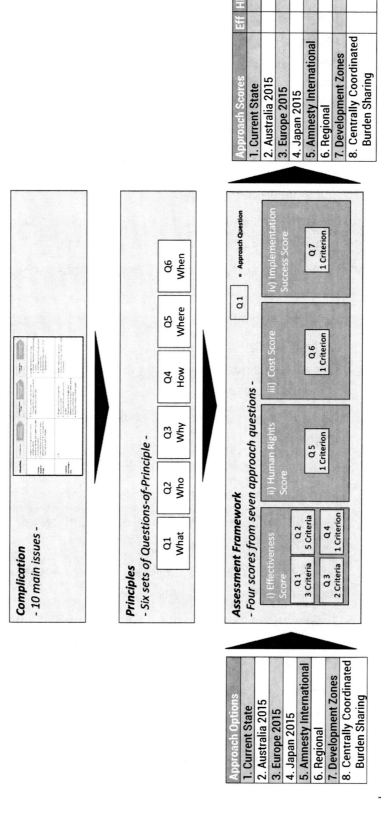

Fig 12.1 › Complication, Principles and Assessment Framework.

The Effectiveness Score

The Effectiveness Score is generated by the four approach questions that have been derived from the main issues outlined in Chapter 11 with the overlay of the questions-of-principle. Within these four questions are eleven criteria and each is provided a score out of ten. The scores are qualitative: 10 means most effective, 1 means least effective. These eleven scores are then averaged to provide an overall effectiveness score. Each criteria was equally weighted.

The first three questions relate to the three steps of the Refugee Journey. The fourth is an over-arching question regarding persistence and scalability.

Q1. How can the number of Forcibly Displaced People be minimised and how can they find protection as safely and as easily as possible? Specific criteria include:

    1.1 Reducing the numbers of new Forcibly Displaced People.

    1.2 Enabling people to find safety as easily as possible and eliminating risk taking behaviour in order to improve protection prospects.

    1.3 Eliminating policies that divert finite resources from improving the plight of refugees, either directly through government spend or indirectly through resultant asylum seeker behaviour.

Q2. How can protection best be provided to asylum seekers and refugees? Specific criteria include:

    2.1 Ensuring the highest possible probability for repatriation.

    2.2 Standardising protection regardless of location.

    2.3 Avoiding overwhelming intakes of asylum seekers and refugees by Countries of First Asylum.

    2.4 Avoiding overwhelming intakes of asylum seekers and refugees by Countries of Second Asylum.

    2.5 Eliminating the diversion of resources caused by the use of protection channels by those without legitimate refugee claims (e.g. economic migrants).

Q3. How can the time spent waiting in limbo for a Durable Solution be minimised? Specific criteria include:

    3.1 Reducing the average time spent waiting in limbo for a Durable Solution. This includes living in temporary accommodation, having little access to paid work, and having no certainty of the future.

> 3.2 Ensuring the human rights of the population of the host nation and of the asylum seekers and refugees are protected across short and long-term horizons. Where cultures are incompatible, assimilation to the host nation is assured.
>
> Q4. How can the approach provide ongoing and scalable protection? Specific criteria include:
>
>> 4.1 Ensuring persistence and scalability of the protection approach considering Countries for First and Second Asylum, asylum seekers and refugees.

The Human Rights Score

The Human Rights Score is generated by the fifth approach question, which reflects the need to protect human rights as discussed in **Q3. Why to protect?** question-of-principle. A qualitative score is provided: 10 means most effective, 1 means least effective.

> Q5. How well does the approach honour the tenets of international law? Specific criteria include:
>
>> 5.1 Adhering to the Refugee Convention and other human rights agreements including the Declaration of Human Rights, the Convention of the Rights of Children and the International Covenant on Civil and Political Rights.

The Cost Score

The Cost Score is generated by the sixth approach question, which provides a qualitative score with regard to the relative financial cost of an approach option: 10 means most costly, 1 means least costly.

> Q6. How costly is implementation?

The Implementation Success Score

The Implementation Success Score is generated by the seventh approach question, which provides a qualitative score with regard to the relative probability that the approach will be adopted and operated in the manner envisaged. Considerations include the complexity of the approach and the likely cooperation across multiple nations. A qualitative score is provided: 10 means most likely to be implemented, 1 means least likely.

> Q7. How probable is successful implementation? Specific criteria include:
>
>> 7.1 Probability of implementation and probability of success once implemented. Considerations include complexity and the likelihood of cooperation across nations.

Assessment Framework

Each approach option is provided with four qualitative scores, each out of ten. Chapters 14 and 15 explore the main Holistic Approach options for the refugee situation. Each option is assessed across the described criteria and provided the four qualitative scores, each out of ten.

Fig 12.2 > The assessment framework. Four scores from seven questions.

1. Effectiveness	Question	Question Criteria	Pros	Cons	Scores / 10	Score
Question 1.	Q1. How can the number of Forcibly Displaced People be minimised and how can they find protection as safely and as easily as possible?	1.1 Reducing the numbers of new Forcibly Displaced People.	- TBC	- TBC	- TBC	
		1.2 Enabling people to find safety as easily as possible and eliminating risk taking behaviour in order to improve protection prospects.	- TBC	- TBC	- TBC	- TBC
		1.3 Eliminating policies that divert finite resources from improving the plight of refugees, either directly through government spend or indirectly through resultant asylum seeker behaviour.	- TBC	- TBC	- TBC	
Question 2.	Q2. How can protection best be provided to asylum seekers and refugees?	2.1 Ensuring the highest possible probability for repatriation.	- TBC	- TBC	- TBC	
		2.2 Standardising protection regardless of location.	- TBC	- TBC	- TBC	
		2.3 Avoiding overwhelming intakes of asylum seekers and refugees by Countries of First Asylum.	- TBC	- TBC	- TBC	- TBC
		2.4 Avoiding overwhelming intakes of asylum seekers and refugees by Countries of Second Asylum.	- TBC	- TBC	- TBC	
		2.5 Eliminating the diversion of resources caused by the use of protection channels by those without legitimate refugee claims (e.g. economic migrants).	- TBC	- TBC	- TBC	
Question 3.	Q3. How can the time spent waiting in limbo for a Durable Solution be minimised?	3.1 Reducing the average time spent waiting in limbo in temporary accommodation, having little access to paid work, and having no certainty of the future.	- TBC	- TBC	- TBC	- TBC
		3.2 Ensuring the human rights of the population of the host nation and of the asylum seekers and refugees are protected across short and long term horizons. Where cultures are incompatible, assimilation to the host nation is assured.	- TBC	- TBC	- TBC	
Question 4.	Q4. How can the approach provide ongoing and scalable protection?	4.1 Ensuring persistence and scalability of the protection approach considering Countries for First and Second Asylum, asylum seekers and refugees.	- TBC	- TBC	- TBC	- TBC
				Effectiveness Score (average)	TBC	

2. Human Rights	Question	Question Criteria	Pros	Cons	Scores / 10	Score
Question 5.	Q5. How well does the approach honour the tenets of international law?	5.1 Adhering to the Refugee Convention and other human rights agreements including the Declaration of Human Rights, the Convention of the Rights of Children and the International Covenant on Civil and Political Rights.	- TBC	- TBC	- TBC	- TBC
				Human Rights Score (average)	TBC	

3. Cost	Question	Question Criteria	Pros	Cons	Scores / 10	Score
Question 6.	Q6. How costly is implementation?	6.1 Total cost (financial and other) of implementation.	- TBC	- TBC	- TBC	- TBC
				Cost Score (larger is more cost)	TBC	

4. Probability	Question	Question Criteria	Pros	Cons	Scores / 10	Score
Question 7.	Q7. How probable is successful implementation?	7.1 Probability of implementation and probability of success once implemented. Considerations include complexity and the likelihood of cooperation across nations.	- TBC	- TBC	- TBC	- TBC
				Implementation Success Score	TBC	

PART 3
Options & Recommendation

Section 3.1

Options Assessment

Part 1
Situation
(Chapters 1-10)

Section 1.1

CH 1-7 Global Review
- Uses the *Refugee Journey* framework to review the global refugee situation. Including:
  - Disruptive Causes and Forcibly Displaced People.
  - Protection (i.e. as asylum seekers or refugees).
  - Durable Solutions (i.e. Repatriation, Local Integration or Resettlement).

Section 1.2

CH 8-10 Australian Review
- Reviews the Australian context including:
  - Australia's migration programs.
  - Australia's humanitarian program.
  - Controversy and debate surrounding Australia's humanitarian program.

Part 2
Complication, Principles & Assessment Framework
(Chapter 11-12)

Section 2.1

CH 11 The Complication
- Summarises the main issues identified through the global and Australian reviews.

Section 2.2

CH 12 Principles & Assessment Framework
- Outlines the Questions of Principle that must be answered to best manage the refugee situation.
- Sets out the approach option assessment framework.

Part 3
Options & Recommendation
(Chapters 13-17)

Section 3.1

CH 13-15 Options Assessment
- Summarises the various Component Policies.
- Summarises and assesses the various Holistic Approaches using the approach option assessment framework.

Section 3.2

CH 16-17 Discussion and Recommendation
- Discusses the trade-offs in selecting the best Holistic Approach Option.
- Recommends an approach and provides a pathway for implementation including Australia's next steps.

CH 13. APPROACH OPTIONS – COMPONENT POLICIES

Component Policies & Holistic Approaches

With the establishment of the key questions to answer and the principles to guide assessment, the approach options can now be reviewed and assessed. There are two broad types of approaches: Component Policies and Holistic Approaches.

Component Policies are initiatives regarding the refugee situation acting in a specific area without being an overall strategy (Holistic Approaches). This chapter details the main Component Policies being discussed and tried around the world. As they are not Holistic Approaches, they have not been assessed against the framework outlined in Chapter 12.

Holistic Approaches are overall strategies regarding the management of the refugee situation. They consider all aspects of the plight of Forcibly Displaced People, beginning with their initial displacement from the Country of Origin, to their claim for asylum, RSD and protection as a refugee, to final attainment of permanent protection through a durable solution. Holistic Approaches must also sit within the global context for refugee management and align with the reality of how other countries are behaving. A summary of the main Holistic Approaches will be provided in Chapters 14 and 15 and each is assessed according to the principles established in Chapter 12.

Component Policies Overview

This book provides an overview of the main components that have been suggested by governments, advocates, and media commentators. As detailed in Figure 13.1, each Policy Component has been categorised within the effectiveness key question and specific sub-point with which it is most relevant.

Fig 13.1 ▶ Component Policies - Overview.

Question	Component Policy #	Component Policy Name
1. How can the number of Forcibly Displaced People be minimised and how can they find protection as safely and as easily as possible?	1a	Attend to Endemic Issues
	1b	Improve Transparency of Commerical Arrangements
	1c	Help Control Population
	1d	Reduce Remittance Costs
	1e	Increase Trade and Direct Foreign Investment
	1f	Restrict Arms Sales to Refugee Countries of Origin
	1g	Coordinate Short and Long-term Support Post Conflict
	1h	Legal Safe Routes to Protection
	1i	Combat Trafficking
	1j	Rescue Those in Danger
	1k	Allow Entry at Borders
	1l	Implement 'No Advantage' Principle (e.g. Dublin Agreement)
2. How can protection best be provided to asylum seekers and refugees?	2a	End Mandatory Detention and Expand Community Processing
	2b	Grant Asylum Seekers the Right to Work
	2c	Protect the Interests of Children
	2d	Independent Oversight of Processing Facilities
	2e	Improve Refugee Status Determination (RSD)
	2f	Fast Determinations of Refugee Status
	2g	Ratify and Uphold the Refugee Convention
	2h	Share Refugee Burden
	2i	Improve Removal and Return of Failed Asylum Seekers
	2j	Full Funding of UNHCR
	2k	Funding of Government Bodies for Asylum Seekers
3. How can the time spent waiting in limbo for a Durable Solution be minimised?	3a	100% Resettlement (or Increase Resettlement Quotas)
	3b	Reduce the Rights for Refugees and Immigrants
	3c	Reduce Immigration
	3d	Allow Refugees to Pay for Citizenship (Indentured Labour)
	3e	Privately Sponsor Resettlement
	3f	Abolish Temporary Protection Visas (TPVs)
	3g	Combat Xenophobia and Racism
	3h	Create a Refugee State
	3i	Update and Ratify the Refugee Convention
	3j	Withdraw from the Refugee Convention

Component Policies Review

Q1. Minimise Forcibly Displaced People

The following policies seek to answer the Effectiveness Question 1. How can the number of Forcibly Displaced People be minimised and how can they find protection as safely and as easily as possible?

1a. Attend to Endemic Issues

Effective protection and ultimate provision of durable solutions for the world's displaced people will be more difficult if and when there are more Forcibly Displaced People. Strategies that minimise the likelihood of countries failing to adequately protect their citizens must be utilised in any comprehensive management approach. Melbourne's Asylum Seeker Resource Centre, recognises that 'greater attention on the endemic issues of war and oppression in refugee-producing countries must be a part of an effective management strategy'[1].

Of course, the tasks of minimising wars and oppression are easier said than done. Civil war is the Disruptive Cause that results in the most displaced people, and low wealth increases the risk of civil war. Given this, improvements in the wealth and economy of the poorer nations should have a positive effect in minimising the potential for Forcibly Displaced People.

In line with the solution principles of all nations contributing in a manner proportional to their ability, efforts to raise the poorest countries out of poverty must be continued. In line with solutions being practical, results learnt from past experiences, especially those where resources have been spent which haven't worked, should be heeded.

1b. Improve Transparency of Commercial Arrangements

The extraction of money away from the public purse, and ultimately the citizens of a nation, is a common feature in many of the poorer nations of the world, including those that are long-time Countries of Origin for refugees. One of the most important areas is in natural resources. For many of the poorest countries of the world, revenues from their natural resources are potentially larger than the foreign aid they receive[2]. In his book, *The Bottom Billion,* economist Paul Collier argues that corruption and mismanagement of these resources within the countries of the Developing World can be minimised and

---

[1] Asylum Seeker Resource Centre, *Asylum seekers and refugees: myths, FACTS + solutions,* 38. Accessed 8 December 2016 <https://www.asrc.org.u/pdf/myths-facts-solutions-info_.pdf>
[2] Paul Collier, *The Bottom Billion* (New York: Oxford University Press, 2007), 113 of 187. iBook edition.

the associated revenues for their societies increased through international charters and guidelines for the resources industry[3].

Collier suggests such a charter for the resources industries could build on international standards proposed by the British government's 2002 Extractive Industries Transparency Initiative. Five steps were outlined[4]:

1. All contracts for mining and extraction must be auctioned off in a transparent process.

2. Contracts must ensure that some of the risks currently borne by developing countries (for example commodity price risk) are shared with the mining companies.

3. All payments of revenue must be transparent. This enables citizens to better understand the revenues the government is receiving on their behalf and should help with budget scrutiny.

4. Transparency in public expenditures.

5. Rules for smoothing public spending in response to revenue shocks. Such a step would include guidelines on how to manage volatility in resource revenues rather than each country having their own ad hoc system.

1c. Help Control Population

Reductions to the high Total Fertility Rates of developing countries decrease the potential for large numbers of displaced people in two ways. The first is simply through a reduction in the potential total of displaced people resulting from disruptive events – a smaller population resulting in smaller numbers displaced. The second is that reduced fertility rates are shown to improve a country's prosperity in the short term[5], which in turn helps to reduce the propensity for civil war (as outlined in Chapter 2).

Hans Rosling is a medical doctor, academic and statistician renowned for his talks statistics and the developing world. He describes four drivers to lower fertility[6] rates in the poorer countries that have not gone through the Demographic Transition (where the majority of the population growth is set to come from):

1. Children survive: possible through improvements in vaccination, medicine, sanitation and nutrition to levels of the developed world.

---

3   Ibid.
4   Ibid.
5   Brigid Fitzgerald Reading, "Education Leads to Lower Fertility and Increased Prosperity," Earth Policy Instititute, May 12, 2011, accessed July 25, 2016 <www.earth-policy.org/data_highlights/2011/highlights13>.
6   Hans Rosling, "Religion and Babies" (Talk presented via TED Tal, April 2012, Doha, Qatar).

2. Many children are not needed for work: possible through economic improvements.
3. Women are getting education and join the labour force: possible through economic improvements and cultural changes towards gender equality.
4. Family planning is accessible, which includes contraception.

1d. Reduce Remittance Costs

Remittance payments help improve the prosperity of poor countries. Remittance payments from immigrants and temporary visa holders in developed countries back to their homeland countries is already an effective way to improve the economy in the developing countries, often far exceeding foreign aid. Removal of costs such as fees for financial transfers and the large perpetual commissions taken by recruitment agents will further enhance the flow of money into these developing countries.

1e. Increase Trade and Foreign Direct Investment

Trade and foreign direct investment into developing nations brings capital and jobs for its inhabitants. This improves a country's prosperity, decreasing the chance for civil war as well as alleviating potential economic migration incentives (as jobs are better at home, and the comparative labour of emigrants will not be as cheap). Such investment will lead to equalisation in living standards across developing and developed nations in the long term. In the short and medium term this often increases migration from the developing country, an example being NAFTA and migration from Mexico to the United States[7].

1f. Restrict Arms Sales to Refugee Countries of Origin

Restrictions of such sales in order to reduce the ongoing detrimental impacts of civil wars. Although such restrictions could prove quite effective if successfully implemented, given the political disparity across the globe the likelihood of a restriction that is adhered to by all countries is very low.

1g. Coordinate Short and Long-term Support Post Conflict

Better support for the recovery of refugee Countries of Origin, post conflict, can improve the number and long-term success of repatriating refugees to their home nation. Coordinating the activities and goals of the humanitarian agencies that provide short-term support, such as the UNHCR, and the development agencies that provide long-term systemic support, such as the World Bank, is a fundamental component of such success. Successful

---

7   James F. Hollifield, Philip L. Martin and Pia M. Orrenius, *Controlling Immigration: A Global Perspective*, Third Edition (United States, Standford Univerity Press, 2014), 28.

coordination of these agencies must first overcome differences in strategies and timelines, as well as competition over scope (i.e. which agency does what).

The following policy components primarily focus on eliminating risk-taking behaviour in order to improve protection prospects.

1h. Legal Safe Routes to Protection

This policy would provide safe routes for asylum seekers to authorised protection zones, most likely countries that are signatories to the Refugee Convention. Consequently, use of people smuggler operations would greatly reduce and dangerous voyages would be undertaken less. This has been recommended internationally by Amnesty International[8] and within Australia by the Asylum Seeker Resource Centre[9].

This policy could manifest as a provision of safe transport between countries where the destination country provides a better quality of life for refugees or a better opportunity for a Durable Solution. The primary risk of such a policy is that it results in concentrations of arrivals at countries that are perceived desirable, which in turn overwhelm that country's ability to function viably. Such an outcome would not only threaten the refugees but the supporting country itself. An example of the potential strains is Germany in 2015.

1i. Combat Trafficking

Active policing and prosecution of people smuggling operations. This component solution has been recommended by Amnesty International in 2015[10]. While these initiatives serve some benefit in reducing the prevalence of their existence and the associated movement of people in an uncontrolled manner, their ultimate control is dependent on removing any advantage from such uncontrolled movements.

1j. Rescue Those in Danger

There have been numerous cases where people have died in attempting to reach developed nations to claim asylum. Multiple groups have called for improved procedures to rescue those in danger as well as adjustment of policies to prevent the likelihood of these events occurring. Although rescue efforts are made when boats reach distress, lives have been

---

8   Tharanga Yakupitiyage, "Amnesty International's 8-Point Plan for Refugee Crises," *Inter Press Service News Agency*, October 14, 2015.
9   Asylum Seeker Resource Centre, *Asylum seekers and refugees: myths, FACTS + solutions*, 36. Accessed 8 December 2016 <https://www.asrc.org.au/pdf/myths-facts-solutions-info_.pdf>
10 Tharanga Yakupitiyage, "Amnesty International's 8-Point Plan for Refugee Crises," *Inter Press Service News Agency*, October 14, 2015.

lost. Further, complexities arise when determining the consequences of combating people smuggling and the subsequent risk asylum seekers face.

In 2013, the ASRC recommended a short-term policy adjustment for Australia to 'remove its harsh people smuggling sentencing laws along with the policy of confiscating asylum seeker boats. These policies only incentivise people smugglers to utilise vessels that are unseaworthy, overcrowded and manned by inexperienced, uninformed and often desperate and underage Indonesians, altogether increasing the risk of a tragedy at sea'[11].

The following policies eliminate the diversion of finite resources from improving the plight of refugees - either directly in terms of government spend, or indirectly through asylum seeker behaviour that creates double-handling.

1k. Allow Entry at Borders

The intent of the Refugee Convention is for signatory states to provide refuge for all refugees provided they have not committed serious crimes. This includes all asylum seekers during their period awaiting Refugee Status Determination. No penalties are to be imposed for illegal entry and no contracting state is to return or 'refouler' a refugee to the area where their life was threatened.

Many signatory states, including Australia, are not currently following the intention of the Refugee Convention. One of the main reasons appears to be the threat of large numbers, such as those experienced in Europe, should states allow entry for all asylum seekers at their borders. The Europe 2015 experience has shown many are willing to claim refugee status in Europe (and potentially other developed nations). Such numbers, if deemed to be above the threshold amounts for the intake nations, may create difficulties in processing all people and in identifying and prioritising those most vulnerable.

1l. Implement 'No Advantage' Principle (e.g. Dublin Agreement)

A 'no advantage' principle, such as that recommended for Australia by the Houston Report dictates, that 'no benefit is gained through circumventing regular migration arrangements'[12]. The objective in the Australian context was to discourage the use of irregular maritime channels (people smugglers) that increase the chance of deaths at sea.

A related philosophy underpins the Dublin Agreement in Europe. This agreement was largely ignored in 2015 with the mass migration in Europe toward Germany. When

---

11 Asylum Seeker Resource Centre, *Asylum seekers and refugees: myths, FACTS + solutions,* 36. Accessed 8 December 2016 <https://www.asrc.org.au/pdf/myths-facts-solutions-info_.pdf>
12 Angus Houston, Paris Aristotle and Michael l"Estrange, "Report of the Expert Panel on Asylum Seekers",(August, 2012), 14.

functioning, the agreement's aim is to reduce uncontrolled people movement that causes an increased burden on desired countries, as well as movement through illegal channels that potentially increases the vulnerability of asylum seekers. It dictates which EU country is responsible for the RSD and if necessary transfers asylum seekers back to the responsible country. Its objective is to reduce the practice of 'asylum shopping' where one person submits multiple applications in different countries (such acts result in greatly duplicated effort), as well as the behaviour of travelling through 'safe' countries on the way to those more desirable.

The Dublin Agreement effectively inundates the entry countries with asylum seekers. As Alexander Betts, Director of the Refugee Studies Centre at the University of Oxford, says, *"it creates a fundamental inequality, by placing a disproportionate responsibility on frontline states like Italy and Greece"*[13].

Q2. Consistent Protection for Refugees and Supporting Nations

The following policies seek to answer Effectiveness Question 2. How can protection best be provided to asylum seekers and refugees?

2a. End Mandatory Detention and Expand Community Processing

Arguments for the cessation of Mandatory Detention include the improvement of the quality of life for the asylum seeker and the elimination of human rights breaches by arbitrary detention. Community Processing is a proposed alternative in that it allows asylum seekers to live in specified residences in the community. Additionally, the operating costs of Community Processing (~A$100,000 per person per year) are significantly lower than those of immigration detention (~A$239,000) or offshore detention facilities (~A$400,000). Expanded use of Community Processing is recommended by the ASRC[14] as it could harbour a larger number of asylum seekers for the same cost. Much of these costs could be removed with the provision of access to employment.

While Community Processing lowers the cost, its extensive use would reduce the deterrence impacts of mandatory detention. This would increase the likely number of asylum seeker arrivals and subsequently the societal risks that too great an influx of asylum seekers may have on the host nation.

---

13   Camila Ruz, "What happens to failed asylum seekers?," *BBC News Magazine,* August 13, 2015.
14   Asylum Seeker Resource Centre, *Asylum seekers and refugees: myths, FACTS + solutions,* 31. Accessed 8 December 2016 <https://www.asrc.org.au/pdf/myths-facts-solutions-info_.pdf>

2b. Grant Asylum Seekers the Right to Work

As mentioned by Oxford Economist and author Paul Collier, the living conditions provided by UNHCR camps are not the main issue impacting a refugee's quality of life. In fact, quite often the conditions are better than many of their neighbouring villages. The biggest issue relates to refugees' inability to work.

> "People are well-fed and their housing conditions are far superior to the African cities with which I am more familiar... The problem with the camps is that people have no autonomy: most especially, they are not allowed to work."

As discussed in Chapter 10, allowing people the ability to work, to earn their own success, is a key to overall happiness. However, allowing refugees the right to work is not a decision without consequence. Potential impacts affect the unemployment rate of the host nation, wages in the host nation, and even the political stability of the ruling government. The right to work may be provided within many different contexts. For instance, it could be provided to refugees as it is to permanent residents (as recommended by the ASRC), or it could be provided to refugees within 'Development Zones' within the host nation[15].

Human rights barrister Julian Burnside suggested that if there are legitimate concerns, then asylum seekers could be required to live in rural areas while they awaited their RSD[16]. Dr Anne Kilcullen has proposed a similar concept whereby local or rural communities could request a certain number of asylum seekers with particular skillsets to fill specific labour needs. Asylum seekers who qualify could be matched with each community[17].

2c. Protect the Interests of Children

The Australian Labor Party's 2015 policy approach to asylum seekers referred to protecting the interests of children. This protection included a statement ensuring that children were out of detention as soon as possible[18]. However, the actual process to be followed was not mentioned. An issue with removing children from detention becomes apparent when considering that their parents would also need to be removed with them as well (as it would be in the children's best interests). An approach to remove all children from

---

15 Alexander Betts and Paul Collier, "Help Refugees Help Themselves: Let Displaced Syrians Join the Labor Market," *Foreign Affairs*, November/December 2015.
16 Jane McAdam and Fiona Chong, *Refugees: Why seeking asylum is legal and Australia's policies are not*, (Sydney: NewSouth Publishing, 2014), 108.
17 Ibid.
18 "A humane and compassionate approach to asylum seekers," Australian Labor Party, accessed July 24, 2016 <www.alp.org.au/asylumseekers>.

detention would signal the end of the deterrence effect of mandatory detention on families with children.

Other aspects in protecting the needs of children include appointing an advocate for the children who is independent of the Department of Immigration and Border Protection and imposing mandatory reporting of any child abuse in all immigration detention facilities[19].

2d. Independent Oversight of Processing Facilities

The Australian Labor Party's 2015 policy approach to asylum seekers also referred to appointing an independent oversight of Australian funded processing facilities. Such governance aims to ensure that people within these facilities are treated humanely and are safe.

2e. Improve Refugee Status Determination

The Refugee Status Determination process is important with regards to the accuracy and number of applicants who are granted refugee status, as well as the efficiency with which they are processed. As discussed in Chapter 5, Australia's approval rates are generally higher than those produced through UNHCR determination processes[20]. There are also a significant number of negative decisions overturned during review[21]. Countries such as the UK and Canada have reviewed their systems and have implemented significant reforms as a result.

2f. Fast Determinations of Refugee Status

All Refugee Status Determinations to be completed within a timely and stated period, such as 90 days. This will reduce the period spent waiting in limbo by asylum seekers. One consequence would be less time spent in detention centres. Another consequence may be an increased number of asylum seekers in line with a reduced deterrence.

2g. Ratify and Uphold the Refugee Convention

The majority of the world's countries have ratified the Refugee Convention. However, in Asia many countries such as Malaysia, Thailand and Bangladesh, have not. These countries may be more willing to ratify the Convention if more formal international agreements that share the burden of supporting refugees were in place.

---

19   Ibid.
20   Sara Davies, " "FactCheck: are Australia's refugee acceptance rates high compared with other nations?," *The Conversation*, August 20, 2013.
21   Angus Houston, Paris Aristotle and Michael l"Estrange, "Report of the Expert Panel on Asylum Seekers",(August, 2012), Attachment 5.

In addition, the intention of the Refugee Convention is not always upheld by signatory nations. Specific breaches include not punishing those who have entered the country illegally, and allowing refugees the right to work. Why do signatory countries conduct these breaches? The most likely reason is a concern that upholding the Refugee Convention risks being burdened with an overwhelming number of refugees and illegitimate economic migrants.

2h. Share Refugee Burden

Burden-sharing is essentially the allocation of refugees throughout a group of supporting nations according to a list of criteria in terms of how many each country could take. Burden-sharing could be in the form of temporary sheltering of refugees or taking in refugees with a view to granting permanent residency. Burden-sharing through permanent resettlement is a more realistic option in burden-sharing as voluntary repatriation is less likely once refugees move further from their Country of Origin. The number allocated to each country may be dictated by a quota or left up to a country to self-determine how much support they will provide to 'do their bit'.

In theory, burden-sharing will help the largest number of refugees as all countries will be accommodating the total number of people they (or a quota system) deem to be their limit. However, it does not guarantee all people will be protected or that Countries of First Asylum are not overwhelmed with refugees, threatening their social and economic stability.

2i. Improve Removal and Return of Failed Asylum Seekers

As stated by the Houston Report in 2012, "It is fundamental to a properly functioning system of international protection that those determined not to be in need of protection, after having undergone a thorough assessment should be returned to their country of origin"[22]. Without such a mechanism, failed claimants will stay in the country, causing further stress on the system and diverting resources away from those who are assessed to need assistance the most. There is generally a low rate of return of failed asylum seekers. In the EU just 40% of failed asylum seekers return to their home country.

Some Countries of Origin do not accept involuntary and undocumented returns, further complicating the outcome for these people. An effective approach may include providing incentives for countries to cooperate and assist with involuntary removals, as well as disincentives for non-compliance.

---

22 Angus Houston, Paris Aristotle and Michael l"Estrange, "Report of the Expert Panel on Asylum Seekers", (August, 2012), 55.

2j. Full Funding of UNHCR

Many of the problems associated with the inconsistent and inadequate protection of asylum seekers and refugees may be mitigated by more funding. In particular, the areas that most need the funding are Countries of First Asylum that shelter the vast majority of refugees. The UNHCR is a ready-made vehicle to help support the quality of life in these refugee camps, and funds would increase protection and positive outcomes for asylum seekers and refugees.

Opponents to funding increases to the UNHCR point to the recent rise in funding requirements linked to the increase in in refugee numbers (from ~US1 billion in 1990s, to US$3.3 billion in 2010 and US$6.6 billion in 2014). Such increases cannot continue indefinitely before they start to place an enormous strain on donor countries. Given the general inefficiencies in large not-for-profit organisations, concern about further increases to the UNHCR is understandable. Regardless of these concerns, the lifting of the quality of life for refugees within countries that offer low standards of protection is obviously dependent on the level of resources provided to the UNHCR.

2k. Funding of Government Bodies for Asylum Seekers

Countries unilaterally funding research and support in relation to asylum seekers and related issues may also provide further benefit through better understanding of the problem. For example, the Houston Report recommended further investment into completing the evidence-base on asylum issues. With a better understanding of the issues comes a better opportunity for effective policies to alleviate these issues.

Q3. Minimise time in limbo and minimise cultural frictions

The following policies seek to answer Effectiveness Key Question 3. How can the time spent waiting in limbo for a Durable Solution be minimised?

3a. 100% Resettlement (or Increase Resettlement Quotas)

Participation in the resettlement program is voluntary for a nation. Currently about 26 nations are involved, and in 2014 about 100,000 refugees were resettled into new countries. This number represents approximately 1% of refugees overall. In effect, about 10% of refugees approved for resettlement are resettled each year.

Increasing the resettlement number to 100% (about 1 million), or a number as close to that as possible, would provide more refugees with permanent protection sooner. If this is not possible, formal guidelines regarding how many refugees a nation could resettle given its population, space and wealth could be established.

Implementation of this policy potentially contravenes the principle of protecting the populations of the intake nations and the viability of liberal democracies. Given the current refugee population, no one country could commit to resettling all refugees without threatening its own viability. Similarly, no group of countries could commit long term to resettling all the world's refugees irrespective of what future numbers may be. What if one billion refugees presented?

A quota system establishing a theoretical maximum based on a country's characteristics such as population and wealth appears more aligned to the principle of protecting the intake population and the host nation. Even then, each country must consider the social and economic impacts of accepting additional resettled refugees. The following example highlights what is possible with burden-sharing.

- The 62 Countries of Second Asylum discussed in Chapter 5 (which have more than 1 million people in population, are Free or Partially according to Freedom House and are high income or upper-middle income according to the World Bank) would be required to resettle refugees.

- Countries of First Asylum (such as Lebanon, South Africa and Turkey) are not required to resettle additional refugees and therefore are omitted from resettlement requests.

- No country is required to resettle more than 50,000 refugees each year. Fourteen countries would be capped at 50,000 resettled refugees each year: Japan, South Korea, Poland, United Kingdom, Italy, Spain, France, Germany, Mexico, Argentina, Brazil, Venezuela and the United States of America.

- High income Countries of Second Asylum resettle refugees equivalent to 0.20% of their population each year. This would mean Australia would resettle close to 48,000 each year.

- Upper-middle income Countries of Second Asylum resettle refugees equivalent to 0.1% of their population each year. This would mean that Malaysia with a population of 30 million would resettle close to 30,000 each year.

Through these rules over 1.3 million refugees are resettled each year, adequately covering the approximate 1 million resettlement requests and well above the average across recent years (prior to 2015) of 100,000 each year.

Fig 13.2 ▶ Volunatry Resettlement. Burden Sharing - 62 Countries of Second Asylum.

Country	2015	Income Group	Freedom Status	Burden Sharing Category	Annual Resettlement Amount
Mauritius	1,273,212	Upper-middle income	Free	UM Income	1,273
Tunisia	11,253,554	Upper-middle income	Free	UM Income	11,254
Botswana	2,262,485	Upper-middle income	Free	UM Income	2,262
Namibia	2,458,830	Upper-middle income	Free	UM Income	2,459
Japan	126,573,481	High income	Free	50,000 Limit	50,000
Mongolia	2,959,134	Upper-middle income	Free	UM Income	2,959
South Korea	50,293,439	High income	Free	50,000 Limit	50,000
Malaysia	30,331,007	Upper-middle income	Partly Free	UM Income	30,331
Singapore	5,603,740	High income	Partly Free	H Income	11,207
Cyprus	1,165,300	High income	Free	H Income	2,331
Israel	8,064,036	High income	Free	H Income	16,128
Kuwait	3,892,115	High income	Partly Free	H Income	7,784
Bulgaria	7,149,787	Upper-middle income	Free	UM Income	7,150
Czech Rep	10,543,186	High income	Free	H Income	21,086
Hungary	9,855,023	High income	Free	H Income	19,710
Poland	38,611,794	High income	Free	50,000 Limit	50,000
Romania	19,511,324	Upper-middle income	Free	UM Income	19,511
Slovakia	5,426,258	High income	Free	H Income	10,853
Denmark	5,669,081	High income	Free	H Income	11,338
Estonia	1,312,558	High income	Free	H Income	2,625
Finland	5,503,457	High income	Free	H Income	11,007
Ireland	4,688,465	High income	Free	H Income	9,377
Latvia	1,970,503	High income	Free	H Income	3,941
Lithuania	2,878,405	High income	Free	H Income	5,757
Norway	5,210,967	High income	Free	H Income	10,422
Sweden	9,779,426	High income	Free	H Income	19,559
UK	64,715,810	High income	Free	50,000 Limit	50,000
Albania	2,896,679	Upper-middle income	Partly Free	UM Income	2,897
Bosnia and H	3,810,416	Upper-middle income	Partly Free	UM Income	3,810
Croatia	4,240,317	High income	Free	H Income	8,481
Greece	10,954,617	High income	Free	H Income	21,909
Italy	59,797,685	High income	Free	50,000 Limit	50,000
Portugal	10,349,803	High income	Free	H Income	20,700
Serbia	8,850,975	Upper middle income	Free	UM Income	8,851
Slovenia	2,067,526	High income	Free	H Income	4,135
Spain	46,121,699	High income	Free	50,000 Limit	50,000
Macedonia	2,078,453	Upper-middle income	Partly Free	UM Income	2,078
Austria	8,544,586	High income	Free	H Income	17,089

Country	2015	Income Group	Freedom Status	Burden Sharing Category	Annual Resettlement Amount
Belgium	11,299,192	High income	Free	H Income	22,598
France	64,395,345	High income	Free	50,000 Limit	50,000
Germany	80,688,545	High income	Free	50,000 Limit	50,000
Netherlands	16,924,929	High income	Free	H Income	33,850
Switzerland	8,298,663	High income	Free	H Income	16,597
Dominican Rep	10,528,391	Upper-middle income	Free	UM Income	10,528
Jamaica	2,793,335	Upper-middle income	Free	UM Income	2,793
Trinidad and T	1,360,088	High income	Free	H Income	2,720
Costa Rica	4,807,850	Upper-middle income	Free	UM Income	4,808
Mexico	127,017,224	Upper-middle income	Partly Free	50,000 Limit	50,000
Panama	3,929,141	Upper-middle income	Free	UM Income	3,929
Argentina	43,416,755	High income	Free	50,000 Limit	50,000
Brazil	207,847,528	Upper-middle income	Free	50,000 Limit	50,000
Chile	17,948,141	High income	Free	H Income	35,896
Colombia	48,228,704	Upper-middle income	Partly Free	UM Income	48,229
Ecuador	16,144,363	Upper-middle income	Partly Free	UM Income	16,144
Paraguay	6,639,123	Upper-middle income	Partly Free	UM Income	6,639
Peru	31,376,670	Upper-middle income	Free	UM Income	31,377
Uruguay	3,431,555	High income	Free	H Income	6,863
Venezuela	31,108,083	High income	Partly Free	50,000 Limit	50,000
Canada	35,939,927	High income	Free	50,000 Limit	50,000
USA	321,773,631	High income	Free	50,000 Limit	50,000
Australia	23,968,973	High income	Free	H Income	47,938
New Zealand	4,528,526	High income	Free	H Income	9,057
					1,330,242

3b. Reduce the Rights for Refugees and Immigrants

A roll back of the legal, political and social rights for immigrants or refugees to a country can arguably allow a country to house more refugees and migrants. A policy could require refugees to remain in rural towns which have job vacancies but are experiencing difficulty in attracting or retaining residents to fill them. This policy is somewhat fulfilled in Australia with the creation of the Safe Haven Enterprise Visa in 2014, albeit applying only to refugees. Another policy would be to limit access to welfare for a certain number of years for new migrants or refugees.

The reduction of such rights could also make it more difficult for unauthorised immigrants to stay through the legal channels generally open to all inhabitants. It avoids the diplomatic costs associated with more stringent border enforcement or imposition of tough new visa restrictions on the nationals of high immigration countries.

Such tiering has deeper risks if applied to citizens. Creating tiered citizenship with regards to rights sets a dangerous precedence for the breach of human rights. Once the first set of rights have been curtailed for part of the population, further rolling back of rights may be very difficult to halt. A large body of research suggests curtailing of welfare rights does not stem the flow of new migrants as it is superseded by the demand pull factors such as job prospects[23].

3c. Reduce Immigration

Suspending or reducing the amount of regular immigration and replacing these positions with refugees would enable a higher intake of refugee and asylum seekers. There would be no additional negative consequences of large population increases to the existing infrastructure or culture.

The negative consequence that would occur is the opportunity cost of the positive impact skilled migrants bring immediately to the economy. Such immediate contributions to the GDP are unlikely to be matched by a corresponding refugee intake. Refugees, for a variety of reasons, contribute less initially to the GDP. In general, refugees are less skilled than skilled migrants and often less ready to work due to various factors including exposure to trauma. The reduced opportunities for people to migrate to a country, due to preferential treatment of refugees, creates incentives for would-be migrants to present as needy (rather than as being able to contribute).

3d. Allow Refugees to Pay for Citizenship (Indentured Labour)

The cost, including welfare payments and educational services, of resettling large numbers of refugees is one concern that limits the number of resettlement places. If this cost, or part thereof, would be repaid over time by the refugee, then arguably a country's willingness to accept refugees would increase. The average cost for Australia to resettle a refugee per year is $14,500 (about A$58,000 over four years[24]). This may be paid upfront or taken on as a debt by the refugee. The debt is then repaid over time in a process similar to the indentured labour schemes of the 17th-19th centuries or, more recently, Australia's Higher Education Contribution Scheme (HECS) whereby the government requires for loans to be repaid out of salaries only once earnings are above a certain threshold.

This scheme potentially increases the number of places available per year by reducing the financial burden of host nations. However, the financial burden may not be the only

---

23 James F. Hollifield, Philip L. Martin and Pia M. Orrenius, *Controlling Immigration: A Global Perspective,* Third Edition (United States, Standford Univerity Press, 2014), 28.
24 Patrick Durkin, "Big Business wants to double Syrian refugees to 25,000," *The Australian,* Feb 3, 2016.

factor limiting the number of refugees taken in each year. A greater issue with this scheme is its arguable abuse of the principle to maintain and expand human rights by requiring vulnerable and disadvantaged people to take on debt to pay for their protected status.

3e. Privately Sponsor Resettlement

Allow private citizens and organisations to sponsor the refugee resettlements through a system where donations may be made to the resettlement costs of refugees. This effectively reduces the economic impact of a given number of resettlement places. It could also lead to an increased number of places. The benefit of this policy component depends on the extent to which the financial burden of refugee resettlements is the limiting factor regarding the yearly refugee intake.

Canada runs a Private Sponsorship of Refugees Program[25]. Sponsors or Sponsoring Groups agree to provide refugees with care, lodging, settlement assistance and support. The duration usually lasts for twelve months or less if the refugee becomes self-sufficient. In some circumstances the period may last as long as 36 months.

3f. Abolish Temporary Protection Visas (TPVs)

The provision of refugees with TPVs allows them to stay and work within the host country for a finite period of time before returning home once repatriation is possible. TPVs can potentially increase the number of refugees a nation can shelter, especially in the capacity of burden-sharing of refugees not planned for resettlement. TPVs do not provide a permanent solution, and may ultimately not be adequate to meet the needs of a very large number of displaced people.

Conversely, removing TPVs and moving all asylum seekers found to be refugees on to permanent protection visas will provide more certainty to all refugees processed in Australia. Although the updated TPVs now provide more rights, they still result in the holder not having any long-term certainty regarding their future. *Lives in Limbo* by Michael Leach and Fethi Mansouri documents the negative mental impacts a prolonged period in limbo can cause[26].

3g. Combat Xenophobia and Racism

Amnesty International's 8-point plan asserts that xenophobic and racist views limit the level and tone of the humanitarian response towards asylum seekers by various countries, which is to the detriment of asylum seekers.

---

25 "Guide to the Private Sponsorship of Refugees Program," Government of Canada, accessed July 24, 2016 <www.cic.gc.ca/english/resources/publications/ref-sponsor/>.
26 Michael Leach & Fethi Mansouri, *Lives in Limbo* (Sydney: UNSW Press, 2004).

> *"...governments must refrain from engaging in xenophobia themselves, for example by implying or directly claiming asylum-seekers and migrants are to blame for economic and social problems. Governments must also reform any laws or policies that explicitly or practically result in racial or other forms of discrimination. Governments must also have effective policies to address xenophobic and racial violence[27]."*

Of course, very large intakes of asylum seekers and refugees (as seen in Lebanon, Jordan and Germany in 2015) can ultimately lead to economic and social problems. However, these countries remain the rare exceptions in the international picture and an argument exists that many countries have the capacity to do much more without risking too great an economic or social disruption.

Xenophobia and racism work both ways. The most common and obvious is any discrimination or intolerance displayed by the state and the majority's attitude towards migrants. However, the opposite also occurs with migrants self-segregating and forming attitudes of distrust and intolerance towards the state and the culture of the majority population.

As discussed in Chapter 7, the correct level of integration of immigrants from different cultures is open for debate. Western values that should be adopted regardless of whether an assimilation or multicultural policy is followed include: the rule of law, secularism, freedom of speech and religion, equality of sexes, and minority rights. Although these expectations may be established, their implementation and enforcement is not guaranteed.

3h. Create a Refugee State

Creation of a new state that accepts refugees who are unable to be repatriated or resettled to other countries. While this allays some of the fears host nations have regarding a massive influx of refugees on their national stability, this policy has a number of significant implementation and operational barriers:

- Land would be required to be provided by a country or countries. This land would need to be donated or purchased permanently.
- Funds and resources would be required to establish the necessary infrastructure.
- Further funds and resources would be required to establish systems of government and courts, and services like police.

---

[27] Tharanga Yakupitiyage, "Amnesty International's 8-Point Plan for Refugee Crises," *Inter Press Service News Agency,* October 14, 2015.

Criticisms of the creation of a refugee state also include the segregation of the problem away from the developed nations, an approach that ultimately may make success of such a state less likely.

3i. Update and Ratify the Refugee Convention

An updated and improved Refugee Convention may include[28]:

- An updated refugee definition that also encompasses temporary displacements and IDPs as well as guaranteeing the rights of displaced people.
- A formalised world response to refugee situations beyond non-refoulement: emergency assistance in safe havens, temporary protection, repatriation, local integration and resettlement.
- A focus on groups (not individuals) and on humanitarian assistance (not a definition of persecution).
- Accountability regarding displacements on countries responsible, which may include sanctions and other interventions as well as provide support for reconstruction and reintegration.
- Direction of resources to where they are most needed (Countries of First Asylum).
- Flexibility regarding how states may choose to help. (For example, Japan sends money, Australia and Canada provide resettlements).

A result of such updates could be a new set of obligations that separates refugee support from migration, meaning that helping refugees does not mandate they migrate to a new country. Alternate options would include: Safe Havens, Temporary Protection, international cooperation for burden-sharing.

3j. Withdraw from the Refugee Convention

In theory, withdrawal from the Refugee Convention would enable a country to commit to a sizable resettlement effort as they would not be burdened by the uncapped obligations of the Convention.

Not all obligations would be eliminated. There would still be a requirement to process asylum seeker claims as asylum from political persecution and a requirement for non-refoulement through the International Covenant in Civil and Political Rights (ICCPR), and the Convention Against Torture and Other Degrading and Inhuman Treatment (CAT). It must be noted that withdrawal may be interpreted as pushing the burden elsewhere and rejecting international standards. The result may be a loss of influence in any forums looking to reshape the international protection framework.

---

28 Adrienne Millbank, "The Problem with the 1951 Refugee Convention,"Parliament of Australia (September 5, 2001).

CH 14. HOLISTIC APPROACHES AND ASSESSMENT – CURRENT STATE

What approach options to the refugee situation are available and how do those options compare?

While numerous Component Policies (reviewed in Chapter 13) have been raised by governments and media commentators, only a handful of realistic Holistic Approaches have been attempted or proposed. The recent approaches adopted by Australia, Germany and Japan differ greatly and will be used as a basis to explore how each would work as a global Holistic Approach. Four other holistic approach ideas will also be reviewed. These seven approach options, plus an 'As-Is' (do nothing) approach, are each assessed against the framework developed in Chapter 12. Each option is scored through which comparisons can be made.

The Holistic Approach options assume a global effort. That is, some involvement from all countries who can provide support for the refugee situation. The probability of successful implementation is a critical factor. What works well in theory may not work in practice for a variety of reasons. For example, many countries may resist implementing certain approaches or, even if all do attempt to adopt an approach, the probability of successful implementation may be low. In both cases, the effectiveness of the approach will be compromised.

The first option reviewed is to change nothing and maintain the current approach. With regard to the refugee situation, this means the current approaches used by countries would all be maintained. These approaches are very diverse. For instance, Saudi Arabia and Japan accept almost no refugees, Australia has strict border controls and offshore processing, and Europe in 2015 had an open-door policy for asylum seekers from war-torn Syria and other countries of the Middle East.

- Approach 1. As-Is 2015

The next three options are ones that were followed by specific countries in 2015. Each option rather different. Australia, Germany and Japan.

- Approach 2. Australia 2015.
- Approach 3. German-led EU 2015.
- Approach 4. Japan 2015.

Finally, four potential Holistic Approaches are reviewed. Aspects of these options have been tried, though not universally or for long periods.

- Approach 5. Amnesty International 8-Point Plan.
- Approach 6. Regional Frameworks.
- Approach 7. Development Zones.
- Approach 8. Centrally Coordinated Burden Sharing.

Each approach is assessed according to the framework outlined in Chapter 12 and provided with four qualitative scores, each out of ten. This methodology is not designed to be scientific; rather its true value is in providing the structure to consider all aspects of the various options prior to making a decision.

It should be noted that none of the options address minimising the disruptive causes that Forcibly Displaced People. In the words of author and international refugee law expert James Hathaway *"No approach of refugee protection, standing on its own, can eradicate the needs for persons to flee from serious harm ... Protection, if carefully designed and delivered, is the critical complement to root cause intervention"*[1].

Holistic Approach Options – Current State

Approach 1. As-Is

How would the refugee problem be managed if the aim was for all countries to maintain an approach similar to that used in 2015?

The first half of the book provides a thorough review of the outcomes of these various approaches. In short, there are 15 million people confirmed as refugees by RSD who are under temporary protection and are awaiting a permanent Durable Solution. The vast majority of these refugees are protected in Countries of First Asylum that neighbour the

---

[1] James Hathaway, "Toward the reformulation of international refugee law: a model for collectivized and solution-oriented protection," 1997 <www.queensu.ca/samp/transform/Hathaway.htm>.

Countries of Origin. These Countries of First Asylum are generally poor and many are overwhelmed by the vast numbers of refugees under their protection.

The standard of protection for refugees in Countries of First Asylum are basic. Accommodation is rudimentary and access to jobs and the associated freedoms money provides are limited. In many cases refugees take the risk to leave the camps and enter the black market workforce in the cities as illegal immigrants. This in turn places pressure on the local job market. Any resultant loss of jobs by locals adds pressure to the society of the host nation.

The wait for a Durable Solution is long. Although a true measure is hard to calculate, a widely-held belief is that the average wait for a Durable Solution may be as high as eighteen years[2]. Repatriations have had limited success and in recent years the number of returns has reduced. Resettlement numbers are also comparatively low – about 100,000 resettlements occur each year, which is less than one percent of the number of refugees.

Due to the quality of life in Countries of First Asylum and the low likelihood of resettlement outcomes, many refugees attempt to reach the more distant resettlement countries to improve their immediate protection standards and their long-term prospects for a permanent solution. Doing this often means taking on considerable risk including engaging people smugglers. The true number of lives lost, thefts committed and people placed into servitude by this risk taking is not known.

The response to such secondary movement is varied across different resettlement countries. Australia's 2015 approach used boat turn-backs and offshore processing on the assumption all arrivals would have been able to seek protection closer to home. The number of asylum seeker arrivals in Australia was very low in 2015 after being high and rising up until 2013 when the policies were introduced. Currently, Australia's approach looks to be sustainable and scalable in terms of its own interests, but places pressure on Countries of First Asylum. Australia's policies have also been criticised internationally as violating many tenets of the Refugee Convention and Human Rights.

The German-led Europe 2015 approach, accepted all people who presented as asylum seekers. The response to Europe's approach was for a massive migration of people from North Africa and the Middle East to Europe. Over one million people arrived by boat or on foot, and more than half of these were subsequently found to have no legitimate refugee claim[3]. The large number of refugee arrivals is placing considerable pressure on the countries of Europe and many agreements of the European Union. Firstly, the financial cost of housing

---

2   Dr. James Milner, "Integrative Thinking and Solutions for Refugees" (Talk presented via TEDxRideauCanal, February 2012).
3   Peter Cluskey, "Most fleeing to Europe are 'not refugees', EU official says," *Irish Times,* January 26, 2016.

and processing the refugees is borne primarily by Germany. Secondly, countries are viewing border control as increasingly important. Many European countries (such as Hungary and Denmark) have shut their borders, breaking the Schengen Agreement. Better control of immigration was one of the key reasons cited by the exit advocates in Britain's Brexit referendum where it voted to exit the European Union. Currently the European approach looks to meet many of the tenets of the Refugee Convention and international human rights law but does not seem scalable for potentially large increases in arrivals. It also does not seem to be sustainable as many additional countries, including Germany, are considering closing their borders.

Other countries, many of them wealthy, such as Japan and Saudi Arabia, take very few refugees and could do more. There are also countries, such as many in South East Asia including Malaysia and Indonesia, who have not signed the Refugee Convention but accept large intakes of refugees. The refugees then work in the black market economies of these countries trying to make ends meet.

Assessment Detail

Effectiveness Score

Q1. Minimise FDP and Enable Easy Protection

1.1 Reducing the numbers of new Forcibly Displaced People. (5/10)

Some current actions are attempting to minimise the disruptive causes of Forcibly Displaced People. Examples include interventions in Syria and peace-keeping in Afghanistan. The complexity is that in many instances such interventions can add to the displacement of people. Key examples being the displacement of millions of Iraqis by the war that removed Saddam Hussein's regime, and the fighting that followed the rise of ISIS within the power-vacuum of Iraq following the departure of America and her allies. This is not to say that Saddam Hussein's regime wasn't in gross violation of human rights and that its removal could have improved the life of the Iraqi population. However, it indicates that international interventions have deep complexities and risk unforeseen consequences.

1.2 Enabling people to find safety as easily as possible and eliminating risk-taking behaviour in order to improve protection prospects. (5/10).

The current policies of Europe enable people to find adequate safety more easily than within countries with tighter border controls such as Australia, or countries who accept very few refugees such as Saudi Arabia. All these policies result in a higher number of people taking risks such as engaging people smugglers in order to improve their situation.

1.3 Eliminating policies that divert finite resources from improving the plight of refugees, either directly through government spend or indirectly through resultant asylum seeker behaviour. (5/10)

The different approaches followed worldwide have varying outcomes regarding the diversion of resources. Europe's approach encourages the use of people smugglers to get people across the Mediterranean and into Europe.

Australia's deterrence policies require a continual cost in maintaining offshore processing centres and border protection. These costs are diversionary as they do not directly support conditions for asylum seekers. As per the Australian experience, these costs would be high initially and settle as the behaviours of asylum seekers change in line with the incentives of such travel.

Average: 5.0

Q2. Best protection levels

2.1 Ensuring the highest possible probability for repatriation. (8/10)

Repatriation is consistently pursued as the Durable Solution of preference by the UNHCR. The probability of repatriation reduces the distance a refugee moves from their Country of Origin. In general, about 80% of refugees remain in a neighbouring Country of First Asylum. Even with the movement of over one million people to Europe in 2015, less than half being refugees, the proportion of refugees being protected in the Countries of First Asylum remains largely unchanged.

2.2 Standardising protection regardless of location. (3/10)

There is currently a great difference in the protection standards experienced by refugees dependent on their location and method of arrival. For instance, those arriving to a resettlement country like Australia with a valid visa would experience far better protection standards than refugees arriving to overwhelmed Countries of First Asylum.

2.3 Avoiding overwhelming intakes of asylum seekers and refugees by Countries of First Asylum. (2/10)

As discussed, there are many Countries of First Asylum experiencing overwhelming numbers of refugees that threaten their viability and social cohesion. These include Turkey, Lebanon and Jordan.

2.4 Avoiding overwhelming intakes of asylum seekers and refugees by Countries of Second Asylum. (4/10)

Many countries in Europe are now concerned about the number of refugees and illegal entrants that arrived in 2015. These countries include Germany, Sweden and France.

2.5 Eliminating the diversion of resources caused by the use of protection channels by those without legitimate refugee claims (e.g. economic migrants). (3/10)

While the use of the asylum seeker pathway as an avenue for economic migrants occurs all over the world, the German-led European experience of 2015 has significantly increased its use. The open-border policy for asylum seekers, coupled with difficulties in extracting those who fail the RSD, provides a great incentive for people seeking to improve their prospects even though they are not refugees.

Average: 3.8

Q3. Reduce waiting time and minimise cultural friction

3.1 Reducing the average time spent waiting in limbo for a Durable Solution. This includes living in temporary accommodation, having little access to paid work, and having no certainty of the future. (5/10)

The time waiting for a Durable Solution varies according to the location and arrival method of the asylum seeker. The figure is very hard to calculate. When considering the total refugee numbers (15 million) and the recent repatriation and resettlement figures (about 100,000 each in 2014) it seems certain the average waiting period is at least ten years.

3.2 Ensuring the human rights of the population of the host nation and of the asylum seekers and refugees are protected across short and long-term horizons. Where cultures are incompatible, assimilation to the host nation is assured. (4/10)

The largest numbers of asylum seekers generally arrive to the Countries of First Asylum or some of the European Countries of Second Asylum (such as Germany). Toward the end of 2015, two highly visible examples of resultant cultural disruptions were experienced in Europe: The Paris shootings and the Cologne sexual assaults on New Years' Eve.

Average: 4.5

Q4. Ongoing and Scalable Protection

4.1 Ensuring persistence and scalability of the protection approach considering Countries for First and Second Asylum, asylum seekers and refugees. (3/10)

The approach adopted by Europe in 2015 saw a massive influx of people into European countries including Germany and Sweden. The immigrant numbers were approximately 1% of the total population. The probability of sustaining such a large number of refugees year after year is low. Australia has one of the world's largest immigrant populations and has averaged a NOM of slightly less than 1% of population. This is with a heavy skew toward skilled migrants who provide an immediate boost to the economy. No Western country has ever taken in 1% of population annually and provided them with provisions such as welfare as outlined by the Refugee Convention.

The approach adopted by Europe in 2015 does not appear scalable. Europe will not be able to absorb ever-increasing numbers of refugees. Countries of First Asylum are also currently expected to absorb uncapped numbers of refugees. Although they are provided with resources and financial support from the UNHCR and do not have the same welfare systems as in resettlement countries, sheltering such uncapped numbers is also unsustainable.

Average: 3.0

Human Rights Score

Q5. Human Rights

5.1 Adhering to the Refugee Convention and other human rights agreements including the Declaration of Human Rights, the Convention of the Rights of Children and the International Covenant on Civil and Political Rights. (6/10)

The qualitative assessment of the As-Is human rights will be used as the baseline from which the human rights score from all other approach options will be assessed.

The German-led European approach attempts to honour the tenets of the Refugee Convention. However there are many other regions of the world not fulfilling all tenets of international human rights law. Australia, although a signatory to all cornerstone instruments, conducts arbitrary detention and administers punishment for arriving without valid entry documentation.

Other countries offer very few places for refugees. Two examples are Japan (a signatory to the Refugee Convention) and Saudi Arabia (not a signatory). Although both provide funding to the UNHCR, the provisions in the Refugee Convention are not being met.

Average: 6.0

Cost Score

Q6. Cost

6.1 Total cost (financial and other) of implementation. (5/10)

The qualitative assessment of the As-Is cost will be used as the baseline from which the cost score from all other approach options will be assessed.

Current efforts to resolve the refugee situation are extensive and the true extent of the cost is hard to estimate. First, there are the costs borne by individual states. In Countries of First Asylum hundreds of refugee camps house millions of people. In addition to the donation of land and resources, local economies and infrastructure are also tested as thousands of refugees move into the cities in an effort to find work to support themselves. In resettlement nations, billions of dollars are spent on myriad policies including deterrence, housing, RSD processing, and the services and social security provided to refugees and permanent residents.

Billions of dollars are also spent through the numerous NGOs, the largest being the UNHCR. The 2014 annual budget for the UNHCR was in excess of US$6 Billion dollars. Only half of the budget was raised from donor states.

Average: 5.0

Implementation Score

Q7. Implementation Probability

7.1 Probability of implementation and probability of success once implemented. Considerations include complexity and the likelihood of cooperation across nations. (9/10)

The qualitative assessment of the As-Is implementation success will be used as the baseline from which the implementation success score from all other approach options will be assessed.

Estimating the implementation of the As-Is state is an oxymoron as by definition it is occurring and is essentially implemented. Logic would dictate a score of ten. However, one area of flux is the German-led European approach – its implementation is still in flux so its score has been lowered slightly.

Average: 9.0

Assessment Summary

The As-Is approach is a mixture of many approaches. It reflects the varying strategies used by different countries and regions based on their needs and concerns. Accordingly, these various strategies draw different reactions from the international community.

States that seldom offer placements, such as Saudi Arabia and Japan, draw some criticism from the international community. However, these countries do provide large donations to the UNHCR. Australia's punitive deterrence measures also draw criticism, particularly with regard to human rights abuses, but its resettlement placements are consistently among the highest in the world. Conversely Lebanon, Jordan, and African countries like Kenya are praised for their generosity in supporting refugees as Countries of First Asylum, yet fears exists around the resultant security and stability with such large influxes of refugees.

It is widely hoped that better strategies exist to manage the refugee situation. This As-Is Approach will be used as the baseline by which other options will be assessed. It represents the easiest implemented pathway that would occur without an impetus to change. To that end, the four scores provided are arbitrary and the value lies in the comparison between these scores and those of the other approach options.

Effectiveness Score: 4.3

Human Rights Score: 6.0

Cost Score: 5.0

Implementation Score: 9.0

Fig 14.1 ▶ Approach 1. As-Is approach.

	Question	Question Criteria	Pros	Cons	Scores / 10	Score
1. Effectiveness						
Question 1.	Q1. How can the number of Forcibly Displaced People be minimised and how can they find protection as safely and as easily as possible?	1.1 Reducing the numbers of new Forcibly Displaced People.	- Nil.	- Attempts to intervene risk unforeseen consequences such as post Iraqi rise of ISIS. - Minimal encouragement for increased refugee presentation.	5	4.7
		1.2 Enabling people to find safety as easily as possible and eliminating risk taking behaviour in order to improve protection prospects.	- Open borders to many European states. - Tight border controls in resettlement countries outside Europe.	- High risk taking to enter Europe.	4	
		1.3 Eliminating policies that divert finite resources from improving the plight of refugees, either directly through government spend or indirectly through resultant asylum seeker behaviour.	- Expense of paying people smugglers continues.	- Expense of paying people smugglers continues. - Expense of diversionary spend continues	5	
Question 2.	Q2. How can protection best be provided to asylum seekers and refugees?	2.1 Ensuring the highest possible probability for repatriation.	- Repatriation pushed as preferred choice by UNHCR. 80% of refugees in neighbouring countries of first asylum.	- Nil	8	5.0
		2.2 Standardising protection regardless of location.	- General, but not complete, adherence to Refugee Convention. European countries attempting to honour convention obligations for all.	- Great difference in the protection standards experienced by refugees dependent on their location and method of arrival	5	
		2.3 Avoiding overwhelming intakes of asylum seekers and refugees by Countries of First Asylum.	- Nil.	- Many countries of first asylum overwhelmed. Incl Turkey, Lebanon and Jordan.	5	
		2.4 Avoiding overwhelming intakes of asylum seekers and refugees by Countries of Second Asylum.	- Mnay resettlement nations control the numbers of arrivals.	- Many countries in Europe overwhelmed. Incl. Germany, Sweden and France.	4	
		2.5 Eliminating the diversion of resources caused by the use of protection channels by those without legitimate refugee claims (e.g. economic migrants).	- Deterrence occurs in countries like Australia, Canada and the USA.	- Large volumes of economic migrants to Europe	3	
Question 3.	Q3. How can the time spent waiting in limbo for a Durable Solution be minimised?	3.1 Reducing the average time spent waiting in limbo for a Durable Solution. This includes living in temporary accommodation, having little access to paid work, and having no certainty of the future.	- Nil.	- High waiting periods for refugees.	5	4.5
		3.2 Ensuring the human rights of the population of the host nation and of the asylum seekers and refugees are protected across short and long term horizons. Where cultures are incompatible, assimilation to the host nation is assured.	- Nil.	- Examples of resultant cultural disruptions in Europe were experienced. Such as the Paris shootings and and the Cologne sexual assaults on New Years' Eve.	4	
Question 4.	Q4. How can the approach provide ongoing and scalable protection?	4.1 Ensuring persistence and scalability of the protection approach considering Countries for First and Second Asylum, asylum seekers and refugees.	- European approach places more onus on wealthier countries.	- Perpetuity of Resettlement nation intake (~1%) in Europe unlikely.	4	4.0
				Effectiveness Score (average)		**4.7**
2. Human Rights	Question	Question Criteria	Pros	Cons	Scores / 10	Score
Question 5.	Q5. How well does the approach honour the tenets of international law?	5.1 Adhering to the Refugee Convention and other human rights agreements including the Declaration of Human Rights, the Convention of the Rights of Children and the International Covenant on Civil and Political Rights.	- European approach attempts to honour the tenets of the Refugee Convention.	- Limitations of other countries such as Australian, Japan, China.	6	6.0
				Human Rights Score (average)		**6.0**
3. Cost	Question	Question Criteria	Pros	Cons	Scores / 10	Score
Question 6.	Q6. How costly is implementation?	6.1 Total cost (financial and other) of implementation.	- Nil.	- Very high cost. - New and complex approach. Probability of successful unknown.	5	5.0
				Cost Score (larger is more cost)		**5.0**
4. Probability	Question	Question Criteria	Pros	Cons	Scores / 10	Score
Question 7.	Q7. How probable is successful implementation?	7.1 Probability of implementation and probability of success once implemented. Considerations include complexity and the likelihood of cooperation across nations.	- High probability in maintaining a current state where country follows its own approach.	- Pressure exists on the current German-led EU approach.	9	9.0
				Implementation Success Score		**9.0**

Approach 2. Australia 2015

How would the refugee problem be managed if the aim was for all countries to adopt an Australia 2015 Approach?

Australia's relatively uncontroversial Offshore program constitutes the UNHCR Durable Solution of Voluntary Resettlement. Conversely, the Onshore Program, for asylum seekers arriving at the border under the Refugee Convention is widely criticised. In terms of providing permanent residencies to refugees, across the two programs Australia has provided approximately 13,750 humanitarian visas each year. This is approximately 0.06% of the country's population.

If each of the 62 Countries of Second Asylum provided the same proportion of permanent places to refugees as Australia, almost one million permanent humanitarian visas would be provided to refugees each year. This effectively meets the volume of UNHCR submissions for resettlement in 2014 and is far in excess of the placements provided through resettlement or local integration in 2014 (about 200,000).

Fig 14.2 ➤ The nations who can help. 62 Countries of Second Asylum.

Country	Continent	Land Size (sq km)	2015	Income Group	GNI per capita*	Freedom in the World	Sum (all UNHCR POC)	Sum UNHCR POC per Pop
Mauritius	Africa	2,040	1,273,212	Upper middle	$9,710	Free	-	0.00%
Tunisia	Africa	163,610	11,253,554	Upper middle	$-	Free	1,135	0.01%
Botswana	Africa	600,370	2,262,485	Upper middle	$7,240	Free	2,847	0.13%
Namibia	Africa	825,418	2,458,830	Upper middle	$5,680	Free	4,264	0.17%
Japan	Asia	377,835	126,573,481	High income	$42,000	Free	12,491	0.01%
Mongolia	Asia	1,565,000	2,959,134	Upper middle	$4,280	Free	15	0.00%
South Korea	Asia	-	50,293,439	High income	$27,090	Free	4,866	0.01%
Malaysia	Asia	329,750	30,331,007	Upper middle	$10,760	Partly Free	270,621	0.89%
Singapore	Asia	693	5,603,740	High income	$55,150	Partly Free	3	0.00%
Cyprus	Asia	9,250	1,165,300	High income	$26,370	Free	7,593	0.65%
Israel	Asia	20,770	8,064,036	High income	$34,990	Free	45,284	0.56%
Kuwait	Asia	17,820	3,892,115	High income	$-	Partly Free	94,652	2.43%
Bulgaria	Europe	110,910	7,149,787	Upper middle	$7,420	Free	17,864	0.25%
Czech Rep	Europe	78,866	10,543,186	High income	$-	Free	5,137	0.05%
Hungary	Europe	93,030	9,855,023	High income	$13,470	Free	18,675	0.19%
Poland	Europe	312,685	38,611,794	High income	$13,730	Free	29,251	0.08%
Romania	Europe	237,500	19,511,324	Upper middle	$9,370	Free	2,542	0.01%
Slovakia	Europe	48,845	5,426,258	High income	$-	Free	2,673	0.05%
Denmark	Europe	43,094	5,669,081	High income	$61,310	Free	26,807	0.47%
Estonia	Europe	45,226	1,312,558	High income	$18,530	Free	88,261	6.72%
Finland	Europe	337,030	5,503,457	High income	$-	Free	15,845	0.29%
Ireland	Europe	70,280	4,688,465	High income	$44,660	Free	10,578	0.23%

Country	Continent	Land Size (sq km)	2015	Income Group	GNI per capita*	Freedom in the World	Sum (all UNHCR POC)	Sum UNHCR POC per Pop
Latvia	Europe	64,589	1,970,503	High income	$15,660	Free	263,224	13.36%
Lithuania	Europe	65,200	2,878,405	High income	$15,380	Free	4,794	0.17%
Norway	Europe	324,220	5,210,967	High income	$103,050	Free	56,220	1.08%
Sweden	Europe	449,964	9,779,426	High income	$61,600	Free	226,158	2.31%
UK	Europe	-	64,715,810	High income	$42,690	Free	153,560	0.24%
Albania	Europe	28,748	2,896,679	Upper middle	$4,460	Partly Free	8,032	0.28%
Bosnia and H	Europe	-	3,810,416	Upper middle	$4,780	Partly Free	144,124	3.78%
Croatia	Europe	56,542	4,240,317	High income	$13,020	Free	19,809	0.47%
Greece	Europe	131,940	10,954,617	High income	$22,090	Free	42,732	0.39%
Italy	Europe	301,230	59,797,685	High income	$34,280	Free	140,277	0.23%
Portugal	Europe	92,391	10,349,803	High income	$21,320	Free	1,057	0.01%
Serbia	Europe	102,350	8,850,975	Upper middle	$5,820	Free	271,573	3.07%
Slovenia	Europe	20,273	2,067,526	High income	$-	Free	330	0.02%
Spain	Europe	504,782	46,121,699	High income	$-	Free	6,593	0.01%
Macedonia	Europe	-	2,078,453	Upper middle	$-	Partly Free	3,175	0.15%
Austria	Europe	83,858	8,544,586	High income	$-	Free	78,913	0.92%
Belgium	Europe	30,510	11,299,192	High income	$47,030	Free	41,684	0.37%
France	Europe	547,030	64,395,345	High income	$43,070	Free	309,414	0.48%
Germany	Europe	357,021	80,688,545	High income	$47,640	Free	455,081	0.56%
Netherlands	Europe	41,526	16,924,929	High income	$51,210	Free	91,385	0.54%
Switzerland	Europe	41,290	8,298,663	High income	$-	Free	83,528	1.01%
Dominican Rep	Latin Am & C'bean	48,730	10,528,391	Upper middle	$6,030	Free	211,354	2.01%
Jamaica	Latin Am & C'bean	10,831	2,793,335	Upper middle	$-	Free	22	0.00%
Trinidad and T	Latin Am & C'bean	-	1,360,088	High income	$-	Free	170	0.01%
Costa Rica	Latin Am & C'bean	51,100	4,807,850	Upper middle	$10,120	Free	23,718	0.49%
Mexico	Latin Am & C'bean	1,972,550	127,017,224	Upper middle	$9,860	Partly Free	4,722	0.00%
Panama	Latin Am & C'bean	78,200	3,929,141	Upper middle	$11,130	Free	18,675	0.48%
Argentina	Latin Am & C'bean	2,766,890	43,416,755	High income	$14,160	Free	4,359	0.01%
Brazil	Latin Am & C'bean	8,511,965	207,847,528	Upper middle	$11,530	Free	47,946	0.02%
Chile	Latin Am & C'bean	756,950	17,948,141	High income	$14,910	Free	2,346	0.01%
Colombia	Latin Am & C'bean	1,138,910	48,228,704	Upper middle	$7,970	Partly Free	6,044,552	12.53%
Ecuador	Latin Am & C'bean	283,560	16,144,363	Upper middle	$6,070	Partly Free	133,744	0.83%
Paraguay	Latin Am & C'bean	406,750	6,639,123	Upper middle	$4,380	Partly Free	166	0.00%
Peru	Latin Am & C'bean	1,285,220	31,376,670	Upper middle	$6,370	Free	1,690	0.01%
Uruguay	Latin Am & C'bean	176,220	3,431,555	High income	$16,350	Free	328	0.01%
Venezuela	Latin Am & C'bean	-	31,108,083	High income	$-	Partly Free	174,027	0.56%
Canada	Northern America	9,976,140	35,939,927	High income	$51,690	Free	165,874	0.46%
USA	Northern America	9,629,091	321,773,631	High income	$55,200	Free	455,048	0.14%
Australia	Oceania	7,686,850	23,968,973	High income	$64,680	Free	57,100	0.24%
New Zealand	Oceania	268,680	4,528,526	High income	$-	Free	1,619	0.04%

*Atlas Method (USD 2014).

Providing humanitarian places is not cheap. Each person granted permanent protection qualifies for the same entitlements (such as social security) as citizens. Australia's budget estimate is A$58,000 per refugee[4]. Using this estimate, the cost of Australia's 13,750 humanitarian visas each year is A$800 million. Thus, providing permanent protection to refugees without external financial support is expensive. Such a policy is only likely to be adopted by wealthy nations.

In addition, Australia provided US$48 million (or A$46 million using December 2012 exchange rate) to the UNHCR in 2012. This was a modest 0.01% of Australia's federal government revenue (~A$341billion). However, it ranked 11th highest in dollars provided by all countries and the EU, and around 2% of the US$2.2 billion donated by all such countries, intergovernmental bodies, UN funds and private donors. A matching of this amount would lift the UNHCR budget significantly. A clear rationale for such a high position is Australia's relative wealth and relatively low number of asylum seekers.

The Voluntary Resettlement program is a burden-sharing activity. Australia is able to provide these places as the number of direct arrivals (either authorised or unauthorised) is very small relative to many developed nations, particularly those in Europe.

Australia housed 51,700 refugees and asylum seekers as of the end of 2014. This is approximately 0.24% of Australia's population and only 0.03% of the world's total number of refugees and asylum seekers. This number is so low due primarily to Australia's remote location and strict laws aiming to deter boat trips to Australia, thus seeking to gain the advantage of being protected within Australia over the protection of their Country of First Asylum. Only asylum seekers arriving with valid visas or refugees through the resettlement program are accepted.

Australia is not alone in its system. In broad terms, Canada's approach is quite similar and is modelled on aspects of Australia's system. Both countries are wealthy and free, and have large resettlement programs. Also, due to their distance, both receive far fewer onshore asylum seeker claims than European nations; Canada receives less boat arrivals than Australia[5]. Both countries use immigration detention for some refugees, for example Canada's grounds for detention include inadequate identification or through irregular arrival as designated by the Minister of Public Safety and Emergency Preparedness[6]. Although both have received criticisms from international agencies, in most recent metrics Canada appears the more generous. It shelters a higher proportion of asylum seekers and refugees per capita and has provided more special placements to Syrian refugees. As previously

---

4   Patrick Durkin, "Big Business wants to double Syrian refugees to 25,000," *The Australian,* Feb 3, 2016.
5   Katie Derosa, "Mandatory detention for refugee claimants has already proved to be a failure, critics say," The Vancouver Sun, November 17, 2012.
6   "Arrests, detentions and removals," Canada Border Services Agency, accessed, March 2016. Cbsa-asfc.gc.ca

discussed, it also has a process to allow private sponsorship for refugee resettlement. The UNHCR donations per capita are similar.

Fig. 14.3 ❯ Country Comparison: Australia and Canada.

Metric	Australia	Canada
Demographics	-	-
Population (2015)	23,968,973	35,939,927
GNI per capita (2014)	$64,680	$51,690
% born overseas	28%	21.8%
% with 1 parent born Overseas	20%	17.4%
A,S, & Refugees	-	-
Asylum seekers Housed (2014)	21,518	16,711
Refugees (2014)	35,582	149,163
Combined % of Population	0.24%	0.46%
Resettlements	-	
2014	11,600	12,300
2014 as % of populaton	0.05%	0.03%
Special Syrian Intake	12,000	25,000
Special Syrian Intake as % of population	0.05%	0.07%
Immigration Detention	-	
Reasons	Unauthorised Arrival	No ID, Irregular Arrivals
Length of Detention	Indefinite	Indefinite
UNHCR	-	
Donation (2014)	$48,200,780	$73,423,460
Donation (2014) per capita	$2,01	$2,04

Such a policy assumes Australia is not a Country of First Asylum, as it would be if, for example, Indonesia became a refugee-producing county. In that regard Australia's policy cannot be emulated by Countries of First Asylum like Kenya, Lebanon or Jordan. These countries would still be required to shoulder the main influx of refugees at considerable cost to their economic and social viability. The refugees have a physical requirement in terms of housing, which is only partially fulfilled through refugee camps. Many refugees do not stay in camps but rather head to the major cities. In cases like Lebanon, where the refugees make up as much as a quarter of the host population, this places a strain on the existing infrastructure. Additionally, the influx of refugees creates an enormous impact on the job market. People are naturally desperate to work for the choices and autonomy that money provides. Whether sanctioned by the government or not, a flood of workers in the host economy results in a decline in the wages for the lower-skilled jobs and the potential loss of jobs for many of the host nation.

The policy can potentially be emulated in Europe. Specifically, turning back boats and foot traffic prior to their arrival within European countries on the assumption asylum seekers have left a Country of First Asylum. In the cases where asylum seekers do arrive, outsourced protection and processing by countries relatively close but outside the EU could be created. This would reflect Australia's offshore processing and no-advantage policy. Enlisted outsource countries would require large payments for such services. Examples may be Morocco, the Ukraine or Belarus. The Australian government is expecting annual offshore processing costs in PNG and Nauru of just under A$400 million after set-up costs of over $A1 billion per year.

Australia's 2015 approach breaches many international agreements, some definitively and others in spirit. Such breaches, including those related to the Refugee Convention, would be emulated by all countries willing to adopt such an approach.

Australia 2015 – Key Approach Points

- Provision of permanent humanitarian visas equivalent to approximately 0.06% of the country's population, largely through resettlement if not acting as a Country of First Asylum. If the 62 identified Countries of Second Asylum each provided resettlement places to a similar extent, over one million permanent humanitarian visas would be provided.
- Donation of 0.01% of GDP to the UNHCR.
- Protection as per the Refugee Convention for authorised arrivals.
- Turn-back policy for attempted unauthorised arrivals.
- Outsourced protection and processing within third countries as a pillar of deterrence.

Assessment Detail

Effectiveness Score

Q1. Minimise FDP and enable easy protection

1.1 Reducing the numbers of new Forcibly Displaced People. (5/10)

The Australia 2015 Approach has no direct action in minimising the disruptive causes of Forcibly Displaced People. Indirectly this approach would limit the number of FDPs who would present as asylum seekers by making the cost of presenting for protection more onerous than for other initiatives. This increased cost is through the low comfort levels in the Countries of First Asylum, limited access to the wealthy Countries of Second Asylum and still long waits for resettlement. This analysis considers such an outcome as a positive on the assumption some asylum seekers are too quick to leave their homeland.

1.2 Enabling people to find safety as easily as possible and eliminating risk-taking behaviour in order to improve protection prospects. (4/10)

The strict deterrence regime would reduce the often dangerous secondary movement of people away from their Countries of First Asylum to the wealthier resettlement nations. Risk-taking behaviour would dramatically reduce. Unfortunately, this approach provides little impetus to improve the low standard of safety experienced in the Countries of First Asylum who are not signatories to the Refugee Convention.

1.3 Eliminating policies that divert finite resources from improving the plight of refugees, either directly through government spend or indirectly through resultant asylum seeker behaviour. (6/10)

The expense of paying people smugglers would be avoided for asylum seekers who are deterred from travelling to a resettlement country through perceptions of advantage being eliminated. This would only be a benefit to refugees should a similarly easy pathway to safety, with a potential Durable Solution, be available.

A continual cost would still be maintained in deterring such efforts, including offshore processing centres and border protection. These costs are diversionary as they do not directly support conditions for asylum seekers. Australian experience indicates these costs would be high initially and settle as the behaviours of asylum seekers change in line with the incentives of such travel.

Average: 5.3

Q2. Best protection levels

2.1 Ensuring the highest possible probability for repatriation. (8/10)

A high proportion of refugees would remain in the Countries of First Asylum, maximising the probability of repatriation. This high proportion results from deterrence measures and the primary engagement of Resettlement nations via resettlement of refugees rather than protection of asylum seekers and refugees prior to a durable solution.

2.2 Standardising protection regardless of location. (3/10)

Significant human rights breaches of 'unauthorised' asylum seekers would occur – the chief breach being the arbitrary detention of all such asylum seekers (including children) for indefinite periods should they not be willing to return to their Countries of Origin. These human rights are effectively subordinated to those human rights protected by the Resettlement nations through maintenance of their viability. These measures are enacted as a deterrence in the hope future attempts do not occur. Such obvious human rights breaches against innocent people brings into question, especially for liberal democracies, the very values a nation claims to support.

Protection standards would still vary across different types of refugees. Those arriving to a Country of Second Asylum with a valid visa, prior to seeking asylum, will receive sanctuary in that country with education, employment opportunities and social security in line with citizens of that nation. This standard of protection would be far better than that experienced by refugees arriving to overwhelmed Countries of First Asylum or arriving without visas to Countries of Second Asylum who would be moved on to outsourced locations through a no-advantage policy.

2.3 Avoiding overwhelming intakes of asylum seekers and refugees by Countries of First Asylum. (2/10)

The pressure borne by the Countries of First Asylum is heavy, sheltering about 80% of asylum seekers and refugees. These pressures include physically and financially housing and feeding refugees, the social implications of large influxes of people from possibly different cultures, and the impact to the local economy. It will be even greater than currently experienced as asylum seekers and refugees are deterred from moving on toward distant countries perceived to be more favourable. Such pressures place these countries at risk of economic and social deterioration. Twenty percent of refugees and asylum seekers have been hosted by Countries of Second Asylum (that is, not Countries of First Asylum). In 2014, the United States, Germany, and France hosted over 1.2 million refugees between them. Almost another one million were hosted across Sweden, Canada, the UK, Italy, the Netherlands, Switzerland, Austria and Norway. With these nations hosting greatly reduced numbers, there would be additional pressure on the Countries of First Asylum. This increase in refugees would be only partially offset by greatly increased resettlement numbers.

2.4 Avoiding overwhelming intakes of asylum seekers and refugees by Countries of Second Asylum. (9/10)

This approach also controls the numbers of arrivals at more distant, resettlement nations. It works to protect the viability of these resettlement nations and ultimately the ongoing human rights which stem to their populations from such viability. Of course, just how much this viability is at threat is debatable, both in the short term and the long term. The influx of refugees to many nations after World War II and their ultimate successful integration is evidence that large numbers are manageable. However, the European experience of 2015 is displaying some dangers of accepting too many arrivals at once. Such dangers include terrorist attacks, financial burdens and a level of civil unrest in the form of fears and protests.

2.5 Eliminating the diversion of resources caused by the use of protection channels by those without legitimate refugee claims (e.g. economic migrants). (9/10)

This approach is anticipated to deter economic migrants from attempting, rationally, to utilise the asylum-seeker channel. Economic migrants reduce opportunities for asylum seekers as they contribute to increased numbers of arrivals and crowd out some legitimate refugees. It is hard to estimate the cost saving of such deterrence but it is known that the EU reported over 60% of the 2015 arrivals had no legitimate refugee claims[7]. It would be unlikely such arrivals would occur under this approach as only legitimate refugees would be resettled to Countries of Second Asylum.

Average: 6.2

Q3. Reduce waiting time and minimise cultural friction

3.1 Reducing the average time spent waiting in limbo for a Durable Solution. This includes living in temporary accommodation, having little access to paid work, and having no certainty of the future. (6/10)

Australia's provision of permanent humanitarian visas (approximately 0.06% of population) is quite generous in global terms. Adoption of this policy by the 62 Countries of Second Asylum would provide permanent residency to over one million people each year. This is up to five times greater than the 2014 numbers, and would help to reduce the waiting periods for refugees. Additional permanent placements may be available in 'outsource countries' through arrangements with these nations.

One assumption around this approach is with the reduction in the asylum seeker arrivals to the resettlement nations, a greater number of permanent places can be provided through resettlement of refugees at levels intake nations can control without threatening their viability.

3.2 Ensuring the human rights of the population of the host nation and of the asylum seekers and refugees are protected across short and long-term horizons. Where cultures are incompatible, assimilation to the host nation is assured. (5/10)

Australia does have some premises in its multicultural policy stipulating all Australians accept the basic structures and principles of Australian society (see Chapter 8). While it is not clear how such stipulations are encouraged or enforced, the practical experience of Australia's multiculturalism appears that immigrant and refugee intakes at previous

---

7   Peter Cluskey, "Most fleeing to Europe are 'not refugees', EU official says," *Irish Times,* January 26, 2016.

levels have led to broad and beneficial integration into society with assimilation across the core areas as described by Australia's multicultural policy. In general, such long term levels can also be expected to be manageable across other resettlement nations.

However, these limitations are not in place for Countries of First Asylum. The large number of people entering could lead to cultural tensions or changes that infringe on the human rights the host population.

Average: 5.5

Q4. Ongoing and Scalable Protection

4.1 Ensuring persistence and scalability of the protection approach considering Countries for First and Second Asylum, asylum seekers and refugees. (6/10)

Australia's 2015 approach is highly likely to be able to continue in perpetuity given the relatively high but controlled resettlement numbers. The chief concern is with the inability of the Countries of First Asylum to handle ever larger numbers of asylum seekers.

The Australian approach is highly scalable with regard to resettlement nations. They will accept refugees primarily through resettlement and not from at-border arrivals. This allows nations to cap their intake at levels they perceive ensures their viability. However, it has limited scalability in relation to Countries of First Asylum. With larger numbers of refugees, these countries are placed under even more pressure with limited burden-sharing from the resettlement nations, outside their resettlement totals. As the numbers continue to increase, conditions for refugees and the countries themselves deteriorate. This may help self-limit the refugee inflow. If it does not, ultimately the Countries of First Asylum will fracture.

Average: 6.0

Human Rights Score

Q5. Human Rights

5.1 Adhering to the Refugee Convention and other human rights agreements including the Declaration of Human Rights, the Convention of the Rights of Children and the International Covenant on Civil and Political Rights. (4/10)

The protection of human rights under the Australia 2015 approach is a mixed bag. Human rights are fully protected for authorised arrivals and refugees resettled through the Offshore Program. Conversely, the deterrence measures and no-advantage principles imposed through offshore detention centres used in the Onshore Program break many human rights.

These include:

- Article 9 of ICCPR prohibits arbitrary detention.
- Article 7 of ICCPR prohibits torture or cruel, inhuman or degrading treatment or punishment.
- Article 10 of ICCPR requires treatment of people with humanity and respect to their inherent dignity.
- Article 3(1) of the CRC requires all actions concerning children, the best interests of the child should be the primary consideration.
- Article 24(1) of the CRC provides that all children have the right to the highest attainable standard of health.
- Article 37(b) of the CRC states that no child shall be deprived of his or her liberty arbitrarily.
- Article 31 of the Refugee Convention which prohibits imposing penalties through entering without authorisation.

Average: 4.0

Cost Score

Q6. Cost

6.1 Total cost (financial and other) of implementation. (3/10)

Overall, it is estimated that a global adoption of Australia's 2015 approach by resettlement nations would result in less cost than currently borne. The most significant reduction in spend would be seen by Europe.

Countries of Second Asylum nations would, in general, increase their spending in three areas: through taking in more permanent migrants; through deterrence and border protection mechanisms; and through increased donations to the UNHCR and assistance programs. They would also expect reduced spending in the housing and processing of refugees.

As a consequence, Countries of First Asylum will be required to shoulder additional cost. While the financial burden of the increased numbers will be covered by increased donations from resettlement nations, many other costs will fall squarely with the Countries of First Asylum. These include the provision of land and natural resources, social cohesion and economic stability.

Average: 3.0

Implementation Score

Q7. Implementation Success

7.1 Probability of implementation and probability of success once implemented. Considerations include complexity and the likelihood of cooperation across nations. (7/10)

The uptake or cooperation of such policies by the international community is not guaranteed. Some Countries of Second Asylum may have difficulty in agreeing to adopt turn-back and offshore (or outsourced) protection policies as they contravene much of the spirit of the Refugee Convention and already receive heavy criticism from many countries. That said, such policies may be accepted in the hope of reducing the number of economic migrants and also due to the larger resettlement intakes than most countries have previously undertaken. Acceptance would also require public perception their country was not one of First Asylum and those needing help were able to find it in Countries of First Asylum.

The success of resettling over one million people depends on the uptake of this approach by the 62 Countries of Second Asylum. In 2014, only 27 countries provided resettlement places. Many of the nations proposed to provide placements of 0.06% of population are likely to resist, citing protection of their cultural or economic viability. For instance, Japan with a population of over 120 million would be expected to resettle over 70,000 refugees each year. In 2014 they housed less than 15,000 refugees. European countries such as France, Belgium and the UK, which are experiencing some social unrest particularly with home grown Islamism, may be very reluctant to increase their resettlement numbers as many of the current refugee-producing nations are Muslim majority nations. These concerns would be somewhat diminished by the reduction in the asylum seekers and temporary refugees being housed in these nations.

Outside the Countries of First Asylum, which appear to have little choice but to generously accept and help the asylum seekers as best they can, the approach allows them to contribute according to resources, specifically as it relates to resettlement numbers.

Average: 7.0

Assessment Summary

Adoption of the Australia's 2015 Approach by the 62 Countries of Second Asylum would be an attempt to reduce secondary travel by providing more resettlement places in wealthy nations, globalising the no-advantage policy and placing more protection and processing obligations on the Countries of First Asylum.

It would move resettlement nations away from one of the tenets of the Refugee Convention which is to protect and not punish asylum seekers for not having appropriate documentation. The benefits sought by such a move include less harm and diversion of resources through the use of people smugglers, less economic migrants and more control of the numbers entering resettlement nations. With this additional control and expected reduction in asylum seeker arrivals, resettlement nations are expected to permanently resettle a greater number of refugees (up to one million each year), which would greatly reduce the average length of displacement for Forcibly Displaced People.

There are a number of implementation challenges involved. Additional pressures would be placed on Countries of First Asylum that would have to be supported by more funding and resources from NGOs such as the UNHCR. Many nations would resist adopting the approach. Countries of First Asylum would be concerned about increasing pressure on their already stressed societies. Some resettlement nations like Japan would be expected to resettle large numbers of refugees for the first time in their history. Other resettlement nations, such as those in Europe may have concerns about breaching the human rights of vulnerable people seeking a better life.

The greatest benefit is the order and control placed around the movement of people. A global no-advantage policy would limit the movement of individual asylum seekers travelling long distances in order to improve their prospects. It would close avenues for economic migrants that crowd out those less able to move. These controls would effectively enhance the ability of resettlement nations, many of them liberal democracies, to protect their viability and the ongoing human rights their viability maintains.

Effectiveness Score: 5.8
Human Rights Score: 4.0
Cost Score: 3.0
Implementation Score: 7.0

Fig 14.4 ▶ Approach 2. Global adoption of the 2015 Australian approach.

	Question	Question Criteria	Pros	Cons	Scores /10	Average
1. Effectiveness						
Question 1.	Q1. How can the number of Forcibly Displaced People be minimised and how can they find protection as safely and as easily as possible?	1.1 Reducing the numbers of new Forcibly Displaced People.	- Limit Forcibly Displaced People presenting as asylum seekers by making the cost of presenting for protection more onerous than with other initiatives.	- No direct action in minimising the disruptive causes.	5	
		1.2 Enabling people to find safety as easily as possible and eliminating risk taking behaviour in order to improve protection prospects.	- Reduced dangerous secondary movement to the wealthier resettlement nations.	- Nil.	5	5.3
		1.3 Eliminating policies that divert finite resources from improving the plight of refugees, either directly through government spend or indirectly through resultant asylum seeker behaviour.	- Expense of paying people smugglers avoided.	- Continual diversionary cost in maintaining deterring efforts.	6	
Question 2.	Q2. How can protection best be provided to asylum seekers and refugees?	2.1 Ensuring the highest possible probability for repatriation.	- The high proportion of refugees remaining in countries of first asylum maximises the probability of repatriation.	- Nil.	8	
		2.2 Standardising protection regardless of location.	- Nil.	- Human rights breaches of 'unauthorised' asylum seekers, such as arbitrary detention. Different protection: authorised vs unauthorised.	3	6.2
		2.3 Avoiding overwhelming intakes of asylum seekers and refugees by Countries of First Asylum.	- Nil.	- Pressure borne by the countries of first asylum is large.	2	
		2.4 Avoiding overwhelming intakes of asylum seekers and refugees by Countries of Second Asylum.	- Controls the numbers of arrivals at more distant, resettlement nations.	- Nil.	9	
		2.5 Eliminating the diversion of resources caused by the use of protection channels by those without legitimate refugee claims (e.g. economic migrants).	- Deterrence of economic migrants.	- Nil.	9	
Question 3.	Q3. How can the time spent waiting in limbo for a Durable Solution be minimised?	3.1 Reducing the average time spent waiting in limbo for a Durable Solution. This includes living in temporary accommodation, having little access to paid work, and having no certainty of the future.	- Five times increase in Resettlement would help to reduce the waiting periods for refugees.	- Nil.	6	
		3.2 Ensuring the human rights of the population of the host nation and of the asylum seekers and refugees are protected across short and long term horizons. Where cultures are incompatible, assimilation to the host nation is assured.	- Cultural friction is limited in Resettlement nations through the control of the annual intake.	- No specific requirement for immigrant people to assimilate culturally. No volume limitations for the countries of first asylum.	5	5.5
Question 4.	Q4. How can the approach provide ongoing and scalable protection?	4.1 Ensuring persistence and scalability of the protection approach considering Countries for First and Second Asylum, asylum seekers and refugees.	- Likley to continue in perpetuity given the relatively high but controlled resettlement volumes.	- High pressure borne by the countries of first asylum.	6	6.0
				Effectiveness Score (average)	**5.8**	

	Question	Question Criteria	Pros	Cons	Scores /10	Score
2. Human Rights						
Question 5.	Q5. How well does the approach honour the tenets of international law?	5.1 Adhering to the Refugee Convention and other human rights agreements including the Declaration of Human Rights, the Convention of the Rights of Children and the International Covenant on Civil and Political Rights.	- Full protection of the human rights of refugees resettled through the Offshore Program.	- Deterrence measures used part of teh Onshore Program, including the use of offshore detention centres, break many human rights.	4	4.0
				Human Rights Score (average)	**4.0**	

	Question	Question Criteria	Pros	Cons	Scores /10	Score
3. Cost						
Question 6.	Q6. How costly is implementation?	6.1 Total cost (financial and other) of implementation.	- Resettlement countries can contribute according to resources.	- Uptake by international community not guaranteed. Limited control of inflows and effort for countries of first asylum.	3	3.0
				Cost Score (larger is more cost)	**3.0**	

	Question	Question Criteria	Pros	Cons	Scores /10	Score
4. Probability						
Question 7.	Q7. How probable is successful implementation?	7.1 Probability of implementation and probability of success once implemented. Considerations include complexity and the likelihood of cooperation across nations.	- Low complexity approach	- Some countries may have moral objectives.	6	6.0
				Implementation Success Score	**6.0**	

Approach 3. German-led EU 2015

How would the refugee problem be managed if the aim was for all countries to adopt an approach similar to the German-led Europe 2015 Approach?

Similar to the Australian approach, countries that are most able to adopt the German-led Europe Approach are the 65 relatively wealthy and free nations of over 1 million people. Germany's open-door policy in 2015 toward asylum seekers from Syria and other war-torn countries – particularly Africa and the Middle East – is broadly in line with the Refugee Convention. Germany's approach was supported by most of the European nations which the asylum seekers had to travel through. This included rescuing sinking boats, accepting boat landings, and allowing passage through their land. In total over one million people arrived in Europe as asylum seekers.

As noted in Chapter 11, by early 2016 it was assessed that 60% of arrivals to the EU did not have legitimate refugee claims. It remains unclear whether there are plans to deport those found not to be refugees, or if any such plans would actually work if attempted.

German-led Europe 2015 – Key Approach Points

- Germany accepts, protects and processes all asylum seekers arriving to its land.
- Germany increasingly provided guidelines with regard to which country's citizens had legitimate claims for refugee status.
- Most European countries asylum seekers had to traverse to arrive in Germany allowed such transit.
- Burden-sharing is sought across countries both in terms of refugee processing and resettlement.

Assessment Detail

Effectiveness Score

Q1. Minimise FDP and enable easy protection

1.1 Reducing the numbers of new Forcibly Displaced People. (2/10)

The German-led European approach of 2015 has no direct action in minimising the disruptive causes of Forcibly Displaced People. Such initiatives would be considered in the scope of foreign policy. This approach increased the number of FDPs who presented as asylum seekers as the opportunity to resettle in a wealthy nation was greatly increased. The result was a presentation of many asylum seekers who were assessed not to be refugees. It is also likely many who would otherwise have stayed at home also decided to present as refugees given the higher chance of a desired outcome being migration into Europe. Using the other end of the same logic as with the Australian Approach, this analysis considers such an outcome as a negative through the assumption that some asylum seekers are too quick to leave their homeland.

1.2 Enabling people to find safety as easily as possible and eliminating risk-taking behaviour in order to improve protection prospects. (8/10)

The overwhelming attractiveness of this approach is that it gives asylum seekers much control and opportunity to improve their protection prospects. With as many as 65 large and wealthy countries honouring the Refugee Convention similar to Germany in 2015, there would be tremendous opportunity for satisfactory protection outcomes to be found by most asylum seekers. The ease of arriving at those countries is also improved as countries en route would be willing to accept asylum seekers and let them pass through should they wish.

The negative of unregulated secondary movement, from a Country of First Asylum to one with perceived advantages would still occur. This is likely to involve people smugglers, particularly along traditional routes (for instance the Middle East to Europe). A practice both costly and dangerous.

1.3 Eliminating policies that divert finite resources from improving the plight of refugees, either directly through government spend or indirectly through resultant asylum seeker behaviour. (9/10)

Outside the use of people smugglers, there is little money diverted to policies or activities that do not directly help asylum seekers.

Average: 6.3

Q2. Best protection levels

2.1 Ensuring the highest possible probability for repatriation. (2/10)

The large amount of secondary movement to resettlement nations would work to move a significant portion of asylum seekers far from their Countries of Origin, reducing the probability for repatriation.

2.2 Standardising protection regardless of location. (6/10)

Discrepancies between protection standards of wealthy resettlement nations and the less wealthy Countries of First Asylum would remain. However, the reduced pressure on these countries would help improve conditions for those refugees who remained. Conversely, increased numbers arriving at resettlement nations would reduce protection standards. Both programs would work toward standardising protection. As asylum seekers and refugees would be freer to move, human rights breaches, institutionalised through government policy, may be less as people would move away from such countries.

2.3 Avoiding overwhelming intakes of asylum seekers and refugees by Countries of First Asylum.(8/10)

The burdens borne by Countries of First Asylum would be largely reduced as many asylum seekers would seek to travel to the more attractive wealthier nations as seen in 2015.

2.4 Avoiding overwhelming intakes of asylum seekers and refugees by Countries of Second Asylum. (3/10)

Very large numbers would arrive at the wealthy Countries of Second Asylum with the rational motivation for an improved life. Such numbers would promote more responsive burden-sharing arrangements. Although a desired outcome, such arrangements are likely to be tolerated only up to levels that do not appear to threaten the viability of the in-taking nation. For instance, Germany's requests for burden-sharing in 2015 went largely unheeded.

2.5 Eliminating the diversion of resources caused by the use of protection channels by those without legitimate refugee claims (e.g. economic migrants). (2/10)

Again, the German-led Europe 2015 Approach resulted in at least 60% of asylum seeker arrivals being determined not to have legitimate refugee claims. The open-border policy for asylum seekers, coupled with difficulties in extracting those who fail the RSD, provides a great incentive for people seeking to improve their prospects even if not refugees.

Not only does it add more cost in terms of RSD processing and protection prior to assessment but it also crowds out attention that should be paid to the legitimate asylum seeker. This approach also risks excluding the less mobile who are not able to make the journey to the country where they desire to be accepted. Certainly some women and children may be able to follow their male family member who travelled in advance, but not all will have such family arrangements. Sadly, such an approach has also been shown to be open to those seeking to enter to inflict acts of terrorism.

Average: 4.0

Q3. Reduce waiting time and minimise cultural friction

3.1 Reducing the average time spent waiting in limbo for a Durable Solution. This includes living in temporary accommodation, having little access to paid work, and having no certainty of the future. (5/10)

With the engagement of up to 62 Countries of Second Asylum in protecting asylum seekers it is likely the numbers of refugees being offered permanent visas will rise. In addition, large numbers of arrivals into countries of asylum will continue to add impetus for burden-sharing mechanisms to be created.

However, intakes beyond the threshold of what countries believe they can manage as permanent residents, without threatening their viability, are an issue. With developed nations likely to be protecting a larger number of refugees and asylum seekers through this method, the number of resettlement places will either decrease, or the country will be put under additional strain.

3.2 Ensuring the human rights of the population of the host nation and of the asylum seekers and refugees are protected across short and long-term horizons. Where cultures are incompatible, assimilation to the host nation is assured. (3/10)

With uncontrolled numbers arriving at resettlement nations, the threat to their economic and cultural viability grows. Towards the end of 2015, examples of resultant cultural disruptions were experienced. Examples toward the end of 2015 included the Paris shootings and the Cologne sexual assaults on New Year's Eve.

Average: 4.0

Q4. Ongoing and Scalable Protection

4.1 Ensuring persistence and scalability of the protection approach considering Countries for First and Second Asylum, asylum seekers and refugees. (3/10)

As outlined in the analysis of the As-Is Approach, the probability of sustaining large inflows year after year is low. The rights guaranteed to refugees through the Refugee Convention result in welfare and housing costs that become enormous with large numbers of additional refugee arrivals every year.

The German-led Europe Approach in 2015 does not appear scalable. The tenets of the Refugee Convention ultimately place a great burden on the resettlement nations. The utilisation of the pathway by economic migrants and the low return rates of those found not to be legitimate refugees add to the pressure borne by rich resettlement nations from people arriving from the developing world.

Average: 3.0

Human Rights Score

Q5. Human Rights

5.1 Adhering to the Refugee Convention and other human rights agreements including the Declaration of Human Rights, the Convention of the Rights of Children and the International Covenant on Civil and Political Rights. (9/10)

The German-led Europe 2015 Approach attempts to honour the tenets of the Refugee Convention. In direct contrast to the Australia 2015 Approach, there is no arbitrary detention, nor is there punishment for arriving without valid entry documentation. Additionally, allowing the flow of asylum seekers to the more wealthy nations would increase the proportion of refugees with access to work opportunities.

Average: 9.0

Cost Score

Q6. Cost

6.1 Total cost (financial and other) of implementation. (8/10)

The German-led Europe 2015 Approach is a high-cost approach due to two key drivers. The first is through housing a greater number of asylum seekers in the developed Countries of Second Asylum, where more money per refugee is provided. This is received in the form of welfare, housing, and integration services. The average spent per refugee is far more than the average spent in Countries of First Asylum. The quality of life is considered by most measures to be much better too.

The second is the incentive to present as an asylum seeker also increases with this approach. This results in more asylum seekers as those who would otherwise have remained in their home countries are enticed to come. This group includes those with legitimate refugee claims as well as those with no legitimate refugee claims at all.

Average: 8.0

Implementation Score

Q7. Implementation Success

7.1 Probability of implementation and probability of success once implemented. Considerations include complexity and the likelihood of cooperation across nations. (2/10)

The most critical issue regarding the German-led Europe 2015 Approach is the uncontrolled and potentially overwhelming numbers of arrivals to participant countries. With no cap on arrivals, the rights of the asylum seekers are placed above those of the nations attempting to help. In extreme cases, this may result in irreversible damage to the economy and social construct of a society. Accordingly, many nations will be reluctant to agree to such an approach. For instance, some European nations closed their borders in 2015 and resisted burden-sharing arrangements. A resultant risk is that with too many nations opting out of the approach, the burden to be carried by each of the remaining nations grows, placing their economies and societies at greater risk.

Average: 2.0

Assessment Summary

The German-led Europe 2015 Approach promises much with the protection of human rights and the shelter of a greater numbers of refugees in wealthy Countries of Second Asylum. The approach will carry a high cost due to the greater number of refugees being housed in the richer resettlement nations. which provide more resources per refugee in line with requirements under the Refugee Convention.

However, the overall effectiveness of the approach is low. By opening up the developed world it does provide fantastic protection for a very large number of people but it also opens up the developed world to a large number of risks. Most of these are driven by the consequences of large and uncontrolled arrivals. The economic burdens of food and shelter, the bureaucratic task of successfully processing people, and the social impact of incorporating a large influx of people, often from a very different culture, are obvious in the short term.

More troubling is the potential influx of large numbers of economic migrants who, by looking for an easy route into a developed country, crowd out true refugees and drain the intake nation's resources. More troubling still is the potential admission of terrorists through inadequate screening due to the number of arrivals. Finally, too large an influx from cultures that cannot or will not assimilate may result in significant cultural tensions. This could result in turning the host society away from values that were once part of its identity.

These threats to the resettlement nations may result in many nations resisting adopting this approach, further reducing the effectiveness of the approach. In reality it is a high-cost solution that is unlikely to be successfully implemented.

Effectiveness Score: 4.5
Human Rights Score: 9.0
Cost Score: 8.0
Implementation Score: 2.0

Fig 14.5 ▶ Approach 3. Global adoption of the 2015 German-led European Approach.

1. Effectiveness	Question	Question Criteria	Pros	Cons	Scores / 10	Score
Question 1.	Q1. How can the number of Forcibly Displaced People be minimised and how can they find protection as safely and as easily as possible?	1.1 Reducing the numbers of new Forcibly Displaced People.	Nil.	- No direct action in minimising the disruptive causes. Encourages increases in refugee presentation.	2	6.3
		1.2 Enabling people to find safety as easily and as possible and eliminating risk taking behaviour in order to improve protection prospects.	- Greatly helps refugees arrive at a country of asylum of their choosin.	- Unregulated secondary movement, from a country of first asylum to one with perceived advantages, would still occur.	8	
		1.3 Eliminating policies that divert finite resources from improving the plight of refugees, either directly through government spend or indirectly through resultant asylum seeker behaviour.	- Little government money diverted to activities that do not directly help asylum seekers.	- Use of People Smugglers would still occur.	9	
Question 2.	Q2. How can protection best be provided to asylum seekers and refugees?	2.1 Ensuring the highest possible probability for repatriation.	Nil.	- Large secondary movement resulting in high volumes of refugees far from their COO.	2	3.8
		2.2 Standardising protection regardless of location.	- Discrepencies remain although reduced countries of first asylum numbers improve conditions for remaining refugees.	Nil.	6	
		2.3 Avoiding overwhelming intakes of asylum seekers and refugees by Countries of First Asylum.	- Country of first asylum burdens greatly reduced.	Nil.	7	
		2.4 Avoiding overwhelming intakes of asylum seekers and refugees by Countries of Second Asylum.	- Large volumes would provide impetus for increased burden sharing arrangements.	- Very large numbers would arrive at the wealthy resettlement nations.	2	
		2.5 Eliminating the diversion of resources caused by the use of protection channels by those without legitimate refugee claims (e.g. economic migrants).	Nil.	- Ecourages arrival of non-refugees.	2	
Question 3.	Q3. How can the time spent waiting in limbo for a Durable Solution be minimised?	3.1 Reducing the average time spent waiting in limbo for a Durable Solution. This includes living in temporary accommodation, having little access to paid work, and having no certainty of the future.	Nil.	- With higher refugee protection requests, Resettlement spots will either decrease or the country will be put under additional strain.	6	4.5
		3.2 Ensuring the human rights of the population of the host nation and of the asylum seekers and refugees are protected across short and long term horizons. Where cultures are incompatible, assimilation to the host nation is assured.	Nil.	- Uncontrolled arrivals threaten economic and cultural viability of resettlement nations.	3	
Question 4.	Q4. How can the approach provide ongoing and scalable protection?	4.1 Ensuring persistence and scalability of the protection approach considering Countries for First and Second Asylum, asylum seekers and refugees.	Nil.	- Rights guaranteed to refugees result in welfare and housing costs for rich Countries of Second Asylum which will be difficult to continue with high year on year asylum seeker entries.	3	3.0
				Effectiveness Score (average)		**4.5**

2. Human Rights	Question	Question Criteria	Pros	Cons	Scores / 10	Score
Question 5.	Q5. How well does the approach honour the tenets of international law?	5.1 Adhering to the Refugee Convention and other human rights agreements including the Declaration of Human Rights, the Convention of the Rights of Children and the International Covenant on Civil and Political Rights.	- Attempts to honour the tenets of the Refugee Convention other human rights agreements including the Declaration of Human Rights, the Convention of the Rights of Children and the ICPPR.	Nil.	9	9.0
				Human Rights Score (average)		**9.0**

3. Cost	Question	Question Criteria	Pros	Cons	Scores / 10	Score
Question 6.	Q6. How costly is implementation?	6.1 Total cost (financial and other) of implementation.	Nil.	Nil.	8	8.0
				Cost Score (larger is more cost)		**8.0**

4. Probability	Question	Question Criteria	Pros	Cons	Scores / 10	Score
Question 7.	Q7. How probable is successful implementation?	7.1 Probability of implementation and probability of success once implemented. Considerations include complexity and the likelihood of cooperation across nations.	Nil.	- Risks through uncapped obligations may limit the uptake by countries.	2	2.0
				Implementation Success Score		**2.0**

Approach 4. Japan 2015

How would the refugee problem be managed if the aim was for all countries to adopt the approach Japan has followed in recent years (including 2015) regarding refugees?

Japan is one of the few developed nations that does not provide a lot of places for refugee protection or for permanent solutions. In 2015, 99% of the 7,586 refugee applicants were rejected – only 27 people were granted refugee status[8]. In the previous year Japan only accepted 11 people from 5,000 applicants[9].

Aside from the limited number of placements, Japan is very generous in terms of donations to the UNHCR and assistance programs. It ranks second behind the United States in terms of dollars donated, US$252 million in 2013. It also recently announced a US$1.6 billion assistance program for Syrians and Iraqis caught up in conflict[10].

In 2015, the Japanese Prime Minister, Shinzo Abe, presented Japan's priorities as tackling internal crises that include a declining birth rate, an ageing population, and an under representation of women in the labour market. The consequence of this policy is that Japan has low numbers of refugees and asylum seekers within its borders. In 2013 Japan housed 2,419 refugees and 10,705 asylum seekers, in total about 0.01% of its population.

If the 62 of the 65 wealthy and free nations (excluding the Countries of First Asylum of Lebanon, Turkey and South Africa), matched Japan's lead in protecting 0.01% of their population as refugees and asylum seekers then only 186,000 would be sheltered rather than over three million by these nations.

Japan 2015 – Key Approach Points.

- Provision of almost no resettlement or local integration places for refugees.

- Provision of very few temporary protection places worldwide, approximately 0.01%. If the 62 rich and free Countries of Second Asylum each provided asylum and refugee places to a similar extent, only 186,000 places would be provided.

- Enormous pressure on the Countries of First Asylum, which are presumed to remain with open borders. If they also closed their borders, then refugees would remain persecuted or would turn and fight for freedom.

---

8   Shusuke Murai, "Japan recognizes only 27 refugees, despite rising numbers of applications," *Japan Times,* January 23, 2016.
9   Justin McCurry, "Japan says it must look after its own before allowing in Syrian refugees," *The Guardian,* September 30, 2015..
10 Ibid.

Assessment Detail

Effectiveness Score

Q1. Minimise FDP and enable easy protection

1.1 Reducing the numbers of new Forcibly Displaced People. (7/10)

The Japan 2015 Approach has no direct action in minimising the disruptive causes of Forcibly Displaced People. Indirectly, if followed by all Countries of Second Asylum, such an approach would limit the number of FDPs who would present as asylum seekers by making the costs of presenting for protection more onerous and the associated benefits less attractive (the reduced benefits being the limited access to the wealthy resettlement countries and still long waits for resettlement). This analysis considers such an outcome as a positive by the assumption that some asylum seekers may be too quick to leave their homeland.

1.2 Enabling people to find safety as easily as possible and eliminating risk-taking behaviour in order to improve protection prospects. (5/10).

By closing their countries to the vast majority of refugees, Countries of Second Asylum would reduce the often dangerous secondary movement of people away from their Countries of First Asylum to the wealthier nations. The implication is that risk-taking behaviour would dramatically reduce. Unfortunately, this approach also increases the difficulty for people who have nowhere else to go to find security.

1.3 Eliminating policies that divert finite resources from improving the plight of refugees, either directly through government spend or indirectly through resultant asylum seeker behaviour. (5/10)

The expense of paying people smugglers would be avoided once asylum seekers have been deterred from travelling to Countries of Second Asylum. This would only be a benefit to refugees should a similarly easy pathway to safety with a potential Durable Solution be available.

A continual cost must still be maintained by the resettlement nations in deterring such efforts, including offshore processing centres and border protection. These costs are diversionary as they do not directly support conditions for asylum seekers. As with the Australia 2015 Approach, these costs are initially high before lowering as asylum seeker behaviours change in line with incentives.

Average: 5.7

Q2. Best protection levels

2.1 Ensuring the highest possible probability for repatriation. (8/10)

All resettlement nations would house very limited asylum seekers and reject most refugee claims. A high proportion of refugees would remain in the Countries of First Asylum, which would maximise the probability of repatriation.

2.2 Standardising protection regardless of location. (2/10)

The extremely low numbers of refugees protected or provided resettlement placements in the Countries of Second Asylum result in two broad outcomes. First, placements and protection in relatively wealthy nations is all but eliminated for millions of refugees – about three million or 20% of the refugee population. Second, protection levels become more standardised around the lower levels experienced at the Countries of First Asylum.

2.3 Avoiding overwhelming intakes of asylum seekers and refugees by Countries of First Asylum. (1/10)

The pressure borne by the countries of First Asylum is large and would increase further. Countries of First Asylum house about 80% of the world's refugees and asylum seekers. Under the Japan Approach, this number would greatly increase to almost 100%, meaning a 25% increase for the Countries of First Asylum.

While this increase is significant it would be somewhat offset by increases in donations commensurate with Japan's generous donations (4th largest overall[11], 13th overall per GDP/16th overall per capita).

2.4 Avoiding overwhelming intakes of asylum seekers and refugees by Countries of Second Asylum. (9/10)

The numbers of arrivals at Countries of Second Asylum would be extremely limited. This would strictly protect the viability of these nations.

2.5 Eliminating the diversion of resources caused by the use of protection channels by those without legitimate refugee claims (e.g. economic migrants). (9/10)

The strict limitations on asylum seekers and refugees would also deter economic migrants attempting to utilise the asylum seeker channel.

Average: 5.6

---

[11] "UNHCR Japan Fact Sheet," accessed 17 August 2016 <www.unhcr.org/5000196c13.pdf>

Q3. Reduce waiting time and minimise cultural friction

3.1 Reducing the average time spent waiting in limbo for a Durable Solution. This includes living in temporary accommodation, having little access to paid work, and having no certainty of the future. (1/10)

The elimination of almost all local integration and resettlement placements in the Countries of Second Asylum would significantly increase the waiting periods for refugees.

3.2 Ensuring the human rights of the population of the host nation and of the asylum seekers and refugees are protected across short and long-term horizons. Where cultures are incompatible, assimilation to the host nation is assured. (5/10)

Due to the incredibly low intake, the Countries of Second Asylum experience little resultant human rights pressures experienced by cultural incompatibility. The increased intake for Countries of First Asylum would proportionally heighten such pressures. In many cases, but not all, the neighbouring countries shared many cultural aspects with the countries of origin. Although this can help mitigate cultural pressures, with large numbers cultural friction leading to disruptions of human rights is likely.

Average: 3.0

Q4. Ongoing and Scalable Protection

4.1 Ensuring persistence and scalability of the protection approach considering Countries for First and Second Asylum, asylum seekers and refugees. (3/10)

The obvious threat to persistence and scalability of a Japan 2015 Approach is with regard to the ability for the Countries of First Asylum to handle continually large numbers of asylum seekers year after year, or a massive intake in one year.

Countries of First Asylum will not only have to shoulder 25% more refugees but with virtually no resettlement occurring, further pressure to locally integrate will be required. Countries of Second Asylum effectively act just as donors to the international cause. A significant risk is the diplomatic breakdown between these countries and the Countries of First Asylum who may well perceive Countries of Second Asylum as not contributing proportionally to the humanitarian effort.

Average: 3.0

Human Rights Score

Q5. Human Rights

5.1 Adhering to the Refugee Convention and other human rights agreements including the Declaration of Human Rights, the Convention of the Rights of Children and the International Covenant on Civil and Political Rights.

A situation where all Countries of Second Asylum take in excessively low numbers of asylum seekers coupled with high rejection rates of refugee applications would seemingly raise questions as to its adherence to the Refugee Convention and other instruments of international law. One requirement that such an approach may breach is the principle of non-refoulement. Such a high rejection rate may lead to the return of refugees to areas of harm.

Average: 1.0

Cost Score

Q6. Cost

6.1 Total cost (financial and other) of implementation. (3/10)

The Japan 2015 Approach by resettlement nations would reduce costs with the most significant reduction in that incurred by Europe.

Countries of Second Asylum would experience cost reductions in housing asylum seekers and refugees as well as services and support for new permanent residents through the resettlement program. These reductions would be partially offset by maintaining deterrence programs and increasing the donations to the UNHCR as Japan ranks relatively high (13th per GDP).

With a complete uptake of the Japan 2015 Approach by Countries of Second Asylum, almost all refugees would be housed in the comparatively low cost Countries of First Asylum. While the financial burden of the increased numbers will be covered by the increased donations from the Countries of Second Asylum, many other costs will fall squarely with the Countries of First Asylum. These include the provision of land and natural resources, social cohesion and economic stability.

Average: 3.0

Implementation Score

Q7. Implementation Success

7.1 Probability of implementation and probability of success once implemented. Considerations include complexity and the likelihood of cooperation across nations. (6/10)

The Japan 2015 Approach is a low complexity approach. Assuming full uptake, it is easy to coordinate. However, the uptake in implementation of such policies by the international community is not guaranteed. Many Countries of Second Asylum may have difficulty in agreeing to such a low intake of asylum seekers and refugees. Resistance would be even more likely than with the Australia 2015 Approach, and it may be accepted in the hope of reducing the number of economic migrants. Acceptance would also require public perception that their country was not a Country of First Asylum and that those needing help were able to find it in such countries.

Countries of First Asylum may respond with disappointment and anger if such policies were followed by all resettlement countries. The risk of a breakdown in relations between Countries of Second Asylum and those of First Asylum would be likely if such an approach was widely followed.

Average: 6.0

Assessment Summary

The Japan 2015 Approach is low complexity and is easy to coordinate but with a low likelihood of widespread implementation. Traditionally about 20% of refugees and asylum seekers are outside Countries of First Asylum, with the Japan 2015 Approach this percentage would reduce to almost zero. Further burden would be added by an ending of all resettlement places by the resettlement countries as well. The added burden on the Countries of First Asylum would be supported by an increase in donations to the UNHCR.

A strength of the Japan 2015 Approach is the elimination of the moral hazard that can attract people into attempting secondary movements to resettlement nations. It also protects the economic and cultural interests of the Countries of Second Asylum. Widespread adoption of the Japan 2015 Approach is likely to attract much criticism with regard to Countries of Second Asylum not adequately contributing. Such criticism would be expected from people both external to and within these nations. Given this criticism, it is an unlikely option even with its low complexity.

Effectiveness Score: 5.0
Human Rights Score: 1.0
Cost Score: 3.0
Implementation Score: 6.0

Fig 14.6 > Holistic Approach Assessments. Approach 4. Japan 2015.

1. Effectiveness	Question	Question Criteria	Pros	Cons	Scores / 10	Score
Question 1.	Q1. How can the number of Forcibly Displaced People be minimised and how can they find protection as safely and as easily as possible?	1.1 Reducing the numbers of new Forcibly Displaced People.	- Would deter many.	- Nil.	7	5.7
		1.2 Enabling people to find safety as easily as possible and eliminating risk taking behaviour in order to improve protection prospects.	- Secondary movement would be reduced.	- Nil.	5	
		1.3 Eliminating policies that divert finite resources from improving the plight of refugees, either directly through government spend or indirectly through resultant asylum seeker behaviour.	- Expense of paying people smugglers avoided.	- Some continual diversionary cost in maintaining deterring efforts.	5	
Question 2.	Q2. How can protection best be provided to asylum seekers and refugees?	2.1 Ensuring the highest possible probability for repatriation.	- Ensures vast majority of refugees reemain in countries of first asylum.	- Nil.	8	5.8
		2.2 Standardising protection regardless of location.	- Large donations to help countries of first asylum to improve standards to some extent.	- Less refugees housed by wealthy developed nations.	2	
		2.3 Avoiding overwhelming intakes of asylum seekers and refugees by Countries of First Asylum.	- Nil.	- Places all the burden on the countries of first asylum.	1	
		2.4 Avoiding overwhelming intakes of asylum seekers and refugees by Countries of Second Asylum.	- Strict border controls and low acceptance rate ensure no pressures on resettlement nations.	- Nil.	9	
		2.5 Eliminating the diversion of resources caused by the use of protection channels by those without legitimate refugee claims (e.g. economic migrants).	- Low intake rates result in little opportunity for utlisiation by non-refugees.	- Nil.	9	
Question 3.	Q3. How can the time spent waiting in limbo for a Durable Solution be minimised?	3.1 Reducing the average time spent waiting in limbo for a Durable Solution. This includes living in temporary accommodation, having little access to paid work, and having no certainty of the future.	- Nil.	- Further increases waiting time as less resettlement or local integration places.	1	3.0
		3.2 Ensuring the human rights of the population of the host nation and of the asylum seekers and refugees are protected across short and long term horizons. Where cultures are incompatible, assimilation to the host nation is assured.	- Negligible impact on countries of first asylum.	- Further increases burden on countries of first asylum. - Potential for backlash towards resettlement nations perceived as selfish and not doing their bit.	5	
Question 4.	Q4. How can the approach provide ongoing and scalable protection?	4.1 Ensuring persistence and scalability of the protection approach considering Countries for First and Second Asylum, asylum seekers and refugees.	- Nil.	- Countries of First Asylum will be required to handle even larger numbers as the current burden sharing provided by Countries of Second Asylum will cease.	3	3.0
				Effectiveness Score (average)		5.0

2. Human Rights	Question	Question Criteria	Pros	Cons	Scores / 10	Score
Question 5.	Q5. How well does the approach honour the tenets of international law?	5.1 Adhering to the Refugee Convention and other human rights agreements including the Declaration of Human Rights, the Convention of the Rights of Children and the International Covenant on Civil and Political Rights.	- Nil.	- Low acceptance rate contravenes the burden sharing aspect of the Refuge Convention.	1	1.0
				Human Rights Score (average)		1.0

3. Cost	Question	Question Criteria	Pros	Cons	Scores / 10	Score
Question 6.	Q6. How costly is implementation?	6.1 Total cost (financial and other) of implementation.	- Very high donations to the UNHCR and assistance programs.	- Nil.	3	3.0
				Cost Score (larger is more cost)		3.0

4. Probability	Question	Question Criteria	Pros	Cons	Scores / 10	Score
Question 7.	Q7. How probable is successful implementation?	7.1 Probability of implementation and probability of success once implemented. Considerations include complexity and the likelihood of cooperation across nations.	- Low complexity with strict border controls and low acceptance rate through RSD.	- More difficult for nations more central and with land borders.	5	5.0
				Implementation Success Score		5.0

CH 15. HOLISTIC APPROACHES AND ASSESSMENT - PROPOSED

Holistic Approach Options – Current State

Approach 5. Amnesty International

The German-led Europe 2015 Approach was a dramatic shift towards welcoming asylum seekers and refugees fleeing persecution and war. It was far more welcoming towards undocumented migrants arriving at its borders who claimed asylum. Even with these actions, the approach falls short of the Amnesty International recommendations, released via an eight-point plan in October 2015. At the time of its release Amnesty International Secretary General Salil Shetty said:

> *"The international refugee protection regime.... risks being left in tatters if world leaders continue in their deplorable failure to protect vulnerable people fleeing war and persecution[1]".*

Effectively an extension of Germany and Europe's 2015 Approach, the eight point plan detailed by Amnesty International is to:

1. Fully fund humanitarian appeals for refugee crises;
2. Fulfil all resettlement needs;
3. Provide safe and legal routes for refugees;
4. Rescue those in danger of death;
5. Allow entry through borders;

---

1 Tharanga Yakupitiyage, "Amnesty International's 8-Point Plan for Refugee Crises," *Inter Press Service News Agency*, October 14, 2015, accessed July 24, 2016.

6. Combat xenophobia and racism;
7. Investigate and prosecute trafficking;
8. Ratify and uphold the Refugee Convention.

Many of these recommendations were included in the analysis conducted regarding the German-led Europe Approach. The new aspects of the Amnesty International recommendations are chiefly around fully-funding the humanitarian appeals for the refugee crises, fulfilling all resettlement needs and providing safe and legal routes for refugees.

Fully funding humanitarian appeals requires a dramatic lift in donations. As the largest and most critical organisation for the provision of protection and support, the UNHCR provides the best example of the current funding shortfall. The UNHCR relies primarily on government and private donations to fund its budget. The latest figures are the 2014 budget, of which only 55% was actually met with donations. Contributions would effectively have to double to make up the shortfall.

Fulfilling all resettlement needs refers to the refugees who were specifically assessed by the UNHCR to need priority resettlement (rather than waiting for repatriation or local integration). In 2014 the number of resettlement submissions was 103,890[2]. The UNHCR's estimate of people requiring resettlement for 2016 is 1,150,000[3]. Providing safe and legal routes for refugees, in combination with allowing entry through borders, will increase the flow of refugees to Countries of Second Asylum as it will lower the dangers currently deterring some of the IDPs or refugees located in Countries of First Asylum. The refugees that moved towards Europe during 2015 represented at the most 3% of the IDPs and refugees from the Middle East and North Africa. If such initiatives entice one in five more people to travel, the annual inflow would be over six million in the years ahead.

Amnesty International Recommendations 2015 – Key Approach Points.

- Provides the open borders and uncapped acceptance of asylum seekers as with the German-led Europe 2015 Approach.
- Provides full funding to the UNHCR through donations.
- Resettlement nations fully meet the resettlement requests (about 1 million annually).
- Provides safe and legal routes for refugees and punishes people smugglers.

---

2   UNHCR, "Projected Global Resettlement Needs 2016," (paper presented at 21st Annual Tripartite Consultations on Resettlement, Geneva, Switzerland, June 29 - July 1, 11.
3   Ibid 10.

Assessment Detail

Effectiveness Score

Q1. Minimise FDP and enable easy protection

1.1 Reducing the numbers of new Forcibly Displaced People (1/10)

This has no direct action in minimising the disruptive causes of FDPs. Such initiatives would be considered in the scope of foreign policy. As with the German-led Europe 2015 Approach, it is likely the Amnesty International Approach will result in the presentation of asylum seekers who would otherwise have been deterred as the perceived costs associated with the claim for asylum were too high. This analysis considers such an outcome as a negative on the assumption some asylum seekers may be too quick to leave their homeland.

1.2 Enabling people to find safety as easily as possible and eliminating risk-taking behaviour in order to improve protection prospects. (9/10)

Even more so than the German-led Europe 2015 Approach, the Amnesty International Approach would help refugees arrive at a country of asylum of their choosing. Countries would be willing to accept the asylum seekers and support their transit.

1.3 Eliminating policies that divert finite resources from improving the plight of refugees, either directly through government spend or indirectly through resultant asylum seeker behaviour. (9/10)

Diversion in spending by both asylum seekers (on people smugglers) and governments (on deterrence and rescue measures) would be minimised.

Average: 6.3

Q2. Best protection levels

2.1 Ensuring the highest possible probability for repatriation. (1/10)

The large amount of secondary movement to Countries of Second Asylum would work to move asylum seekers far away from their Countries of Origin, reducing the probability for repatriation.

2.2 Standardising protection regardless of location. (6/10)

Asylum seekers are given a large amount of control and opportunity to improve their protection prospects. With the pathways even easier and safer to the attractive Countries of Second Asylum, the numbers will increase and maximise the reduction in the burdens borne by Countries of First Asylum.

This reduced number would help to improve the protection standards provided by Countries of First Asylum, bringing them closer to those of Second Asylum. Once again, the arrival of large numbers will compel these nations to seek burden-sharing arrangements. However, it is unlikely they will be met for ever-greater numbers of refugees.

2.3 Avoiding overwhelming intakes of asylum seekers and refugees by Countries of First Asylum. (9/10)

Discrepancies between protection standards in wealthy Countries of Second Asylum and the less wealthy Countries of First Asylum would remain. However, as with the German-led Europe 2015 Approach, the reduced pressure on the Countries of First Asylum would help improve conditions for those refugees who remain. Also, as the asylum seekers and refugees would be freer to move, human rights breaches institutionalised through government policy may be less as people would move away from such countries.

2.4 Avoiding overwhelming intakes of asylum seekers and refugees by Countries of Second Asylum. (2/10)

The uncapped and potentially overwhelming number of arrivals to certain countries is the biggest concern. As the risks and barriers associated with moving are reduced, a greater proportion of IDPs or refugees staying in rudimentary conditions at Countries of First Asylum will be enticed to move abroad. This could overwhelm many countries if a large proportion of the 38 million IDPs migrate. When considering the viability of an intake nation to maintain ongoing protection of the human rights of its citizens, this approach cannot be considered a compelling option if the outcome is perceived to threaten its economic and social stability.

2.5 Eliminating the diversion of resources caused by the use of protection channels by those without legitimate refugee claims (e.g. economic migrants). (2/10)

Large numbers of non-refugees such as economic migrants or terrorists are encouraged to attempt to enter developed nations as was seen in Europe in 2015. This risks significant security issues and adds cost to RSD processing and protection efforts prior to their assessment, and draws attention away from legitimate asylum seekers. This approach also risks the crowding out of those less mobile that are not able to make the journey to their desired country for acceptance. They must rely on resettlement regimes.

Average: 3.6

Q3. Reduce waiting time and minimise cultural friction

3.1 Reducing the average time spent waiting in limbo for a Durable Solution. This includes living in temporary accommodation, having little access to paid work, and having no certainty of the future. (5/10)

Using 2014 numbers, full resettlement is roughly one million people per year. This conveniently matches a resettlement intake of 0.06% of population discussed with the adoption of the Australian approach. So at first glance this looks like an achievable task provided all countries can be convinced to sign up. Remember countries such as Japan have not traditionally resettled many refugees at all.

An alternative sharing of the resettlement burden across the 65 wealthy and free nations was described in Chapter 13. Countries of First Asylum were exempt, no country was required to resettle more than 50,000 refugees each year. High-income countries resettle refugees equivalent to 0.20% of their population each year, and upper-middle income countries resettle refugees equivalent to 0.1% of their population each year. Over 1.3 million refugees could be resettled each year through this mechanism. However, the social impacts of this in addition to large scale negative economic and social burdens on Countries of Second Asylum would be enormous.

3.2 Ensuring the human rights of the population of the host nation and of the asylum seekers and refugees are protected across short and long-term horizons. Where cultures are incompatible, assimilation to the host nation is assured. (2/10)

Uncontrolled numbers arriving at Countries of Second Asylum threaten economic and cultural viability. Towards the end of 2015, examples of resultant cultural disruptions were experienced, such as the November 2015 Paris shootings and the Cologne sexual assaults on New Year's Eve 2015.

Average: 3.5

Q4. Ongoing and Scalable Protection

4.1 Ensuring persistence and scalability of the protection approach considering Countries for First and Second Asylum, asylum seekers and refugees. (2/10)

The probability of Countries of Second Asylum sustaining large inflows year after year without significant impacts to their economies and social cohesion is low. The rights guaranteed to refugees through the Refugee Convention result in welfare and housing costs that become enormous with large arrivals year after year.

The Amnesty International Approach does not appear scalable. The tenets of the Refugee Convention ultimately place a great burden on wealthy nations with welfare systems. The utilisation of the pathway by economic migrants, and the low return rates of those found not to be legitimate refugees will add to the pressure borne by rich Countries of Second Asylum from people arriving from the developing world.

Average: 2.0

Human Rights Score

Q5. Human Rights

5.1 Adhering to the Refugee Convention and other human rights agreements including the Declaration of Human Rights, the Convention of the Rights of Children and the International Covenant on Civil and Political Rights. (9/10)

The Amnesty International Approach honours the tenets of the Refugee Convention. There is no arbitrary detention, nor is there punishment for arriving without valid entry documentation. Additionally, allowing the flow of asylum seekers to the more wealthy nations would increase the proportion of refugees with access to work opportunities.

Average: 9.0

Cost Score

Q6. Cost

6.1 Total cost (financial and other) of implementation. (9/10)

The Amnesty International Approach has all the costs of the German-led Europe 2015 Approach with additional costs in the creation and maintenance of safe pathways to supporting nations, and the fulfilment of all humanitarian funding requests. Given this, it is considered to be the most expensive of all the approach options covered.

A greater number of asylum seekers being sheltered in the wealthy Countries of Second Asylum will result in a higher average spend per refugee. The improved conditions for many, plus the easier pathways for arrival, will result in increased numbers of people requesting asylum. The requirement that ensures the safe travel of the asylum seekers will also require extensive investment.

Additional costs also come from fully meeting the humanitarian funding requests. The 2014 target budget was only 55% met, meaning the likely target figure for 2016 will be at least double what was donated in 2014. Many of the wealthy countries that would be expected to increase their donations are also the countries called upon to help with protecting and resettling refugees. For instance, Germany ranked fifth in total donations and Sweden seventh. A potential opportunity lies with greater donations from the wealthy oil-producing nations. The United States was the highest donor providing US$1.3 billion, Saudi Arabia donated only US$29 million and Qatar only US$5 million. This pattern is consistent through most of the oil-rich nations. Only Kuwait is donating over US$100 million. Fulfilling the humanitarian budget may be possible if these nations are convinced to donate.

Average: 9.0

Implementation Score

Q7. Implementation Success

7.1 Probability of implementation and probability of success once implemented. Considerations include complexity and the likelihood of cooperation across nations. (1/10)

The key issue with the Amnesty International Approach is that a full resettlement effort must be provided along with open borders for accepting refugee arrivals as well as the doubling of donations to the UNHCR and relevant agencies. Together, this triumvirate will place an enormous amount of strain on the wealthy Countries of Second Asylum.

As with all approaches dealing with resettlement numbers, the situation becomes more difficult with each country that does not commit to help. With resettlement targets to be met and the avenues for arrival to developed nations made easier it is highly possible that more refugees than ever before will present. If this occurs, the numbers to be assessed and submitted for resettlement will increase in the short term and probably persist as the top refugee countries of origin have high fertility rates. With developed nations likely to be protecting a larger number of refugees and asylum seekers, the numbers of resettlement places they offer will either decrease or these countries will be put under additional strain.

Average: 1.0

Assessment Summary

Adoption of the Amnesty International Approach would provide great support to the Forcibly Displaced People of the world in the short term. If functional, the transit to Countries of First Asylum and Countries of Second Asylum would be safe. This would enable asylum seekers to travel to where they could find protection as easily and effectively as possible. It would most likely take some pressure off the Countries of First Asylum and could level out the standards of protection between these countries and the countries in the developed world.

A commitment to meet 100% of resettlement needs removes some incentive for travelling long distances in order to improve the prospects of a durable solution. However, this only applies to the 10% deemed to require resettlement. The other 90% could still seek a life in a developed nation like Australia, the US, or in Europe while being protected as refugees. Travel to these countries may still be perceived as a way to a better quality of life as well as a higher chance for permanent residency in a developed nation.

The key drawback of the approach is the large financial requirements and the risk of ever-increasing numbers that will threaten the viability of supporting nations. In order to meet UNHCR budgetary needs, donations would need to at least double with the key donors including additional costs for supporting the transit of asylum seekers and policing people smugglers. Safe and easy pathways to the developed world would surely attract record numbers of asylum seekers and economic migrants which could swamp supporting nations with numbers above what they would be able to accommodate.

Effectiveness Score: 4.0
Human Rights Score: 9.0
Cost Score: 9.0
Implementation Score: 1.0

Fig. 15.1 > Approach 5. Global adoption of the 2015 Amnesty International Approach

	Question	Question Criteria	Pros	Cons	Scores / 10	Score
1. Effectiveness						
Question 1.	Q1. How can the number of Forcibly Displaced People be minimised and how can they find protection as safely and as easily as possible?	1.1 Reducing the numbers of new Forcibly Displaced People.	Nil	- No direct action in minimising the disruptive causes. - Encourages increases in refugee presentation.	1	6.3
		1.2 Enabling people to find safety as easily as possible and eliminating risk taking behaviour in order to improve protection prospects.	Greatly helps refugees arrive at a country of asylum of their choosing, even moeso than German-led Eurpoe approach.	Secondary movement from a Country of First Asylum to one with perceived advantages, would be regulated.	9	
		1.3 Eliminating policies that divert finite resources from improving the plight of refugees, either directly through government spend or indirectly through resultant asylum seeker behaviour.	Diversion in spending by both asylum seekers (on people smugglings) and governments (on deterrence and rescue measures measures) would be minimised.	Nil	9	
Question 2.	Q2. How can protection best be provided to asylum seekers and refugees?	2.1 Ensuring the highest possible probability for repatriation.	Nil	- Large secondary movement, even moreso than with German-led Europe, resulting in high volumes of refugees far from their country of origin.	1	3.4
		2.2 Standardising protection regardless of location.	Discrepncies remain although reduced countries of first asylum numbers improve conditions for remaining refugees.	Nil	6	
		2.3 Avoiding overwhelming intakes of asylum seekers and refugees by Countries of First Asylum.	Country of First Asylum burdens greatly reduced.	Nil	8	
		2.4 Avoiding overwhelming intakes of asylum seekers and refugees by Countries of Second Asylum.	Large volumes would provide impetus for increased burden sharing arrangements.	Very large numbers would arrive at the wealthy resettlement nations.	1	
		2.5 Eliminating the diversion of resources caused by the use of protection channels by those without legitimate refugee claims (e.g. economic migrants).	Nil	Ecourages arrival of non-refugees.	1	
Question 3.	Q3. How can the time spent waiting in limbo for a Durable Solution be minimised?	3.1 Reducing the average time spent waiting in limbo for a Durable Solution. This includes living in temporary accommodation, having little access to paid work, and having no certainty of the future.	Nil	- With higher refugee protection requests, Resettlement spots will either decrease or the country will be put under additional strain.	6	4.0
		3.2 Ensuring the human rights of the population of the host nation and of the asylum seekers and refugees are protected across short and long term horizons. Where cultures are incompatible, assimilation to the host nation is assured.	Nil	Uncontrolled arrivals threaten economic and cultural viability of resettlement nations.	2	
Question 4.	Q4. How can the approach provide ongoing and scalable protection?	4.1 Ensuring persistence and scalability of the protection approach considering Countries for First and Second Asylum, asylum seekers and refugees.	Nil	- Low likelihood of existing in perpetuity.	2	2.0
				Effectivess Score (average)		**4.2**

	Question	Question Criteria	Pros	Cons	Scores / 10	Score
2. Human Rights						
Question 5.	Q5. How well does the approach honour the tenets of international law?	5.1 Adhering to the Refugee Convention and other human rights agreements including the Declaration of Human Rights, the Convention of the Rights of Children and the International Covenant on Civil and Political Rights.	Attempts to honour the tenets of the Refugee Convention.	Nil	9	9.0
				Human Rights Score (average)		**9.0**

	Question	Question Criteria	Pros	Cons	Scores / 10	Score
3. Cost						
Question 6.	Q6. How costly is implementation?	6.1 Total cost (financial and other) of implementation.	Nil	- Very high cost - Many resettlement nations may resist agreeing to uncontrolled numbers of asylum seekr entries.	9	9.0
				Cost Score (larger is more cost)		**9.0**

	Question	Question Criteria	Pros	Cons	Scores / 10	Score
4. Probability						
Question 7.	Q7. How probable is successful implementation?	7.1 Probability of implementation and probability of success once implemented. Considerations include complexity and the likelihood of cooperation across nations.	Nil	- Larger resettlements, uncapped refugee intakes and doubling of donation stress supporting nations.	1	1.0
				Implementation Success Score		**1.0**

Approach 6. Regional Frameworks

Description

In 2015, the Australian Labor Party released a policy plan to develop a regional approach. Its proposal included three key initiatives: to increase donations to the UNHCR by almost ten times to A$450 million in order to support improved protection standards within South East Asia; to maintain a policy of offshore processing; and to almost double the Resettlement to 27,000 by 2025.

How would the refugee problem be managed if the aim was for all countries to contribute to a Regional Framework Approach as proposed by the Australian Labor Party in 2015?

A number of regions would be created in which the countries undertake to cooperate in a regional approach. In the current distribution of refugee Countries of Origin, the Countries of First Asylum are generally less developed than the more distant, developed countries that asylum seekers and refugees attempt to enter in order to improve their prospects. A Regional Framework Approach aims to standardise the protection levels and durable solution outcomes across a region, thereby reducing this movement.

Countries of First Asylum would be provided with financial and technical assistance from the more wealthy countries in the region and, if needed, the UNHCR. This assistance would help provide the possible protection standards for asylum seekers and refugees. This would include a guarantee of non-refoulement, the right to work, quick RSD, and access to housing and social security. Close burden-sharing arrangements would also be sought to transfer refugees to limit excessive strain on countries where intake populations become an issue. Such transfers would be coordinated between the countries and effectively eliminate much of the market for people smugglers.

It is anticipated that a reduction in asylum seeker arrivals to the more distant developed countries would occur as protection and durable solution outcomes are improved in the Countries of First Asylum. To support this, a no-advantage policy similar to that recommended by the Houston Report would be employed. Offshore processing for such arrivals to Australia is a component of this in the South East Asia context.

Through improved conditions in Countries of First Asylum and enforcement of no-advantage policies in relation to secondary movements from Countries of First Asylum to those of Second Asylum, the numbers of arrivals to Countries of Second Asylum is expected to be relatively low. For Australia, this would also keep current levels relatively low, for Europe the aim would be a dramatic reduction in numbers. The expectation is that with reduced refugee numbers, the number of Resettlement places can increase. For example, Australia would almost double its intake to 27,000 by 2025, which would be approximately 0.1% of the population. If all the 65 relatively wealthy and free nations followed suit about 1.8 million refugees would be resettled each year, well above the current annual UNHCR submissions for resettlement.

Regional Frameworks – Key Approach Points.

- Countries group into regions such as Europe, Asia Pacific, Africa, North America and South America.
- Countries of First Asylum provide financial and technical assistance to improve protection standards. This would be provided by regional neighbours and the UNHCR.
- No-advantage policies are enforced to limit incentives for secondary movements from Countries of First Asylum.
- Countries of Second Asylum to increase their annual intake to 0.1% of population in order to provide more durable solutions for refugees and ease the pressure on the Countries of First Asylum.

Assessment Detail

Effectiveness Score

Q1. Minimise FDP and enable easy protection

1.1 Reducing the numbers of new Forcibly Displaced People. (4/10)

Similar to all previous approaches, a regional approach has no direct action in minimising the disruptive causes of FDPs. Such initiatives would be considered in the scope of foreign policy. A well-functioning Regional Framework Approach may encourage previously disenchanted, persecuted people to present as asylum seekers but not to the same extent as the German-led Europe or Amnesty International approaches.

1.2 Enabling people to find safety as easily as possible and eliminating risk-taking behaviour in order to improve protection prospects. (9/10)

Protection standards at the Countries of First Asylum would be lifted and the incentives for asylum seekers to take excessive risks to improve their protection prospects reduced. These risks include the engagement of people smugglers.

1.3 Eliminating policies that divert finite resources from improving the plight of refugees, either directly through government spend or indirectly through resultant asylum seeker behaviour. (9/10)

The expense of paying people smugglers would be avoided for asylum seekers who are deterred from travelling to a Country of Second Asylum as perceptions of advantage have been eliminated. The policies for the Regional Framework Approach around secondary movements from Countries of First Asylum are similar to those already employed through the Australia 2015 Approach. Thus a similar negative aspect is the continual cost in deterrence such as through off-shore processing centres and border protection. These costs are diversionary as they do not directly support conditions for asylum seekers. These costs would reduce as the behaviours of asylum seekers change in line with the incentives.

Average: 6.0

Q2. Best protection levels

2.1 Ensuring the highest possible probability for repatriation. (8/10)

As the capacity of the Countries of First Asylum is increased, a greater proportion of refugees will remain closer to their Countries of Origin. This maximises the probability of repatriation.

2.2 Standardising protection regardless of location. (8/10)

Levels of protection are standardised by improving the Countries of First Asylum through targeted funding and technical assistance. This would be significant in South East Asia where many countries have yet to sign the Refugee Convention nor adhere to its requirements. Burden-sharing arrangements, if appropriately established, would also standardise protection levels by reducing excessive concentrations of asylum seekers and refugees in some countries.

2.3 Avoiding overwhelming intakes of asylum seekers and refugees by Countries of First Asylum.(5/10)

Through capacity development and burden-sharing arrangements, the Countries of First Asylum are somewhat protected from being overwhelmed with refugee numbers. However, due to the uncapped obligations of the Refugee Convention, this outcome is still highly probable.

2.4 Avoiding overwhelming intakes of asylum seekers and refugees by Countries of Second Asylum. (7/10)

This approach controls the numbers of arrivals at the resettlement nations, protecting the viability of these nations and ultimately the ongoing human rights that stem to their populations from such viability.

2.5 Eliminating the diversion of resources caused by the use of protection channels by those without legitimate refugee claims (e.g. economic migrants). (8/10)

The Regional Framework Approach deters economic migrants from attempting to utilise the asylum seeker channel. Again, the reduction in migrant numbers could be quite significant given EU reports from the 2015 experience.

Average: 7.2

Q3. Reduce waiting time and minimise cultural friction

3.1 Reducing the average time spent waiting in limbo for a Durable Solution. This includes living in temporary accommodation, having little access to paid work, and having no certainty of the future. (7/10)

The average time waiting in limbo is likely to reduce significantly with a functioning Regional Framework Approach. The approach would result in countries resettling from 1 to 1.8 million refugees each year, being dependent on the proportion of wealthy nations agreeing for the first time to resettle refugees, or offer more resettlement places. Given the additional expense of a Regional Framework Approach it is likely that some nations may negotiate to provide more funding and resettle less refugees.

3.2 Ensuring the human rights of the population of the host nation and of the asylum seekers and refugees are protected across short and long-term horizons. Where cultures are incompatible, assimilation to the host nation is assured. (5/10)

A Regional Framework Approach outlines no specific requirement for immigrant people to assimilate culturally if certain cultural aspects are deemed to be incompatible. Such potential cultural friction is limited in Countries of First Asylum through the control of the annual intake to 0.1% of the population. However, these limitations are not in place for the Countries of First Asylum. The large numbers of intake could potentially lead to cultural tensions or changes that infringe on the human rights of their population.

Average: 6.0

Q4. Ongoing and Scalable Protection

4.1 Ensuring persistence and scalability of the protection approach considering Countries for First and Second Asylum, asylum seekers and refugees. (6/10)

If successfully implemented, a Regional Framework Approach is likely to endure. Capacity building and burden-sharing arrangements provide a solid framework for Countries of First Asylum to handle large refugee numbers year after year. Controlled resettlement numbers at the 0.1% of population would ensure Countries of Second Asylum are not overwhelmed.

Regional approaches are also reasonably scalable. Capacity building enables Countries of First Asylum to house more refugees in better conditions. Burden-sharing arrangements enable regions to improve the handling of larger volumes of refugees. One consequence that will add to the strain of the supporting countries is that improved conditions within Countries of First Asylum will result in more refugees presenting for a given situation.

Average: 6.0

Human Rights Score

Q5. Human Rights

5.1 Adhering to the Refugee Convention and other human rights agreements including the Declaration of Human Rights, the Convention of the Rights of Children and the International Covenant on Civil and Political Rights. (7/10)

The offshore processing of asylum seekers who attempted secondary movements to developed nations would trigger similar human rights breaches to 'unauthorised' asylum seekers as with the Australia 2015 Approach. For example, arbitrary detention of all such asylum seekers, including children, for indefinite periods. Once again, such human rights breaches, although undesirable, are required in order to protect the human rights within the resettlement nations. Such justification becomes harder to maintain if the numbers being housed in Countries of First Asylum become overwhelming.

Average: 7.0

Cost Score

Q6. Cost

6.1 Total cost (financial and other) of implementation. (6/10)

The cost of building and maintaining a Regional Framework Approach lies somewhere between the cost of Australia 2015 Approach and the cost of the German-led Europe 2015 Approach.

Cost is borne by Countries of First Asylum in housing large numbers of refugees in accordance with the tenets of the Refugee Convention. In support of this, financial and administrative resources are donated by the more developed countries. While the cost per refugee is increased from the current cost in these Countries of First Asylum, it is far less than what would be borne should they be housed in the Countries of Second Asylum. By this logic, for a given amount of resources, more refugees can be supported in the Countries of First Asylum.

This cost is not without some risk. Many Countries of First Asylum, that would receive funds and technical assistance to build capacity, have histories of corruption, fraud and waste. The opportunity for diverting or frittering away money provided for capacity building requires a high level of governance and oversight.

Additional expenses are borne by resettlement nations through an expanded resettlement program, the proposal in this case being 0.1% of the nation's population. Expenses are also required to maintain a deterrence program for people looking to access resettlement nations through secondary movements.

Average: 6.0

Implementation Score

Q7. Implementation Success

7.1 Probability of implementation and probability of success once implemented. Considerations include complexity and the likelihood of cooperation across nations. (4/10)

A Regional Framework Approach increases the possibility of countries being involved by allowing some scope for them to contribute according to their ability and skill set. For instance, countries with money but less space or appetite for protecting or resettling refugees (such as Singapore or Japan) could donate larger sums of money to the program. Poorer countries that are Countries of First Asylum could house and process the refugees with the support of the UNHCR and wealthier countries. Finally, resettlement numbers to countries like Australia could be raised with the knowledge their cost of housing and protecting refugees will decrease.

However, for all the positive possibilities of a Regional Framework Approach, there are some significant implementation issues. The first is the large financial investment required to build capacity. The second is the international cooperation and the reliance and trust placed on other countries. Indonesia, for instance, is a country with a history of corruption and disregard to people smuggling activities and a well-functioning Regional Framework Approach will require full cooperation with and involvement from Indonesia.

Third, a Regional Approach as per the Refugee Convention still requires an uncapped obligation to accept, house and process asylum seekers. This could ultimately overwhelm a Country of First Asylum. Accordingly, the uptake by a significant enough proportion of nations may not occur. Countries of First Asylum may resist agreeing to honour many aspects of the Refugee Convention, particularly those that grant permission to work and alternatives to detention. Similarly, resistance may come from more developed nations due to the expectation to resettle a larger number of refugees each year. Many of the nations proposed to provide resettlement placements up to 0.1% of population are likely to resist, citing protection of their cultural or economic viability. Again, these concerns would be somewhat diminished by the reduction in the asylum seekers and temporary refugees being housed in these nations.

Average: 4.0

Assessment Summary

Targeting the worldwide adoption of a Regional Framework Approach has a number of benefits in terms of burden-sharing and the development of consistent protection standards by improving those of less developed nations. This improvement, in theory, more quickly protects the human rights of vulnerable people. It would be possible for many more countries to provide adequate protection standards. A Regional Framework Approach also has an advantage in that countries contribute what they can in terms of skills, money and their protection.

The biggest issue concerning a Regional Framework Approach are its implementation and the need for full cooperation. It may not be possible to get a high take-up by countries as all will be required to provide more. This is also part of its attractiveness. Countries of First Asylum will be required to provide better housing, freedom of movement and work rights. Resettlement nations will be required to resettle more refugees, and whoever can provide funds will be asked to provide funds. The large transfer of resources across jurisdictions does expose this approach to theft and corruption. Many of the Countries of First Asylum have histories of such waste. Examples in South East Asia include Indonesia[4], Thailand[5] and Vietnam[6]. Even without the risks of fraud and deception, the coordination requirements make implementation difficult. A Regional Framework Approach requires cooperation between multiple countries, dealing with emotive and critical matters such as human rights and national security. It will not be easy to implement.

Effectiveness Score: 6.5
Human Rights Score: 7.0
Cost Score: 6.0
Implementation Score: 5.0

---

4 Lateef, S. Et al; "Indonesia - Combating corruption in Indonesia - enhancing accountability for development (English)," World Bank, 2003, accessed 17 August 2016, <http://www.documents.worldbank.org/curated/en/548131468774967556/Indonesia-Combating-corruption-in-Indonesia-enhancing-accountability-for-development>
5 Transparency International, *Global Corruption Barometer 2013,* 25 February 2014.
6 Ibid.

Fig. 15.2 ▶ Approach 6. Global adoption of Regional Approaches (Labor 2015)

1. Effectiveness	Question	Question Criteria	Pros	Cons	Score / 10	Score
Question 1.	Q1. How can the number of Forcibly Displaced People be minimised and how can they find protection as safely and as easily as possible?	1.1 Reducing the numbers of new Forcibly Displaced People.	Nil	- No direct action in minimising the disruptive causes. - Minimal encouragement for increased refugee presentation.	4	6.0
		1.2 Enabling people to find safety as easily as possible and eliminating risk taking behaviour in order to improve protection prospects.	Would lift standards of Countries of First Asylum and reduce risk taking incentives for asylum seekers.	Nil	7	
		1.3 Eliminating policies that divert finite resources from improving the plight of refugees, either directly through government spend or indirectly through resultant asylum seeker behaviour.	Expense of paying people smugglers avoided.	Continual diversionary cost in maintaining deterring efforts. Expected to reduce in time.	7	
Question 2.	Q2. How can protection best be provided to asylum seekers and refugees?	2.1 Ensuring the highest possible probability for repatriation.	With increased capacity in Countries of First Asylum, a greater proportion of refugees to be closer to their countries of origin.	Nil	8	7.2
		2.2 Standardising protection regardless of location.	Standardised level of protection through targeted funding and technical assistance to Countries of First Asylum.	Nil	8	
		2.3 Avoiding overwhelming intakes of asylum seekers and refugees by Countries of First Asylum.	Capacity development and burden sharing arrangements help mitigate impacts of large volumes.	Due to the uncapped obligations of the Refugee Convention, large intakes still highly probable.	5	
		2.4 Avoiding overwhelming intakes of asylum seekers and refugees by Countries of Second Asylum.	Controls the numbers of arrivals at more distant, resettlement nations.	Nil	8	
		2.5 Eliminating the diversion of resources caused by the use of protection channels by those without legitimate refugee claims (e.g. economic migrants).	Deterrence of economic migrants.	Nil	7	
Question 3.	Q3. How can the time spent waiting in limbo for a Durable Solution be minimised?	3.1 Reducing the average time spent waiting in limbo for a Durable Solution. This includes living in temporary accommodation, having little access to paid work, and having no certainty of the future.	High resettlement numbers help to reduce the waiting periods for refugees	Nil	7	6.0
		3.2 Ensuring the human rights of the population of the host nation and of the asylum seekers and refugees are protected across short and long term horizons. Where cultures are incompatible, assimilation to the host nation is assured.	Cultural friction is limited in Resettlement nations through the control of the annual intake	- No specific requirement for immigrant people to assimilate culturally. - No volume limitations for the countries of first asylum.	5	
Question 4.	Q4. How can the approach provide ongoing and scalable protection?	4.1 Ensuring persistence and scalability of the protection approach considering Countries for First and Second Asylum, asylum seekers and refugees.	Nil	- Low scalability due to economic and cultural pressures on the intake nations.	6	6.0
				Effectiveness Score (average)		6.5

2. Human Rights	Question	Question Criteria	Pros	Cons	Scores /10	Score
Question 5.	Q5. How well does the approach honour the tenets of international law?	5.1 Adhering to the Refugee Convention and other human rights agreements including the Declaration of Human Rights, the Convention of the Rights of Children and the International Covenant on Civil and Political Rights.	TBC	TBC	7	7.0
				Human Rights Score (average)		7.0

3. Cost	Question	Question Criteria	Pros	Cons	Scores /10	Score
Question 6.	Q6. How costly is implementation?	6.1 Total cost (financial and other) of implementation.			6	6.0
				Cost Score (larger is more cost)		6.0

4. Probability	Question	Question Criteria	Pros	Cons	Scores /10	Score
Question 7.	Q7. How probable is successful implementation?	7.1 Probability of implementation and probability of success once implemented. Considerations include complexity and the likelihood of cooperation across nations.	Countries can contribute in different ways.	Big reliance on less developed countries, some with histories of corruption and economic waste.	4	4.0
				Implementation Success Score		4.0

Approach 7. Development Zones

The Development Zone policy component was raised by Alexander Betts and Paul Collier in 2015 as an approach specifically for the forcibly displaced Syrian population[7]. If successfully implemented, the approach has many benefits, not least being that refugees are given opportunity and autonomy through work which potentially helps rather than threatens the local economy.

How would the refugee problem be managed if Development Zones were aimed to be established throughout the world much like those proposed by Betts and Collier in 2015?

Development Zones are separated areas that act as economies-in-a-bubble. A number would be set up in various countries around the world, usually Countries of First Asylum. They would house refugees from the neighbouring country and have infrastructure sufficient not only to house refugees but to also allow commercial enterprises to operate. Such enterprises could be in any industry including manufacturing or agriculture and would include international firms as well as firms that have been displaced from the Country of Origin. Schools and job training facilities would also exist within the zones. The infrastructure of the Development Zones may be pre-existing or it may even be developed by some of the resident businesses. The businesses would employ mainly the refugees of the country it was designed to support as well as workers of the host nation.

The Development Zones would have their own economy. Depending on the location, the currency used may be that of the Country of Origin or a major international currency like the Euro or the US Dollar. Such segregation would limit the impact to the host economy. In particular it would avoid a flood of refugees hitting the host nation workforce, which threatens to lower minimum wages and take jobs away from local residents. Contributing international businesses would establish operations in the Development Zones. International governments can contribute by providing financial incentives for businesses to set up in these areas as well as subsidies to host nations who will be required to contribute land and infrastructure for the creation of these Development Zones.

The establishment of Development Zones will provide an environment where refugees waiting for a Durable Solution can progress their schooling or work life. With the successful establishment of Development Zones, the social and financial pressure on Countries of First Asylum is reduced, as is the flow of refugees to Countries of Second Asylum. To ensure secondary movement is limited, deterrence measures including boat turn-backs and no-advantage policies would be necessary. As a consequence, resettlement

---

[7] Alexander Betts and Paul Collier, "Help Refugees Help Themselves: Let Displaced Syrians Join the Labor Market," *Foreign Affairs,* November/December 2015.

countries would be expected to increase the numbers of refugees resettled. The Australia 2015 Approach (0.06% of population) is used in this example, resettling up to one million refugees per year across the 62 Countries of Second Asylum.

Emergency refugee camps will continue to be used. Rather than housing refugees for long terms, these will be temporary facilities. Refugees will be transferred to Development Zones shortly after RSD.

Development Zones – Key Approach Points

- Emergency Camps still used to initially house and process asylum seekers.
- Land and infrastructure provided by host countries to create Development Zones where separate economies-in-a-bubble are created. Following RSD, most refugees will be moved to these zones where they will have full work rights.
- Reduced financial and social pressures on Countries of First Asylum.
- Deterrence measures employed to halt secondary movements from countries of First Asylum to Countries of Second Asylum.
- With the reduced flow of asylum seekers to Countries of Second Asylum, these countries increase their annual resettlement intake to a target of 0.06%.

Assessment Detail

Effectiveness Score

Q1. Minimise FDP and enable easy protection

1.1 Reducing the numbers of new Forcibly Displaced People. (4/10)

Similar to all previous approaches, Development Zones offer no direct action in minimising the disruptive causes of FDPs. Such initiatives would be considered in the scope of foreign policy. A well-functioning Development Zone may encourage previously disenchanted, persecuted people to present as asylum seekers but not to the same extent as the German-led Europe or Amnesty International approaches.

1.2 Enabling people to find safety as easily as possible and eliminating risk-taking behaviour in order to improve protection prospects. (7/10).

A Development Zone dramatically lifts the standards in the Countries of First Asylum and reduces incentives for asylum seekers to take excessive risks and travel further to improve their protection prospects. Having access to work and education should improve living standards and autonomy within the Country of First Asylum. It should reduce the impetus for refugees to expend resources and risk moving further afield with the goal to improve their situation. Incentives to travel are reduced as resettlement becomes more likely through a significant rise in resettlement numbers.

1.3 Eliminating policies that divert finite resources from improving the plight of refugees, either directly through government spend or indirectly through resultant asylum seeker behaviour. (7/10)

The use of people smugglers would be avoided. Many asylum seekers would be deterred from travelling to a Country of Second Asylum as perceptions of advantage have been eliminated. Development Zones will not by themselves eliminate secondary movement. Border protection efforts must also be employed to stop secondary movements. Diversionary cost must therefore be borne in deterrence efforts that would include off-shore processing centres. These costs would be high initially and lower as the behaviours of asylum seekers change in line with the incentives.

Average: 6.0

Q2. Best protection levels

2.1 Ensuring the highest possible probability for repatriation. (8/10)

Development Zones will enable a greater capacity for refugees to be housed close to their Countries of Origin. Through this, the probability of repatriation is maximised.

2.2 Standardising protection regardless of location. (8/10)

Development Zones hold the greatest hope for a scalable approach that improves the standard of living enjoyed by refugees as they wait for a permanent solution. If successfully implemented, small economies will flourish where refugees are able to educate, train and work to advance their lives. The location of Development Zones in the Countries of First Asylum and the associated shut down of secondary movement eliminates the advantages provided to refugees who are more mobile.

By pursuing their own autonomy and educational and career aspirations, refugees are able to contribute to their own financial situation in a way not previously allowed. Added benefits come from the potential additions to funding through businesses as well as development agencies focusing on re-development of nations following wars.

2.3 Avoiding overwhelming intakes of asylum seekers and refugees by Countries of First Asylum.(7/10)

Well-functioning Development Zones could host large numbers of refugees with minimal impact to the economies of host nations. The negative consequences, such as black market employment of desperate refugees undercutting the indigenous labour force, would be reduced.

2.4 Avoiding overwhelming intakes of asylum seekers and refugees by Countries of Second Asylum. (7/10)

The numbers of arrivals at Countries of Second Asylum are controlled, protecting the viability of these nations and ultimately the ongoing human rights that stem to their populations from such viability. As discussed in Approach 1, just how much this viability is at threat is debatable.

2.5 Eliminating the diversion of resources caused by the use of protection channels by those without legitimate refugee claims (e.g. economic migrants). (8/10)

Opportunities for economic migrants to utilise the asylum channel are greatly reduced as the vast majority of intakes into the Countries of Second Asylum are through the resettlement channel.

Average: 8.0

Q3. Reduce waiting time and minimise cultural friction

3.1 Reducing the average time spent waiting in limbo for a Durable Solution. This includes living in temporary accommodation, having little access to paid work, and having no certainty of the future. (9/10)

The average time waiting for a Durable Solution through the Development Zone Approach would be similar to the Australia 2015 Approach or the Regional Framework Approach where pressure on the Countries of Second Asylum to house refugees is reduced allowing them to increase their resettlement quotas.

The big advantage with the Development Zone Approach is that the waiting time for a Durable Solution may not be perceived by many refugees as in limbo at all. If successfully implemented, some refugees will be improving their skills and careers working in a viable industry that will hopefully transfer back to the Country of Origin when conditions allow.

3.2 Ensuring the human rights of the population of the host nation and of the asylum seekers and refugees are protected across short and long-term horizons. Where cultures are incompatible, assimilation to the host nation is assured. (7/10)

As with all approaches that have the majority of refugees stay in the Countries of First Asylum, large numbers of asylum seekers could lead to cultural tensions or changes that infringe on the human rights of their population. However, as the Development Zones would be separated, semi-autonomous regions, the approach provides the least total impact on the culture and viability to these countries. Potential cultural friction is also limited in Countries of Second Asylum through the control of their annual resettlement intake.

Average: 8.0

Q4. Ongoing and Scalable Protection

4.1 Ensuring persistence and scalability of the protection approach considering Countries for First and Second Asylum, asylum seekers and refugees. (8/10)

Of all approaches, Development Zones allow for the greatest sharing of the refugee load. They limit the burden on both the Countries of First Asylum and Second Asylum nations. As such they are the approaches with the greatest longevity and scalability.

Average: 8.0

Human Rights Score

Q5. Human Rights

5.1 Adhering to the Refugee Convention and other human rights agreements including the Declaration of Human Rights, the Convention of the Rights of Children and the International Covenant on Civil and Political Rights. (6/10)

The offshore processing of asylum seekers who attempted secondary movements to developed nations would trigger similar human rights breaches to 'unauthorised' asylum seekers as the Australian 2015 Approach. For example, arbitrary detention of all such asylum seekers, including children, for indefinite periods. Once again, such human rights breaches, although undesirable are required in order to protect the human rights within the resettlement nations. Such justification becomes harder to maintain if the numbers being housed in Countries of First Asylum become overwhelming.

The segregation of refugees into separate Development Zones has negative social and human rights consequences regarding the freedoms afforded to refugees. Isolating refugees from the main society of the host nation creates a sense of exclusion and isolation for the refugees. Restrictions of travel to within the Development Zones, by necessity small in obtaining their use, will create a sense of imprisonment and further amplify a sense of isolation.

The potential of greedy business managers to exploit refugees desperate to work, through under payment and poor working conditions, requires a robust and continual monitoring regime. This function cannot rest with the host nation itself and could be filled by the UNHCR or other NGOs.

Average: 6.0

Cost Score

Q6. Cost

6.1 Total cost (financial and other) of implementation. (7/10)

The creation and maintenance of Development Zones is a high-cost approach. Host nations will be required to donate or lease land and infrastructure. The creation of a separate economic zone, probably using different currencies from the host nation, would add administrative costs.

International governments would be required to provide funding and incentives to help attract businesses to the areas. Businesses themselves will also be required to undertake significant risk in opening operations in such an untested and possibly volatile environment.

Average: 7.0

Implementation Score

Q7. Implementation Success

7.1 Probability of implementation and probability of success once implemented. Considerations include complexity and the likelihood of cooperation across nations. (5/10)

The support required by host nations and the business community is large and, as such, not guaranteed. The donation or leasing of land and infrastructure is an enormous opportunity cost, especially if businesses are allowed to be run autonomously. Many host nations would be hesitant in allocating premium land and infrastructure to such enterprises. Likewise, businesses would also be tentative in allocating too much capital to enterprises operating in such tenuous environments. These concerns may allay in time, especially if early schemes prove successful. Additional funding would also be required from the international community to provide incentives for businesses to establish and operate in a new and high-risk environment.

The success of Development Zones will vary according to the capabilities of refugees as well as the quality of the land and infrastructure provided by the host nation. Development Zones for Syrian refugees appear viable as the population predominantly speak the same language as their hosts, most are educated and many have manufacturing skills. The same confluence of characteristics will not always be present. For instance, the work opportunities for many refugees from Somalia with limited education arriving to areas in Kenya with limited manufacturing facilities would be much less. The most likely outcome would be agricultural work on predominantly barren land.

Even with Development Zones, uncapped obligations to accept, house and process asylum seekers could ultimately disrupt an overwhelmed Country of First Asylum. Accordingly, the uptake by a significant enough proportion of nations must occur.

Average: 5.0

Assessment Summary

Development Zones is an uncommon but not untried approach. Worldwide implementation of such an approach would provide protection and autonomy to refugees in a scalable way with fewer burdens on the economies and societies of the supporting nations. This would apply to both the Countries of First Asylum and Second Asylum. If effectively implemented, it will help refugees develop skills to be used when provided with a Durable Solution. It also improves the infrastructure of the host nation and potentially helps lay the foundations for the economic redevelopment of the Country of Origin.

Although the approach has worked before in isolated examples, it is likely to have varying degrees of success dependent upon the specifics of each situation. These specifics include the quality of the land and infrastructure provided as well as financial and operational support provided by the international community and businesses. The engagement and uptake from the refugees themselves is also a critical factor, although analysts suggest many refugees are very willing to work. Development Zones do require a strong monitoring program as they do have the potential to result in exploitation of vulnerable people desperate to work.

Effectiveness Score: 7.5
Human Rights Score: 6.0
Cost Score: 7.0
Implementation Score: 4.0

Fig. 15.3 ▶ Approach 7. Global adoption of Development Zone (Betts & Collier 2015).

1. Effectiveness	Question	Question Criteria	Pros	Cons	Scores/10	Score
Question 1.	Q1. How can the number of Forcibly Displaced People be minimised and how can they find protection as safely and as easily as possible?	1.1 Reducing the numbers of new Forcibly Displaced People.	- Nil	- No direct action in minimising the disruptive causes. - Minimal encouragement for increased refugee presentation.	4	6.0
		1.2 Enabling people to find safety as easily as possible and eliminating risk taking behaviour in order to improve protection prospects.	- Would lift standards of Countries of First Asylum and reduce risk taking incentives for asylum seekers.	- Nil	7	
		1.3 Eliminating policies that divert finite resources from improving the plight of refugees, either directly through government spend or indirectly through resultant asylum seeker behaviour.	- Expense of paying people smugglers avoided.	- Continual diversionary cost in maintaining deterring efforts. Expected to reduce in time.	7	
Question 2.	Q2. How can protection best be provided to asylum seekers and refugees?	2.1 Ensuring the highest possible probability for repatriation.	- With increased capacity in Countries of First Asylum, a greater proportion of refugees to be closer to their countries of origin.	- Nil	9	8.0
		2.2 Standardising protection regardless of location.	- Small economies will flourish where refugees are able to educate, train and work to advance their lives.	- Success will vary according to the type of refugees and the land and infrastructure of the host nation	8	
		2.3 Avoiding overwhelming intakes of asylum seekers and refugees by Countries of First Asylum.	- Can host large numbers of refugees with minimal impact to the economies of the host nation.	- Due to the uncapped obligations of the Refugee Convention, large intakes still highly probable.	7	
		2.4 Avoiding overwhelming intakes of asylum seekers and refugees by Countries of Second Asylum.	- Controls the numbers of arrivals at more distant, resettlement nations.	- Nil	9	
		2.5 Eliminating the diversion of resources caused by the use of protection channels by those without legitimate refugee claims (e.g. economic migrants).	- Deterrence of economic migrants.	- Nil	7	
Question 3.	Q3. How can the time spent waiting in limbo for a Durable Solution be minimised?	3.1 Reducing the average time spent waiting in limbo for a Durable Solution. This includes living in temporary accommodation, having little access to paid work, and having no certainty of the future.	- High resettlement numbers help to reduce the waiting periods for refugees. - Waiting time may not be perceived as limbo.	- Nil	9	8.0
		3.2 Ensuring the human rights of the population of the host nation and of the asylum seekers and refugees are protected across short and long term horizons. Where cultures are incompatible, assimilation to the host nation is assured.	- Cultural friction is limited in Resettlement nations through the control of the annual intake. - Reduced impact on Countries of First Asylum.	- No specific requirement for immigrant people to assimilate culturally. - No volume limitations for the countries of first asylum.	7	
Question 4.	Q4. How can the approach provide ongoing and scalable protection?	4.1 Ensuring persistence and scalability of the protection approach considering Countries for First and Second Asylum, asylum seekers and refugees.	- Best chance of perpetuity.	- Nil	8	8.0
				Effectiveness Score (average)		7.5

2. Human Rights	Question	Question Criteria	Pros	Cons	Scores/10	Score
Question 5.	Q5. How well does the approach honour the tenets of international law?	5.1 Adhering to the Refugee Convention and other human rights agreements including the Declaration of Human Rights, the Convention of the Rights of Children and the International Covenant on Civil and Political Rights.	- Attempts to honour the tenets of the Refugee Convention.	- Offshore detention breaches the Refugee Convention. Segregation of refugees into separate Development Zones has negative social and human rights consequences.	6	6.0
				Human Rights Score (average)		6.0

3. Cost	Question	Question Criteria	Pros	Cons	Scores/10	Score
Question 6.	Q6. How costly is implementation?	6.1 Total cost (financial and other) of implementation.	- Nil	- Very high cost - New and complex approach. Probability of successful unknown.	7	7.0
				Cost Score (larger is more cost)		7.0

4. Probability	Question	Question Criteria	Pros	Cons	Scores/10	Score
Question 7.	Q7. How probable is successful implementation?	7.1 Probability of implementation and probability of success once implemented. Considerations include complexity and the likelihood of cooperation across nations.	- Nil	- TBC	3	3.0
				Implementation Success Score		3.0

Approach 8. Centrally Coordinated Burden Sharing

International refugee law expert James Hathaway suggests that the Refugee Convention has been increasingly marginalised with regard to refugee protection. To change this, he proposes an approach (which will be referred to as Centrally Controlled Burden Sharing) that changes the way refugee law is implemented. He posits that "the obligations are right, but the mechanisms for implementing these obligations are flawed in ways that too often lead states to act against their own values and interests - and which produce needless suffering amongst refugees"[8].

How would the refugee problem be managed if the aim was for all countries to contribute to Centrally Controlled Burden Sharing?

The approach is summarised by five principles[9]:

1. **Reform must address the circumstances of all states, not just the powerful few.** Share out fairly and in a binding way the burdens and responsibilities of the less developed world, including financial contributions and guaranteed resettlement opportunities.

2. **Plan for, rather than react to, refugee movements.** Commitments to pre-determined financial sharing and human responsibility sharing (protection of refugees and resettlements) made prior to refugee movements. Factors such as GDP and arable land may be used as starting points.

    An example of responsibility sharing using the 2014 refugee numbers, pre-commitments could be distributed across all 65 wealthy and free countries, the 62 Countries of Second Asylum as well as South Africa, Lebanon and Turkey (Countries of First Asylum). Each country would take in a percentage according to their GDP, countries of 'high income' taking in three times the amount per GDP as countries of 'upper-middle income'.

In this scenario the Countries of First Asylum take in a greatly reduced amount. For example:

- Turkey, an upper-middle income country containing about 4% of the population of Countries of Second Asylum, would be required to shelter 1.9% of the refugees (about 270,000 - a number far less than the 1.6 million people it supports as a Country of First Asylum).

- Australia as a high-income country would be required to shelter more refugees per capita than Turkey. Although a much smaller population, a similar commitment in terms of refugee burden-sharing would be made. About 1.7% or 250,000, which is almost five times its current share.

---

8 "A global solution to a global refugee crsis" James C. Hathaway. 29 February 2016. Opendemocracy.net
9 Ibid.

- The United States, high income and 17% of the relevant population would be committed to shelter 23.0% of the refugees, almost 3.3 million.
- Germany's commitment would be 830,000. Less than the number that arrived there in 2015.

Fig. 15.4 > Centrally Coordinated Burden Sharing Example (using 2014 data).

Country	2015	Income Group	GNI per capita Atlas method (USD) 2014	Freedom in the World	2014 Current State	Refugees to Take	Percentage of Refugees
Mauritius	1,273,212	Upper middle	$9,710	Free	-	4,328	0.03%
Tunisia	11,253,554	Upper middle	$-	Free	901	38,251	0.27%
Botswana	2,262,485	Upper middle	$7,240	Free	2,645	7,690	0.05%
Namibia	2,458,830	Upper middle	$5,680	Free	1,767	8,358	0.06%
South Africa	54,490,406	Upper middle	$6,800	Free	112,192	185,213	1.29%
Japan	126,573,481	High income	$42,000	Free	2,560	1,303,707	9.06%
Mongolia	2,959,134	Upper middle	$4,280	Free	6	10,058	0.07%
South Korea	50,293,439	High income	$27,090	Free	1,173	518,022	3.60%
Malaysia	30,331,007	Upper middle	$10,760	Partly Free	99,381	103,095	0.72%
Singapore	5,603,740	High income	$55,150	Partly Free	3	57,719	0.40%
Cyprus	1,165,300	High income	$26,370	Free	5,126	12,003	0.08%
Israel	8,064,036	High income	$34,990	Free	39,716	83,060	0.58%
Kuwait	3,892,115	High income	$-	Partly Free	614	40,089	0.28%
Lebanon	5,850,743	Upper middle	$9,800	Partly Free	1,154,040	19,887	0.14%
Turkey	78,665,830	Upper middle	$10,840	Partly Free	1,587,374	267,385	1.86%
Bulgaria	7,149,787	Upper middle	$7,420	Free	11,046	24,302	0.17%
Czech Rep	10,543,186	High income	$-	Free	3,137	108,595	0.75%
Hungary	9,855,023	High income	$13,470	Free	2,867	101,507	0.71%
Poland	38,611,794	High income	$13,730	Free	15,741	397,701	2.76%
Romania	19,511,324	Upper middle	$9,370	Free	2,182	66,319	0.46%
Slovakia	5,426,258	High income	$-	Free	799	55,890	0.39%
Denmark	5,669,081	High income	$61,310	Free	17,785	58,392	0.41%
Estonia	1,312,558	High income	$18,530	Free	90	13,519	0.09%
Finland	5,503,457	High income	$-	Free	11,798	56,686	0.39%
Ireland	4,688,465	High income	$44,660	Free	5,853	48,291	0.34%
Latvia	1,970,503	High income	$15,660	Free	183	20,296	0.14%
Lithuania	2,878,405	High income	$15,380	Free	1,007	29,684	0.21%
Norway	5,210,967	High income	$103,050	Free	47,043	53,673	0.37%
Sweden	9,779,426	High income	$61,600	Free	142,207	100,728	0.70%
UK	64,715,810	High income	$42,690	Free	117,161	666,573	4.63%
Albania	2,896,679	Upper middle	$4,460	Partly Free	104	9,846	0.07%
Bosnia and H	3,810,416	Upper middle	$4,780	Partly Free	6,890	12,952	0.09%
Croatia	4,240,317	High income	$13,020	Free	726	43,675	0.30%
Greece	10,954,617	High income	$22,090	Free	10,604	112,833	0.78%
Italy	59,797,685	High income	$34,280	Free	93,715	615,916	4.28%
Portugal	10,349,803	High income	$21,320	Free	699	106,603	0.74%
Serbia	8,850,975	Upper middle	$5,820	Free	43,751	30,084	0.21%
Slovenia	2,067,526	High income	$-	Free	257	21,296	0.15%

Country	2015	Income Group	GNI per capita Atlas method (USD) 2014	Freedom in the World	2014 Current State	Refugees to Take	Percentage of Refugees
Spain	46,121,699	High income	$-	Free	5,798	475,053	3.30%
Macedonia	2,078,453	Upper middle	$-	Partly Free	883	7,065	0.05%
Austria	8,544,586	High income	$-	Free	55,598	88,009	0.61%
Belgium	11,299,192	High income	$47,030	Free	29,179	116,382	0.81%
France	64,395,345	High income	$43,070	Free	252,264	663,272	4.61%
Germany	80,688,545	High income	$47,640	Free	216,973	831,092	5.77%
Netherlands	16,924,929	High income	$51,210	Free	82,494	174,327	1.21%
Switzerland	8,298,663	High income	$-	Free	62,620	85,476	0.59%
Dominican Rep	10,528,391	Upper middle	$6,030	Free	608	35,786	0.25%
Jamaica	2,793,335	Upper middle	$-	Free	22	9,495	0.07%
Trinidad and T	1,360,088	High income	$-	Free	83	14,009	0.10%
Costa Rica	4,807,850	Upper middle	$10,120	Free	20,744	16,342	0.11%
Mexico	127,017,224	Upper middle	$9,860	Partly Free	1,837	431,732	3.00%
Panama	3,929,141	Upper middle	$11,130	Free	17,271	13,355	0.09%
Argentina	43,416,755	High income	$14,160	Free	3,498	447,193	3.11%
Brazil	207,847,528	Upper middle	$11,530	Free	7,490	706,474	4.91%
Chile	17,948,141	High income	$14,910	Free	1,773	184,866	1.28%
Colombia	48,228,704	Upper middle	$7,970	Partly Free	213	163,929	1.14%
Ecuador	16,144,363	Upper middle	$6,070	Partly Free	122,161	54,875	0.38%
Paraguay	6,639,123	Upper middle	$4,380	Partly Free	153	22,566	0.16%
Peru	31,376,670	Upper middle	$6,370	Free	1,303	106,649	0.74%
Uruguay	3,431,555	High income	$16,350	Free	272	35,345	0.25%
Venezuela	31,108,083	High income	$-	Partly Free	173,600	320,413	2.23%
Canada	35,939,927	High income	$51,690	Free	149,163	370,181	2.57%
USA	321,773,631	High income	$55,200	Free	267,222	3,314,268	23.02%
Australia	23,968,973	High income	$64,680	Free	35,582	246,880	1.71%
New Zealand	4,528,526	High income	$-	Free	1,349	46,644	0.32%

3. **Embrace common but differentiated state responsibility.** All states provide first asylum, but where a refugee arrives has no influence on where they are protected. People will be allocated according to the pre-determined rules regarding responsibility sharing. Beyond this there is flexibility for how different states contribute for different refugee situations. Help may be in the form of protection for the duration of risk, resettlement, or exceptional immediate resettlement. All states would be required to make contributions to financial burden-sharing and the human responsibility sharing (protection of refugees and resettlements) with no trade-offs between the two.

4. **Shift away from national, and towards international, administration of refugee protection.** The UNHCR to centralise administration of quotas, allocate refugees and funds. Also, the UNHCR to centralise RSD and group assessments to reduce processing costs by eliminating the duplicate RSD efforts occurring in multiple countries.

5. **Protection for duration of risk, not necessarily permanent immigration.** Protection with a view to return home. However, if no solution found after 5-7 years, then resettlement is guaranteed. Further, unaccompanied minors, plus victims of severe trauma, will require immediate permanent integration.

Centrally Coordinated Burden Sharing – Key Approach Points

- Share out in a binding way the burdens of the less developed world.
- Commitments to pre-determined financial sharing and human responsibility sharing.
- All states provide first asylum arrival point that has no influence on protection location.
- Some flexibility for how different states contribute for different refugee situations.
- UNHCR administers centralised RSD, group assessments, funds allocation and refugee quotas and allocations.
- Protection with a view to repatriation. Guaranteed resettlement after 5-7 years.

Assessment Detail

Effectiveness Score

Q1. Minimise FDP and enable easy protection

1.1 Reducing the numbers of new Forcibly Displaced People. (3/10)

Centrally Coordinated Burden Sharing will lift the quality of protection for all refugees. It will also provide certainty with a worse case of repatriation after seven years. Lifts in these outcomes will increase the proportion of refugees presenting who may otherwise have not. This analysis considers such an outcome as a negative on the assumption some asylum seekers will be too quick to leave their homeland, however the extent of these false presentations would be less than the German-led Europe 2015 Approach.

1.2 Enabling people to find safety as easily as possible and eliminating risk-taking behaviour in order to improve protection prospects. (8/10).

The use of people smuggling and secondary movement should reduce considerably through this method. One key unknown is whether there is still a perceived advantage in seeking first asylum by arriving at a wealthy nation. Although stated policy would be that location of first asylum plays no factor on the long-term protection, the machinations in practice may prove different as the cost of transferring people could be avoided by allowing them to stay where they present.

1.3 Eliminating policies that divert finite resources from improving the plight of refugees, either directly through government spend or indirectly through resultant asylum seeker behaviour. (9/10)

Most duplicate or diverted spending is eliminated through Centrally Coordinated Burden Sharing. The use of people smuggling is anticipated to reduce, with one caveat regarding the perception any advantage in arriving at a wealthy nation. Most critically, the centralisation of RSD will eliminate duplicate bureaucracies across countries as well as eliminate duplicate effort caused by the prevalence of asylum shopping where the one asylum seeker presents at multiple countries resulting in each undertaking RSD.

Average: 6.7

Q2. Best protection levels

2.1 Ensuring the highest possible probability for repatriation. (3/10)

Repatriation rates are likely to fall for two reasons. First, more people will be located further away from their countries which decreases the likelihood of repatriation. Second, a knowledge of guaranteed resettlement after seven years may influence some candidates to resist repatriation however they can.

2.2 Standardising protection regardless of location. (8/10)

A high standardisation of protection standards will be achieved through the financial sharing and responsibility sharing requirements. Standards will be further enhanced if refugees are allowed work rights. However, in this scenario the perception by many will be that the quality of life will be higher in the more wealthy countries.

2.3 Avoiding overwhelming intakes of asylum seekers and refugees by Countries of First Asylum.(7/10)

Clearly the responsibility sharing aspect will greatly reduce the pressure felt by Countries of First Asylum. One caveat being that with likely increases to the number of refugee presentations, there will still be great pressures placed on these countries.

2.4 Avoiding overwhelming intakes of asylum seekers and refugees by Countries of Second Asylum. (7/10)

The responsibility sharing aspect will increase the pressure felt by Countries of First Asylum, especially if countries agree to a proportional quota rather than a set number. As per the example, commitments made for current numbers would result in countries like Turkey, Lebanon, Germany and Sweden receiving fewer refugees than they currently do. This reduction is borne across all the other nations. Countries like the United States, Japan, Canada and Australia are all required to take in more refugees. The United States sheltering 3.3 million (from 150,000 in 2014), Japan 1.4 million (from less than 3,000), Canada 370,000 (from 149,000) and Australia 260,000 (from 36,000).

The proportional commitments are effectively uncapped obligations. With the improved prospects and guarantees regarding resettlement it is likely that increases to the number of asylum seekers presentations, and then refugees following RSD, will occur.

2.5 Eliminating the diversion of resources caused by the use of protection channels by those without legitimate refugee claims (e.g. economic migrants). (5/10)

Although all asylum seekers will be required to go through a centralised RSD, this is unlikely to deter all economic migrants. Anecdotal evidence suggests many people are still able to attain refugee status through RSD with fabricated stories. The level of precision with RSD checks will remain low for some time yet.

Average: 6.0

Q3. Reduce waiting time and minimise cultural friction

3.1 Reducing the average time spent waiting in limbo for a Durable Solution. This includes living in temporary accommodation, having little access to paid work, and having no certainty of the future. (9/10)

If upheld, the knowledge of a guaranteed resettlement following seven years eliminates all feeling of uncertainty for refugees. Seven years as a worse case is far better than the widely quoted 17-year figure for the average length of displacement,

3.2 Ensuring the human rights of the population of the host nation and of the asylum seekers and refugees are protected across short and long-term horizons. Where cultures are incompatible, assimilation to the host nation is assured. (5/10)

In small numbers, Centrally Coordinated Burden Sharing will work well as no country should be overwhelmed and the standards for refugees would be lifted. However, larger numbers will likely result in negative consequences. A quota system utilising proportions is effectively an uncapped obligation leading to the potential to overwhelm participant countries.

Average: 7.0

Q4. Ongoing and Scalable Protection

4.1 Ensuring persistence and scalability of the protection approach considering Countries for First and Second Asylum, asylum seekers and refugees. (6/10)

The financial and responsibility (human) sharing aspects of this solution provide it with some persistence and scalability. However, beyond the strategy of sharing the burdens there are plans to manage a large number of refugees without impacting the host society (as with Development Zones). Further, the approach will encourage more people to present including some economic migrants who would risk happily fabricating a story as no deterrence measures are in place.

Average: 6.0

Human Rights Score

Q5. Human Rights

5.1 Adhering to the Refugee Convention and other human rights agreements including the Declaration of Human Rights, the Convention of the Rights of Children and the International Covenant on Civil and Political Rights. (9/10)

Centrally Coordinated Burden Sharing honours the tenets of the Refugee Convention through a new interpretation of the law. If successfully implemented it would do well in protecting the human rights of refugees. There is no arbitrary detention, nor is there punishment for arriving without valid entry documentation. Refugees would be able to work and an increased number would be protected in the more wealthy nations.

Average: 9.0

Cost Score

Q6. Cost

6.1 Total cost (financial and other) of implementation. (8/10)

Centrally Coordinated Burden Sharing is a very high-cost approach. A greatly expanded UNHCR would be required to conduct the RSD, coordinate the quotas and allocate refugees. This expense is somewhat reduced by the elimination of the duplicate bureaucracies of RSD in each country, overall creating a more efficient system. However, additional costs would be incurred within each country through the guarantee of work rights, the guarantee of resettlements, and the likelihood that with a more attractive and certain outcome, the numbers presenting will increase.

Average: 8.0

Implementation Score

Q7. Implementation Success

7.1 Probability of implementation and probability of success once implemented. Considerations include complexity and the likelihood of cooperation across nations. (4/10)

The likelihood of implementation is low. The key issues being the enhanced powers of the UNHCR, for instance in managing all RSD and the uncapped obligations (through a proportional quota) on distant and wealthy nations. For true responsibility sharing, agreements across countries need to be made in terms of the proportion of refugees each country takes in as well as the proportion of refugees each will resettle. However, this does not guarantee a limit to the number required to be housed.

Although Countries of First Asylum have been dealing with this for many years, until Europe in 2015 this has rarely been experienced by developed nations. Each time it has, borders were closed. The added issue is that if successfully implemented, this new system is likely to encourage many more legitimate and economic refugees to present than the current systems (outside Europe 2015) do.

Average: 4.0

Assessment Summary

Centrally Coordinated Burden Sharing has many benefits. First, by predetermined proportional quotas and financial burden-sharing it will lift and standardise the quality of protection experienced by refugees. Second, it attempts to remove the link between the country an asylum seeker arrives at and where they will stay as a refugee or be resettled. This eliminates much of the diverted spending on people smuggling and deterrence activities. Third, the centralised RSD further creates efficiencies by eliminating duplicated bureaucracies and the associated asylum shopping it attracts.

Perhaps the two biggest qualities of the approach are the implicit guarantees that refugees will be able to work within the countries they are sheltered in (and resettle to), and of repatriation if after 5-7 years the situation at their Country of Origin has not improved.

The negative is in regard to the uncapped obligation that is expected to be endured by all countries. This obligation exists in the advanced commitment to accept a proportion of all refugees deemed by the UNHCR in addition to committing to resettling a proportion that have reached their 5-7 year threshold or qualify for immediate resettlement (for example as a victim of trauma). Such commitments make it impossible for a country to control its migration intake, a core aspect of sovereign rights since the treaty of Westphalia in 1648.

This negative is likely to be further amplified as such updates to the refugee system would attract far more people to present as refugees. Many would have legitimate cases but would have remained in the situation with less attractive options, others still will be economic migrants attracted by the prospects that if they can pass RSD a better life immediately awaits. The elimination of the link between the country of presentation and actual asylum is a worthy pursuit; however, economics may lead to a process outcome that creates an advantage to those who present in the country they hope to remain in.

These negatives make Centrally Coordinated Burden Sharing unlikely to achieve universal support from many countries. Thus, the probability of successful implementation is low.

Effectiveness Score: 6.1
Human Rights Score: 9.0
Cost Score: 8.0
Implementation Score: 3.0

Fig. 15.5 ▶ Approach 8. Global adoption of Centrally Coordinated Burden Sharing.

1. Effectiveness	Question	Question Criteria	Pros	Cons	Score / 10	Score
Question 1.	Q1. How can the number of Forcibly Displaced People be minimised and how can they find protection as safely and as easily as possible?	1.1 Reducing the numbers of new Forcibly Displaced People.	- Nil.	- No direct action in minimising the disruptive causes. - Encourages an increased refugee presentation.	3	6.7
		1.2 Enabling people to find safety as easily as possible and eliminating risk taking behaviour in order to improve protection prospects.	- Lift standards of Countries of First Asylum, protection is shared across countries not necessarily where people arrive. Reduce risk taking incentives for asylum seekers.	- Nil.	8	
		1.3 Eliminating policies that divert finite resources from improving the plight of refugees, either directly through government spend or indirectly through resultant asylum seeker behaviour.	- Expense of paying people smugglers avoided.	- Nil.	9	
Question 2.	Q2. How can protection best be provided to asylum seekers and refugees?	2.1 Ensuring the highest possible probability for repatriation.	- Nil.	- More asylum seekers are moved away from countries of first asylum. Reducing likelihood of repatriation.	3	6.0
		2.2 Standardising protection regardless of location.	- Lift standards of Countries of First Asylum, sharing of funds across countries.	- Nil.	8	
		2.3 Avoiding overwhelming intakes of asylum seekers and refugees by Countries of First Asylum.	- Burden sharing occurs through a management from the UNHCR. Quotas based on number better than % (which is uncapped).	- Through an increased likelihood of repatriation (5-7 years) they there is likely to be an increase in presentations.	7	
		2.4 Avoiding overwhelming intakes of asylum seekers and refugees by Countries of Second Asylum.	- Burden sharing occurs through a management from the UNHCR. Quotas based on number better than % (which is uncapped).	- Through an increased likelihood of repatriation (5-7 years) they there is likely to be an increase in presentations.	7	
		2.5 Eliminating the diversion of resources caused by the use of protection channels by those without legitimate refugee claims (e.g. economic migrants).	- Nil.	- Through an increased likelihood of repatriation (5-7 years) there is likely to be an increase in economic refugee attempts.	5	
Question 3.	Q3. How can the time spent waiting in limbo for a Durable Solution be minimised?	3.1 Reducing the average time spent waiting in limbo for a Durable Solution. This includes living in temporary accommodation, having little access to paid work, and having no certainty of the future.	- Period capped at 5-7 years. Assuming resettlement placements are viable.	- Assumes resettlement placements are viable.	9	7.0
		3.2 Ensuring the human rights of the population of the host nation and of the asylum seekers and refugees are protected across short and long term horizons. Where cultures are incompatible, assimilation to the host nation is assured.	- Nil.	- If refugee and resettlement quotas are by pro-portion, uncapped obligations may result in loss of sovereignty regarding borders in the short term for the host nation.	5	
Question 4.	Q4. How can the approach provide ongoing and scalable protection?	4.1 Ensuring persistence and scalability of the protection approach considering Countries for First and Second Asylum, asylum seekers and refugees.	- Burden sharing helps booth with scalability and persistence.	- Strong positive outcomes for the refugees are likey to encourage presentations.	6	6.0
				Effectiveness Score (average)		**6.4**

2. Human Rights	Question	Question Criteria	Pros	Cons	Scores / 10	Score
Question 5.	Q5. How well does the approach honour the tenets of international law?	5.1 Adhering to the Refugee Convention and other human rights agreements including the Declaration of Human Rights, the Convention of the Rights of Children and the International Covenant on Civil and Political Rights.	- Attempts to honour the tenets of the Refugee Convention other human rights agreements including the Declaration of Human Rights, the Convention of the Rights of Children and the ICPPR.	- Nil.	9	9.0
				Human Rights Score (average)		**9.0**

3. Cost	Question	Question Criteria	Pros	Cons	Scores / 10	Score
Question 6.	Q6. How costly is implementation?	6.1 Total cost (financial and other) of implementation.	- RSD more economical through centralisation.	- Larger beuaracracy through centralised system.	8	8.0
				Cost Score (larger is more cost)		**8.0**

4. Probability	Question	Question Criteria	Pros	Cons	Scores / 10	Score
Question 7.	Q7. How probable is successful implementation?	7.1 Probability of implementation and probability of success once implemented. Considerations include complexity and the likelihood of cooperation across nations.	- Countries can contribute in different ways.	- Big reliance on less developed countries, some with histories of corruption and economic waste.	3	3.0
				Implementation Success Score		**3.0**

Fig. 15.6 > Approach Scoring.

	Question	Question Criteria	Approach 1 As is	Approach 2 Aust 2015	Approach 3 German-led Europe	Approach 4 Japan 2015	Approach 5 Amnesty International	Approach 6 Regional	Approach 7 Development Zones	Approach 8 Centrally Coordinated Burden Sharing
1. Effectiveness										
Question 1.	Q1. How can the number of Forcibly Displaced People be minimised and how can they find protection as safely and as easily as possible?	1.1 Reducing the numbers of new Forcibly Displaced People.	5	5	2	7	1	4	4	3
		1.2 Enabling people to find safety as easily as possible and eliminating risk taking behaviour in order to improve protection prospects.	4	5	8	5	9	7	7	8
		1.3 Eliminating policies that divert finite resources from improving the plight of refugees, either directly through government spend or indirectly through resultant asylum seeker behaviour.	5	6	9	5	9	7	7	9
Question 2.	Q2. How can protection best be provided to asylum seekers and refugees?	2.1 Ensuring the highest possible probability for repatriation.	8	8	2	8	1	8	9	3
		2.2 Standardising protection regardless of location.	5	3	6	2	6	8	8	8
		2.3 Avoiding overwhelming intakes of asylum seekers and refugees by Countries of First Asylum.	5	2	7	1	8	5	7	7
		2.4 Avoiding overwhelming intakes of asylum seekers and refugees by Countries of Second Asylum.	4	9	2	9	1	8	9	7
		2.5 Eliminating the diversion of resources caused by the use of protection channels by those without legitimate refugee claims (e.g. economic migrants).	3	9	2	9	1	7	7	5
Question 3.	Q3. How can the time spent waiting in limbo for a Durable Solution be minimised?	3.1 Reducing the average time spent waiting in limbo for a Durable Solution. This includes living in temporary accommodation, having little access to paid work, and having no certainty of the future.	5	6	6	1	6	7	9	9
		3.2 Ensuring the human rights of the population of the host nation and of the asylum seekers and refugees are protected across short and long term horizons. Where cultures are incompatible, assimilation to the host nation is assured.	4	5	3	5	2	5	7	5
Question 4.	Q4. How can the approach provide ongoing and scalable protection?	4.1 Ensuring persistence and scalability of the protection approach considering Countries for First and Second Asylum, asylum seekers and refugees.	4	6	3	3	2	6	8	6
			4.7	5.8	4.5	5.0	4.2	6.5	7.5	6.4
	Question	Question Criteria	Approach 1 Aust 2016	Approach 2 Aust 2016	Approach 3 German-led Europe	Approach 4 Japan	Approach 5 Amnesty International	Approach 6 Regional	Approach 7 Development Zones	Approach 8 Centrally Coordinated Burden Sharing
2. Human Rights										
Question 5.	Q5. How well does the approach honour the tenets of international law?	5.1 Adhering to the Refugee Convention and other human rights agreements including the Declaration of Human Rights, the Convention of the Rights of Children and the International Covenant on Civil and Political Rights.	6	4	9	1	9	7	6	9
			6.0	4.0	9.0	1.0	9.0	7.0	6.0	9.0
	Question	Question Criteria	Approach 1 Aust 2016	Approach 2 Aust 2016	Approach 3 German-led Europe	Approach 4 Japan	Approach 5 Amnesty International	Approach 6 Regional	Approach 7 Development Zones	Approach 8 Centrally Coordinated Burden Sharing
3. Cost										
Question 6.	Q6. How costly is implementation?	6.1 Total cost (financial and other) of implementation.	5	3	8	3	9	6	7	8
			5.0	3.0	8.0	3.0	9.0	6.0	7.0	8.0
	Question	Question Criteria	Approach 1 Aust 2016	Approach 2 Aust 2016	Approach 3 German-led Europe	Approach 4 Japan	Approach 5 Amnesty International	Approach 6 Regional	Approach 7 Development Zones	Approach 8 Centrally Coordinated Burden Sharing
4. Probability										
Question 7.	Q7. How probable is successful implementation?	7.1 Probability of implementation and probability of success once implemented. Considerations include complexity and the likelihood of cooperation across nations.	9	6	2	5	1	4	3	3
			9.0	6.0	2.0	5.0	1.0	4.0	3.0	3.0

PART 3
Options & Recommendation

Section 3.2
RECOMMENDATION AND IMPLEMENTATION

Part 1 — Situation (Chapters 1-10)

Section 1.1
CH 1-7 Global Review
- Uses the *Refugee Journey* framework to review the global refugee situation. Including:
  - Disruptive Causes and Forcibly Displaced People.
  - Protection (i.e. as asylum seekers or refugees).
  - Durable Solutions (i.e. Repatriation, Local Integration or Resettlement).

Section 1.2
CH 8-10 Australian Review
- Reviews the Australian context including:
  - Australia's migration programs.
  - Australia's humanitarian program.
  - Controversy and debate surrounding Australia's humanitarian program.

Part 2 — Complication, Principles & Assessment Framework (Chapter 11-12)

Section 2.1
CH 11 The Complication
- Summarises the main issues identified through the global and Australian reviews.

Section 2.2
CH 12 Principles & Assessment Framework
- Outlines the Questions of Principle that must be answered to best manage the refugee situation.
- Sets out the approach option assessment framework.

Part 3 — Options & Recommendation (Chapters 13-17)

Section 3.1
CH 13-15 Options Assessment
- Summarises the various Component Policies.
- Summarises and assesses the various Holistic Approaches using the approach option assessment framework.

Section 3.2
CH 16-17 Discussion and Recommendation
- Discusses the trade-offs in selecting the best Holistic Approach Option.
- Recommends an approach and provides a pathway for implementation including Australia's next steps.

CH 16. DISCUSSION AND RECOMMENDATION

Approach Option Summaries

Humanitarian Approaches can only be agreed to, not enforced.

A persistent principle in international relations has been the right for sovereign nations to control their domestic affairs. Management of population growth and its make-up through immigration and humanitarian efforts is a significant component of such sovereignty. This explains, to some extent, the variety of approaches toward refugees adopted by countries such as Australia, Germany and Japan. It is the combined interactions of these various approaches as well as the social and economic characteristics of the countries themselves that have contributed, both in presentation of and response to, the current refugee situation.

That said, it is incorrect to suggest approaches by countries to humanitarian crises are completely without external influence. Sovereign freedoms with regard to humanitarian responses are somewhat constrained for countries that have ratified the Refugee Convention and other instruments of international human rights law. The word 'somewhat' carries meaning in relation to the many countries where these international laws have not been reflected in the country's own laws. If a country has not reflected international laws in their domestic laws they are not compelled to follow any of these commitments. There is no global authority to enforce international laws. As such, humanitarian approaches can only be agreed to, not enforced.

The current worldwide response is an amalgam of approaches with many flaws. The hope is that an improved response can be found.

Some countries, such as Australia and Canada, have treated asylum seekers with a valid visa very differently to those without. Japan and Saudi Arabia resettle very few refugees. Countries like Lebanon, Pakistan and Ethiopia neighbour countries in crisis, so are flooded with refugees as Countries of First Asylum. Recently, rich European countries Germany and Sweden have opened their lands to refugees and have been met with an unprecedented flow of arrivals, resulting in the current global situation, along with the many issues described in the first half of this book. Although humanitarian approaches cannot be enforced, if a widely agreed best practice can be defined, then countries could provide support around such an approach.

Options were assessed according to criteria based on the principles discussed in Chapter 12.

The options in this book are assessed in terms of their merit in being the aligned approach international support should be based upon. The objectives were articulated in seven questions, the answers to which produced four scores regarding each approach option. A balance is required between the human rights of individuals external to a nation and the viability of the nation itself and the human rights of its citizens.

Approaches honouring Human Rights

Three approaches best protect the human rights for asylum seekers and refugees: The German-led Europe 2015 Approach; the Amnesty International Approach; and Centrally Coordinated Burden Sharing. In particular, they allow arrival by anyone claiming asylum and do not punish people with regard to the legality of their arrival should they not claim asylum. The Amnesty International Approach goes even further by recommending legal and safe passage to the countries of asylum to minimise the danger for those seeking asylum. None of these approaches mandate a cap on the obligations of host nations, although Centrally Coordinated Burden Sharing does have prescribed burden-sharing arrangements to proportionally share responsibilities.

Each of the three has clear limitations, both in probability of successful implementation as well as the consequences of a successful implementation. Of the three, Centrally Coordinated Burden Sharing is clearly the best alternative. It has a better overall outcome and a higher chance of implementation.

Other common advantages of these approaches are:

- Maximising the number of refugees living in the better conditions under protection of more wealthy nations. Centrally Coordinated Burden Sharing having the important process step of a proportional distribution.
- Limiting the diversion of resources through nations spending on deterrence measures.

Centrally Coordinated Burden Sharing has unique advantages in that it:

- Eliminates the duplication of RSD systems across many countries, which also will eliminate the practice of asylum shopping.

- Guarantees refugees a resettlement spot after 5-7 years, meaning that the distress associated with living with an uncertainty is somewhat reduced.

The overall effectiveness of these three approaches is reduced by a number of negative consequences that apply to each. Although all three are impacted Centrally Coordinated Burden Sharing, due to its use of pre-committed proportional quotas and by de-linking the country of presentation with the country of asylum and resettlement, avoids the worst of these outcomes. These negative consequences include:

- Massive influxes into the distant resettlement nations have a number of implications:
  - Large financial pressure on nations under the Refugee Convention that must provide welfare and services equivalent to those for their citizens.
  - Decreased probability of repatriation back to the Countries of Origin.
  - Pressure on the wealthy nations, many of whom are the biggest donors to the UNHCR and aid efforts.
  - Potential cultural strains on Countries of Second Asylum. Particularly with militant fundamentalist Islam (or Islamism), which appears unlikely to culturally coexist with the secularism and freedoms of liberal democracies. Such strains may take a long time to eventuate but are arguably starting to materialise in European nations such as the United Kingdom, Belgium and France.
- Wide scale opportunistic use of the humanitarian channel by people without a legitimate asylum claim to enter more wealthy Countries of Second Asylum.
  - Most are likely to be economic migrants. Their presence diverts resources from activities seeking to help asylum seekers. It adds to economic instability through increasing black market labour force supply, and adds to social instability through increasing the proportion of new immigrants within a country.
  - Some, as seen in Europe, will have criminal intentions reducing security and further adding to the social instability.
- Incentives for more asylum seekers to present than otherwise would have. This further drains the population of the countries they are fleeing and adds further pressure on supporting nations to which they flee.

Of the three approaches that most honour the human rights of asylum seekers, Centrally Coordinated Burden Sharing provides the outcomes and highest potential for implementation success. However, for each of the three approaches, the many material negative consequences outweigh the positive benefits. In addition, the extensive support and services Countries of Second Asylum are required to provide under the Refugee Convention make these approaches very expensive.

It is these negative consequences – some immediate, others being potential threats – and the high cost of implementation which reduce the likelihood of their worldwide adoption. The more countries that decline adopting these approaches, the greater the burden on those that do. Consequently, not only is broad uptake considered unlikely, but successful implementation is also considered a low probability.

Approaches most easily implemented

The two most easily implemented approaches, at least from an execution point of view, are those operated by Australia and Japan in 2015. Not only are they the most easily implemented but they are also the lowest cost approaches. They also share the same significant negative of contributing to human rights breaches for many asylum seekers and refugees. That said, both are moderately successful in fulfilling the criteria as set out by the principles discussed in Chapter 12. In fact, both provide better overall outcomes than the European and Amnesty International Approaches.

Of the two, the Australia 2015 Approach is more compelling as it provides better outcomes, including a higher level of generosity toward asylum seekers. This generosity would result in less resistance to a worldwide adoption of the Australia 2015 Approach by Countries of Second Asylum. However, both approaches would be widely criticised. A worldwide Japan 2015 Approach may be perceived as selfish and xenophobic; a worldwide Australia 2015 Approach as breaching human rights. It is this limited global acceptance that is the largest barrier to successful implementation. Apart from their acceptance by other countries, both are relatively simple to implement and of similarly (and relatively) low cost.

In addition to the similarities regarding implementation ease and low cost, these approaches share other positive aspects:

- Relatively generous donations to the UNHCR. In terms of USD per GDP, in 2013 Australia ranked 18th and Japan 7th[1].
- Control of the numbers arriving to Countries of Second Asylum. The expectation is that the vast majority of the protection and RSD is done at the Countries of First Asylum. This would ultimately lower the prevalence of people-smuggler activities.
- This provides the greatest opportunity for repatriation through the majority of refugees remaining at Countries of First Asylum.

---

1 "Donor Profiles," UNHCR, accessed 28 November 2016 <www.unhcr.org/4a31169d.pdf>

PART 3. OPTIONS & RECOMMENDATIONS > CH 16. DISCUSSION AND RECOMMENDATION   373

- A minimisation of the numbers of asylum seekers presenting through the removal of increased incentives and lower costs in presenting.
- Minimisation in the numbers of economic migrants and criminal migrants.

The approaches also share significant negative aspects:

- Increased pressure on Countries of First Asylum through minimal burden-sharing. This is partially offset by the financial donations to build capacity in these countries.
- Resources spent in deterring asylum seekers from making secondary movements to the Countries of Second Asylum.

Assuming successful implementation, the Australia 2015 Approach is more effective in meeting the outcomes of the principles set in Chapter 12. Its positive aspect, not shared with the Japan 2015 Approach, is that a high number of refugees are resettled each year. Almost one million people would be resettled annually if all Countries of Second Asylum agree to undertake the approach. An almost tenfold increase rate from current resettlement numbers would reduce the average amount of time spent waiting in uncertainty for a Durable Solution.

A negative aspect of the Australia 2015 Approach not shared with the Japan 2015 Approach is the human rights breaches inflicted by Australia's Onshore Program against unauthorised arrivals. These include arbitrary detention and differentiated and punitive treatment toward asylum seekers for arriving without valid documentation. Such worldwide adoption of these requirements would require alterations to the Refugee Convention and international human rights laws. Potential alterations to the Refugee Convention include the non-derogable uncapped obligation to protect and process all arrivals to a country, regardless of whether they came from their Country of Origin or from elsewhere.

Both the Australia 2015 and Japan 2015 Approaches have obvious and dramatic negatives that would attract much criticism if proposed to be adopted worldwide. A Japan 2015 Approach would appear as though the resettlement nations are absconding from their international responsibilities. An Australia 2015 Approach would appear to sanction direct breaches of the human rights of some of the world's most desperate and vulnerable people.

If adopted globally, the reality of either approach is an overall improvement in terms of the principles defined in Chapter 12. Most of these better outcomes are through the reduction of asylum seeker presentations to Countries of Second Asylum, many of which are those with no legitimate claim to refugee status. A global adoption of the Australia 2015 Approach by Countries of Second Asylum has the significant positive benefit of increasing the annual resettlement volume by almost ten times and greatly reducing the average time taken for a Durable Solution.

Approaches with high effectiveness

Two highly effective approaches that mostly honour the human rights of asylum seekers and refugees are the Regional Framework and the Development Zone Approaches. Both are high cost with high complexity and are therefore not guaranteed to be successfully implemented. However, they do offer a relative effectiveness well above any of the other approach options investigated. In comparing the two, the Development Zone Approach is less likely to be successfully implemented, but will provide the best effectiveness of all if achieved. Or in investment terms, it is higher risk with higher returns.

In terms of human rights, both aim to improve the quality of protection experienced in Countries of First Asylum. This is done through significant investment in new infrastructure and processes. However, both are systems that would run a deterrence mechanism much like Australia's offshore processing to reduce secondary movement from Countries of First Asylum. The hope is for the number of people within these facilities to be extremely low, due both to improved conditions in Countries of First Asylum, and the deterrence systems themselves. Regardless, the human rights of any people unfortunate enough to be sent to these facilities will be compromised.

Both approaches require international cooperation between Countries of First and Second Asylum. Here lies part of the implementation complexity. Cooperation across multiple countries each with their own agenda, let alone customs and behaviours, reduces clarity and control and adds more chances for failure. Many Countries of First Asylum, integral to the process, have histories of corruption which will add further risk to breakdowns in the agreed procedures and obligations.

Both options are also high cost as they require significant investment to develop infrastructure, bureaucracy and processes. Much of the infrastructure will be housed in the Countries of First Asylum. The financial investment will need to come from the wealthy Countries of Second Asylum, but Countries of First Asylum will be responsible for the majority of the refugees during their period of protection.

As discussed, for all the negative aspects in terms of complexity and cost of implementation, the Regional Framework and Development Zone Approaches provide the most effective outcomes, provided they are successfully implemented. They share many positive aspects:

- The standard of life for refugees and asylum seekers would be improved in the Countries of First Asylum. Associated with this is a more consistent quality of protection, as well as the likelihood of a Durable Solution not dependent on the location of the refugee.
- The highest proportion of refugees remain in Countries of First Asylum, which increases the probability for repatriation. It decreases the chances of refugees

undertaking dangerous travel from Countries of First Asylum to Countries of Second Asylum.

- Countries of Second Asylum would be expected to provide additional placements for resettlement due to the reduced temporary protection requirements. Not only does this provide more placements in the developed world, but also reduces the length of time spent by refugees in a temporary status without certainty of their eventual outcome.
- The prevalence of people smugglers as well as illegal economic or criminal migrants would be minimised.
- Large numbers of asylum seekers would be handled year after year with the least disruption to both Countries of First Asylum and Countries of Second Asylum.

There are comparatively few negatives in terms of effectiveness that both approaches share:

- Countries of First Asylum may still be overwhelmed by large intakes of asylum seekers; and,
- Governments will still operate deterrence measures that will divert resources from helping asylum seekers and refugees.

These shared aspects result in the Development Zones and Regional Approaches holding a similar trade-off of risk versus reward with regard to the management of the refugee situation. When compared to the other options, both provide a better possible outcome (effectiveness) but a high cost and complexity in implementation and therefore a considerable amount of implementation risk. When comparing the two, the Development Zone Approach offers the most positive outcome but with a lesser chance of success.

The positive aspects unique to the Development Zone Approach not shared with the Regional Approach are:

- It enables refugees to work, earn money and even advance their careers within organisations that are likely to continue if they repatriate home, without impacting the local economies of job markets in a material way. For instance, the existence of a black market for labour in the local cities would be greatly reduced. It maximises the human capital of the refugees who are able and willing to work. A fully active adult workforce also provides the best opportunity for children to be fully educated, as it should utilise many of the refugees who can teach.
- International businesses would be encouraged to invest in the Development Zones to improve the assets of the host nation that can be utilised following the departure of the refugees.

- Businesses based, or to be based, in Countries of Origin can be operated from the Development Zones, ready to be transplanted when repatriations begin. This is expected to have positive benefits for redevelopment on the Country of Origin.
- The separate Development Zones will minimise the opportunities for social or cultural frictions due to overwhelming numbers of people. In this way it is more scalable than the Regional approach as it can handle even greater numbers.

The main negative aspects of the Development Zones relate to the probability of their success:

- The likelihood of success varies greatly across different refugee situations. Development Zones for scenarios like Syria, with a largely educated population, present as highly viable. Conversely, the situation for the poorly educated Somalians staying in camps in arid landscapes in Kenya is less likely to create a successful Development Zone.
- The Countries of First Asylum will be required to donate large sections of land and, ideally, infrastructure to support the creation and continuation of what is probably going to be multiple Development Zones. Not all nations will be ready to donate or even lease such assets.
- The level of bureaucracy in coordinating separate economic zones with separate currencies will be very large. This adds to the complexity and cost, further increasing the resistance from countries to participate.

Either solution represents an attempt for the best-case outcome according to the principles by which the assessments have been conducted. However, both provide a degree of risk in terms of whether or not they can be implemented successfully. Failure of implementation will not only result in a massive waste of resources, but almost certainly deep suffering and pain and wasted years for the millions of refugees who were placed into such scenarios. Of the two solutions, the Regional Approach appears the safer option with more humble aspirations, and the Development Zone Approach the option with the potential for the greatest good.

Comparing the Approaches

The four assessment scores for the As-Is Approach and various approach options can be charted to provide a visual tool for assessing the various merits of each. Again, the assessment criteria are dependent upon the principles outlined in Chapter 12.

Figure 16.1 Approach Scoring shows a ball representing each of the approach options.
- The Y-axis signifies how effective the option is in meeting the four key questions outlined in Chapter 12. These include improvements across the three statuses of the

PART 3. OPTIONS & RECOMMENDATIONS > CH 16. DISCUSSION AND RECOMMENDATION   377

Refugee Journey and an overarching assessment of the persistence and scalability of the approach. The higher up the chart an approach is, the more effectively it meets the assessment objectives.

- The X-Axis signifies the relative likelihood of implementation success. The approach options further to the right being those more likely to be successfully implemented. Successful implementation means an approach would achieve the effectiveness represented by the Y-axis. Implementation success is dependent upon the probability of the international community agreeing to align to this approach and the complexity and ease of implementation once attempted.

- The size of the ball represents a relative cost undertaken by the countries supporting the humanitarian effort. The larger the ball the higher the cost. This representation considers financial costs as well as resources such as land across all countries.

- The ball colour represents to what extent each approach adheres to the Refugee Convention and international human rights law in relation to the rights of asylum seekers and refugees. White (signifying complete adherence) to black (little adherence).

Fig. 16.1 > Comparison of Holistic Approach options.

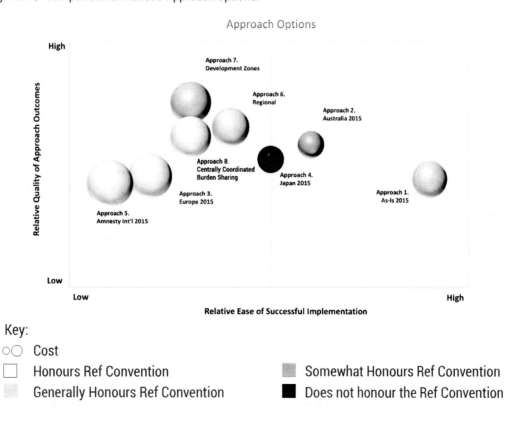

Selecting the best approach

Comparing the benefits and risks of the approach options reveals two important trade-offs. The most critical is the balance required between the human rights of vulnerable individuals originating from countries external to the supporting nations against the viability of the supporting nations and the associated human rights of their citizens (current and future).

Another important trade-off is between the potential effectiveness of the approach in meeting the objectives with the likelihood of implementation success. In short, some approaches could ultimately do much good, but are complex to implement and thus not guaranteed success. Not only does failure to implement threaten disaster for the vulnerable displaced people of the world, but it would also cost supporting nations large amounts of resources and potentially impact their viability. At its most dire outcome, implementation failure could result in dramatic and hard-to-reverse economic and social breakdowns within the countries trying to help.

Centrally Coordinated Burden Sharing is the preferred Refugee Convention Approach

Both the German-led Europe 2015 and Amnesty International Approaches threaten the human rights of the intake nations through the potential breakdown of the Countries of Second asylum through uncapped obligations as prescribed by the Refugee Convention. A glimpse of the potential magnitude of long-distance human movement was provided during the European summer of 2015. Not only is it extremely onerous and destabilising to provide for all asylum seekers under the tenets of the Refugee Convention, as discussed in Chapter 5 it is also now clearly exploited by a large group of people with no legitimate claim for refugee status. Most people individually mean no harm, but in enormous numbers they can bring about serious social upheaval, if not immediately, then almost certainly in the longer term.

Both approach options fully honour the tenets of international human rights law and the Refugee Convention but are untenable according to the principles outlined in Chapter 12. These principles include:

- Both refugees and populations of the supporting intake nations should be protected, with those of the intake nations protected as a priority.
- Protection should be provided to maintain and expand human rights, on occasion requiring the subordination of the human rights of refugees to maintain and enhance global stability, specifically that of liberal democracies.
- Protection should be provided to effect a practical outcome.

Centrally Coordinated Burden Sharing offers an exciting new implementation of the Refugee Convention that adheres to the tenets of international human rights law yet reduces, without eliminating, the uncapped burden on nations. With the pre-commitments to burden-sharing with regard to finances, refugee in-take and resettlements (after a refugee has waited 5-7 years), the standard of protection experienced by refugees will be made more consistent, durable solutions provided faster, and no one country will carry an inordinate proportion of the burden. In this aspect Centrally Coordinated Burden Sharing mitigates some of the major concerns regarding full adherence to the Refugee Convention.

The major limitation, both philosophical and practical, of Centrally Coordinated Burden Sharing is that pre-commitments to burden-sharing in terms of percentage eliminates an aspect of sovereign control. Specifically control over the number (rather than percentage) of people a country accepts as refugees and resettles in any given year, as well as their financial commitments to the global humanitarian effort.

Centrally Coordinated Burden Sharing is the best known attempt to honour the tenets of international law while mitigating the concerns of sovereign states regarding border control and social and economic security. Acceptance of an approach that doesn't honour these tenets will require a review and change to the associated human rights instruments in order to enable concerned nations that want to help to be able to fully adhere to the tenets of international laws without potentially sacrificing their own viability.

The Australia 2015 Approach is easily implemented

The Australia 2015 Approach offers a low complexity and low-cost approach with many positives from the As-Is Approach. It would significantly increase resettlement numbers worldwide and as a result decrease the average time refugees wait for a Durable Solution. It would significantly reduce the secondary movement of refugees, and the associated people smuggling and economic migration.

However, it still places great burdens on the Countries of First Asylum, requires alterations to the Refugee Convention and persists with a level of human rights breaches. For a worldwide uptake of such an approach the Refugee Convention and international human rights law would need to be updated.

Both the adoption of the Australia 2015 Approach and the proposed alterations to the Refugee Convention and international human rights laws will be considered reprehensible at first sight by most, and still unacceptable after consideration by many. The instinctive rejection of such treatment of innocent and vulnerable people will ultimately make a global uptake of this approach a challenge. According to the principles outlined in Chapter 12, it will provide better overall outcomes than the German-led 2015 Europe Approach.

Regional and Development Zones offer more

The best outcomes are possible through the complex and multinational Regional and Development Zone approaches. Both provide a good balance between protecting the human rights of asylum seekers and refugees as well as protecting the viability of the supporting nations. However, they are not without negative consequences, and both share a major weakness in a low probability of successful implementation as they are costly and highly complex.

Of the two approaches, the Development Zones offer the most effective possible outcome. Not only do they provide employment and educational opportunities to refugees, but they also alleviate pressure on Countries of First Asylum through segregating the refugee economy. This minimises the potential negative impact a large influx of people desperate to work may have on the low-paid end of the host nation workforce. Through better insulating the Country of First Asylum from dramatic economic and social consequences, the Development Zone Approach offers the most scalability.

Development Zones also shield Countries of Second Asylum from large influxes of refugees through secondary movement. Through improved conditions in the Countries of First Asylum, secondary movement would not be accepted. Associated to this, a significant drop in the attempted utilisation of the humanitarian channel from economic and criminal migrants is also expected. This drop will enable resettlement countries to provide a greater number of resettlement places. In 2014 just over 100,000 places were offered. The number is so low partly because many such nations are managing large numbers of refugees and asylum seekers. With fewer refugees arriving at Countries of Second Asylum, more resettlement places are available to provide durable solutions. As with the Australia 2015 Approach, it would be possible for an almost immediate ten-fold increase (up to one million each year) in the number of resettlement places.

For all its potential benefits, Development Zones come with a significant chance the implementation will not be successful. It requires agreement and input from multiple Countries of First Asylum, businesses and the wealthy resettlement nations. Most importantly, the refugees themselves must see the benefit of working and living within the zones. It must be recognised that these zones are more workable in some regions than others. Their efficacy is not consistent worldwide. Thus, even with full agreement, the coordination of such zones would be highly complex.

The Regional Approach provides many of the benefits with a higher chance of success. Although there would be more pressure on Countries of First Asylum, the implementation risk would be lowered as the additional bureaucracy of segregated zones would not be required. The Regional Approach presents as a more probable but less perfect approach option.

Recommendation

The approach to adopt must best balance the two important trade-offs:

- Human Rights of asylum seekers versus protection of supporting nations; and
- Overall effectiveness of the approach when implemented versus the probability of its implementation success and the consequences of failed implementation.

The approach that best balances these needs is management of the refugee situation through a number of Development Zones. These Development Zones are created as extensively as possible in addition to a number of Regional Frameworks. As discussed, such approaches will require a review and potential change to the associated human rights instruments. Given the complexity of establishing these zones, a multi-step implementation plan is required (outlined in Chapter 17).

The analysis revealed a potential alternative in adopting Centrally Coordinated Burden Sharing that provided clear benefits in terms of refugee protection and resettlements. Its effectiveness was limited according to two key issues:

- Pre-commitments to burden-sharing in terms of percentage eliminates an aspect of sovereign control.
- The guaranteed protection of asylum seekers and those determined to be refugees through RSD (a process which can be manipulated) and their guaranteed resettlement after 5-7 years results in a moral hazard which will induce a massive increase in the number of refugee presentations. This will lift the total refugee numbers much higher and increase the financial, protection, and resettlement burdens of all supporting nations.

CH 17. IMPLEMENTATION AND AUSTRALIA'S LEAD

Multi-step implementation to a Development Zone Approach

The recommended approach is to build a global system that controls the flow of asylum seekers into Countries of Second Asylum, while progressively improving the plight of asylum seekers and Countries of First Asylum that are sacrificing and risking the most in helping them. This involves a transition from current policies initially to an Australia 2015 Approach, then to enhance Countries of First Asylum through a Regional Framework Approach to provide a platform upon which Development Zones can be progressively implemented as required.

The approach is best described through four steps:

1. Recognition there is no easy answer.
2. Adoption of an Australia 2015 Approach by Countries of Second Asylum, especially in Europe.
3. Building capacity through Regional Frameworks and piloting Development Zones.
4. Adoption of Development Zones for all major refugee situations, supported by the continuation of Regional Frameworks.

Step 1. Recognition There is no Easy Answer

The first half of this book provided a detailed overview of all the complexities of the refugee situation. There are millions of refugees who wait long periods of time for a Durable Solution. That number is likely to be just the tip of the iceberg as many more potential refugees remain in their homeland as IDPs or have yet to present as asylum seekers. The countries that can help represent about 25% of the world's population and are not able to support all refugees without risking their own viability. There are many more complicating factors. In short there is no easy answer which resolves all problems without harm or risk.

Thus, not all asylum seekers and refugees can be provided immediately with help that is equivalent to the standards of the residents of Countries of Second Asylum. The demand for resettlement in a Country of Second Asylum is greater than the supply of places. As a consequence, the allocation of places must be controlled in a manner as orderly as possible - a difficult objective when people are fleeing for their lives, and all countries trying to help asylum seekers are risking their stability and long term viability.

What is a critical reality to accept, is all approach options have at least some negative aspects. The recommended approach is no different. However, it is considered according to the principles defined in this book to be the best approach. In order for it to be adopted, the negative aspects need to be accepted and managed as best they can, with the understanding they are part of what is currently the approach which provides the best long term outcome.

Step 2. Global Adoption of an Australia-Like Approach with review of Refugee Convention

The primary objective of Step 2 is to regain order with regard to the management of the refugee situation. This includes reducing uncontrolled mass movement of people over long distances, the reduction in the number of economic migrants, and controlled burden-sharing between Countries of First and Second asylum.

The first action is to minimise all long-distance secondary movement from Countries of First Asylum. This includes movement of asylum seekers from countries like Malaysia and Indonesia to Australia, as well as movement from the Middle East and North Africa to Germany and Sweden.

This would only be achieved with a widespread recognition that certain international laws, or at a minimum their current interpretation, are creating unforeseen consequences limiting the overall effectiveness of management efforts. Additionally, strict border controls and deterrence measures are required by Countries of Second Asylum.

Review of the Refugee Convention

The Refugee Convention is reviewed to create flexibility around the uncapped obligation of all nations to accept, protect and process refugees at a level equal to that of their citizens. The result will be a requirement for refugees to head to the easiest nation of safety. Movements deemed not to be so will result in asylum seekers returning to those countries or to detention and processing centres much like those used for Australia's Onshore Program.

Additionally, there is also flexibility for nations to provide lesser services to asylum seekers and refugees in order to support more people. Two examples in the Refugee Convention where updates could help nations support more people without threatening their viability are Articles 24 and 26.

- Article 24: Labour, Legislation and Social Security requires that refugees are to be provided with social security equal to that of citizens of the host nations. When required to help enormous numbers of people, such an obligation becomes prohibitive and limits other options that still help save lives but are not so generous.

- Article 26: Freedom of Movement requires refugees to be provided with full rights to move around countries, again limiting the application of certain policies which may help a country take a greater number or refugees without hurting their viability. For instance, some Australian country towns have requested to house refugees, but incentives provided do not effectively result in refugees staying long term. Most refugees head to the bigger cities where there are better services and infrastructure. Such a move is better for each individual, but together places further stress on the cities, and potentially creates segregation into cultural groups which threatens to eventuate in social disruption. A requirement for refugees to stay in such towns seems likely to help these towns, as well as enable Australia to support more refugees.

Adoption of Border Control, Turn-backs and Offshore-like Processing

Countries of Second Asylum adopt strict policies of border control and deterrence much like those in the Australia 2015 Approach. For Australia and Canada, this means the continuation of its deterrence policies of 2015, such as boat turn-backs and offshore processing. For Europe this means the establishment of such policies.

This has very large consequences for Europe. States of the EU such as Greece, Italy and Spain must adopt a 'no-advantage policy' much like Australia's policy, including boat turn-backs and offshore processing. Countries of First Asylum such as Lebanon, Turkey, Jordan and Morocco must be required to house asylum seekers and refugees as best they can and not allow travel onward to distant resettlement nations. Given demand for people wanting resettlement outweighs the supply of places, such uncontrolled movement either results in some taking the limited places, or Countries of Second Asylum risking their viability by accepting more people. Either outcome is unacceptable, through either lack of fairness or potential global destabilisation.

This means the tough, horrid conditions of detention centres, such as those operated through Australia's offshore processing regime in Manus Island and Nauru, will be opened and operated globally as a deterrent to secondary movement. This is immediately required for arrivals to the EU. The unfortunate reality of these centres is that they currently breach aspects of international law.

There is no doubting the operation of such punitive centres, used in this approach to limit the amount of secondary movement to Countries of Second Asylum, results in horrid outcomes for many vulnerable and innocent people. It is the hope and expectation that, if the policy is strictly controlled, the numbers held in such facilities will diminish as people will cease to undertake the secondary voyages departing Countries of First Asylum. Additionally, transfers to Countries of First Asylum should also be possible if able to be negotiated.

There are always exceptions to the rule and there will be some cases where arrivals to Countries of Second Asylum had no easier choice. The necessary flexibility to allow for such arrivals to be handled without incurring the strict deterrence processes should be included. However, given the current footprint of the refugee Countries of Origin, the expectation is such arrivals would be the minority. Refugee arrivals greater than a very small number would imply a breakdown and a deliberate targeting of Countries of Second Asylum. Such targeting would need to be shut down on the assumption it will ultimately be seen a pathway for maximising the chance to obtain one of the limited places in a Country of Second Asylum.

Increase in Resettlement Numbers

Adoption of border control, turn-backs and offshore-like processing policies by all the Countries of Second Asylum would increase pressure on Countries of First Asylum through the reduction in refugee numbers travelling to these nations. The proportion of refugees (20% in 2014) that move toward Countries of Second Asylum would instead remain in Countries of First Asylum. This pressure on the Countries of First Asylum will be partially reduced by increased resettlement numbers in the Countries of Second Asylum. As opposed to asylum seekers requiring RSD, these are people already defined as refugees. Although voluntary, a world-wide recommendation for resettlement targets for countries, based on wealth and population, could be agreed.

In following Australia's 2015 approach, the 62 Countries of Second Asylum could resettle up to one million collectively each year. This represents only 0.06% of the population and still a fraction of the annual immigration intake of many nations. An opportunity to resettle even more refugees is open to each nation depending on their own assessment of what they can handle. For example, Australia takes in up to 1% of its population in migrants each year indicating, at least from an infrastructure and social integration stand point, more refugees could be resettled each year without significant impact. In 2015, Australia agreed to a special intake of 12,000 Syrian refugees in a special humanitarian effort.

Financial and Expert Support for Countries of First Asylum

In all stages of this approach, the Countries of First Asylum bear the majority of the refugee burden - certainly in terms of physical numbers. International support is required to enable these countries to cope as best they can. This support becomes more formalised in Steps 3 and 4, but is initially provided through donations to the countries and aid agencies (e.g. UNHCR) enlisted to help. It can also be provided through expertise to support tasks such as RSD. With the removal of the burden of large numbers of asylum seekers to house and process, Countries of Second Asylum will be expected to increase donations and support efforts on top of their resettlement numbers, which are the first steps in the development of Regional Frameworks.

Step 3. Regional Capacity and Pilot Development Zones

The objective of Step 3 is to improve both the conditions for refugees within Countries of First Asylum, as well as the long-term viability of these countries. This is done through the development of a series of Regional Frameworks. Step 3 will also test the efficacy and implementation issues regarding Development Zones through some pilot programs. Ultimately the creation of Regional Frameworks is the broad approach upon which targeted Development Zones can sit.

Development of Regional Capacity

The financial and technical assistance provided to Countries of First Asylum is further expanded through enhancing the ability of these countries to better support asylum seekers and refugees. Such enhancement includes faster and more effective RSD, better accommodation for refugees, as well as better schooling and working opportunities. Much of these improvements will need to be financed from the more wealthy Countries of Second Asylum. This was recognised in Labor's plan, which was used as the model for this approach.

Burden-sharing in the form of increased resettlement placement offered by Countries of Second Asylum still occurs. As does the opportunity for special one-off intakes such as that conducted by many nations in 2015 for the Syrian refugees. Unfortunately the deterrence mechanisms and their associated breaches of current international human rights laws are still required. The expectation is that with improvement in the conditions of Countries of First Asylum, the numbers attempting secondary movement further diminish.

Pilot some Development Zones

Development Zones are highly complex and their successful implementation is not guaranteed. Eventually, separate Development Zones for each major refugee Country of

Origin will be required, but the implementation risk of trying something so complex can be minimised by slowing building it over time. Initially some trial zones should be piloted to highlight how implementation may best occur, and identify any implementation issues on a smaller scale.

The pilot programs would need to run 3-5 years prior to attaining a true understanding of their relative success or not. This would help define the practical considerations of a Development Zone from the arrangements with countries of asylum, the management of the land and infrastructure, as well as the incentives required to attract international and local businesses into the area. They would also provide valuable information about the response from refugees who worked and studied in these zones.

As the likelihood for success appears dependent on specifics such as land quality, infrastructure, business support and the characteristics of the refugee community, one or two of the most promising refugee situations can be chosen as pilot cases for Development Zones. One example would most likely be a Development Zone in Lebanon for Syrian refugees as outlined by Paul Collier and Alexander Betts in their October 2015 article[1].

Step 4. Globalise Development Zones

The objective of Step 4 is to globalise the use of Development Zones where the environment is appropriate for use. The expectation is that these zones will provide the best quality of life for refugees while waiting for a Durable Solution. Within Development Zones, refugees will not only be safe and housed, they will be able to work for an income or have the opportunity to complete their secondary education or take on additional studies.

Regional Approaches Remain in Operation

The Development Zones will be augmentations to working Regional Frameworks that include large annual placements of refugees into Countries of Second Asylum. In some situations it may be possible to move straight to Development Zones without the capacity development of a Regional Framework. However the expectation is that Development Zones cannot cater to all populations and require additional support for refugees. Thus, Regional Frameworks must remain in operation, including the annual resettlement placements provided by Countries of Second Asylum.

---

1   Alexander Betts and Paul Collier, "Help Refugees Help Themselves: Let Displaced Syrians Join the Labor Market," *Foreign Affairs*, November/December 2015.

Slow, Deliberate Roll-out

Development Zones are envisaged to be protected outposts of the refugee Country of Origin. Within these zones, the citizens of a Country of Origin can continue working in its businesses and maintaining its communities. Given the massive bureaucratic effort in the creation and operation of Development Zones, roll-out will have to be slow. Assuming their success and ongoing need, the Development Zones created for the pilot program will be continued. In addition, five or six refugee Countries of Origin will each have some Development Zones initiated. As they are intended to emulate a stable version of a Country of Origin, each Development Zone is designed to be for the refugees of just one Country of Origin.

Gradually, the major refugee-producing countries would have induced a number of Development Zones to support the refugees fleeing their country. In 2014, the top ten refugee-producing countries accounted for over 75% of the world's refugees. The initial Development Zones will be built for these countries.

Three long-term objectives are sought as knowledge and expertise around Development Zones improves:

1. Development Zones are established for all major refugee Countries of Origin. This will reduce the pressure on the economies and societies of the Countries of First Asylum.

2. The response time from a significant refugee-producing event to the establishment of a Development Zone is enhanced to further limit the stress on refugees as well as Countries of First Asylum.

3. The event of closing Development Zones and the associated return of land and infrastructure to the donor country has been proven and a repeatable process developed.

Australia's Lead

Australia can act immediately in two ways to influence the global move towards Development Zones supported by Regional Frameworks.

Step 1. Immediate Adoption of a Regional Framework

Adoption of Regional Framework policies will provide immediate benefits. The first is the increased resettlement numbers offered by Australia to 27,000 (approximately 0.1% of population), effectively doubling the country's humanitarian intake. This is a significant annual increase but also one which appears manageable in terms of economic and social implications.

The second benefit is the commencement of building capacity in the region, specifically the protection and RSD standards of countries including Indonesia, Malaysia and Thailand. It will not be easy and the improvement will likely be slow and expensive. However, it is a necessary and critical first step for greater regional cooperation, which is required for any chance of a successful Development Zone Approach. The process of closer engagement should start as soon as possible. This is driven by an annual donation to the UNHCR of A$450 million, making Australia the fifth largest donor country, and sends a strong signal of Australia's concern for the best possible management of the refugee situation. With this move, Australia can then act to encourage other wealthy nations in the region such as Japan, South Korea, Malaysia and Singapore, to join discussions around improving the conditions experienced by refugees in the region.

The Regional Framework Approach will contextualise Australia's continuation of the Pacific Solution not as a means of ignoring their obligations to an international problem, but as a necessary component for an optimal outcome. It should also improve Australia's international standing as it commences lobbying for global changes to international agreements and laws around refugees.

Step 2. International Lobbying

In addition to increasing its humanitarian efforts, Australia should commence lobbying internationally on two agendas. The first is for a global approach by Countries of Second Asylum through multiple steps toward a Development Zone Approach – a cessation of the influx of asylum seekers and those without legitimate claims into Europe being the immediate priority. Supporting the move toward a Development Zone Approach, Australia will also lobby for an associated re-framing of the Refugee Convention and other key articles of international humanitarian law in order to allow for the current global context.

As previously discussed, the key areas of flexibility are sought with regard to what are derogable human rights. The goal being to provide the necessary flexibility around obligations on signatory countries in order to enable them to protect their viability in times of high numbers. Examples of such obligations include:

- Uncapped requirement to protect and assess those who claim asylum in your territory.
- Provision of social security at the same level accorded to nationals of the country.
- No penalties with regard to method of entry.
- Freedom of movement of refugees within a country's territory.
- No arbitrary detention.
- No arbitrary detention of children.

Step 3. Explore Potential for Pilot Development Zone.

Explore the potential creation of a pilot Development Zone within the region – one possibility would be for the Rohingya People. The pilot would run for 3-5 years initially, with a view for extension. Ideally such a zone would be in a location geographically close to Myanmar and culturally similar to the Rohingyans. Potential places include Malaysia, Bangladesh or Thailand. Failing any agreement from a close country, a pilot could also be considered in Australia.

CONCLUSION

The world is made up of many and varied people. In researching and completing this book, I encountered two broad perspectives regarding the refugee situation.

One group responded in relation to the humanity involved. They were compelled by the individual horrors endured by innocent people because of (in general) man-made events and the man-made laws controlling the management of the fall-out of those events. For them, the critical element of Australian society and that of any nation looking to help, was to protect the human rights of those fleeing danger and persecution.

The second group responded to the mechanics involved. They were compelled by the facts revealing the risks of what might occur without the man-made laws that manage the fall-out of those events. For this group, the critical element was primarily to protect the nations looking to help, even if it meant the subordination of some human rights of refugees. I find myself in this second group. Of course, we must strive for an approach which both protects the nations helping, as well as the human rights of refugees. If such an approach becomes known, then I will be its strongest advocate.

With regard to understanding the refugee situation, on one level it is very simple. A great many people are in desperate need due to issues they did not create, nor can they control. Without help which protects their human rights, their lives are at risk. However, once the search for an approach to fix this situation commences, the complexities become apparent. The current numbers of refugees are so large, that laws and policies created to help often have unforeseen and detrimental consequences. Effective help ultimately requires the balance of a number of competing issues, all with some negative consequences.

It is the more difficult problems which require more attention, focus and sacrifice. Balancing the human rights of refugees with the sovereignty and viability of supporting nations is one of these problems. It is very difficult, requires sacrifice from many areas, and is not easy to get international alignment. The last time there was impetus for such wholesale changes to address such problems was after World War II. The Refugee Convention, expanded and slightly adjusted in 1967, has not changed since that agreement.

Statistics alone, given the age of these laws, indicate the Refugee Convention and related international human rights laws are due for review and potential change. The growing abuse of aspects of international human rights laws by many liberal democracies suggest either the morality of such nations is declining or the laws are becoming prohibitive in some way. Adherence to human rights laws supported the mass migration to (and growing negative consequences for) Europe in 2015. This provides evidence that it is time for a review of these laws.

With regard to freedoms, a well-known consideration is for the pursuit of as much freedom as possible provided it doesn't do any harm, "My right to swing my fist ends where your nose begins". The same principle should apply with regard to supporting those fleeing danger and persecution. Nations should help as much as possible, provided it doesn't adversely damage their society. Such provisions enabling nations to self-protect exist in the form of derogable rights within human rights law. However, their breadth is not extensive enough in the Refugee Convention or human rights laws with regard to refugees.

If the laws are to be reviewed, it is not to allow nations to punish innocent people. Instead, it will be to allow nations to best help those in need, without threatening their own viability. It is clear there is a better way. We just have to create it.

Index

A

asylum seeker 21, 24, 25, 26, 28, 29, 31, 54, 56, 58, 59, 63, 64, 65, 66, 67, 68, 69, 72, 75, 76, 82, 85, 90, 93, 97, 98, 99, 101, 106, 112, 117, 118, 119, 120, 121, 122, 123, 124, 126, 129, 143, 150, 154, 165, 181, 187, 195, 201, 202, 204, 205, 206, 208, 209, 210, 211, 212, 214, 216, 217, 218, 219, 220, 221, 223, 225, 226, 227, 228, 229, 230, 231, 232, 233, 234, 235, 238, 239, 242, 243, 244, 245, 246, 253, 254, 258, 259, 260, 261, 262, 263, 266, 267, 269, 271, 274, 278, 279, 280, 281, 282, 283, 284, 288, 289, 290, 293, 295, 297, 298, 302, 303, 305, 307, 308, 309, 310, 311, 313, 314, 315, 316, 317, 318, 319, 320, 322, 323, 324, 325, 326, 327, 328, 329, 331, 332, 333, 334, 335, 336, 337, 338, 339, 340, 341, 342, 343, 344, 345, 346, 347, 349, 350, 351, 352, 354, 355, 359, 360, 361, 362, 365, 366, 367, 369, 370, 371, 372, 373, 374, 375, 377, 378, 380, 381, 383, 384, 385, 386, 387, 390

Australia's Offshore Program 227, 237

Australia's Onshore Program 227, 230, 373, 384

B

border fixity 37, 50

C

Christopher Hitchens 168

Countries of First Asylum 29, 83, 89, 90, 106, 109, 110, 111, 116, 124, 126, 127, 135, 136, 139, 158, 161, 244, 256, 260, 261, 264, 266, 269, 283, 284, 285, 291, 294, 295, 297, 298, 299, 300, 302, 306, 307, 308, 309, 311, 312, 313, 314, 315, 317, 318, 320, 322, 323, 324, 325, 326, 327, 328, 329, 332, 333, 334, 335, 337, 339, 340, 341, 342, 343, 344, 345, 346, 347, 348, 349, 350, 351, 352, 354, 355, 356, 360, 361, 363, 365, 366, 369, 372, 373, 374, 375, 376, 379, 380, 383, 384, 385, 386, 387, 389

Countries of Second Asylum 90, 93, 106, 109, 110, 111, 116, 141, 157, 260, 261, 266, 269, 285, 286, 298, 302, 303, 307, 309, 310, 312, 313, 315, 318, 320, 321, 322, 323, 324, 325, 326, 327, 328, 329, 332, 333, 334, 335, 336, 337, 339, 340, 341, 342, 343, 344, 347, 348, 349, 351, 352, 355, 356, 361, 365, 366, 371, 372, 373, 374, 375, 380, 383, 384, 385, 386, 387, 388, 390

Country of Origin 25, 28, 41, 54, 55, 56, 64, 65, 73, 77, 83, 90, 91, 93, 99, 117, 119, 120, 122, 131, 135, 138, 139, 140, 150, 157, 158, 195, 212, 215, 224, 261, 264, 273, 283, 297, 348, 351, 354, 363, 373, 376, 387, 389

Cultural Assimilation 157, 165, 166

D

Demographic Ignorance 153

Disruptive Causes 21, 23, 25, 29, 31, 37, 40, 42, 44, 47, 55, 99, 181, 239, 271, 294, 296, 307, 315, 316, 322, 324, 333, 339, 341, 347, 349, 355, 365, 367

Dr. James Hathaway 294, 356

Durable Solutions 21, 22, 25, 29, 56, 72, 83, 85, 89, 91, 100, 122, 125, 131, 138, 143, 157, 162, 163, 181, 239, 246, 248, 258, 259, 263, 271, 275, 341, 367, 379, 380

F

Forcibly Displaced People 6, 11, 16, 17, 21, 25, 28, 29, 30, 31, 32, 37, 48, 52, 54, 55, 57, 98, 106, 121, 143, 163, 181, 239, 241, 242, 243, 245, 247, 249, 251, 253, 255, 256, 261, 262, 263, 266, 269, 271, 273, 274, 275, 294, 296, 302, 307, 314, 315, 316, 322, 324, 329, 333, 337, 339, 341, 347, 349, 355, 359, 365, 366, 367, 396

I

Internally Displaced People (IDP) 28, 55, 59, 122, 163
International Covenant on Civil and Political Rights (ICCPR) 95, 231, 267, 269, 299, 302, 311, 315, 319, 322, 327, 329, 336, 339, 344, 347, 352, 355, 362, 365, 366
International Covenant on Economic, Social and Cultural Rights (ICESCR) 95
Irregular Maritime Arrivals (IMAs) 65, 67, 202, 227
Islam 53, 59, 153, 157, 169, 170, 171, 176, 177, 178, 179, 247, 371

L

liberal democracy 257
Lifeboat Ethics 253
Local Integration 21, 131, 135, 136, 137, 143, 157, 159, 181, 239, 246, 249, 258, 260, 263, 271, 291, 303, 323, 326, 329, 332, 367

M

Mandate Refugees 28, 29, 30, 31, 33, 98, 99, 100, 101, 113, 116, 137, 142, 162, 163
Mandatory Detention 25, 96, 123, 204, 211, 225, 228, 229, 231, 232, 234, 274, 280, 282
multiculturalism 166, 167, 168, 178, 179, 187, 188, 198, 247, 310
Multiculturalism 157, 165, 166, 167, 168, 198
Mutual Regard 152, 155, 167, 174

N

Net Overseas Migration 143, 144, 184, 186, 189
Non-derogable Human Rights 95
Non-refoulement 65, 74, 75, 85, 117, 125, 199, 235, 257, 291, 327, 340

O

Operation Sovereign Borders 67, 214, 226, 229, 235

P

Pacific Solution 59, 66, 67, 93, 110, 112, 123, 127, 206, 209, 211, 226, 229, 232, 233, 390
Paul Collier 42, 112, 124, 128, 148, 149, 152, 155, 275, 281, 348, 388
people smugglers 25, 56, 58, 59, 69, 117, 124, 141, 235, 242, 279, 295, 296, 297, 302, 308, 314, 315, 317, 324, 329, 332, 333, 338, 340, 341, 347, 350, 355, 365, 375
population 22, 29, 31, 32, 34, 35, 36, 40, 41, 42, 44, 45, 46, 52, 53, 54, 59, 60, 63,

INDEX

64, 77, 81, 84, 89, 102, 103, 104, 105, 106, 107, 110, 111, 114, 115, 116, 121, 123, 126, 128, 134, 137, 143, 144, 146, 147, 149, 150, 151, 152, 153, 154, 155, 161, 163, 166, 170, 171, 172, 173, 174, 179, 183, 184, 185, 186, 187, 188, 189, 190, 191, 198, 209, 223, 228, 243, 244, 247, 249, 251, 252, 253, 254, 255, 256, 257, 260, 262, 267, 269, 274, 276, 284, 285, 288, 290, 296, 298, 299, 302, 303, 305, 306, 307, 310, 311, 313, 315, 319, 322, 323, 325, 326, 329, 335, 339, 340, 341, 343, 345, 346, 347, 348, 349, 351, 353, 355, 356, 357, 361, 365, 366, 369, 371, 376, 383, 386, 389

population growth 35, 36, 52, 53, 146, 151, 154, 155, 171, 185, 187, 190, 191, 276, 369

R

refugee 21, 22, 23, 24, 25, 26, 27, 28, 29, 30, 37, 54, 55, 56, 59, 60, 61, 62, 63, 65, 66, 71, 72, 73, 74, 75, 76, 77, 78, 79, 80, 82, 83, 84, 85, 86, 87, 88, 89, 94, 95, 97, 98, 99, 100, 101, 102, 103, 104, 105, 111, 113, 114, 115, 116, 117, 118, 121, 122, 124, 125, 126, 128, 129, 131, 132, 134, 135, 157, 158, 163, 179, 181, 194, 195, 199, 200, 202, 203, 210, 211, 212, 214, 215, 216, 218, 219, 221, 222, 223, 224, 225, 226, 228, 231, 233, 235, 236, 237, 238, 239, 241, 243, 244, 245, 247, 248, 249, 254, 257, 258, 264, 266, 267, 269, 271, 274, 277, 278, 279, 280, 282, 283, 290, 291, 295, 296, 299, 302, 303, 307, 308, 311, 312, 313, 315, 316, 317, 319, 320, 321, 322, 327, 329, 331, 332, 335, 336, 339, 342, 344, 345, 347, 352, 355, 356, 362, 365, 366, 367, 369, 371, 373, 377, 378, 379, 384, 385, 386, 390, 393, 394, 399

Refugee Convention 22, 24, 25, 26, 27, 28, 30, 37, 55, 56, 59, 61, 62, 65, 66, 71, 72, 73, 74, 75, 76, 80, 83, 85, 87, 89, 94, 95, 97, 98, 99, 100, 101, 102, 103, 104, 105, 111, 116, 117, 118, 121, 122, 124, 125, 126, 128, 129, 131, 194, 195, 199, 202, 215, 223, 225, 231, 233, 235, 237, 238, 243, 244, 249, 254, 257, 258, 264, 267, 269, 274, 278, 279, 282, 283, 291, 295, 296, 299, 302, 303, 307, 308, 311, 312, 313, 315, 316, 317, 319, 320, 321, 322, 327, 329, 332, 335, 336, 339, 342, 344, 345, 347, 352, 355, 356, 362, 365, 366, 369, 371, 373, 377, 378, 379, 384, 385, 390, 393, 394

Refugee Status Determination (RSD) 27, 29, 63, 72, 117, 118, 274

resettlement 24, 25, 29, 57, 59, 82, 89, 90, 93, 110, 111, 112, 116, 125, 136, 137, 138, 139, 141, 142, 158, 159, 160, 161, 170, 187, 195, 200, 202, 210, 211, 214, 215, 216, 225, 227, 230, 232, 237, 238, 243, 258, 260, 263, 283, 284, 285, 288, 289, 291, 295, 297, 298, 299, 300, 302, 303, 305, 306, 307, 308, 309, 310, 311, 312, 313, 314, 315, 316, 317, 319, 321, 322, 323, 324, 325, 326, 327, 328, 329, 331, 332, 334, 335, 337, 339, 341, 342, 343, 344, 345, 346, 347, 348, 349, 350, 351, 352, 355, 356, 358, 359, 360, 361, 363, 365, 371, 373, 375, 379, 380, 381, 384, 385, 386, 387, 388, 389

Resettlement 21, 22, 83, 112, 131, 137, 138, 139, 140, 141, 142, 143, 157, 159, 160, 161, 164, 181, 199, 215, 239, 244, 247, 249, 271, 274, 284, 286, 287, 289, 295,

302, 303, 305, 308, 315, 322, 332, 339, 340, 346, 347, 355, 367, 386
Responsibility to Protect (R2P) 37, 47, 49, 92, 95

S

secularism 168, 290, 371
Sharia 41, 173, 175, 176, 177, 178
sovereignty 28, 48, 50, 60, 92, 186, 247, 255, 365, 369, 393

T

terrorism 46, 174, 178, 179, 318
The Report of the Expert Panel on Asylum Seekers (Houston Report) 226
Total Fertility Rates (TFR) 276

U

United Nations High Commissioner for Refugees (UNHCR) 80
United Nations Relief and Works Agency (UNRWA) 98

V

Voluntary Repatriation 83, 131, 132, 133, 157, 246, 249

W

Wahhabism 179, 180
White Australia policy 167, 183, 187

ABOUT THE AUTHOR

Andrew Bennetts is a management consultant with an interest in the global refugee situation. Since 2003 he has defined and managed complex business issues for some of Australia's largest companies. Across a range of industries including Agriculture, Automotive, Construction, Finance and Telecommunications, Andrew has provided structure to help understand complexities and assess business options. *The Mess We're In – Managing the Refugee Crisis* is his first book and applies the same analytical rigour, effectively employed in business, to the refugee crisis.

ACKNOWLEDGMENTS & THANK YOU

Adrienne Millbank - Amanda Spedding - Anna Forsyth - Ben Silluzio - Brett Dawson

Brook Hely - Carmel McConnell - Charles Powles - Chris Berg

Cornelia Murariu - Dan Evans - David Potaznik - David Uren - Doug Cocks

Dr Bob Birrell - Dr Katharine Betts - Elizabeth Traynor - Glen Smith - Greg Hargrave

Ian Harper - Ira Alvarez - Jake Avent - James Bennetts - James Skerrett - Jamin Silluzio

Jessie Taylor - John Roskam - Julian McMahon - Julie Postance - Kieran Whaley

Kon Karapanagiotidis - Kylie Evans - Lou Silluzio - Luke McConnell - Marcus MacLean

Mary Bennetts - Michael McGrath - Neil May - Paul Ronalds - Peter Green

Philip Ruddock - Ray Bennetts - Ray Hughes - Richard Alston

Sally Sweeney - Stephen Lording - Subu Hebbar

CPSIA information can be obtained
at www.ICGtesting.com
Printed in the USA
LVOW09s1956140517
534490LV00006B/368/P